WOMEN IN ANCIENT SOCIE

Women in Ancient Societies

An Illusion of the Night

Edited by

Léonie J. Archer
Research Fellow in Energy and the Environment
Oxford Institute for Energy Studies

Susan Fischler
Lecturer in Ancient History
University of Birmingham

and

Maria Wyke
Honorary Research Fellow
University College, London

Routledge   New York

Editorial matter and selection © Léonie J. Archer,
Susan Fischler and Maria Wyke 1994
Text © The Macmillan Press Ltd 1994

Published in the
United States of America
by Routledge
29 West 35 Street
New York, NY 10001

ISBN 0 415 90881 7 CL
ISBN 0 415 90882 5 PB

A CIP catalog record for this book
is available from the Library of Congress.

Reprinted and bound 1995
in Great Britain by
Antony Rowe Ltd, Chippenham, Wiltshire

Contents

List of Plates   vii

Acknowledgements   ix

Notes on the Contributors   x

Introduction   xiv

1   Gender Bias in Archaeology   1
    Lucia Nixon

2   Women in Ancient Egyptian Wisdom Literature   24
    Annette Depla

3   Notions of Community and the Exclusion of the Female
    in Jewish History and Historiography   53
    Léonie J. Archer

4   The Problem of Women Philosophers in Ancient Greece   70
    Richard Hawley

5   An Ancient Theory of Gender: Plato and the Pythagorean
    Table   88
    Sabina Lovibond

6   Producing Woman: Hippocratic Gynaecology   102
    Helen King

7   Social Stereotypes and Historical Analysis: The Case of the
    Imperial Women at Rome   115
    Susan Fischler

8   Woman in the Mirror: The Rhetoric of Adornment in
    the Roman World   134
    Maria Wyke

9   Early Christianity and the Discourse of Female Desire   152
    Averil Cameron

10   Reading Between the Lines: Sarah and the Sacrifice
    of Isaac (Genesis, Chapter 22)   169
    Sebastian Brock

11   Public and Private Forms of Religious Commitment among
      Byzantine Women   181
      Judith Herrin

12   Women in Anglo-Saxon Poetry   204
      Fiona Gameson

13   Recycling Ancient Material: An Orthodox View of
      Hindu Women   233
      Julia Leslie

14   The Witch and the Wife: A Comparative Study of Theocritus,
      Idyll 2, Simonides, *Idyll* 15 and *Fatal Attraction*   252
      Laura Gibbs-Wichrowska

      General Bibliography   269

      Bibliography of Works Cited   271

      Index   302

List of Plates

1. Funerary relief depicting process of adornment.
   Third century AD, from Gallia Belgica.
   Reproduction in Museo della Civiltà Romana, inventory no. 2245.

2. Funerary relief depicting instruments of adornment.
   Second century AD, from Pisa.
   Reproduction in Museo della Civiltà Romana, inventory no. 3416.

3. Bridal Casket of Secundus and Projecta, depicting adornment of
   Venus and the bride.
   Fourth century AD, from Esquiline, Rome.
   British Museum.

4. Bronze mirror case depicting erotic scene.
   First century AD.
   Antiquarium Comunale, inventory no. 13694, Rome.

5. Ivory female bust, from end of a hairpin.
   Fourth century AD.
   Antiquarium Comunale, Rome, inventory no. 18522.

Acknowledgements

Photographs courtesy of the photographic archives of the Antiquarium Comunale and the Museo della Civiltà Romana, Rome, and the Trustees of the British Museum, London.

The excerpts from Theocritus, *Idyll* 2 are from Barris Mills, *The Idylls of Theocritus*, Purdue University Press, copyright 1963 by Purdue Research Foundation, West Lafayette, Indiana 47907. Reprinted with permission.

Notes on the Contributors

Léonie J. Archer is a member of Wolfson College, Oxford. Until 1989 she was Fellow in Jewish Studies of the Graeco-Roman period at the Oxford Centre for Postgraduate Hebrew Studies. In 1989 she made a major career change and took up an appointment as Research Fellow in Environmental Studies at the Oxford Institute for Energy Studies. Before turning to her new career, she co-founded the Oxford 'Women in Antiquity' seminar series, involved herself with various gender studies enterprises, and published a number of articles on Jewish women in antiquity. These include a contribution to the 1983 Cameron–Kuhrt collection, essays on 'The Virgin and the Harlot in the Writings of Formative Judaism' for *History Workshop Journal* (1987) and '"In thy blood live": Gender and Ritual in the Judaeo-Christian Tradition' for the Channel 4 book *Through the Devil's Gateway* (ed. A. Joseph, 1990). Her own book, *Her Price is Beyond Rubies: The Jewish Woman in Graeco-Roman Palestine* was published in 1990. Léonie now devotes herself full-time to work on the environment.

Sebastian P. Brock is Reader in Syriac Studies at the University of Oxford and Fellow of Wolfson College, Oxford. His areas of academic interest cover Syriac literature and biblical translation in antiquity, on both of which he has published extensively. Works of particular relevance to this volume and to women's studies are *Holy Women of the Syrian Orient* (with S. A. Harvey, Berkeley, 1987), 'The Holy Spirit as feminine in early Syriac tradition', in *After Eve: Women, Theology and the Christian Tradition* (ed. J. Martin Soskice, London, 1990), and '"Come, compassionate Mother . . . Come, Holy Spirit": a forgotten aspect of early eastern Christian imagery', *Aram* 3 (1991).

Averil Cameron is Professor of Late Antique and Byzantine Studies, King's College, London. In addition to, and also generally informing, her work on antiquity, Averil is interested in cultural history and the sociology of knowledge. She has published widely on later Roman history. Of particular relevance to this volume is her co-edited collection of essays on *Images of Women in Antiquity* (with A. Kuhrt, London, 1983). Most recently, Averil has edited *History as Text* (London, 1989), which includes a chapter by her on 'Virginity as Metaphor', and authored *Christianity and the Rhetoric of Empire* (Berkeley and Los Angeles, 1991).

Annette Depla, a graduate in ancient history and archaeology from the Open University, divides her time between bringing up a young family and teaching Egyptology part-time in the Department of Continuing Studies at the University of Birmingham. Her main academic interests are iconography, wisdom literature and etymology. She is currently bringing to completion her doctoral thesis.

Susan Fischler is Lecturer in Ancient History at the University of Birmingham. She specialises in Roman history, and prior to taking up her post in 1989 at Birmingham she held a temporary appointment at St John's College, Oxford. While a graduate student at Oxford she co-founded the 'Women in Antiquity' seminar from which the papers in this volume are taken. She is currently preparing for publication her doctoral thesis on the public position of Roman imperial women in the Julio-Claudian period.

Fiona Marion Gameson is Tutor in Medieval Literature and Music at the Centre for Medieval and Renaissance Studies, Oxford. She is a graduate student at Trinity College, Oxford, where she is bringing to completion her doctoral thesis on women in Anglo-Saxon poetry.

Laura K. Gibbs-Wichrowska divides her time between living in the USA and Poland. Until recently, she was Editorial Assistant of *Psychological Bulletin*, Vanderbilt University. In 1988, she attained her M.Phil. in European Literature from the University of Oxford, and returned to the USA to gain qualification as a secondary school teacher. Laura works on Polish translations and prepares commentaries on English poems for students of English as a second language. She is currently living and working in Poland.

Richard Hawley is Lecturer in Classics at Balliol College, Oxford, and, from 1989, co-organiser of the Oxford 'Women in Antiquity' seminar. He is presently completing his doctoral thesis on women in Greek drama, and intends to write a book on attitudes toward Aspasia from antiquity to the present day. His interests span women in Greek literature of the Roman imperial period and ancient women in modern popular fiction. He has published 'The unexamined classicist: the place of women's studies in classics', *Classical Association National Newsletter* 1 (1990), 'Aspasia: Athens' First Lady', *Omnibus* 21 (1991), and has contributed to *The Bloomsbury Guide to International Women's Writing* (ed. C. Buck, 1991).

Judith Herrin is Stanley Seeger Professor of Byzantine History at Princeton University, an appointment which she took up subsequent to her work with the Oxford seminar. She has contributed chapters on Byzantine and Early Christian subjects to a number of collections, including *Culture, Ideology and Politics*, edited by R. Samuel and G. Stedman Jones (1982). She has forthcoming, in a Festscrift for A. P. Kazhdan, an essay on the Council *in Trullo* on women. Her general areas of academic interest include literacy in Byzantium and women and orthodoxy in modern Greece and Russia.

Helen King is Lecturer in History at St Katherine's College, Liverpool Institute of Higher Education, and Member of the General Synod of the Church of England. She has published widely on women and medicine in the ancient world, and is currently area adviser for women's studies on the Oxford Classical Dictionary. Her publications include 'Bound to bleed: Artemis and Greek Women', in *Images of Women in Antiquity* (ed. Cameron and Kuhrt, London, 1983); 'Sacrificial blood: the role of the amnion in ancient gynaecology', *Helios* 13/2 (1987); 'The daughter of Leonides: reading the Hippocratic corpus', in *History as Text* (ed. Cameron, London, 1989); 'Using the past: nursing and the medical profession in ancient Greece', in *Anthology of Nursing* (ed. Holden and Littlewood, London, 1991).

Julia Leslie is Lecturer in Hindu Studies at the School of Oriental and African Studies, University of London, and Senior Member of the Centre for Cross-Cultural Research on Women, Oxford. She has travelled widely in south Asia and is an expert on orthodox Hindu practices and classical Indian law. She has published many essays on the roles and rituals of orthodox Hindu women, and her doctoral thesis on Sanskrit religious law relating to women was published in 1989. As well as her extensive writing in this area, Julia is also a prize-winning novelist. She currently has in the press an edited collection of essays, *Rules and Remedies in Classical Indian Law* (Leiden).

Sabina Lovibond is Fellow and Tutor in Philosophy at Worcester College, Oxford. Her main academic interests are in feminist theory and meta-ethics, which she incorporates in her study of ancient philosophy. Sabina has published widely, and works relevant to this collection include *Realism and Imagination in Ethics* (Oxford, 1983), 'Feminism and Postmodernism', *New Left Review* 178 (1989), 'Plato's Theory of Mind', in *Companions to Ancient Thought 2: Psychology* (ed. Stephen Everson, Cambridge, 1991), and *Ethics: A Feminist Reader* (jointly edited with Elizabeth Frazer and Jennifer Hornsby, Oxford, 1992).

Lucia Nixon is Assistant Professor of Classics at the University of New Brunswick at Saint John, Canada. She has done extensive archaeological field work, excavating in the UK, Italy, Turkey and Greece. Since 1987 she has co-directed the Sphakia Survey in south-west Crete with Jennifer Moody. Preliminary field reports from the Survey have been published in *Echos du Monde Classique/Classical Views* (Vols 32–4, 1988–90), and in 1987 she published 'Changing views of Minoan society', in *Minoan Society* (eds Krzyszkowska and Nixon, Bristol). Her other published work includes 'Women and Men in Oxford' (*Oxford Magazine*, 1986) and 'The Anthropology of Homecoming at Queen's' (*Queen's Quarterly* 94, 1987).

Maria Wyke is an Honorary Research Fellow in the Department of Greek and Latin at University College, London. Until 1992 she was College Lecturer in Classics at Newnham and Corpus Christi Colleges, Cambridge. In 1984 she completed her doctoral thesis on women in Roman love elegy. Since then she has published widely on this subject. She is currently writing a book on Classics and popular cinema for the Routledge New Ancient World series and is pursuing her interest in film studies at the British Film Institute.

Introduction

This book represents the fruits of some of the research currently being undertaken in British universities on women's lives and their representations in various ancient societies. The papers derive from the first three years of an ongoing seminar series at the University of Oxford entitled 'Women in Antiquity'. The seminar started in 1985 as a response to the intellectual and often emotional isolation experienced by students and faculty staff engaged in research on women in the ancient world. No women's studies course existed at the University of Oxford; neither was there any women's history course within the ancient history programme. This was, and still is, a real omission and not a case of women's studies having been integrated into a curriculum that recognises the problems of gender. The British Academy and the discipline of ancient history, at least so far as Oxford is concerned, have a long way to go before that stage in the evolution of women's studies is reached.

The book mirrors the seminar series and, it is hoped, is but the first record of the debates conducted in Oxford. It provides a forum for the exchange and development of ideas and methods at a crucial period in the growth of women's studies in this country. It clearly reflects the differing degrees to which the various disciplines have developed in their approach to the female in antiquity and the extent to which they are or are not isolated from the influence of work in other fields.

Some disciplines are clearly just beginning the process of women's history, doing the valuable and very necessary spadework of collecting and collating evidence in pursuit of a lost history. Their primary concern at this stage is with women's history rather than with feminist history or study. Others are analytically and methodologically more mature, and have clearly benefited from contact with developments in the thinking of such modern disciplines as linguistics, social anthropology and literary criticism. Techniques have been borrowed, and while their imposition on ancient material may not always be a comfortable one, it is a useful step on the evolutionary road.

By definition, the study of women draws on and bridges a range of traditionally isolated and self-contained disciplines. Unlike in the USA, in Britain this interdisciplinary approach has not yet been institutionalised. Great individual effort is needed, and volumes such as this, which gather together a range of approaches, are both useful tools and barometers of progress. As perceptions and analytical techniques change, so the need for sourcebooks, specialised studies and especially anthologies increases. One American feminist scholar recently commented that an anthology of hetero-geneous essays is now the most widely utilised vehicle in the USA for exploring the issue of 'woman'. We need to build up a similar wide-ranging dissemination of interdisciplinary information from within Britain. *Women in Ancient Societies: An Illusion of the Night* picks up upon the only other British anthology on women in antiquity (eds Cameron and Kuhrt, Croom Helm, 1983) and is indebted to it. We see this volume as a continuation of the story and hope that it will not be as long before the appearance of a third collection of essays.

Contributors to this volume, from Oxford and elsewhere, include social and legal historians, archaeologists and art historians, philosophers, literary critics, classicists and experts in religious studies. All at the time of writing were involved full-time with academic work: Léonie Archer, founder and co-organiser of the seminar, was a Fellow in Jewish Studies at the Oxford Centre for Postgraduate Hebrew Studies, though she has now moved on to working on environmental matters; Sebastian Brock was and still is lecturer in Syriac at the University of Oxford; Averil Cameron, one of the editors of the 1983 *Images of Women in Antiquity*, was Professor of Ancient History at King's College, London, and now is Professor of Late Antique and Byzantine Studies at the same college; Annette Depla was a student of the Oxford Oriental Faculty, which she left to dedicate her time to bringing up two children; Susan Fischler, also founder and co-organiser of the seminar, was a graduate student in Roman history at Oxford and has since secured a lectureship at Birmingham University; Fiona Gameson is a graduate student in Oxford, working on Anglo-Saxon history, and Richard Hawley was also a graduate student, working on ancient Greek history, and now combines his research with teaching in London; Judith Herrin was an itinerant scholar but now has secured a chair in Byzantine history at Princeton University; Helen King was teaching classics at Newcastle and, shortly after presenting her paper, moved on to Liverpool where she now lectures in history at the Institute of Higher Education; Julia Leslie was a member of the Centre for Cross-Cultural Research on Women, Oxford, and now has a lectureship at the School of Oriental and African Studies in London; Sabina Lovibond was and still is a Fellow in philosophy at Worcester College, Oxford; Lucia Nixon, also an itinerant scholar at the time of writing and an archaeological field director, now lectures at the University of New Brunswick in Canada; and Maria Wyke, co-organiser of the seminar, was a research fellow at Queen's College, Oxford, and is now an Honorary Research Fellow at University College, London.

As can been seen from this list, particular attention was given to encouraging the work of younger scholars, and their contributions to this volume complement the papers of more established academics. All of the contributors bring the different skills, expertise and perceptions of their various disciplines, together with individual insights, to the subject of women in antiquity. Unusually, antiquity in this collection of essays is defined as running from the second millennium BC to AD 1000 and beyond to later centuries where the continuation of classical traditions and their influence may clearly be seen. The customary parameters of 'ancient history' are therefore substantially and appropriately extended both to accommodate the different stages of historical development in the various societies examined and to move antiquity from the geographic and chronological confines within which it is normally treated in mainstream western scholarship. Given the expanded time-frame and interests, geographic and cultural coverage is also extensive, ranging from ancient India to Anglo-Saxon England, material remains to symbolic systems.

In choosing the papers for publication, the editors' aim has been to present a cross-section of the work presented at the seminar series and to bring together perspectives on women in ancient cultures which throw light on each other – both in terms of subject matter and in terms of discipline interest and development. We are sorry that space does not permit publication of all the original seminar contributions. The papers collected here are diverse. No editorial overview has been imposed, but considerable effort has been made by the editors, working with the contributors, to make the texts, individual subjects, methodologies and arguments as clear and accessible as possible to specialist and non-specialist readers alike.

We hope that readers will not confine themselves to their own particular area of interest. To encourage the interdisciplinary dialogue and exchange of ideas, notes have been arranged according to the Harvard system of citation: for full publication details of works referred to, readers will have to look beyond a specific paper or area of immediate interest to them and consult the extended bibliography compiled from all of the papers at the back of the book. A separate list of recommended general publications is also appended. This list comprises works which the editors and contributors felt had been of particular use and of significance for their own research. Not surprisingly, many titles repeated themselves in the submissions from our various authors, reminding us not only of the interdisciplinary nature of this business but also of the overlaps in the perspectives and methods of the papers in this particular collection.

Although treating diverse cultures and periods, all the papers share certain problems and reveal certain themes. All examine, in various ways, the issue of text: text as problematic source of information; woman as text; the interrelationship of text and society; society as text; and text as authority. Text is thus variously defined and analysed. Regarding text as source, all the contributors have the difficulty of culling information from a male-stream tradition, of looking through a male author's eyes, of reading between the lines and dealing with 'woman' as all-too-often a male-ordered construct or representation. The question immediately presents itself as to whether we can ever have access to women's lived experiences. Woman appears as a definitional tool, the 'other'. She is body and sexual being, inferior to man, a threatening enigma to be feared and controlled. In these and other senses, woman is mapped onto: she is text.

In addition to the problem of accessibility to reality, there is the fact that the text itself is not straightforward. There are tensions, both in the attitude of the ancient writers to the construct that they and society have created (and need for the chosen social order); and at the interface between this abstract and the actuality of daily existence. 'Woman' may in some senses be homogeneous; women are not. An example of the tension is to be found in the treatment of elite women. For most of the societies discussed in this volume, women in the sources tend to be upper-ranking. This is problematic not only for the present-day researcher trying to reach all women, but also for some of the ancient writers who, on some level at least, recognise disjunctions both within the image and between the image and the 'reality'. The homogeneity and seeming wholeness of the image 'woman' is fractured at the most simple level by the need to accommodate the existence of different social strata. Clearly, there are differences and tensions between what is said about elite and non-elite, Christian and non-Christian, Greek and Roman and, above all, indigenous and non-indigenous women. Frequently, the characteristics ascribed by the ancient authors to the concept Woman are not applied to their descriptions of particular upper-class women. Yet, at the same time, it is those very women who are regarded as displaying *par excellence* the potential for female ingenuity and manipulation of men, that is, the standard traits of the constructed woman. Because of their position of relative power, upper-ranking women are seen as especially threatening to men and to the construction of the social order. In some senses they are the embodiment of male fear regarding 'woman'.

Where women are concerned, and whatever their social standing, the categories and boundaries which the text and its constructs generate are fluid and easily crossed over. This is the case no matter how rigid and concrete the ancients would like matters to be. In setting woman up as a definitional tool, in placing women in various categories, the system and the text, inevitably, reveal further tensions. Women are seen as mothers, wives, daughters; as prostitutes and seductresses; witches and midwives; as saints, goddesses and military heroes; queens; church functionaries; patronesses and much more. The categories and roles inevitably interweave and the image and/or expectations of one impinge upon the other. So, to be wife is to be potential adulteress and manipulator; to be saint is to deny biological femaleness; to be public figure is to cross into the male domain; to be goddess or military hero is to mediate between men; to be defined as purely sexual as prostitute or virgin is the height of danger. Women who seem to fail to fulfil a given role are questioned, possibly feared. They can no longer be conveniently and completely categorised, and therefore ordered. Women who do fulfil the role assigned to them are often suspect, for by occupying a single category they are regarded as completely 'other' and therefore possessing power (in a threatening rather than a formal sense). Whichever, it is a no-win situation.

One theme running throughout the texts is that whatever categories women occupy or are accorded they are deemed to be in need of male supervision and control. At the heart of all the ancients' assessments of 'woman' and her many roles in society is the all-informing notion of 'the other' and an understanding of woman as body. 'The other' is always inferior to the male norm. Women could never be fully-fledged public, that is male, figures. While they could potentially occupy many different social categories, there was never an equivalence with a male counterpart. 'Queen' did not equal 'King', 'deaconess' did not equal 'deacon', either in authority or function. The 'body' and 'femaleness' precluded such elevation. Although, as the essays in this volume show, the treatment of women as body not surprisingly varied in detail from society to society, one common feature in our sources is the idea of woman as more body than mind, as sexual being rather than social being, as physical entity as opposed to fully political, spiritual or legal person. Even with this all-pervasive theme, the texts still evince tension: patently women at times acted other than body; they too exercised authority (albeit circumscribed) in spiritual and political realms; in some instances they were given explicit power over their own bodies as, for example, in the case of self-diagnosis in Greek medical practices. Whatever the permutations in reality and individual circumstances, however, it was the idea that was important and that informed attitude and social ordering. The idea, as enshrined in text, ritual, law and philosophy, had authority. The woman's body was an informing text, for men and women, of the need for male control.

Throughout the texts with which we have to deal, therefore, there are tensions, tensions both within the image that is created and between that image and the specificities of daily existence. Ironically, the sex over which most effort was made to define and to categorise is the one which remains the most ambivalent and fluid. Men can be defined in contrast to the 'other' which they set up; women, despite all efforts, remain aloof.

The text had – and has – authority. Some of our contributors look at the way in which texts explicitly determined women's lives and lifestyles in specific cultures, prescribing the activities to be pursued as, for example, in the case of the expected expressions of female piety in the later Christian centuries or the gendered division of labour in the daily ordering of an orthodox Hindu household. Other contributors examine the overarching influence of text and the interplay between text and society and the creation of philosophies and ideas. Others again look at the text's (and texts') continuing authority and the recycling of so-called 'ancient' material into the canons of later centuries. It is the case that, while all ancient texts are to some extent culturally-specific, they have an undoubted ring of familiarity to the twentieth-century reader. There is no continuum of cultural specifics, but fundamental patterns for conceptualising the female clearly persist to be reused and moulded for a new present time. Moreover, antiquity has a certain authority in the modern mind, a fact which lends additional impetus to the persistence of the text. These points are drawn out by several contributors who analyse the continuation of ancient 'text' in modern popular culture – and in academic disciplines.

As researchers and writers on women in antiquity, we too are implicated in the text that we seek to analyse. It continues to have authority over us. It dictates what we see or don't see. In a sense we only present, and thus perpetuate, the text as received. Additionally, we write from within a context, both cultural and, more narrowly, academic, which in various ways is shaped by the received text. In many respects *Women in Ancient Societies* follows on from previous texts and stands in a tradition. We should therefore avoid any feelings of complacency.

In other respects, however, this volume – like women's studies in general – is different. By questioning our sources, by refusing simply to reproduce them or present just what they choose to tell us, we break with the tradition. We are aware of the text. We consciously respond to it. We challenge it.

The subtitle, 'An *Illusion of the Night*', reflects very much the concerns of the original Oxford seminar and the purpose of our studies. It derives from a combination of various patristic writings on the origin of woman and the view adopted by some that she was the result of a male emission in the night. The woman in antiquity, in some senses, never really existed; she was always an illusion, a pleasurable but unsettling construct of male imagination. As a woman grounded in reality, she is missing from the outset. In similar vein it could be said that women's studies, in general, is missing from the British academy. To some extent it too is an 'illusion of the night'

– or rather, is viewed as such by many of our (usually male) colleagues. People engaged in the study of women in history are also often viewed as unsettling, as not doing 'real' academic work. And so on.

Despite appearances, our choice of subtitle is not negative! Illusions can be challenged. And by challenging them, we can disturb an apparently settled order, in antiquity and today. The title simply draws attention to a particular state of affairs – which all of us are setting about changing.[1]

Léonie Archer
Susan Fischler
Maria Wyke

NOTE

1. We are pleased to say that the seminar 'Women in Antiquity' is now accorded far greater prominence in the Oxford student listings than ever could have been the case in 1985.

1 Gender Bias in Archaeology[1]

Lucia Nixon

Archaeologists are often accused of the uncritical projection of their own norms and values on to the past. In their splendid article 'Archaeology and the Study of Gender', Margaret Conkey and Janet Spector show that such presentist back-projection includes the unquestioning application of our own gender ideology. They make the point that much archaeological research is therefore biased with respect to gender.[2]

In this chapter I want to look at three different examples of gender bias in archaeology. First, I look at how women and men are portrayed in reconstructions of life in the Stone Age. Next, I consider the Minoans and Mycenaeans in terms of misapplied gender polarity, and how it affects comparisons of these two archaeological cultures. In the third section, I discuss the division of labour in archaeology – what women do, what men do, and how this affects their respective careers. Finally, I suggest some ways in which archaeology might benefit if the problems and distortions caused by gender bias were eliminated.

HUMAN EVOLUTION AND THE STONE AGE

In this section I want to look briefly at both popular and scholarly reconstructions of life in the palaeolithic period, with two questions in mind: how are women and men portrayed, and how are archaeological data analysed in order to find out about them? The Stone Age is a period for which we have relatively little data, yet the lack of good evidence has not resulted in a shortage of reconstructions of palaeolithic life, both popular and scholarly. When I taught an introductory archaeology course, I found plenty of jokes about the Stone Age; indeed, I could put together a whole lecture about evolution, subsistence, technological developments, and so forth, but I soon realised that there were problems, and that I would not be able to use these jokes as I had planned.

Here are two jokes about palaeolithic transport, which illustrate some of the difficulties (Figs. 1 and 2). The first shows an early experiment in transport, where only men are present. The second shows a caveman dragging a woman by her hair; in this case she is giving a backseat commentary on his 'driving'.

Figures 1 and 2 represent two types of joke about the Stone Age, in which either women are absent; or they are present, but negatively portrayed. Both women and men tend to be shown in situations that reflect highly-stereotypical gender roles, with an additional twist: even though women are always depicted in appropriately female contexts (cooking in or near the

Fig. 1. *Early experiments in transportation (G. Larson)*

Fig. 2. *'Watch out for those rocks, stay away from the tar pits, don't go through the puddles . . . '.*

cave, looking after children), they are almost never shown in a positive light. They contribute nothing, indeed they sometimes actively impede the march of male progress. Thus women, if they are there at all, refuse to bring meat (procured by skilful male hunters) home to the cave; they are unable to cook properly; and they scold their creative sons for 'writing' (i.e. painting) on the walls of the family cave. Images like that in Fig. 3 are

Fig. 3.

therefore very rare. But men are always there, evolving as they should, hunting to provide food for the family, and making important new discoveries which will benefit everyone.

The visual focus on men is reinforced verbally in captions and punchlines using the so-called generic pronoun (he, man, etc.). For example, a caveman arrives at a dinner party given by a woman who has not quite finished her preparations. Is she behind schedule? No, he is 'Early Man'. Or take the

Fig. 4. *The Anthropologist's Dream (G. Larson)*

joke where one cave woman says to another 'I saw a Cro-Magnon man today. Wow!' These jokes would not be funny if phrases like 'Early Man' and 'Cro-Magnon Man' really did include women as well as men.

Another joke (Fig. 4) makes it clear what the goals of an anthropologist (or archaeologist) really are – to find both a *Homo habilis* skull and a blonde woman. This joke suggests that those who investigate the most ancient human past are therefore probably men; and that the past as reconstructed by them consists of men and their activities, with women as a negative influence in the background. In the world of jokes, the study of the Stone Age boils down to men studying older men.

Until I began collecting these jokes, I had not realised how many powerful images of Stone Age life there were, ready to be used and reused – the caveman with his club; the shapeless over-the-shoulder garment made of (usually spotted) animal skin, worn by both sexes; the common association of people with already-extinct creatures like pterodactyls and sabre-toothed tigers. The success of such jokes is not dependent on their archaeological accuracy, but instead on our ability to recognise a familiar situation, no matter how remote the chronological context: the impractical male inventor, the whining female backseat driver. In other words these jokes resemble *The Flintstones*, the animated cartoon series set in the Stone Age, but also known as an accurate reflection of mid-twentieth century AD American sex roles.[3] Both the jokes and the cartoon series tell us more about our own time than they do about the palaeolithic.

Of course, the material discussed so far is popular rather than scholarly, though the impact of syndicated newspaper jokes like Gary Larson's 'The Far Side' and cartoons like *The Flintstones* should not be underestimated.[4] Let us turn now to scholarly reconstructions of life in the Stone Age for women and men.

We begin with language. A brief survey of book titles suggests that scholarly works do not avoid the so-called generic pronoun – *Man Makes Himself*; *Prehistoric Men*; *Man the Tool-Maker*; *Man the Hunter*; *Man, Settlement and Urbanism*; *Bones, Ancient Men and Modern Myths*.[5] Many of these books are still cited and used in classes; the older publications have been reprinted many times.

The naming of fossil remains confirms that there is in archaeology as in other disciplines a strong tradition of good old-fashioned sexist language, whose general limitations are concisely discussed by Spender.[6] We are all familiar with nicknames like 'Neanderthal Man' yet, as archaeologists, we are also taught that the sexing of single skeletons – let alone fragments – can be difficult. But perhaps names like 'Peking Man' are truly generic, and do include both female and male? The following example suggests otherwise.

A number of hominid skeletons were found in Ethiopia in 1974, including an unusually complete female. Her scientific name is *Australopithecus afarensis*, yet her nickname is neither 'Afar Man', nor 'Afar Woman' but Lucy, after the Beatles song 'Lucy in the Sky with Diamonds'.

The use of the so-called generic pronouns 'he' and 'man' seems to be connected with the exclusion of women, both verbal and visual, from reconstructions of human evolution. Scholars referring to people as 'man' can find it easy to forget that women were always present with men, and that they too changed and evolved.

Johanson and Edey's book about the Ethiopian skeletons, promisingly entitled *Lucy. The Beginnings of Humankind*, uses the so-called generic pronoun throughout – except to refer to Lucy herself. In the book, only one female is shown: a leopard has carried off (and presumably killed) a woman to a conveniently high tree; below are two men, one brandishing a stick, who were unable to 'rescue' her. A two-page chronological diagram of hominid and human reconstructions shows only men evolving, a drawing to illustrate primate locomotion includes only a male hominid. And finally, the reconstructions of *A. afarensis* depict a very masculine-looking individual, and the accompanying text makes it clear that this was the artist's intention. The only (flesh and blood) reconstruction of Lucy – described as one of the oldest and most complete fossil skeletons discovered so far – is on the cover (of the British paperback edition).[7]

The overemphasis on men and the near-exclusion of women are also apparent at the methodological level; indeed they are enshrined in the most powerful scholarly model for human life in the Stone Age. The Man the Hunter model, as propounded by Washburn and Lancaster (Lee and DeVore, 1968), makes two major assumptions: 1) that hunting by males was crucial for human survival; 2) that hunting by males influenced human evolution, leading to increased brain-size, and new developments in hominid/human society.[8]

Now suppose that another book had appeared in 1968, suggesting that gathering by females was the single most important strategy for human survival – gathering is, after all, known to be more reliable in terms of the quality and quantity of food collected than is hunting, which is unpredictable and often dangerous – and that gathering by females led to an increase in brain-size, and to the emergence of early societies in which labour was rigidly divided by sex, and where the female contribution was technologically innovative, socially beneficial, and always more highly valued. Imagine the scholarly outcry that might have followed – how is it possible to exclude men from a scholarly reconstruction of an important phase of *human* development? How can it be academically respectable to provide a gender-specific model for which little or no direct evidence exists? These are exactly some of the criticisms that have been made of the Man the Hunter model.

It seems, then, that scholarly interpretations of Stone Age life are disturbingly similar to the jokes and cartoons discussed earlier, with respect to language and visual detail. In both cases, there seems to be a strong connection between he/man language and reconstructions that either exclude women or limit them to stereotypical dependence. Even determined attempts to reconstruct the past accurately are distorted by the effects of gender bias.

Thus in Binford's aptly named *Bones. Ancient Men and Modern Myths*, the research questions are defined as follows:

> What was early man like? Did he hunt his food? Did he live in bands? Did he share his food, did he . . . , did he . . . ? We want to know what our ancestors were like and how they lived. We also want to know the forces at work that molded our ancestors so that we 'modern men' were the evolutionary outcome.[9]

More recent work suggests that other questions could usefully be asked. For example, was hunting really the crucial strategy for survival in the Stone Age? In terms of the quality and quantity of food collected, gathering is known to be more reliable than hunting. Margaret Ehrenberg has used ethnographic parallels and archaeological evidence to propose that Woman the Gatherer was indeed more important to Stone Age societies.[10]

And what about the whole concept of survival of the fittest with its associated concepts, scarcity and competition? Gross and Averill (1983) have analysed these two abstract notions in the context of human evolution. They begin by noting that the survival of the fittest is a nineteenth-century idea that suggests both competition and scarcity. Seen through this perspective, life is an unremitting competition for scarce resources, such as food, territory – and females. Thus men would choose women to propagate themselves, but uncontrolled female reproduction could at any time result in scarce resources, which would then have to be acquired through competition.

But there are other possible views of evolution. For example, there is now evidence that among primates it is often *females* who select their mates and that they prefer intelligent males to aggressive ones. Females therefore play an important role in determining the genetic heritage of their offspring. If this is true for early humans, then the concept of competition may no longer be helpful. As for scarcity,

Why not see nature as bounteous, rather than parsimonious, and admit that opportunity and cooperation are more likely to abet novelty, innovation, and creation than are struggle and competition? Evolution in this perspective can be seen not as a constant struggle for occupation and control of territories but as a successive opening of opportunities. . . .[11]

It may no longer be necessary, or appropriate, to view the Stone Age through the brutal perspective of compulsory competition and inescapable scarcity, nor to keep Man the Hunter as the centre of attention.[12]

MINOANS, MYCENAEANS AND MISPLACED GENDER POLARITY

Gender polarity is very common in the way that we look at objects, activities, and concepts, as the following list will perhaps show: dolls, domestic science/home economics, intuition; building blocks, engineering, logic. Most of us would agree, without necessarily thinking it appropriate, that the first three are commonly associated with women, the second three with men. Archaeologists tend to assume that this way of seeing the world is natural, and that this is how people have always seen the world. As a result we may use our own presentist, polarised view to account for differences in human groups without even realising it, and therefore without stopping to consider whether doing so will actually advance our understanding of ancient societies.

Those studying Bronze Age Aegean archaeology are often struck by the difference between the Minoan and Mycenaean civilisations. Here I will briefly introduce Minoan Crete and Mycenaean Greece (roughly 1600–1100 BC), and then discuss how misplaced gender polarity came to be used to 'explain' this difference.

Among the best-known features of Minoan Crete are the large structures we call palaces. A glance at the plan of Knossos reveals an imposing complex some 15 600 sq. m in area (excluding the settlement around it).[13] Neither the palace nor the settlement was fortified but this does not mean that the Minoans did not have weapons; swords/daggers of roughly the same date have been found at a number of sites.[14]

Grander Minoan buildings, including houses as well as palaces, were decorated with wall-paintings, like the Blue Bird and Monkey Fresco from Knossos; and the Cat and Pheasant Fresco from Hagia Triada.[15] These two paintings represent one type of Minoan wall-painting; they are highly stylised scenes painted in brilliant colours, showing animals in a setting of plants and flowers. It was paintings like these that led archaeologists to characterise the people that produced them as the carefree nature-lovers of the Bronze Age.[16]

Of particular interest are the 'miniature frescoes' from Knossos which do include people. In the Sacred Dance and Grove, women in the foreground lead a dance or conduct a ritual in an area marked off by special walkways. Behind them, and outside the special area, are three olive trees and crowds of spectators. Some of the female spectators are seated, and the rest are shown as disembodied heads. But most of the spectators are male. Some, at the same scale as the women in the foreground, are standing; many more are shown in the same artistic shorthand, as disembodied heads.[17]

In the Temple and Grand Stand Fresco, only women are shown as complete figures, either sitting or standing. Once again there is a crowd of spectators in the background, some of whom are female. In general the women are definitely more conspicuous than the men in the picture, shown only as disembodied heads. They are the centre of attention in the wall-painting as preserved.[18]

Evans used the latter fresco to suggest that women had some special role in Minoan society, remarking that 'the non-admission of male spectators among them may well . . . be a sign of female predominance characteristic of the matriarchal stage', and also that women may have a superior social position which allowed them to associate freely with men.[19] He says too that 'Women among the Minoans, as is well illustrated by their occupation of the front seats of the Grand Stands, took the high rank in Society, just as their great Goddess took the place later assigned to Zeus.'[20]

Yet Evans's view of the relative status of Minoan women and men was not always consistent. Most people would agree that people of 'the higher rank in Society' will usually have more and better space – a larger house, the corner office. In the area called the domestic quarter at Knossos in the south-east section of the palace, there are two similar sets of rooms, one larger and one smaller. Because women and men are shown separately in both the Sacred Dance and Grove Fresco and the Temple and Grand Stand Fresco (and because the *Iliad* and *Odyssey* describe separate quarters for women), Evans assumed that these two sets of rooms must have been used as women's and men's quarters, though there are of course other possibilities. Then, because the excavators of the mainland palace at Tiryns had assigned a smaller room to women and a larger one to men, Evans named the smaller set of rooms at Knossos the Queen's Megaron. The larger, known as the Hall of the Double Axes, was therefore for men.[21] Thus though the Knossian wall-paintings suggested a 'matriarchal' society to

Evans, he still thought that men should have more space in the palace. Even though Evans's ideas are inconsistent, no one has ever suggested reversing his names for the two sets of rooms; nor has the notion of Minoan matriarchy disappeared from serious scholarship, despite the lack of any evidence (apart from that of the frescoes) to confirm or disprove it.[22]

These criticisms are not intended as fundamental disparagement of Evans and his work. As his biographer says:

> Time and Chance had made him the discoverer of a new civilization . . . . Fortunately it was exactly to his taste: set in beautiful Mediterranean country, aristocratic and humane in feeling; creating an art brilliant in colour and unusual in form . . . .[23]

Most popular and scholarly assessments of Minoan civilisation were, at least to begin with, as positive and enthusiastic as this one.[24]

On the Greek mainland, the later Bronze Age saw the development of Mycenaean culture. The Shaft Graves of Grave Circle A at Mycenae, excavated by Schliemann in the 1870s, contained a wide variety of grave goods as well as skeletons. The objects associated with male burials included gold masks (at least one does have a beard and moustache); and daggers with inlaid decoration, showing animals being hunted and killed, by other animals or by men.[25]

Initial reaction to the objects found in these graves was not favourable:

> If the criteria by which we are in the habit of judging of the art of the Greeks and other ancient races are applied to these Mycenaean antiquities, we shall find that they rank very low in the scale. They present to us, it is true, considerable vigour and invention in the designing of mere patterns and ornaments, but in almost every case in which the representation of animal life is attempted we see a feebleness of execution, the result of barbarous ignorance . . . . To begin with the gold masks . . . we confess that it was not without a shudder that we first beheld these hideous libels on the 'human face divine'. . . .[26]

Further work at Mycenae revealed the details of the heavy fortifications, such as the Lioness Gate leading on to the citadel. Within the citadel a structure called a palace was excavated; comparison with Knossos reveals that it was neither as large nor as complex.[27]

Both women and men are depicted in Mycenaean frescoes, but there are no wall-paintings where women seem to be the centre of attention; indeed, women and men do not often appear together in the same picture, though it is sometimes hard to be sure of this when only fragments are found. At Pylos, for example, women are shown in processions, and in a scene with possible religious overtones; men can be in processions too, but are also represented as hunters and warriors.[28] It is worth noting that while there are Cretan procession frescoes, hunting and fighting scenes seem to occur only on the mainland.

From this necessarily brief appraisal of Minoan and Mycenaean art and architecture, it is easy to understand why Mycenaean culture was at first seen as negatively barbarous, while the Minoans were considered positively civilised. But even at this stage, the difference between the two cultures has not been explained (or particularly well described), just polarised as good (Minoan) and bad (Mycenaean).

Popular and scholarly opinion of a culture can change dramatically, however, sometimes more than once, as Elizabeth Rawson showed in the case of the Spartans.[29] Current views of the Minoans are not what they were, as this quotation from an otherwise useful handbook will show:

> The standard view today, however, sees the Mycenaeans as Greeks and the Aegean world as under Greek domination after the conquest of a non-Greek Crete by people from the mainland *c.* 1450. But this raises the problem of how a people later to display such genius, enterprise, and originality, could in the vigour of this youthful stage in their history submit to a slavish dependence not only on a non-Greek, half-Oriental civilization such as the Minoan, but also on the civilizations of the Near East in general . . . . On the assumption that the Mycenaeans were Greeks it has to be admitted that the native Greek genius was in some mysterious way stifled by the influence of that seductive fairyworld, the civilization of Minoan Crete; and that it was only rescued from this suffocating constraint with the collapse of the Mycenaean world and the harsh impetus of the entry of the semi-barbarous and as yet uncontaminated Dorian Greek tribes . . . .

Despite their seductive and contaminating influence, the Minoans were not all bad, because 'something peculiarly European has been detected in the art of Minoan Crete, something which was inherited by the Mycenaean world . . . .'[30]

This marked shift in judgement is connected, I believe, with the decipherment of Linear B. The first Linear B tablets were found by Evans at Knossos in the early 1900s; it was nearly 40 years before others were excavated on the mainland. They all date to the period when Mycenaean dominance in the Aegean had overtaken even the Minoans. When Linear B was deciphered in 1954, the tablets turned out to be written in a very early form of the Greek language, thus transforming the hitherto mute Mycenaeans into Greek-speakers. The tablets are lists of commodities and people, and they make it clear that those in charge of the palaces were men, though women were important in several areas of the economy.[31] Thus Mycenaean Greece could be described as a 'patriarchal' society.

A list of nouns and adjectives culled from standard handbooks shows that scholars have a sharply polarised view of Minoan and Mycenaean art and culture.[32]

Minoans	*Mycenaeans*
graceful	stiff
delicate	harsh
finer	cruder
spontaneous	ponderous
miniature	monumental
gay	severe
impressionistic	stylised
movement	restraint
crowded	simple
lovely	handsome
exuberant	disciplined
organic	tectonic

Most people would have no difficulty in knowing which column is associated with women, and which with men. Furthermore these associations are occasionally made explicit ('The high esteem of the female is also discernible in the religion of the more masculine Mycenaean civilization . . .').[33]

In terms of our own cultural heritage, the Greeks are us, so they must be good. People who are not Greeks, who are not part of the same cultural tradition (no matter what they have contributed to our European heritage), are probably bad. The Minoans are not Greeks, which is not good, and then there is the additional problem of 'matriarchy' as well. So other polar opposites can be added to the list above.

non-Greek	Greek
Oriental	European
'matriarchal'	'patriarchal'
feminine	masculine
bad	good

We can now see how misplaced gender polarity works: a difference between two cultures is noticed, though never clearly articulated as an issue. The two cultures are polarised as feminine and masculine, and values are then assigned to these poles: bad and good, or good and bad (the assignment of these values can change, as we have seen). Here the end-result is to polarise the Minoans as feminine, non-Greek, and bad; the Mycenaeans as masculine, Greek, and good.[34]

It should also be noted that this view of the Aegean Bronze Age involves not only a static construction of polar opposites, but a dynamic sequence of events, in which the 'matriarchal' Minoans are subjugated by the 'patriarchal' Mycenaeans. This story follows a pattern that occurs in the fifth-century BC historian Herodotus' account of the Lycians (I.173), and in Varro's explanation (first century BC) of the origin of male democracy in Athens (quoted by St Augustine, *City of God*, 18.9). Pembroke has shown that far from being a real situation, the Lycian matriarchy was part of a mythical statement to bolster a contemporary Greek patriarchy, based on the worst possible alternative.[35] In other words, the hypothetically matriarchal past has been used to validate and reinforce the patriarchal 'present', whether Lycian, Athenian, or archaeological. The implication is that 'matriarchy' and 'patriarchy' are mythically imprecise terms which tell us little about the cultures to which they are applied. It is up to us as archaeologists to avoid such terms, and instead to determine the balance of female and male power as accurately as we can instead of making *a priori* assumptions about it.

Thus-misplaced gender polarity is not useful, for several reasons. First, it leads to inaccuracy. For example, it is extraordinary to view Mycenaean art as monumental, Minoan as miniature. This is achieved by ignoring the size and complexity of Minoan architecture, and by overemphasising Mycenaean fortifications. Such a view involves a rather revealing value judgement on aesthetically pleasing and functional residential design on the one hand, and high defence spending on the other.

Second, misplaced gender polarity leaves us where we started. We have two more or less contemporary civilisations that differ from one another in some respects, and after 90 years of scholarship since the later discovery of Minoan culture, we have not explained the difference. Nor has anyone tried to see if the differences between the Minoans and Mycenaeans were outweighed by the obvious similarities between them. All we have done is to show that *we* think of difference in feminine and masculine terms; once again this says more about us than it does about the Aegean Bronze Age.

THE DIVISION OF LABOUR IN ARCHAEOLOGY

The archaeologist currently dominating the world of popular culture is surely Indiana Jones. He is the James Bond of fieldwork, dashing all over the world and grappling with the forces of evil in order to recover the Lost Ark or the Holy Grail. In his world, women play a subordinate, often sexual role (see Fig. 4 for another example).[36] But in the world of fiction, there is also Frances Wingate, the intrepid archaeologist and devoted mother in Margaret Drabble's novel *The Realms of Gold*, who conducted her own excavations in the African desert.[37] Does either one of these characters correspond to real life? What is the division of labour in archaeology?

In her article 'Socio-politics and the Woman-at Home Ideology', published in 1985, Joan Gero hypothesises a strong similarity between the professional roles of male and female archaeologists, and the kinds of reconstructions they produce, such as the Man the Hunter model:

> We are alerted to certain strong parallels between the male who populates the archaeological record – public, visible, physically active, exploratory, dominant and rugged, the stereotypic hunter – and the practising field archaeologist who himself conquers the landscape, brings home the goodies, and takes his data raw! . . . Corresponding, then, to the stereotyped male, we expect to find the female archaeologist secluded in the base-camp laboratory or museum, sorting and preparing archaeological materials, private, protected, passively receptive, ordering and systematising, but without recognised contribution to the productive process. The women-at-home archaeologist must . . . do the archaeological housework.

Gero also analysed statistics on prestigious National (i.e. American) Science Foundation (NSF) funding, in order to test her hypothesis that the division of labour in archaeology reflects traditional sex roles. The figures show that NSF gives fieldwork a very high priority, but the success/failure rate for these grants also shows that women have much more difficulty in getting funding for their own fieldwork (15 per cent success rate), while men are more than twice as likely (35 per cent) to be successful. Women do better (28 per cent) when they apply for NSF grants for non-field-oriented projects; but the success rate for men was the same no matter what kind of project they applied for.[38] The implication is that fieldwork is man's work and that women should not be doing it; but that being in charge of any kind of project is suitable for men. Gero's findings seem to suggest that Indiana Jones is closer to real life than Frances Wingate.

Foreign archaeologists in Greece (the country in which I have done most of my own fieldwork) provide a good case for the study of the division of labour in archaeology. Because Greek law limits the number of permits for excavation and survey (three each per country), there is competition at the national level for permission to work in Greece, as well as competition for funding. The foreign archaeological schools exist to help with applications to do archaeological fieldwork in Greece, as well as to provide research facilities and a convenient base for those studying the ancient world. Until 1983 no woman had ever been director of a foreign school in Greece; to date only the Canadian Archaeological Institute (1983–86, 1986–87) and the British School at Athens (1989–) have had female directors. The picture is somewhat better for female Assistant Directors, the first of whom was appointed in 1981; currently four foreign schools have employed women in this position (Canada, Australia, Sweden, Switzerland).

As far as I have been able to determine, the American School of Classical Studies is the only foreign school to publish lists of directors, projects, and dates of field seasons, which makes it possible to compare women and men in terms of the number of projects, and their duration (see Table 1.1)

Table 1.1 ASCS projects and seasons, by gender, 1900–80

1900–1940	No. of projects	Total no. of seasons
women	5 (22.7 per cent)	18 (14.2 per cent)
men	18	108
TOTALS	22 (M/F shared project in 1 instance)	126

1940–1980	No. of projects	Total no. of seasons
women	2 (7.4 per cent)	10 (5.9 per cent)
men	28	158
TOTALS	27 (shared project in 3 instances)	168

From this table it emerges very clearly that women direct fewer projects of shorter duration, and that the situation does not seem to have improved over time.[39]

It has not been possible to obtain such figures for all of the foreign archaeological schools, but to the best of my knowledge there have only ever been fifteen women who have initiated their own field projects in Greece, i.e. women who have obtained both the permit and the funding necessary to excavate or survey (the countries represented are Australia, Canada, the US, the UK and Sweden). I know of three other women who have been asked to head major projects already underway; plus others who have co-directed with men. To put these numbers in perspective, we have only to recall that six of the foreign schools have existed for over a century, during which time they each had three excavation permits.

Why is it that more women do not direct field projects? Is it because women do not do fieldwork in Greece, and therefore do not gain the necessary experience?[40] A look at the footnotes naming project staff in final and preliminary reports will usually show that as many women as men will be listed and thanked. But most of the men will usually be out in the trenches, or climbing every mountain in their survey area, while the women will usually be working 'at home' – in charge of the field lab, or storerooms (commonly known as the *apotheke*), cataloguing, drawing, getting supplies – in short, doing the archaeological housework. So there are plenty of women doing archaeology in Greece, but they tend to be assigned to jobs which are not considered suitable experience for directing a field project. Running an *apotheke* is an important job because it involves the management and record-keeping of field data and finds; but I have yet to hear of a field director in Greece, female or male, who has been in charge of one.

Though it is difficult to quantify it in precise terms, the distribution of foreign women and men working in archaeology in Greece, seems uneven, indeed asymmetrical, with men predominating as prestigious field directors, and women usually relegated to the obscure seclusion of the *apotheke*. No doubt future research would reveal sexual stereotyping in other areas of archaeological training such as graduate school; e.g. the choice of 'suitable' thesis topics (boys do architecture, girls do jewellery); and the relative success rates in the completion of higher degrees (less encouragement given to female students, who may be seen only as potential cataloguers; more attention paid to male students as the groundbreaking fieldworkers of the future).[41]

If we return now to the fifteen or so female field directors in Greece, that is, women who have been successful in some sense because of their involvement in a prestigious archaeological activity, it quickly becomes apparent that nearly all of us have had unconventional careers. Men have jobs in archaeology, usually with tenure, and also direct field projects; women who direct field projects do not necessarily get jobs in archaeology. For women it seems to be an either/or proposition; for men, both/and. Now perhaps having an unconventional career is not such a bad thing. The trouble is that without a permanent job in archaeology it is difficult to get funding for fieldwork, or even to participate in any general decision-making within the discipline.

There is another difference between female and male field directors in Greece; most male directors are married, most female directors are not. Let us consider briefly why that may be. A male archaeologist can still expect to marry someone who will arrange her life around his. Thus when male archaeologists marry they may get help to support them financially. They may get help with their dissertation work, either intellectually or practically (typing, making the coffee). They will get someone who will not only have the children but look after them as well, and here it is important to remember that most granting agencies forbid the use of their funds for childcare expenses. Male archaeologists will often get someone who will follow them into the field, perhaps to run the *apotheke* (the traditional reward for this was the opportunity to publish the finds that no one else was interested in); or perhaps to arrange meals and run errands, while taking care of the children. In short, male archaeologists when they marry acquire a built-in source of support, that is, wives.[42]

If a female archaeologist marries, she does not get a wife, she gets a husband, who is unlikely to arrange his life around hers in the manner described above. If a female archaeologist decides to remain single, and therefore to forgo the kind of private life that her male counterparts take for granted, she may reduce her chance of being sidetracked, but she will still have to do without the support that men traditionally get from their wives.[43]

And there is no doubt that people directing field projects do need support. The actual fieldwork is physically challenging and often logistically complicated; obtaining permits, raising the money, organising personnel and, above all, seeing the project through to the final publication are heavy responsibilities. If men usually have wives who provide much of the support necessary to keep the project going, and women do not, it is not surprising that more men than women will be field directors.

But part of the reason that directing a field project is so demanding is the way that the work is structured, so that officially only one person – the 'principal investigator' of the grant proposals – is in charge. I say 'officially', because in fact directors of field projects are a bit like Olympic competitors: many people support them, but only the athlete wins the medal. Surely there is something wrong with the structure of work, as well as the division of labour, if one person has all the responsibility and credit for a particular project, but at the same time requires a large amount of support, often affecting another person's whole life. It is worth noting that female field directors have begun to subvert this structure, by co-directing with other women and with men. But as long as women have less access to 'wifely' support, and as long as the structure of archaeological fieldwork remains unchanged, women will continue to have a harder time than men, if they wish to play any sort of decision-making role in archaeology.

Research on male–female socialisation suggests that men are encouraged to be point-dependent and women tend to be field-dependent, i.e. men cannot see the wood for the trees and women cannot see the trees for the wood.[44] Archaeological training is biased toward point-dependence, in that we are taught to take things apart, often at the expense of putting them together in order to look at the big picture. One result of this analytical 'male' training is that the final report of a survey or excavation will often present long, detailed lists of discrete data, with relatively little space left for 'female' synthesis. Women have long excelled at one particular type of synthesis, though it is considered very much outside the sphere of hard scholarship. I am referring to the much-maligned historical novel, a genre which requires an author to put many different kinds of information together in order to produce a plausibly accurate story. This process could be described in archaeological jargon as taking a hypothesis on a test-drive in order to check out the latest model. After all, both a model and a story are reconstructions of the past; the difference between them is that a story has to be much more complete in order to be plausible. In order to achieve that degree of detail the person producing the story often has to ask many more questions.

Jean Auel, Mary Renault, Pauline Gedge, Sybille Haynes, Colleen McCullough, and Rosemary Sutcliffe have all written interestingly about life in the past, from the Stone Age to Egypt, from Minoan Crete and Mycenaean Greece to the classical world, from the Etruscans to Roman Britain; their books make it possible to see one view of an ancient society very clearly, and to suggest others, in a way that most excavation and survey reports do not.[45] Surely the best way to conduct archaeological research is to use both approaches, 'male' analysis and 'female' synthesis. But approaches to the past will continue to be limited to male ways of thinking and working until there are more women in archaeology at the decision-making level.

CONCLUSIONS

In the first three sections of this chapter I hope to have demonstrated that both archaeology and archaeologists are adversely affected by gender bias. I would like now to make some general suggestions for making archaeology a more rigorous and a more human discipline.

First of all, he/man language has to go. Referring to people in the past and archaeologists in the present as 'he' reinforces the idea that only men have ever been important and that the role of women has always been negligible. Second, visual reconstructions should both include women, and show them in a positive light.

Third, objects such as stone blades and bone needles have no gender; the archaeologist starts by examining the artefact and assessing its physical attributes, but she does not begin by 'knowing' who made or used it; that must be determined, if it is possible to determine it, by careful interpretation. Similarly, cave- and wall-paintings do not come with a key to explain the identity and status of the human beings they depict; rooms and structures are not excavated with labels saying who lived in them and what they did there.

Furthermore, the methodological problems of recognising gender and status that we encountered in the prehistoric examples discussed in the first two sections apply to historic periods as well, when the availability of written evidence often leads archaeologists and historians alike to think that they already 'know' who made the objects and used the structures. Thus in Iron Age Greece, we know that in the Orientalising, Archaic, and Classical periods women should be seen as active patrons of the arts rather than merely passive consumers.[46] But what about women as producers, that is as artists? The representation of a woman painting a vase has long been known; there is also a vase-painter's name, Douris, which could well be a variant of a common Greek woman's name, Doris.[47] These two points suggest that sometimes women took part in the production of vases, just as they are known to have participated in other professions.[48]

Fourth, archaeology has come to pride itself on being a problem-oriented discipline. But being problem-oriented is no protection against bias if only certain problems are addressed. So, for example, 'What was the division of labour in ancient societies?' and 'How can we study it using material evidence?' are questions that have only recently been defined as archaeological problems worth serious consideration. The prevailing tendency had been to assume that we already knew what women and men did, and to use imprecise words like 'matriarchy' and 'patriarchy' to describe what we thought we knew. Unexamined assumptions about who did what in the past produce the kind of presentist reconstructions of the past that say more about us than they do about any other period except our own. But now that we are asking the right questions, it should be possible to get a more accurate view of ancient societies.[49]

To sum up: if what you look for in archaeology is what you find, then *whom* you look for is *whom* you find. If you look only for men, that is all you will get. And if only men do the looking, then archaeology is reduced to the sad spectacle of men studying older men.

Why does any of this matter? After all, archaeology is thought of as an ivory-tower discipline with little connection to the real world which we all inhabit, where the past is neither here nor there. But 'the past', however defined, is very useful, which is why people always want to have the right kind of past, from the right kind of family history, to the right kind of precedents for state ideology. Thus the past as reconstructed by archaeologists, heritage experts, ethnic minorities and national majorities can be used to reinforce and validate the present, and can therefore affect the future as well. No one should therefore be surprised if Man the Hunter is used to justify anything from territorial aggression to modern family policies; after all, if that is how human beings have been since the Stone Age, that must be how we really are, and should continue to be. We must be accurate and meticulous in our interpretations of the past if only because of the uses to which they can be put in the future.[50]

This chapter began partly as the result of teaching an undergraduate course in archaeology. There will eventually, I hope, come a time when it is not necessary to spend classroom time on the problem of gender bias in archaeology, because all archaeological method and theory will work on the premise that women as well as men have always had an important role in the past – but that time has not yet come. It is therefore useful and appropriate to call the problem by its real name, using words like woman, gender, even the f-word (feminist), rather than terms like human. We must realise that our discipline is still a branch of 'men's studies', and we must continue to discuss the problem of gender bias in an explicit way, even as we work towards a truly human archaeology.

NOTES

1. Earlier versions of this paper were given from 1986 to 1988, in various places. I would like to thank the members of these audiences, and the editors of this book for their comments, which have helped to improve the essay; I am, of course, responsible for the faults that remain. I am also grateful to the staffs of the Ashmolean Library, Oxford, and the Ward Chipman Library, University of New Brunswick at Saint John for their help. My husband Simon Price and our daughter Elizabeth Nixon provided much-needed support during the writing of this chapter.
2. Conkey and Spector (1984), p. 3. See also Gero and Conkey (1991).
3. Levinson (1975).
4. E.g. Larson (1985), from which Figures 1 and 4 were taken. The journal *Antiquity* now includes Larson jokes on a regular basis; note also the editor's report on a new computer game, 'Caveman Ugh.Lympics', Chippindale (1989), pp. 419–20.
5. Childe (1936); Braidwood (1948); Oakley (1949); Lee and DeVore (1968); Ucko, Tringham, and Dimbleby (1972); Binford (1981).
6. Spender (1980), pp. 147–57.
7. Lucy and he/man language and reconstructions in Johanson and Edey (1981): use of so-called generic pronouns, pp. 22–3; leopard with woman in tree, p. 71, and note that there is no mention in the text of whether the skull with leopard tooth-holes (on which the drawing is based) was ever sexed; 'human'

evolution pictures, pp. 290–1; primate locomotion, p. 323, reconstructions of *A. afarensis*, pp. 358–61. For the comments of the artist, Jay Matternes, about his reconstructions, see pp. 385–6.

There has been some improvement: in Weaver *et al.* (1985), while only men evolve (pp. 574–6, and pp. 584–5), women do appear in reconstructions of Stone Age life – and they are not just cowering in the back of the cave (pp. 594, 598, 615). There is even a picture of a female archaeologist (p. 582).

8. Washburn and Lancaster in Lee and DeVore (1968), summarised by Conkey and Spector (1984), pp. 6–9. Tracing the origins of the Man the Hunter model is a research project that would definitely be worth doing. The earliest visual representation of Man the Hunter that I could find is an enormous oil-painting, signed F. Cormon and dated 1883, which takes up most of a wall in the Salle d'Archéologie Comparative in the Musée des Antiquités at Saint-Germain-en-Laye, and seems to represent male hunters returning to the shack where they live with their women and children. On the left, men with weapons, dressed in over-the-shoulder furry garments, arrive at a large shack. A dead animal lies at their feet. In the centre is an older man who seems to be making stone tools. On the right is a group of naked women sitting on a bench outside the shack with some children.

9. Binford (1981), p. 249.

10. Ehrenberg (1989), pp. 51–60; and cf. pp. 99–107. Trigger (1989), pp. 334–5 and 399 comments on the dangers of using modern ethnographic parallels for ancient hunter–gatherer societies, with special reference to Binford. He does not discuss women or gender bias.

11. Gross and Averill (1983), pp. 81, 85.

12. See for example the work of Zeller (1987), whose conclusion is that hominid children could have contributed significantly to their own and their mother's subsistence base, and that such a contribution would be an important factor in the successful increase of human populations. Thus far from reproducing uncontrollably, hominid/human mothers reared children who survived to be a precious and enabling community resource. Cf. also Haraway (1990) who discusses other perspectives in primate studies, including sociobiological feminism.

13. Demargne (1964), fig. 157.

14. Evans (1921–36), IV.2, suppl. pl. LXVIII.

15. Ibid., II.2, pls X, XI; Demargne (1964), fig. 198.

16. Miller (1941, repr. 1980), pp. 123–4.

17. Evans (1921–36), III, pl. XVIII.

18. Ibid., pls XVI, XVII.

19. Ibid., III, p. 58.

20. Ibid., III, p. 227.

21. Ibid., III, pp. 349–50 and plan E.

22. Buchholz and Karageorghis (1973), p. 22; Cadogan (1976), p. 9. For further discussion see Nixon (1983) and Ehrenberg (1989), pp. 63–6 and 109–118. See also n. 35 below.

23. Evans (1943), p. 350.

24. Glotz (1925), pp. 303–5.

25. Demargne (1964), figs. 256–71 (masks); inlaid daggers, figs. 263–6.

26. Newton (1880), p. 271.

27. Demargne (1964), fig. 291 (Lioness Gate); fig. 290 (plan of Mycenae); Renfrew (1972), p. 243 (comparison of size of palaces at Knossos and Mycenae).

28. Lang (1969), pp. 86–90, 62, 131–2, and pls 1, M, and R (scenes with women), 64–5, 68–71, 71–6 (scenes with men).

29. Rawson (1969). I am grateful to Helen Brock for this reference.

30. Hood (1978), pp. 240–1.

31. Billigmeier and Turner (1981).

32. Compiled from Matz (1962), Buchholz and Karageorghis (1973); Hood (1978); Higgins (1981).

33. Buchholz and Karageorghis (1973), p. 22. Non-archaeologists have picked up on the Minoan:Mycenaean/feminine:masculine dichotomy; compare the treatment of the two cultures in Renault (1958, 1962). More recently Michael Wood, in his BBC series *The Search for Troy*, described Minoan Crete as 'a culture of luxury' while flutes trilled in accompaniment; trumpet-blasts announced his panegyric to the Mycenaean empire; I am grateful to Margaret Laird for these observations.

34. The association between women, Minoans, and 'non-Greek, half-Oriental' is an important one. Said (1978) made the connection between Oriental *men* and effeminacy, but never explored the significance of the link for women.

35. Pembroke (1967), Lefkowitz (1986). If the hypothetical era of matriarchy is anathema for some, it has become a lost golden age for others, such as Rohrlich-Leavitt (1977), Eisler (1987) and Cross (1990).

36. Once again the influence of popular culture should not be underestimated: one of the male graduate students working on the field project that I co-direct in Crete has shown up every year with full Indiana Jones regalia, including a bullwhip.

37. Drabble (1975).

38. Gero (1985), pp. 344–7.

39. Lord (1947), pp. 295–308; Meritt (1984). It should be noted that these figures have been taken directly from the ASCSA lists, which count women and men who have directed smaller projects on larger sites separately, e.g. Agnes Stillwell in the Potter's Quarter at Corinth; these women are not included in the total of fifteen female field directors. The figures stop too soon to show the small but definite upsurge in female directors of surveys in the 1980s (three Americans, as well as one Canadian and one Swede). Survey archaeology is cheaper and less time-consuming than excavation, and has only recently become respectable in Greece. For a brief period, survey was perhaps 'suitable' for women because of its relative lack of prestige. But the number of survey permits is now limited, just like excavation permits, and my prediction is that women will have a harder time in future getting permission (from their own countries) to apply to do survey work.

40. Waterhouse (1986), p. 132 tells us that women were not permitted to reside at the British School at Athens, nor to take part in excavations until 1910; other foreign schools may have had similar prohibitions.

41. In general, the division of labour in the academic world is based on the same old sexual stereotypes – with men taking conspicuous decision-making roles

at the top, and women confined to the lower ranks of the hierarchy, however it is defined; cf. the figures in Nixon (1987); CUWAG (1988); DeWitt and Nixon (1988). Thus even stay-at-home female classics professors encounter difficulties in getting their work accepted that their male colleagues seldom face; see Lefkowitz (1981), pp. 82–3.

42. Wives of male students at the British School were expected to help support their husbands financially, as reported by Waterhouse (1986), p. 147. In North America wives providing financial support for husbands in graduate school call their work a PHT (Putting Hubby Through). As for intellectual support, PhD dissertations written by men commonly acknowledge their wives' help. I have now seen a two-wife dissertation in a discipline that also involves fieldwork, in which the author thanks both his wives for the clearly crucial difference their contribution made to his research.

Bernard (1972) has pointed out that marriage is beneficial for men, and that men know this (most divorced and widowed men remarry); she also discusses the corollary, that marriage is not so beneficial to women. In Greek archaeology, not only are most male field directors married, but many of them have been married more than once. I call this the Schliemann Syndrome, after the illustrious excavator of Troy and Mycenae, himself married twice. As readers of Bernard would expect, these husbands (and their careers) have benefited, but their wives (or functional equivalents) have not always fared so well. For example, it is very rare for both first and second wives to have jobs in archaeology. For a somewhat similar situation in the business world, see Connelly (1989).

43. Needless to say, single female archaeologists, like other women who decide against marriage and long-term relationships with men, risk being called promiscuous or frigid; the sexual conduct of single male archaeologists is seldom criticised in the same terms.

All research involving fieldwork poses problems for women (for the usual stereotypical reasons), and much of what I have to say here applies to anthropology as well; cf. Friedl (1970), Clark Forbes (1983), and Butler and Turner (1987), especially their comments on the (positive) effect of children on professional objectivity and subjectivity (pp. 18–21).

44. Spender (1980), pp. 164–5; Gilligan (1982).

45. Auel (1980), Renault (1958, 1962), Gedge (1977, 1978), Haynes (1987), McCullough (1990), Sutcliffe (1978, 1986). I am grateful to Catherine Farrell for the McCullough reference.

46. Ridgway (1987), pp. 400–4.

47. Vase with female vase-painter, Green (1961); Anne Bowtell kindly furnished this reference. I am grateful to Jim Coulton for the observation about Douris/ Doris.

48. Lefkowitz and Fant (1982), pp. 27–31.

49. See Conkey and Spector (1984), pp. 21–7 and Sørensen (1988), pp. 14–18 for other suggestions on improving archaeological method and theory.

50. For an example of prehistoric archaeology being used as part of a positive argument for future change, see Arwill-Nordbladh (1989) on Montelius and the early Swedish women's movement.

2 Women in Ancient Egyptian Wisdom Literature
Annette Depla

This chapter presents a study of women in Ancient Egypt, and will concentrate on data provided by a discrete group of documents, known to modern scholars as Wisdom, or Didactic Literature, and to the Egyptians as Instructions. The chapter will deal only with the Pharaonic period (2900–332 BC), as changed attitudes towards women emerge with the Graeco-Roman period, as do new problems regarding the analysis of source material.

Table 2.1 Period demarcations (Hornung (1982), p. 261)

Date	Chronological divisions	Dynasties
c.2900–2628	Archaic	I and II
c.2628–2134	Old Kingdom	III–VIII
c.2134–2040	First Intermediate Period	IX–XI
c.2040–1650	Middle Kingdom	XI–XIV
c.1650–1551	Second Intermediate Period	XV and XVI Hyksos
1551–1070	New Kingdom	XVII–XX
1070–664	Third Intermediate Period	XXI–XXV
664–332	Late Period	XXVI–XXX
332 BC–AD 395	Graeco-Roman Period	

PROBLEMS OF SOURCES: WOMEN, THE SILENT SEX

Unlike the case for men, no vernacular treatise on women – guidelines as to how they should behave or their accepted place in society – survives in the body of ancient Wisdom literature. Also, there are no autobiographies by women in the Pharaonic period. The first examples derive from the Graeco-Roman period and fall outside the chronological scope of this paper. There are no examples of Didactic literature for or by women. Thus, we do not know what was expected of women, nor what rites of passage, if any, were undergone, or the major landmarks in their careers as wives and mothers. References to women within the Wisdom texts are incidental, often laconic and enigmatic. Their history has instead to be constructed from data contained within the entire cultural assemblage currently available to Egyptologists: wills and testaments; transmission deeds; depositions; depictions in temple reliefs; tomb murals, and statuary.

In spite of the variety of material, the overall picture is far from complete, and at times appears contradictory. For example, administrative documents such as those listed above show that women had a degree of economic independence and could initiate unilateral action to administer, distribute, defend, or increase their personal property.[1] On the other hand, Didactic literature, which was written by men, for men, implies dependence on the part of the females and reduces women to ancillary actors in the advancement of the male career.

A further problem is the variable survival rate of the material: one locale, genre, or era may be over-represented in the historical record because of the fortuitous survival of artifacts and texts. A notable example is Deir el-Medina, the village that housed the artisans that worked on the royal tombs at Thebes.[2] Its preservation under desert sand has offered archaeologists a rare opportunity to study an entire village and its associated archives. However, the specialised skills of the inhabitants and their unique relationship with the Crown urges caution when generalising about village life throughout Egypt. The variable survival rate of the texts means that in order to have sufficient data to study, it is necessary to consider material from a large chronological span. This carries a number of hazards. No society, no matter how conservative, remains entirely static, and comparisons of texts separated by millennia must be treated with extreme caution even if seeming to treat the same subject. Identification of trends is fraught with difficulty, and even when patterns in the material may be tentatively discerned, they are at times in turn contradicted by evidence from other archaeological and historical sources.

Additionally, analysis of textual material is often hampered by our, as yet, limited knowledge of the language. Even where translations are possible, there are still instances where the sense of the passage remains obscure. We are equally hampered by our Christian concepts of morals and theology, and the acceptance of state interference in our lives – concepts and interference which did not pertain in ancient Egyptian society where, for example, marriage was effected simply by the start of cohabitation, without religious ceremony or involvement of secular authority.[3] Moreover, and paradoxically, the very popularity of the Instructions has led to a number of problems for the modern scholar. The texts were copied over and over again, being used in scribal schools to develop literary skills as well as to promote the philosophy contained within. Large numbers of ostraca survive inscribed with school exercises which are by their very nature incomplete and distorted.[4] Most of the 'complete' texts that survive are later copies and have suffered in the course of transmission. Often textual corruptions appear to be due to incomprehension on the part of the copyist, but recognition of this fact is not necessarily of help to the modern scholar. With these problems and lacunae in mind, however, it remains the case that we can say something, however, tentatively, about women in ancient Egyptian society. We shall start by reading between the lines of the Didactic Literature.

SOCIAL BACKGROUND OF THE DIDACTIC LITERATURE

The writers of Didactic Literature naturally took it for granted that the readers of the Instructions would be conversant with the basic assumptions and mores of Egyptian society. Those that are relevant to this study are summarised below.

The Egyptians perceived the state, nature and religion as being completely intertwined and indivisible. This found expression in the concept of *Maat*, a word difficult to translate, partly because of the breadth of its meaning at any one time, and partly because of the subtle changes in meaning that evolved over millennia. At its most simple, *Maat* meant living in accordance with divine rule. It encompassed humanitarian aims and also order, harmony and restraint. Chaos, or *Isft*, was greatly feared by the Egyptians. *Isft* included passion, anger and recklessness as well as war, famine and natural disasters. Each member of society strove to live in *Maat*, that is, in an obedient, self-contained moral life.[5]

Another core concept or myth which informed Egyptian society was the tale of the god Osiris, his sister–wife Isis, and their son, Horus (conceived by Isis from the revivified remains of her husband). Isis ministers to the body of her assassinated husband, and nurtures their son in secret, protecting him and seeking justice for him: this provided an image of perfect womanhood. This myth formed part of the bedrock of Egyptian life. Every king was believed to be the embodiment of Horus, and consequently, semi-divine. At death, he became Osiris.[6] The rituals which the royal household took to themselves on the basis of the myth were gradually appropriated by the people: for example, the elder son acting as a Horus figure for his parents during their funerary rites.[7] Significantly, the role of the heroic mother was lauded over and above that of loyal wife. This explains the importance of the king's mother in Egyptian society.[8] The triad, father, mother and child, was a popular feature in religious iconography and, in addition to the Osiris, Isis, Horus complex, other deities appear in the same type of relationship.[9] The divine informed, and conformed, to the ideal family unit – namely, the nuclear family.

The kinship terminology employed by the ancient Egyptians confirmed the primacy of this familial unit. Only the members of the nuclear family had specific designations: father, mother, son, daughter, brother, sister. Other familial relationships were expressed through compounds of these terms, for example, maternal uncle = brother of the mother, maternal grandmother = mother of the mother. The Egyptian family was constantly splitting into new units as each child married and established a household.[10] At the same time, these nuclear cells seem to have been part of an extended family system, as yet imperfectly understood but evinced by references in literary and sapiential writing such as 'Do not say my mother's brother has a house' and 'Because of his mother's father, he is assigned to the stable.'[11] It is interesting to note that it is the maternal relatives that seem to have primacy in these texts.

WISDOM LITERATURE AND LITERACY

Three media were used for the transmission of information, beliefs and ideals: oral (evinced by such phrases as 'on this day a declaration made by . . .', 'and any scribe who will read out this stela'),[12] pictorial, and documentary. While there is evidence for the oral transmissions of the principles that formed the foundation of this Wisdom genre, it is impossible to quantify the extent of that method of dissemination. This chapter will concentrate on surviving written material. In written form, 'wisdom' was presumably only accessible to a very small section of Egyptian society since it is estimated that only one per cent of the population were literate. Most of the readership would have been male, and literacy, in varying degrees, appears to have been confined to the royal household, temple staff, scribes, workmen attached to royal tombs, and workmen employed in provincial necropoli.[13] Internal evidence argues that where women were members of the above categories, they too possessed a degree of literacy.[14] The literate classes had access to a wide variety of both entertaining and edifying literature, and the most popular genre in the latter category was Wisdom Literature – the Instructions.

It is difficult to assess how far the maxims of wisdom percolated into the illiterate sections of society. Incidental information in legal documents suggests that the broad principles inherent in living in accordance with *Maat* were acknowledged at every level of society. Members at the lowest rung of society would not have had to worry about behaviour at a banquet, but do seem to have been aware of their rights in the pursuance of justice.[15]

Wisdom Literature was known throughout the Near East from the third millennium BC to well after the second century AD.[16] Biblical Wisdom Literature includes, for example, Proverbs, Job, Ecclesiastes, and Wisdom Psalms.[17] Egyptian documents provide the earliest as well as some of the latest examples of the genre.

Wisdom in the ancient Near East was not an abstract concept relating to discernment or knowledge. It was rather concerned with the practicalities of daily life. Wisdom was the adherence to a series of precepts and admonitions concerning one's relationship with the gods (or God) and fellow men, whereby success in this life would be achieved and happiness in the afterlife assured. In ancient Egypt, wisdom was synonymous with obeying Divine Ordinance; a life that rejected these guidelines was associated with chaos and evil. In a broad context, therefore, Wisdom Literature can be seen as religious, though to the modern eye, much of it is concerned with material and social success rather than spiritual qualities.

The Instructions normally take the form of an elder male addressing a younger male. In the Old and Middle Kingdoms (c. 2628–1650 BC) the author is said to be a father advising his son. During the New Kingdom (1551–1070 BC), this device was modified and examples where an older scribe instructs his apprentice appear alongside the earlier form. There appear to be four exceptions to this format, (a) the Instruction to Kagemni, (b) the Loyalist Instruction, (c) the Instruction of the High Priest Amenemhet, and (d) the Onomasticon of Amenemope. In the conclusion to the Instruction of Kagemni, it appears that the father addresses all his children. However, the pronouns and verbal forms in the body of the text indicate that a single male was being addressed, and it is possible that Kagemni, as the 'eldest son', was to be responsible for the dissemination and implementation of the Instruction among his siblings.[18] The Loyalist Instruction and the Instruction of the High Priest Amenemhet are indisputably addressed to all the children of the respective authors, whilst the Onomasticon of Amenemope is said to be an Instruction to 'teach the ignorant'.[19] There is not a single extant example of an Instruction written by a father for his daughter, nor by a mother for her son, or a mother for her daughter.

The contents of the Instructions are matched by the claims in autobiographical texts inscribed on tomb walls.[20] Like the Didactic Literature, these biographies also seem to have been the sole province of men. Careers were really only open to men, and with a successful career came a number of responsibilities. These two factors were irrevocably linked and provide the subject matter for both types of textual dissemination.

While this much can be said with certainty, in other respects there is a disjunction between social experience and representation in the texts. Thus, the texts describe a society in which a young, healthy male provides and cares for the weak, including widows and the aged of both sexes, and establishes a household by which his name is perpetuated. In actuality, daughters as well as sons were expected to care for their parents, and one's maternal ancestry was as important as the paternal line.[21]

Moreover, the information contained in these Instructions reflects the opinions and aspirations of a small section of Egyptian society, namely, those of the aristocratic and wealthy males. It is assumed throughout that its audience had sufficient resources to have a son or sons educated, and to support a wife and daughters. Men were expected to provide for their families. Not only is this implicit in the Instructions, but it is also acknowledged elsewhere in Egyptian documents, for example in the tale of the Eloquent Peasant, where he and his protagonist make provision for the Peasant's wife and children.[22] Egyptian sapiential writings indicate that it was only when a man failed in his duty that his dependants were obliged to go to work. This clearly identifies the economic level of society for whom the Instructions were written and reveals the texts as ignoring the fact that women could and did earn their livings as brewers, wet nurses, clothing manufacturers and more.[23]

Within Egyptian sapiential writings, advice is given, *inter alia*, concerning the correct treatment of, and behaviour towards, women. I have identified six categories of women in the material: (a) mothers, (b) wives, (c) widows, (d) women outside the family circle, (e) maidservants, (f) 'those who give pleasure'. It is noteworthy that no advice is given *vis-à-vis* the relationship between father and daughter in Pharaonic Wisdom Literature. This omission is best understood in the context of the purpose of these

Instructions. As mentioned, Wisdom Literature provided a framework for a successful life. One of the external signs of a successful life was a successful career. Getting married and establishing a household showed wisdom and stability, while at the same time establishing one's independence in the community. In theory, the success or otherwise of a man's life depended upon informed decisions on the choice of career, friends and wife. Such 'information' was to be found within the Instructions (at least for the wealthy and educated). Daughters did not directly impinge upon the furtherance of one's career and had no explicit cultic role to play in the funerary ceremonies. Marriage does not seem to have been an instrument for career advancement, and marrying outside one's own circle was discouraged.[24] There is no evidence in Pharaonic literature that a father chose a suitable husband for his daughter. Rather, marriage was on the basis of mutual attraction and a girl's choice of partner was largely influenced by her mother's approval, rather than that of her father. Education of a female child was also the responsibility of the mother.[25] For these several reasons, the category we would expect to find of 'daughter' does not appear in the texts and we are left with the six groups listed above.

The discussion of women in Egyptian Wisdom Literature which follows has been based on a study of all the examples of the Literature known to me, including material that falls outside the chronological confines of the Pharaonic Period. The latter is included for comparative purposes. The chapter represents an initial survey of material available. In examining the data, a number of questions remain unanswered. It is hoped that these will be resolved by research at a later date. The subject matter is presented chronologically, in three sections: Old, Middle and New Kingdoms. After a brief description of each example, the relevant excerpts are quoted and analysed, with the results being summarised and synthesised in the conclusion. Standard translations are used throughout, except in cases where there are lexical difficulties, or the sense of the passage is obscure, when the translation is my own.

WOMEN IN THE OLD KINGDOM

The Old Kingdom (2628–2134 BC) was a period of relative prosperity and stability with 'no obvious challenge to, or major malfunction in, the social order'.[26] Instructions from this period are resolutely upper-class, reflecting the mores and attitudes of the wealthy Egyptian male. Three texts are traditionally assigned to the period, namely, the Instruction to Kagemni, the Instruction of Hordjedef, and the Instruction of Ptah-hotep.[27] Four groups of women can be isolated within these texts: (a) wives, (b) women of other households, (c) mothers and (d) maidservants. The unifying themes in the Instructions are the establishment and maintenance of the household, and living in peace with the community at large. While women are generally portrayed in a positive light, they are also shown to be in need of male protection and support. What does not emerge from the Wisdom Literature of this time is that women could participate fully in some of the most essential and important activities of ancient Egyptian society. They could enjoy the same burial rites as their husbands, and benefit from priestly stipends attached to mortuary chapels.[28]

1 The Instruction of Kagemni

This is an incomplete work of which only the final portion survives. The only reference to a woman is a comparative one. The text is very corrupt at this point, but seems to use the tenderness of a mother to her child as a yardstick against which the 'harsh man's' behaviour is judged.[29] As will be seen later in this chapter, motherhood was the pinnacle of female achievement in the eyes of society. Mothers were regarded as paragons. For someone to be kinder than a mother was to be altogether quite remarkable. Unfortunately, the sentence before this one is too corrupt for translation and so we do not know the context of the statement.

2 The Instruction of Hordjedef

Only the beginning survives of this fragmentary work. It contains the earliest example of a maxim which was a recurring theme in Didactic Literature, namely the establishment of a household:

> If you are an excellent one,
> You should found your household.
> Marry a woman, Mistress of the Heart;
> A son will be born to you.[30]

References in autobiographical texts confirm the importance of this 'landmark'.[31]

There are various interpretations of the phrase 'Mistress of the Heart'. It could mean someone in control of herself (self-control being an attribute greatly admired by the Egyptians), or simply a lovable woman. Other commentators have rendered the phrase as 'a hearty wife' or a 'strong woman'.[32]

3 The Instruction of Ptah-hotep

This is the longest sapiential text attributed to an Old Kingdom figure. Several of its maxims have been the subject of recent research. The text consists of 37 maxims, of which only two deal exclusively with women, namely numbers 21 and 37. I quote maxim 21 in full:

> If you are excellent, you shall establish your household,
> And love your wife according to her standard;
> Fill her belly, clothe her back,
> Perfume is a prescription for her limbs.
> Make her happy as long as you live!
> She is a field, good for her lord.
> You shall not pass judgement on her.
> Remove her from power, suppress her;
> Her eye when she sees (anything) is her storm wind.
> This is how to make her endure in your house.
> You shall retain her. A female
> Who is in her own hands is like rain:
> She is sought for, and she has flown away.[33]

This is a very complex passage. It appears to have a bipartite form; lines 1–7 relating to a positive attitude on the part of the husband, while lines 8–13 portray a negative attitude towards a wife. Lines 1–7 expand the theme first noted in Hordjedef, namely the founding of a household. The husband is exhorted to love, provide for and protect his wife. The elements food, clothes and oil are later found as the constituents in Maintenance Deeds drawn up by men for their wives after marriage.[34] It has been suggested that line 6, 'She is a field, good for her lord', is a sexual metaphor referring to the procreation of a son, a recurring theme in Wisdom Literature. Other similes for wives found in later Wisdom texts describe them as 'stone surface' (for carving) and a 'stone quarry'.[35] Elsewhere the phrase 'open her with a chisel' is used as a metaphor for intercourse, and figures of speech comparing women to minerals and stones are generally best understood as sexual imagery.[36] The passivity of women inherent in 'stone', is reflected in the imagery of a ploughed field (line 6 of the quotation) and is confirmed by representations of women in ancient Egyptian art, where women are portrayed in static modes in contrast to the vigorous poses of their spouses.[37]

Line 7 'You shall not pass judgement on her' appears to be a concise precursor of an injunction found in Ani not to criticise one's wife, but to observe and admire her skill in managing the house.[38]

The following six lines introduce a different attitude towards women. The wife is portrayed as unpredictable, potentially violent but at the same time of great value. Consequently, she needs to be controlled and kept from wielding power outside the home. These 13 lines encapsulate the dualistic nature of women acknowledged in Egyptian society; what might be termed the conflict between the 'good' and the 'bad' woman.[39] Women who conform to the role demanded of them by society, namely (heroic) mother and loyal wife, were to be highly favoured and were deemed good. Women were not, however, suited to positions of authority outside the home because of their unpredictability and intransigence – the image of the storm wind (line 9) indicates loss of control, an attitude synonymous with *Isft* and unacceptable in a career-minded male. This may be seen as the opposite of Mistress of the Heart who represents the ideal wife, mentioned in Hordjedef.

Both sexes were seen as having dual natures. In men the tension was between natures personified as Horus and Seth (good and evil); in women the conflict is represented as being between Sakhmet and Bast.[40] Sakhmet, the lioness goddess, represented the violent and unpredictable, and Bast, also a lioness goddess but sometimes shown as a cat, was a goddess of pleasure, music, dance and healing.

It seems to me that lines 7–13 can be elucidated by reference to two myths – The Destruction of Mankind,[41] and The Myth of the Sun's Eye.[42] In the tale of The Destruction of Mankind, Re the Sun-God and the King of the gods, instructs his Eye, identified here with Sakhmet, to slay mankind in punishment for plotting against him. It appears that after the initial massacre, Re repents of his decision, but has to resort to a strategy to restrain Sakhmet since it is implied that she could not be recalled by reason. Similarly, in The Myth of the Sun's Eye, Thoth, the god of wisdom and, by extension, reason, is sent to entice the Sun's Eye back to Egypt from whence she had left to the detriment of Re and all Egypt. It is an errand fraught with danger. Thoth encounters the Sun's Eye in her docile form of cat, but her violent form of lioness is never far away. He successfully woos the Sun's Eye back and the wellbeing of Egypt and all her denizens, divine and mortal, is assured. The husband in our text can be paralleled to Re; his wife is then his Eye. Just as Sakhmet had to be controlled by Re, so the husband had to control his wife; and just as the prosperity of Egypt depended upon the return of the Sun's Eye, so the prosperity of a man's house depended on his wife's stability. The value of the wife is underlined by the reference to 'rain' – a very rare and valuable commodity in Egypt, though notoriously difficult to summon or control.

The last maxim of this work, number 37, also concerns advice about the treatment of a wife. The verse contains a number of lexical difficulties. The latest research has produced the following translation:

If you marry a fat woman
With a happy disposition and known by her town.
If she unites these two qualities
And time with her is pleasant,
Do not put her aside, but let her eat
So that she laughs with all her heart
One will say (then) . . .
A happy woman controls [her water?][43]

Implicit in this passage are the qualities a man should seek in a wife. Good companionship seems to have been valued higher than good looks: divorce, here referred to as 'to put aside', on the grounds of physical inadequacies, is treated with derision in some texts. Despite this, fatness in women was not a desirable thing. Egyptian art presented the ideal female as thin and svelte. Representations of fat women are extremely rare. Two notable examples are known: (a) the Queen of Nubia shown in a relief in the mortuary temple of Hatshepsut at Deir el-Bahri and (b) fecundity figures from reliefs from the temples of Sahure and Niuserre.[44] Men, on the other hand, with the exception of the king, had two modes of representation on official monuments. Muscular, trim figures were used to symbolise the vigour of youth, while successful and comfortable old age was expressed by rendering the male with a large belly and double chin.[45]

The young man is advised therefore that while his wife may not conform visually to the feminine ideal, a happy disposition and a good reputation were not to be despised. 'Known by her town' was the figure of speech used to denote respectability. As will be seen, in the New Kingdom texts, the stranger, rootless and unknown, was anomalous in Egyptian society and a threat to its stability. This maxim confirms the xenophobic attitude of the Egyptians.

The meaning of the last word translated here as 'her water' is as yet unknown. Cannuyer has suggested that it derives from the root 'celestial waters', hence the translation here.[46] Comparison with Maxim 21 suggests this is possible. Maxim 21 warns that an unhappy and angry woman will dissipate like water, whereas Maxim 37 appears to reverse the simile to say that a happy woman will control (conserve?) her water; that is to say, she will continue to contribute to the marriage relationship. In a country whose livelihood was dependent on the successful management of water, the imagery of restrained and/or dissipated water must have been a powerful one.

As mentioned earlier, 'to put aside' is an allusion to divorce. Divorce is well-attested in ancient Egypt.[47] Objection to the dissolution of a marriage does not seem to have been for religious reasons but was linked to the desire for a stable society, the need to protect the inheritance of one's heirs and to ensure that there were successors to perform funerary rites. The underlying concern seems to have been title and usufruct of property: whereas marriage instituted new property complexes through marriage contracts, divorce could lead to communal disruption and legal disputes. Heavy fines could be imposed on a husband who divorced his wife, no doubt to act as a deterrent. A woman does not seem to have been subject to the same financial penalty. Divorce was enacted by the woman leaving the conjugal home whether or not she initiated proceedings. In essence then, divorce made a woman and her children homeless. While the community prided itself on the care given to widows, divorcees and children, divorce no doubt placed a burden on local resources which was better avoided wherever possible. Clauses assuring women of financial compensation in the event of divorce are attested in marriage contracts, but the amount varied from family to family and no doubt the poorer sections of society fared worse than those where women had inherited wealth. Even for the more wealthy, the level of compensation does not seem to have been particularly generous and most women would have faced economic difficulties after the dissolution of their marriage.[48]

There are three other maxims in Ptah-hotep that mention women, namely, numbers 1, 18 and 19. Maxim 1 states:

Good speech is hidden more than greenstone
yet may be found among the serving girls
on the grindstone.

These lines can best be understood in the context of a very consciously hierarchical world and warn the addressee that intelligence was not the monopoly of the upper classes. Neither could it be assumed that men were *a priori* cleverer than women.

Maxim 18 is preserved on a number of different manuscripts and in the version from P. Prisse reads:

If you want to make a friendship last
in a house you enter,
whether as lord, or brother, or friend,
in any place you enter,
beware of approaching the women!
The place where this is done cannot be good;
there can be no cleverness in revealing this.

A thousand men are turned away from their good:
a little moment, the likeness of a dream,
and death is reached by knowing them.
It is a vile thing, conceived by an enemy;
one emerges from doing it
with a heart (already) rejecting it.
As for him who ails through lusting after them, no
plan of his can ever succeed.[49]

I take the expression 'to know' in the biblical sense and understand this passage as a prohibition against unlawful intercourse. What is not clear in this version of the maxim is whether the male perpetrator of the crime was committing rape or adultery. Although many terms are known for sexual congress from ancient Egypt, the distinctions are not yet fully understood. At the present level of knowledge of the Egyptian language it is not possible to distinguish between accounts of rape and acts of intercourse with consent. This is particularly important when dealing with texts in which men are accused of having illicit intercourse with women, some married, some single.[50] Was it rape or adultery in society's eyes? As yet, there is insufficient data to be able to answer the questions.

An alternative version of the maxim intercollates two more lines between lines 8 and 9 of the quotation. They are as follows:

One is made a fool by limbs of faience
and then she turns into carnelian.[51]

This has been interpreted by some scholars as referring not only to adultery but to the dangers of wily women. The limbs of faience (green) are contrasted with the woman's temper of carnelian (red) which serve as imagery to represent the tension between the cool/good woman and the hot/bad woman. Literary texts indicate that the consequence of adultery was often death at the hands of the aggrieved party.[52] Death was not only meted out to the woman but to the guilty male as well. There is no evidence that death was a statutory penalty and we know of no cases where the cuckold husband took such violent revenge. Nevertheless, a number of later Instructions continue to warn the addressee that violation of a married woman could lead to death. The authors were either basing this on known cases, or believed that passions ran so high in such cases that death was a distinct possibility at the hands of the injured husband. Surviving legal texts show that the actual punishment for the adulterous male was usually financial, and for the woman divorce, rather than death.

Very little is known about the mechanisms employed by society to adduce if someone was guilty of adultery. So far as can be judged, cases rested on accusations by one party against the activities of fellow villagers. These could be refuted, by the taking of oaths, or acknowledged in the presence of a local court. The President of the court seems to have been empowered to negotiate a settlement between the parties.[53]

Maxim 18 provides one of only three references to adultery in Didactic Literature from the Pharaonic Period; the other two are to be found in the Instruction of Ani, dating to the New Kingdom, and will be discussed below.

Conclusions based on this extremely limited material must be tentative, but one can postulate that the ancient Egyptians acknowledged that both sexes were capable of, and responsible for, adultery. In the Old Kingdom, the man seems to be the initiator, whereas in the New Kingdom material the woman is responsible.

The following Maxim, Number 19, is a warning against greed. The likely scenario is a dispute over property of which there are many examples from Ancient Egypt.[54] The text states:

Beware of an occasion of rapacity.
It is a serious disease and incurable.
The one who enters it cannot exist.
It makes ill-disposed fathers and mothers
and brothers of mothers.
It drives apart wife and husband.

Whereas elsewhere in Egyptian culture, the family norm seems to have been the nuclear family, there appears to be a reference here to an extended system in operation as well, with its reference to 'brothers of mothers'. Its full significance is unknown. Further examples of this extended kinship pattern occur in two New Kingdom texts. What is noteworthy is that it is the mother's extended family that has primacy in these texts. In the case of the Instruction of Ani the text reads.

Buy a house, or find and buy one,
Shun contention,
Don't say, 'My mother's father has a house'[55]

and in P. Anastasi III we read

Because of his mother's father he is assigned to the
stable which has five slaves.[56]

Implicit in these examples is the fact that children could expect to inherit property from their mother. Transmission deeds and wills show that mothers could bequeath not only property to children of either sex but also offices, for example Pesset who bequeathed her office of Overseer of Physicians to her son Akhethotep.[57] Interestingly, the most frequent parent mentioned in dedicatory inscriptions and autobiographical texts is the mother.[58]

WOMEN IN THE MIDDLE KINGDOM

With the breakdown of centralised government in the First Intermediate Period, c. 2134 BC, probably exacerbated by natural disasters such as low Nile floods, texts appear in which the accepted order is questioned and pessimism about the future appears alongside descriptions of chaos. Although the Instructions of the Middle Kingdom (c. 2040–1650 BC) retain their prescriptive nature, they also reflect the developments around them. The treatise of kingship cited below could only have developed in an atmosphere where the supremacy of the monarchy had been challenged. Indeed, of the six sapiential texts assigned to the Middle Kingdom, two purport to be by kings for their successors.[59] One is by an aristocrat to his son, while the other three appear to be the first non-aristocratic Instructions.[60] Of the six texts, only three have references to women and these are to be found in the two 'royal' Instructions and in the non-aristocratic Satire on Trades.

A new group of women is introduced in the material from the Middle Kingdom, namely widows. This group was missing in the literature of the Old Kingdom, and its appearance in the material of the Middle Kingdom probably reflects demographic changes brought about by the natural disasters and civil unrest that characterised the First Intermediate Period. It also reflects the general mood of pessimism that pervades other forms of Egyptian literature of this period.[61]

The three references to widows in Pharaonic Wisdom Literature show them to be vulnerable to attack and abuse. Attempts to defraud widows are attested in legal documents, although theoretically a widow and her property were protected by law.[62]

1 The Instruction Addressed to King Merikare

This Instruction is preserved on three fragmentary papyri that only partly complement each other. Unfortunately, the most complete text is also the most corrupt, with numerous scribal errors and lacunae.

The opening quatrain of the verses concerned with the administration of justice includes the only reference to women in the work:

Do justice, then you endure on earth;
Calm the weeper, don't oppress the widow.[63]

Similar sentiments are expressed in autobiographical texts where, among the virtues usually listed, were the following: '[I was] a father to the orphan, a husband to the widow, brother to the divorced woman.'[64] While neither orphans, widows nor divorcees were disadvantaged in law, all fell outside the scope of the nuclear family unit. They no longer had a relationship with a pivotal male figure – father, husband or brother – and this may well have rendered them anomalous in Egyptian society.

2 Instruction of King Amenemhet I for his Son Sesostris

As in the Instruction to King Merikare, women are only mentioned once. King Amenemhet states that in spite of his beneficence to the state and the dangers he had faced on the country's borders, he had found treachery and ingratitude in the Palace. It is in the description of the attack on the King that women are mentioned:

For I had not prepared for it,
had not expected it,
had not foreseen the failings of the servants.
Had women ever marshalled troops?
Are rebels nurtured in the Palace?
Does one release water that destroys the soil,
And deprive people of their crops?[65]

Palace conspiracies occurred sporadically throughout Egyptian history. The earliest recorded example is to be found in the Autobiography of Weni from the Old Kingdom.[66] In almost every instance, female members of the royal household were active in the intrigue. The rhetorical question about women marshalling troops and the nurturing of rebels has a twofold purpose. It describes in an idiomatic form how the Palace conspiracy was formulated. It obviously involved women of the royal household and, probably, younger sons of the king. At the same time the lines are redolent of bitterness since this disloyalty was unexpected. Women and children were expected to support and defend the head of the household, not topple him from power. Untamed water referred to in the last line was a simile for unrestrained power synonymous with anarchy, and occurs elsewhere in Wisdom Literature in respect of women. This imagery of destruction may also reflect the disastrous aftermath of civil war that swept over the country following the assassination attempt on the king.

3 Satire on Trades

The third and last text to be discussed in this section, The Satire on Trades, is the earliest example of an Instruction belonging to the Scribal School. It represents a new development in sapiential writings, which had previously been the province of the aristocracy and royalty. The text is a consciously biased work, exaggerating the hardships endured in other livelihoods. There are no references to the positive side of other careers described, nor to the discomforts a scribe might face while on attachment to government offices.

All extant manuscripts of the Satire on Trades are marred by textual corruptions. Women are mentioned five times. Three references are to mothers, and two to womankind in general.

As already noted, mothers were held in high regard in ancient Egypt. Moral obligation as well as affection formed a strong bond between mothers and their offspring. In this context the statement from the beginning of the work – 'I'll make you love scribedom more than your mother'[67] – evokes a career of great dedication and satisfaction. The respect accorded to mothers is also reflected in the injunction

> Don't tell lies against your mother,
> The magistrates abhor it.[68]

Given the preeminence of the heroic mother in Egyptian mythology and the status of mothers generally, such behaviour would be tantamount to sacrilege. In autobiographies, men were at pains to list among their virtues the fact that they 'did not defame mother'.[69] The two lines quoted above seem to refer to some type of inter-family dispute. Litigation regarding inheritance rights and property are well-attested and could last generations.[70] However, I know of no surviving legal documents from the Pharaonic Period where a son takes his mother to court or vice versa.

The third reference to mothers states: 'Praise god for your father and your mother who set you on the path of life.'[71] This is evidence of the respect accorded to both parents and the joint responsibility parents had in promoting the education of their children.[72]

The pain and discomfort experienced by women in labour is acknowledged in a verse that outlines the life of a weaver or basket maker:

> The weaver in the workshop,
> He is worse off than a woman
> With knees against his chest.
> He cannot breathe air.[73]

Representations of weaving appear in a number of tombs and were most popular in the Middle Kingdom. The craft was not confined to one particular sex. Weavers are shown in profile with their knees up to their chest. Later drawings from the New Kingdom, of men in particular, show them sitting on low seats with their legs spread widely.[74] Drawings and paintings of women in childbirth provide the best parallels for the squatting position adopted by weavers. The New Kingdom variant can be seen as analogous to a woman squatting on a birth stool. The lack of breath referred to obviously recalls the discomfort of parturition. Medical texts and literary works show that men had a surprisingly good knowledge of the events of childbirth. Representations of birth were used to decorate temple walls and frequently included male deities as witnesses.[75]

Another verse in the Satire on Trades concerns the woes of a washerman and has been cited as evidence of menstrual taboo in ancient Egypt.[76] The standard translation reads:

> His food is mixed with filth and there
> is no part of him which is clean.
> He cleans the garment of a woman in menstruation.[77]

It must be said, however, that the verse abounds with lacunae and unknown words. If the original Egyptian text is consulted, it becomes apparent that a different interpretation is to be preferred. A more accurate translation would be:

> His food is mixed with filth and
> there is no part of him that is clean.
> It is in a woman's skirt that he puts himself
> and then he is in a heavy state.

Even within the context of a satirical work which consciously distorts reality, there must have been some expectation that some of the barbs would hit home and that young apprentice scribes would acknowledge the validity of the basic premise of the work, namely, that of all the careers open to a young man, scribedom provided the greatest opportunities for personal advancement. In this light there must have been something risible about a man in a woman's skirt and that could well be the import of this verse.

The orthography of the word at the end of the sentence which I have translated as a 'heavy state' is ambiguous. While the writing has some similarities with the ancient Egyptian word for menstruation, the determinative speaks against it. It could be read as 'natron' (a type of salt), 'establish', or 'heavy'. The determinative clearly indicates that the word designated a bad state.[78] Neither 'natron' nor 'establish' provide an appropriate meaning in the circumstances. 'Heavy' in the *OED* meaning of 'hard to bear, grievous, sore, distressful' occurs in marriage contracts where compensation for divorce is arranged: 'If I repudiate the woman . . . and I make the heavy fate catch her . . . I shall give to her'.[79] In this context, 'heavy fate' is apparently synonymous with great distress, and this approximates more closely with the state of the washerman than the possible alternative meanings given above.[80] As for menstrual taboo generally in ancient Egypt, there is insufficient evidence to substantiate it.[81] The association of the word for menstruation with a bad or contaminating state is a modern interpretation not borne out by securely attested examples of context and word in Pharaonic texts. Such securely attested examples carry the sign for a liquid issuing from lips which has an entirely neutral status.[82]

WOMEN IN THE NEW KINGDOM

In the so-called Second Intermediate Period, the lead-up to the New Kingdom, a weakened centralised government (Dynasties XV and XVI) was challenged by the invasion of the Hyksos. As a result, Egypt was divided for about 100 years. Under King Ahmose of the XVIII Dynasty, the Hyksos were finally driven out and the nation reunited. Through the New Kingdom, subsequent monarchs extended their power beyond Egypt's borders northwards into Palestine and as far south as modern Sudan. It was a period of great prosperity and security. However, the second half of the XXth Dynasty (c. 1150 BC) saw a decline in the Egyptian economy, coupled with the loss of her empire. Kings of the closing years of the New Kingdom were largely ineffectual. Their weak government allowed the proliferation of independent states within the country during the Third Intermediate Period.[83]

Of the many surviving Instructions from the New Kingdom, only a few provide us with information on women. They are the Instruction of Ani and the Instruction of Amenemope, and two groups of texts designated respectively as Educational Instructions and Ancient Writings.[84]

Women in New Kingdom Wisdom Literature can be divided into two categories: those of the immediate family (wife, mother and widows) and those outside the family (women who give pleasure and potential adulteresses).

Themes first identified in the Old Kingdom, such as establishing a household, reverence for mothers and injunctions against illicit intercourse, are expanded in the New Kingdom. We learn more of what men expected other men to do for their families, and of their broader social responsibilities, but as ever very little about a woman's duties to her family and the community at large. In the interaction between men and women, whether recommended or prohibited, it is once again the man who is pivotal. There are, however, two new aspects of womankind which are introduced into sapiential texts in this period. One is the appearance of a woman who regards herself as free to take the initiative in sexual matters; the other is a woman who gives pleasure. Very little is known about the latter. A euphemism for sexual relations was 'spending a pleasant hour together', and 'women who give pleasure' might be identified as courtesans. There is no evidence for prostitution in the modern sense.[85] There is no criticism of these women's behaviour on moral grounds. Pre-marital intercourse did not attract moral censure. These 'entertaining' ladies were to be avoided simply because they distracted a young scribe from the rigorous training required to attain a successful career. References to the women occur in contexts of drinking, eating to excess and losing control:

> Now you are seated in front of the wench, soaked in anointing oil,
> your wreath of *ishtepen* at your neck, and your drum on your belly.
> Now you stumble and fall over your belly anointed with dirt.[86]

1 The Instruction of Ani

The best-preserved copy of this work survives on a manuscript dating to the XXIst or XXIInd Dynasties.[87] Unfortunately, the beginning of the text is badly damaged, and the copy as a whole is full of lacunae and corruptions. Some of the gaps can be filled in and errors rectified by comparison with other versions. Like the Satire on Trades, this Instruction is addressed to a non-aristocratic audience. Women are mentioned as wives, mothers and women who are 'strangers'.

Wives are referred to three times in the text. The first example is as follows:

> Take a wife while you're young
> That she make a son for you;
> She should bear for you while you're youthful.
> It is proper to make people.
> Happy the man whose people are many.[88]

This first example has clear antecedents in Ptah-hotep and Hordjedef of the Old Kingdom. Later in the manuscript there are a number of lines relating to the treatment of the wife within the household:

Do not control your wife in her house,
when you know she is efficient;
Don't say to her, 'Where is it? Get it'
when she has put it in the right place.
Let your eye observe in silence
Then you recognise her skill;
It is a joy when your hand is with her.
There are many who don't know this.
If a man desists from strife at home
he will not encounter its beginning.
Every man who founds a household
should hold back the hasty heart.[89]

This maxim has two functions. It prompts the ideal of marriage and warns the man against divorce. The rest of the maxim urges a harmonious relationship, and forms the context in which advice against divorce might be given.

The third reference to a wife comes from a maxim about rank and hierarchy:

A woman is asked about her husband,
A man is asked about his rank.[90]

It is unlikely that these lines suggest that a wife's individuality was subsumed into her husband's. Rather it reflects the career structure and promotion possibilities in Egyptian society. It was perfectly possible for a man to move up from the social class in which he was born. This social mobility was one of the fruits of a scribal education, but was occasionally witnessed also in other careers like the military.[91] The weight of evidence suggests that women were rarely educated, though exceptions are known. Examples of female scribes, doctors and other administrators occur throughout the whole of Egyptian history, but in no great numbers: these posts were outside the main career structure enjoyed by men and were confined to the households of queens and other high-born ladies. Opportunities for women to move up the social scale on their own account were restricted. In these circumstances, a woman's rank was linked to her husband.[92] Rank rather than gender was the ultimate arbiter in determining who was 'head' of the house. A fragmentary ostracon preserves the line 'Do not marry a woman who is richer/greater than you, so that you do not . . .', while in the demotic Instruction of Ankhsheshonq the author advises, 'If a wife is of nobler birth than her husband he should give way to her.'[93] The majority of Egyptians seem to have married spouses from within their social circle, a practice which, among other things, would preserve the norm of a male being the household head.[94]

The Instruction of Ani contains a paean of praise for mothers, admonishing the addressee to 'double the food your mother gave you, support her as she supported you'. The verse outlines all the sacrifices the mother made for the child and her commitment to his well-being. In the closing lines, the addressee is urged to establish a household, and to show as much dedication to his own child as did his own mother towards him, 'lest she raise her hands to god and he hears her cries'. In this verse it is clear that mothers were active in promoting their sons' education: 'When she sent you to school and you were taught to write, she kept watch over you daily.'[95]

The third category of woman discussed in Ani is 'the woman who is a stranger':

Beware a woman who is a stranger.
One who is not known in her town.
Don't stare at her when she goes by.
Don't know her carnally.
A deep water whose course is unknown
Such is a woman away from her husband.
'I am pretty', she tells you daily
when she has no witnesses;
She is ready to ensnare you.
A great deadly crime when it is heard . . .[96]

There are two underlying dangers implied in the passage. One is the danger of the unknown, the stranger; the other is the danger of becoming embroiled in adultery.

Ancient Egyptian villages were insular, xenophobic communities.[97] It appears that few travelled beyond the confines of their natal locality. Within the close confines of village society, a complex interaction of family relationships was established. Strangers, male or female, threatened this framework. This is tacitly acknowledged in Ankhsheshonq where a father is advised, 'Do not let your son marry a woman from another town, lest he be taken from you.'[98] If the ideal was the stable community, then its opposite, rootlessness as represented by strangers, was the embodiment of chaos and disorder. Demotic Instructions in particular warn against leaving one's village and of the dangers outside the city.[99] Being known in one's town was synonymous with respectability, as was seen in Ptah-hotep's maxim. Line 2 here underscores the disreputable nature of the wandering woman.

Adultery, like the stranger, threatened the fabric of society. Evidence of actual cases of adultery surviving from ancient Egypt are few and far between. It is clear that adultery not only undermined the complex family alliances within the village and compromised the status of a woman's offspring, but also affected property and inheritance rights. In one particular case an adulterous couple were warned that, unless they went to court to legalise the liaison, they would receive summary justice from the community.[100] Whereas Ptah-hotep regarded the male as the instigator in illicit sexual encounters, here we see the blame placed on the woman. Extant textual evidence suggests that 'woman as temptress' was a new theme introduced during the New Kingdom. What exactly precipitated this literary development is hard to identify, but it is the case that the New Kingdom was a period of unprecedented military and economic expansion. The country experienced large-scale demographic changes, as slaves, immigrants and mercenaries converged on Egypt. No doubt interactions between these alien groups and the native residents led to tensions and feelings of unease within village communities. The 'woman as temptress', 'a stranger, not known in her town', were symptomatic of this social upheaval.

Adultery is here identified as 'a great deadly crime'. This is paralleled by legal documents from the Third Intermediate period and later which, according to the usual translation, describe adultery as 'the great crime that is found in a woman', so placing the burden of guilt upon her.[101] However, this translation ignores the wide range of the preposition *m* and the evidence of mores from other sources, and reflects a modern interpretation rather than the actual ancient practice. There is no evidence that women were regarded as intrinsically evil, as was the case, for example, in Europe in the later centuries of the Christian era. The crime was the *act* of illicit intercourse with a married woman.[102] A more accurate translation would be 'the great crime that is found with (occurs with) a married woman'. Marriage contracts state that if a woman is divorced following her adultery, she forfeits the compensation normally granted to divorcees. There is no information as to what redress a woman had against her husband if he were found committing adultery.

A second possible allusion to adultery may be seen in Column IX, lines 6–7 of Ani:

Do not go after a woman;
Let her not steal your heart.[103]

Contemporary love poetry, however, also describes the debilitating effects of passion and this last quotation may in fact have more in common with women being perceived as distractions rather than relating to adultery *per se*.[104]

2 Instruction of Amenemope

The Institution of Amenemope is completely preserved on a papyrus dating to the period of the XXII–XXV Dynasties. In this long text women are mentioned twice, and only as widows. The first example is as follows:

> Do not be greedy for a cubit of land
> Nor encroach on the boundaries of the widow.[105]

The person who engaged in this kind of fraud was an enemy of humankind and would incur divine retribution. In the context of an agricultural society such as Egypt, someone who moved boundary markers was depriving another of his livelihood and inheritance.[106] This maxim makes no reference to a widow's legal position, which is known to have been secure in theory.[107] The second example states,

> Do not pounce on a widow when you find her
> in the fields,
> and then fail to be patient with her reply.[108]

This sentence has been interpreted as an injunction not to prosecute a widow gleaning in fields other than her own without giving her a fair hearing. The importance of impartial justice is a regular theme in the texts.[109]

3 Educational Writings

The Satire on Trades discussed above was the precursor of a genre of writings focused on the career of a scribe and known to modern commentators as Educational Instructions. This genre had its *floruit* during the New Kingdom.[110] The corpus of careers satirised was increased to include the soldier, charioteer and stable-master, which was consistent with the increased military aspect of the New Kingdom. It is very introspective literature, giving no explicit advice regarding relationships with, or treatment of, women. However, the social responsibilities of a male to his household are implicit in the cautionary tales that form the framework for this genre. Certain other themes are carried over from earlier material. For example, in the most complete papyrus from this collection the constancy of a mother's love is extolled and used as a symbol of supreme satisfaction born of commitment to duty.[111] The sexual imagery of the 'wife as stone' discussed already in the context of Maxim 21 of Ptah-hotep, also appears in this material.[112]

4 Ancient Writings

A collection of ostraca and papyri has recently been identified as components of a work modern scholars call 'Ancient Writings'.[113] Only two of these ostraca need mention here. The first concerns the old and mothers:

> Mock not an old man nor an old woman in their infirmity
> lest they utter curses against you in your old age.
> Do not sate yourself alone if your mother is a
> have-not; it will surely be heard by . . .[114]

Earlier parallels suggest that it was the local god who would take the necessary steps to rectify this lack of filial duty. The theme of the second ostracon – 'Do not marry a woman richer than you' – concerns a subject discussed already in the section concerning the inadvisability of marrying outside one's own rank.

CONCLUSIONS

According to the writings analysed above, a woman's place was centred in the home. Men were not comfortable with the idea of women wielding power outside the domestic domain and the didactic literature presented here suggests that steps were taken to circumscribe a woman's power outside the house. The procreation and rearing of children were the wife's prime duty. Mothers were very highly regarded, to such an extent that widowed mothers took precedence over their daughters-in-law in household matters.[115] Childlessness could be grounds for divorce. It also had other legal ramifications. To circumvent the law, the husband of a childless couple adopted his wife as his daughter so that she, rather than his siblings, could inherit the estate after his death.[116]

Establishing a household had a literal as well as a metaphorical sense. Dissolution of the marriage either by death or divorce rendered the wife homeless, though not without an income.[117] If founding a household was in accordance with *Maat*, then its dissolution must have been a manifestation of *Isft*. Widows, divorcees and orphans were therefore symptoms of underlying chaos, and ministering to them would have been tantamount to restoring *Maat*. The care of the disadvantaged restored social and religious equilibrium.[118]

The recurring references to the procreation of a son did not indicate an antipathy towards daughters. It reflects a ritual necessity since a son was required to supervise the burial of his parents. This role was of vital importance, both from a mythopoeic point of view and from the economic. The law was 'he who buries, inherits'.[119] In every other respect daughters and sons seem to have had equal status in their parents' regard.

There were no legal injunctions to curtail the activities of women, nor were they denied any cultic rites. It appears that women were free to travel without a male chaperone. In fact Ramasses III boasted that under his rule a woman could travel safely throughout Egypt.[120]

Woman as 'temptress' occurs for the first time in the New Kingdom texts, although the greatest number of references to this theme is to be found in the Graeco-Roman material.[121] It is not a major topic in Pharaonic Wisdom Literature.

Throughout the Pharaonic period, women who conformed to the social ideal as daughter, wife and mother were treated with respect and had a certain amount of independence. Lack of education prevented most women from achieving personal success outside the home, though there was no active policy to deny them this opportunity since we do know of female scribes and doctors.[122]

The feelings and thoughts of ancient Egyptian women are largely unrecorded. Brief glimpses can be found in letters and in economic, legal and poetic texts. These generally show compliance with the *status quo*, which is to be expected given that the whole of Egyptian society was predicated on the maintenance of *Maat*, making rebellion tantamount to evil. Such freedom as women had was exercised within the constraints of a consciously hierarchical and patriarchal society.

NOTES

1. Allam (1989b).
2. Bruyere (1924–53).
3. Pestman (1961), p. 10; Eyre (1984), pp. 100f; Lichtheim (1980), p. 128.
4. Lichtheim (1976), pp. 167–78. Ostraca were flakes of stone or pottery inscribed with ink or paint. In Ancient Egypt they functioned in much the same way as note-pads or scrap paper today, for draft reports, lists, school exercises etc.
5. Bleeker (1929); Hornung (1982), pp. 213–16; Shirun-Grumach (1985), p. 173f.; Frankfort (1977), p. 14; Wilson (1977), pp. 105–9 and pp. 82–6.
6. No standard version of the myth exists. It has to be reconstructed from a wide variety of materials, for which see Griffiths (1960), Lichtheim (1976), pp. 214–23, Rundle Clark (1978), pp. 97–180; Te Velde (1980), col. 25–7.

7. Gardiner (1961), pp. 107–46.
8. Redford (1986), p. 168, n. 24; Redford (1967), p. 65, n. 42; Griffiths (1966), p. 140 and n. 92; Garland (1968), p. 35f.
9. Hornung (1982), p. 218.
10. Troy (1986), pp. 104–7; Černy (1957), pp. 51–5.
11. See, respectively, Lichtheim (1976), p. 139 and Caminos (1954), p. 96.
12. Gardiner (1940), p. 24, 1.14–15; Eyre and Baines (1989), p. 109; Sethe and Helck (1928), pp. 79–80; Shupak (1989).
13. Baines and Eyre (1983), pp. 65–9; Lesko (1990) argues for a larger proportion of the population being literate.
14. Baines and Eyre (1983), pp. 81–5; Ward (1989), p. 35f.; Bryan (1985), pp. 17–32; Fischer (1989), pp. 13f.
15. Peet (1930); Gardiner (1940), pp. 23f.; De Buck (1947), pp. 152–164; Goedicke (1963), pp. 71–92; Lichtheim (1976), p. 160, ch. 23 and 26 and (1975), pp. 169–84.
16. Kitchen (1980).
17. Other comparative literature has been published by Pritchard (1950); Ruffle (1979), pp. 29–68.
18. Théodoridès (1971), p. 297.
19. Lichtheim (1975), p. 128; Gardiner (1910), pp. 87–99; Gardiner (1947), I, 2.
20. Lichtheim (1975), pp. 18–27; (1976), pp. 18–20; (1980), pp. 13–41.
21. Gardiner (1940), p. 24; Černy (1945), pp. 29–53; Hoffman (1979), pp. 322f.; Fischer (1989), p. 3; Lesko (1989c), p. 31; Redford (1986), p. 213; Troy (1986), pp. 102–4.
22. Lichtheim (1975), pp. 170 and 173.
23. Caminos (1954), p. 55; Allam (1989), p. 22f, Černy (1973), pp. 175–81.
24. Posener (1951), pp. 184–5.
25. Simpson (1973), p. 304 (13); Lichtheim (1976), p. 183 and p. 190.
26. Kitchen (1979), p. 237; Gardiner (1961), pp. 72–106.
27. It is argued by some Egyptologists, such as Lichtheim (1975), pp. 6f., that these works were pseudepigraphical and were attributed to eminent writers and an early date to give them added weight and validity.
28. Fischer (1989), p. 23.
29. Lichtheim (1975), p. 60, n. 8.
30. Posener (1952), p. 113.
31. Lichtheim (1976), p. 12.
32. Lichtheim (1975), p. 58; Simpson (1973), p. 340; Posener (1952), p. 113.
33. Parkinson (1991), p. 55.
34. Pestman (1961), pp. 145ff.
35. See Lichtheim (1976), pp. 176 and (1980) 178; Badawy (1961), p. 144.
36. Manniche (1978), p. 54.
37. Robins (1990), p. 21.
38. See Lichtheim (1976), p. 143.
39. Troy (1984), pp. 77–81; (1986), pp. 7–9 and p. 24.
40. Te Velde (1980), col. 25–7; Troy (1984), p. 78 and n. 8.
41. Lichtheim (1976), pp. 197–9; Troy (1986), p. 24.
42. De Cenival (1988); Smith (1984), col. 1082–7; Boylan (1922); Bleeker (1973).
43. Translation after Cannuyer (1986), pp. 92–103.

44. Naville (1898), plate LXIX, 3rd Register; Baines (1985), pp. 110f.
45. Darby, Ghalioungui and Grivetti (1977), p. 60.
46. Cannuyer (1986), p. 102.
47. On divorce, see Pestman (1961), pp. 58–79; Allam (1981); Eyre (1984), pp. 98–101 and n. 81.
48. Pestman (1961), pp. 13f.
49. Parkinson (1991), pp. 68–9.
50. Černy (1929), pp. 243–58; Eyre (1984), pp. 93f. and n. 17.
51. Troy (1984), p. 77.
52. On punishments for adultery see Simpson (1973), pp. 16–18; Manniche (1978), pp. 61f.; Eyre (1984), pp. 97–100; Lichtheim (1976), p. 137 and (1980), p. 177; Volten (1955), p. 272 1.7.
53. Eyre (1984), p. 100; Černy (1929), pp. 243–58; Janssen (1988), pp. 134–7 and nn. 12, 13.
54. Allam (1989b), passim.
55. Lichtheim (1976), p. 139.
56. Caminos (1954), p. 96.
57. Ogdon (1986), p. 62f.; Ghalioungui (1983), p. 92.
58. Fischer (1989), pp. 8–11; Ward (1989), p. 43; Redford (1967), p. 65, n. 4 and (1986), p. 168, n. 24.
59. Lichtheim (1975), pp. 97–100 and pp. 135–9.
60. Lichtheim (1975), p. 128; Kitchen (1979), p. 281; Lichtheim (1975), pp. 184–92; Fischer (1982), pp. 45–50.
61. See, for example, Lichtheim (1975), pp. 149–62.
62. Pestman (1961), p. 88; Gaballa (1977); Allam (1989b), pp. 25f.
63. Lichtheim (1975), p. 100.
64. Lichtheim (1975), p. 172; Stewart (1979), plate 18. 13.
65. Lichtheim (1975), p. 137.
66. Lichtheim (1975), pp. 18–23.
67. Lichtheim (1975), p. 185.
68. Lichtheim (1975), p. 191.
69. Ghalioungui (1983), p. 73; Edwards (1965), p. 25, plate 11.2, line (X + 8) of inscription.
70. Gaballa (1977); Allam (1989b), pp. 25–6 and 29.
71. Lichtheim (1975), pp. 191.
72. Lichtheim (1976), p. 141.
73. Lichtheim (1975), p. 188.
74. On weaving, see Ling Roth (1978); Hayes (1953), pp. 264f.
75. On childbirth, see Robins (1988), p. 67; Harris (1971), p. 120, plate IIb; Brunner (1964); Pillet (1952), pp. 77–93 and fig. 8; Ghalioungui (1973), pp. 114–16, n. 178 and fig. 14; Lepsius (1849–59), Abt. IV, plate 60b; Goedicke (1985), pp. 19–26; Ebbell (1937); Lichtheim (1975), pp. 220f.
76. Robins (1988), p. 67; Frandsen (1986), col. 135–42.
77. Simpson (1973), p. 334.
78. Gardiner (1979), G37.
79. Pestman (1961), p. 61.
80. Möller (1918), p. 10, c(6), d(4/5) and p. 14, n. 6; Clère (1949); p. 38 and p. 42.
81. Janssen (1980), pp. 127–52.

82. Gardiner (1979), D26.
83. Kitchen (1986).
84. Lichtheim (1976) pp. 135–63; Kitchen (1979), pp. 281, 282.
85. Manniche (1978), p. 33; Eyre (1984), pp. 95–6; Černy (1973), pp. 175–81; Goedicke (1967), pp. 97–102.
86. Caminos (1954), p. 182.
87. See Lichtheim (1976), pp. 135–6 for text and further discussion.
88. Lichtheim (1976), p. 136.
89. Lichtheim (1976), p. 143.
90. Lichtheim (1976), p. 140.
91. Lichtheim (1975), pp. 66 and 71; Lichtheim (1976), pp. 12–15.
92. Bryan (1985), pp. 17–32; Ward (1989), p. 37; Ghalioungui (1983), p. 92; Ogdon (1986), pp. 62f.; Troy (1986), pp. 76–9; Robins (1990), pp. 18–21.
93. Posener (1951), pp. 184–5; Lichtheim (1980), p. 180.
94. Pestman (1961), p. 4.
95. All citations of Ani from Lichtheim (1976), p. 141.
96. Lichtheim (1976), p. 137.
97. Cannuyer (1989), pp. 53f.
98. Lichtheim (1980), p. 171.
99. Lichtheim (1980), pp. 207–8; Cannuyer (1989), pp. 48f.
100. Janssen (1988), p. 135.
101. Möller (1918), pp. 6–7 and 11.
102. On adultery, see Eyre (1984), pp. 95 and 100–5.
103. Lichtheim (1976), p. 143.
104. Lichtheim (1976), p. 185.
105. Lichtheim (1976), p. 151.
106. Marzal (1965), p. 101.
107. Eyre (1984), pp. 102f.; Pestman (1961), p. 88.
108. Lichtheim (1976), p. 161.
109. Lichtheim (1976), pp. 21–4, (1975) 169–84.
110. Kitchen (1979), p. 282.
111. Lichtheim (1976), pp. 169.
112. Lichtheim (1976), p. 176.
113. Kitchen (1979), p. 281.
114. Gardiner (1957), pp. 43–5.
115. James (1962), letter II.
116. Pestman (1961), p. 75; Gardiner (1940), pp. 23f.
117. Pestman (1961), p. 77.
118. Stewart (1979), UCII, plates 18 l. 13 [l = line].
119. Allam (1989a), p. 128 and n. 22; Janssen and Pestman (1968), p. 140.
120. Lichtheim (1976), p. 137; P. Harris quoted by Eyre (1984), p. 101.
121. Lesko (1989c), p. 101.
122. Ward (1989), p. 35; Fischer (1989), p. 21.

3 Notions of Community and the Exclusion of the Female in Jewish History and Historiography
Léonie J. Archer

For some years now, my particular area of research interest has been the period of formative Judaism, a period which lasted from about 600 BC to AD 200 and saw the emergence in essence of what may be termed modern, rabbinic Judaism – a religious system quite distinct from that of the early books of the Bible and one which continues to shape and inform Jews and Judaism today. These centuries of formative Judaism saw the development of new laws, new definitions, theologies, philosophies and social structures. They were times of intense fluidity and change, when monotheism first really emerged as a rigorous and normative system and when the Law – that huge body of commandments designed to embrace virtually every aspect of Jewish daily existence – gradually took shape and preeminence in Jewish life.[1] My concern has been to examine the changing position, image and status of women within Palestine during these developments.[2]

Many things could be said, in the context of the present collection of essays, about women's lives and representations in this all-important period. I have chosen to look at notions of community in Jewish history and historiography, and I stress the historiography (in particular modern historiography) part of the title. I have chosen this topic both as a unifying theme for the various aspects of women's lives that I would like to present here, and, more importantly, because 'community' was, and still is, central to Jewish religious and social thought and practice. As will be seen in the course of this chapter, the word and its attached meanings deserve attention in a book whose explicit agenda is women's history and gender.

An idea of community was very important to the Jews of antiquity, and that idea has been taken up wholesale by modern writers. In the Old Testament (henceforth called Bible), the word for community appears 169 times, and the various allied, and often interchangeable, terms like 'assembly', 'covenant' (see below) or 'people' some three or four thousand times.[3] In the secondary literature on Jews and Judaism it is difficult to find one

53

work which does not contain the word 'community' (or allied term) either in its title or a chapter heading, and the word is always sprinkled liberally throughout the text. To mention just three works which I shall be drawing on in this chapter and which may be taken as representative of the modern historiographic genre: there is the completely revised and up-dated four-volume edition of the nineteenth-century work by the German scholar Emil Schürer, *The History of the Jewish People in the Age of Jesus Christ*, the final volume of which appeared in 1987 edited by Fergus Millar, Geza Vermes and Martin Goodman; the second is a two-volume work entitled *The Jewish People in the First Century*, edited by Shemuel Safrai and others, published in 1974 and 1976, which contains contributions by a great many of today's leading Jewish scholars on various aspects of life in ancient Palestine; and the third is the older but still widely-read *A Social and Religious History of the Jews* by Salo Baron, again multi-volumed and originally written in the 1930s but revised and considerably extended between 1952 and 1983. I shall also draw on the same author's *The Jewish Community*, published in 1942. All of these books, especially the revised Schürer, are central reference works for the student of Jewish antiquity. All, in their surveys of Jewish history, life and law make great use of the term 'community'. Similarly, the *Oxford English Dictionary* has as its largest sub-entry under the heading 'community' the term's biblical usage, both the original Hebrew and then its translations through Greek, Latin and the various English forms. Another sub-entry, this time concerned with the definition of community as a body distinct from its neighbours, has as its chief example the so-called 'Jewish Community'. 'Community', therefore, is a very important term of Jewish self-definition and organisation, and a much-used tool of analysis by modern historians of Jewish antiquity and later periods.

I say 'tool of analysis' but this is in fact something of a misnomer. Rather it is an assumption-filled, value-laden, semi-descriptive label from which the analysis flows and by which the analysis is dictated. The process may conveniently be imagined in terms of a bicycle wheel, the analysis fanning out like spokes from the hub and the hub being viewed as some kind of static, immutable and all-embracing entity, never in itself to be questioned or examined. The problem is that, unrecognised by most of the riders of that bicycle, some of the spokes on the wheel are missing and the centre itself is not as coherent and comprehensive as they would like to imagine.

'Community' is not a neutral or static term. It is multi-faceted and multi-tiered and, given the male-stream tradition of historical experience (in terms of power, authority and public decision-making) and, consequently, the male-stream tradition of historiography, it is also heavily gendered. It falls into the same category as other so-called descriptive or analytical terms of reference such as 'democracy' or 'people', where rule has not in fact been by the totality of the given society or where women have not been counted in the reckoning. These words at least have received some attention in recent years in the context of women's history and gender studies, as, for example, in the increased sensitivity regarding the use of 'democracy' without qualification for fifth-century BC Athens, or 'people' in study of the aspirations of the seventeenth-century Levellers in this country. 'Community', as far as I know, has not – that is, apart from one excellent related paper by Lyndal Roper (1987) which discusses the use of *gemeiner Mann* in sixteenth-century Reformation Germany.

As I mentioned earlier, modern scholars – at least in so far as Judaism is concerned – have adopted wholesale the ancients' use of the word 'community'. They have perpetuated the bias of the male-stream experience of history and historiography, and continue to be both gender-blind and gender-bound in their writings. Indeed, as we shall see in the course of this paper, modern writers are if anything more gender-blind than their ancient counterparts.

What I would like to do here, therefore, is reapproach the word 'community' and examine the actual applicability of the term in its various contexts in Jewish antiquity. All too often the term, as used by both ancient and modern writers, is not as all-embracing and inclusive as our texts would have us believe. On the one hand and as we shall see, the community which is presented in the ancient sources as mainstream, normative and inclusive of all members of the Jewish population (if on occasion only through representation by a smaller body) is often exclusive of women – a fact seemingly not recognised by modern authors in their representations of Jewish life in antiquity. (Indeed, this is an instance when modern texts often carry a heavier load of gender-blindness than the primary sources, for the latter often did draw distinctions between male and female activity which twentieth-century writers then appear to ignore.) On the other hand, types of community not taken as part of the mainstream definition are accorded little or no recognition in either the ancient or the modern sources and barely graced with any collective title. These unrecognised communities, in reality part of the fabric of 'the community' and not satellites around it, often involved women. The questions to be asked, therefore, are what comprised 'the community'? Who defined it? Where did status lie? And how have ancient definitions and perceptions been perpetuated in modern representations of social ordering and community (fed as they are not only by information from the past but also by modern writers' own cultural context)? In consequence of my concern to trace the continuation of bias, or gender-blindness, I shall structure the chapter loosely around the definitions of community and congregation as given in that recognised authority of semantic history and meaning, the *OED*.

The first area to look at is that which the *OED* labels 'Co-Religionists', that is, a body of people sharing in common the same religious beliefs and practices – and here I would stress the word practices. Judaism was, and still is, grounded in two fundamentals: the Covenant and the Law.

The Covenant, or 'contract' between God and the Jews, was established early on in Hebrew history. As recorded in the Bible, it was a special and exclusive contract, with obligations on both parties, which separated the Jews from other nations and set them up in special relation with God as His Chosen People. The external sign of the covenant was circumcision, a ritual which heralded a male's entry into the covenant and into the potential for full participation in his people's religion and cult. Without it he could not, as an adult, function in civil or religious affairs. It was a physical sign of his membership of the community and so fundamental to Jewish thought that it and the word for covenant are used interchangeably and synonymously in the texts.[4] The biblical law which decreed that circumcision be the mark of entry into the covenant and that it take place early on in a child's life – the ritual had had other significances before this legislation and previously had occurred at puberty or in adulthood[5] – reads as follows:

> And God said unto Abraham: 'And as for thee, thou shalt keep my convenant, thou and thy seed after thee throughout their generations. This is My Covenant, which ye shall keep, between Me and you and thy seed after thee: every male among you shall be circumcised in the flesh of your foreskin; and it shall be a token of a covenant betwixt Me and you. And he that is eight days old shall be circumcised among you, every male throughout your generations . . . . My Covenant shall be in your flesh for an everlasting covenant. And the uncircumcised male who is not circumcised in the flesh of his foreskin, that soul shall be cut off from his people; he hath broken My Covenant.' (Genesis 17:9–14)[6]

For a girl there was no similar, substitute *rite de passage*. She was a member of her people by birth and no further ritual of entry into the covenant was accorded her – despite the fact that within the framework and terms of reference of Jewish ritual practice, various substitutes, such as ritual slaughter of an animal or the cutting-off of the girl's first hair, were readily available.[7] Her accountability as a Jew was determined patrilineally, and her membership of the Covenant was both passive, unritualised and by association with males – similar, in fact, to that of a male who, for whatever reason, had not been circumcised. The much-vaunted principle of matrilineality with respect to Jewishness, that is, the transmission of Jewishness by the female line, only came about in later centuries and, in fact, it may be debated whether strictly speaking it ever came about at all. Louis Jacobs recently argued that our use of the term matrilineal in this context is a convenient but misleading shorthand and that the transmission of Jewishness was and is dependent upon the same patrilineal principles at work everywhere else in society and upon rabbinic understanding of what constitutes lawful marriage and therefore lawful offspring.[8] The subject is, however, complex and deserving of a whole other study. For this chapter and for our purposes, it is sufficient to recognise that at least for the majority of the period we are looking at – that of formative Judaism – clearcut patrilineality was unquestionably the rule.

Regarding the historic shift, decreed in the Genesis passage, of the ritual of circumcision from a *rite de passage* at adulthood to a covenantal entry on the eighth day of life, Baron remarks:

> they [the legislators] advanced the time of the performance from the age of thirteen to the early days of infancy, severing its intrinsic connection with *male* pubescence and made of it instead an eternal symbol of God's covenant with the Jewish *people*. (my italics)[9]

As just mentioned, only boys had a ritualised entry to the Covenant; presumably they were the representatives of the people. One suspects, however, that authors such as Baron were not even seeing them as representatives. It is more likely that in keeping with a long line of traditional thinking, the words 'covenant', 'community', and 'people' simply bring to his and other authors' minds the male members of society.

The all-embracing Covenant had therefore a decidedly male bias, and, in fact, was on occasion referred to in the Bible as the 'brotherly covenant'.[10] The people of the Covenant, both men and women, were called *bene Israel* (literally 'sons of Israel', Israel being the name of one of the patriarchs of biblical history) and from early on in the period, i.e. the time of the revised Covenant, their God was Yahweh, a male deity.[11]

Still with the definition of community as 'Co-Religionists', we come to the second fundamental of Judaism: the Law. This was the huge body of biblical and post-biblical commandments, with all their rabbinic refinements and commentary, which governed virtually every aspect of Jewish daily existence and, as the practical manifestations of the Covenant, served to differentiate the Jews as a nation apart. Although, according to the narrative of Exodus, women were present at the original delivery of the Law by God to Moses at Mount Sinai and at the subsequent national assembly recorded in Deuteronomy of oath-renewal to keep the Covenant, they were over the succeeding centuries of the post-exilic period declared exempt by the (male) religious leaders from the obligation to fulfil those commandments which were both positive and dependent on a certain time of the day or year[12]. They were, however, bound by all of the negative commands and failure to observe those resulted in the full weight of the penal code descending. This exclusion from the positive precepts accounted for nearly half the total number of commandments, despite the fact that according to the tenth chapter of Nehemiah both men and women of the restored community in Palestine, following the exile to Babylon in the sixth century, had entered into a curse to 'observe and to do all the commandments of the Lord our Lord and His ordinances and His statutes'.[13]

With this exemption, which was effectively an exclusion eventually formalised as such in rabbinic statute, women had no responsibility, for example, to circumcise their sons (a particularly significant exemption) or to take them to the Temple in Jerusalem for the ritual redemption of the first-born; they were exempt from making the thrice-yearly pilgrimage to Jerusalem at the feasts of Passover, Pentecost and Tabernacles; from living in the ceremonial booths which were erected at the feast of Tabernacles; from shaking the ritual palm branch (the *lulab*) at the same feast, or sounding the ram's horn (the *shofar*) at new year; from wearing phylacteries (ritual prayer-boxes, *tefillin*) or going to synagogue, and even from reciting the daily affirmation of faith, the *shema*: 'Hear O Israel, the Lord our God the Lord is One'.[14] If they did observe any of the commandments from which they were exempt, the rabbis placed them in the category of 'one who is not commanded and fulfils', a talmudic expression meaning the action was without value.[15] Women were also denied any significant education in the Law, despite the fact that the Graeco-Roman period witnessed the growth throughout Jewish Palestine of a formal system of schooling at both primary and advanced levels, an education programme described by one present-day writer as

> a comprehensive system of schooling designed to bring knowledge of the Torah [Law] to all members of the Jewish community, rich and poor, aristocrat and ordinary citizen alike.

I must confess that that present-day writer was myself, writing in the Cameron-Kuhrt collection of 1983. With some saving grace, however, I did follow my piece of gender-blind prose with the statement that women had no part in the schooling system.

I mention trips to Jerusalem which was, of course, where the great Temple lay – the central institution in Jewish religion until its destruction by Rome in AD 70. Regarding the duty to make pilgrimage there on high holidays, the author Salo Baron in *A Social and Religious History of the Jews* writes (on the basis of rabbinic law) that 'only old, sick, or abnormal men, as well as women, small boys and slaves were exempted' from the duty to travel.[16] All others, that is, all healthy adult males, were under a religious obligation to go there three times a year.

The main activity of the Temple was animal sacrifice, which was conducted by a male priesthood. Women, although not obliged, were permitted to attend the Temple, but in the main they were only allowed into an outer, less-hallowed area of the precinct which was called the Court of Women – a title which was, in fact, something of a misnomer as men had free access to this court. Women were, however, only allowed there if they were neither menstruating nor had recently given birth. If either of these was the case, then they were barred access altogether. As the first-century AD historian Josephus wrote:

> All who ever saw our Temple are aware of the general design of the building and the inviolable barriers which preserve its sanctity. It had four surrounding courts, each with its special statutory restrictions. The outer court was open to all, foreigners included; during their time of impurity women alone were refused admission. To the second court all Jews were permitted and, when uncontaminated by any defilement, their wives; to the third, male Jews [alone], if clean and purified; to the fourth, the priests . . . .[17]

The business of sacrifice was conducted in the Court of Priests, and to this court male Israelites were permitted to bring their private offerings, which were then sacrificed by the priests at the altar of unhewn stone. Only rarely were women granted admission to this inner court for, as the Mishnah records,

> The rites of laying on of hands, [on the beast's head before its slaughter], of waving, bringing near [the meal-offering], taking the handful and burning it, wringing the necks of the bird-offerings, sprinkling the blood [of the offering on the altar] and receiving the blood . . . all these are performed by men but not by women.[18]

Occasionally, however, and despite the mishnaic ruling, women were permitted to perform the ritual of laying-on of hands – presumably on those occasions when the offering was of a particularly personal nature (such as a 'sin-offering' to remove taboo from an individual or the sacrifice demanded for the purification after childbirth), but the somewhat intriguing comment of the Gemara (the post-AD 200 commentary on the Mishnah) regarding this practice was 'Not that it was customary for women, but that it was to appease the women'.[19] We shall return to this quotation later.

Upkeep of the vast Temple complex and cult was by means of a half-shekel tax which, according to Baron, Safrai, Stern and others on the basis of Exodus 30:14–15, 'was levied on every Jew over the age of twenty'. In fact, the biblical text clearly states that it was only levied on men, a fact that the modern-day authors undoubtedly know but often fail to present clearly in their discussion of the subject. For them, all too often it appears that (and certainly reads as if) male Jews = all Jews = the Jewish community. This is a clear instance of the increased bias or blindness, mentioned at the start of this chapter, of modern-day writers compared with their ancient sources.

The annual tax was brought in person or by agents to Jerusalem and together with the regular pilgrimages meant that the city had a constant influx of visitors. On this state of affairs, Safrai *et al.* in the book *The Jewish People in the First Century* have the following comment. As with the previous quotations from modern writers, I shall simply leave their words for your perusal with no further analysis, for the perpetuation of a gendered understanding of 'Jew', 'people' and 'community' and the definition of all three as that which falls in the male public arena is all too evident from what they say:

> These visits did much to bind the individual Jew . . . to the city and the land . . . they influenced the whole character of Judaism . . . Jews went on pilgrimage to Jerusalem and stayed there, got to know personally the teachers of Torah, and became personally and directly linked with what was happening in the city . . . . *Every member of the people of Israel who had something to say and wanted a public platform made his way to Jerusalem* . . . [on returning home] . . . they had a vital link with the actuality and development of Judaism which went beyond the pronouncements of its authorities and sages and matters affecting public life as a whole. (my italics)[20]

Still under the heading of Co-Religionists, I would like now to turn very briefly to another sub-definition of community, that is, community as a congregation or assembly, and look at the synagogue, a Greek word which literally translates as 'gathering' or 'coming together'. The synagogue was an institution which seems to have developed from the Jews' experience of the exile to Babylon in the sixth century BC.[21] In Palestine it continued in existence alongside the Jerusalem Temple until the latter's destruction in AD 70, and thereafter became the primary Jewish institution, the focal point in every Jewish community; that is, town. The synagogue's purpose was twofold: (1) instructional, that is, educational in the Holy Law through public readings and through schooling classes attached to the synagogue, and (2) liturgical, that is, structured services of worship with prayer, readings and sermons. Obviously the two overlapped in function and purpose.[22]

As already mentioned, women were excluded from the process of formal education.[23] They were also exempt from the obligation to go to synagogue. If they did go – and this was one of their primary ways of gaining access to knowledge of the Law through the readings and sermons – they were accorded no active participation. Men conducted the services. They read aloud from the Holy Scrolls and prayed their prayers to God the King and Father in the male language of their revered ancestors.[24] Women, if present, most probably sat apart from the men in consequence of the period's taboos about the free mingling of the sexes and thus were physically distanced in some way from the meetings' activities.[25] They could not be called upon to read from the scrolls because, due to their lack of obligation to fulfil that commandment, they were ineligible to act as agents or representatives of the 'community'. As the Talmud so nicely puts it, 'All are qualified to be among the seven [who read on sabbath mornings], even a minor and a woman, but a woman should not be allowed to come forward to read out of respect for the congregation'.[26] Commenting on this state of affairs, in a book unusually devoted to a study of women in Judaism, the present-day scholar Rafel Loewe writes:

> the ineligibility of women . . . (to act) . . . as leaders in prayer for congregations including men (rests) on the principle that whereas obligation may be fulfilled by a plurality of those liable to it acting cooperatively, one of their number taking the lead and the others consciously fulfilling their obligation in unison with him, the situation would be quite otherwise were the quasi-representative figure not under an obligation of precisely analogous quality to that of the remainder of the congregation.[27]

Services could only take place if ten adult males were present, no matter how many women might be there, and members of the synagogue community were called *bene ha-knesset*, 'sons of the assembly', *knesset* being the Aramaic for synagogue.

To turn then to the second main area of definition, that is, the Civil Community, the *OED* describes this as 'a body of people organised into a political, municipal, or social unity . . . *a body of men living in the same locality . . . a body to which all alike belong, the public*' (my italics).

Strictly speaking, there was no division in Jewish society between the civil and the religious, the secular and the sacred: all formed the holy community living according to divine commandment. For the purposes of ease of presentation here, however, I somewhat artificially separate the two spheres. In the discussion that follows, though, it should be remembered that in reality there was no division.

The internal constitutional definition of a town in Jewish Palestine (and I say 'internal' to make clear the distinction between Jewish towns and the Greek-constituted *poleis* which were to be found all over Palestine) was the presence of ten resident adult males, that is, a number sufficient to form the quorum necessary for a synagogue service (a fact which highlights the absence of the modern-day secular–sacred divide and the centrality of religion to Jewish social ordering). It has been reckoned that in the seventh century BC there were about 400 towns and cities in Palestine. By the turn of the eras these units must have increased considerably both in size and number, for the estimated population-count for first-century Palestine is around two-and-a-half million.[28]

Community organisation for the early biblical period was by clan, district rulers, heads of prominent families, religious leaders, and, in particular, city elders, an institution which continued in the post-exilic period – all of whom were male. Regarding the city elders, Baron in *The Jewish Community* comments that in their appointment and function an 'egalitarian principle' was at work: one did not have to be noble to be something; elders were not elected but were representative because they came from a recognised clan or family, and their deliberations at the city gate (where according to the Bible they usually met) 'undoubtedly gave every citizen opportunity to express his views'. Jewish social organisation was, in his opinion, 'a political and religious democracy' (pp. 43–8). Baron does not consider the fact that women were not allowed (or at least expected) to frequent the public places of the city, let alone hold office, and so had no part in these deliberations. Equally there is no consideration of the way in which he uses the all-embracing terms 'democracy' and 'citizenship' with application only to men.

The municipal organisation for the later Graeco-Roman period (and here I am speaking only of those cities with a purely or predominantly Jewish population) was by a council of seven judges, plus three synagogue functionaries and an 'assembly of men in the city'. There were additionally the religious leaders – the sages – and various officials for specific tasks such as the inspector of markets, and various trade, social and charitable associations. According to Safrai *et al.*, 'the appointment of the leadership was debated in public and the leadership was only accepted with the full approval of the public'. That public again only comprised men, a point not noted (or perhaps not recognised) by the authors. Safrai *et al.* continue:

An important aspect of . . . the civic leadership was the broad basis on which it was founded . . . authority belonged to the community and the assembly. Fundamentally the ruling authority was the gatherings of local citizens to deal with civic matters, and of all Jews to deal with national matters.[29]

Similar comments to those given above for the quotations from Baron obviously apply here too.

The services which this supposedly democratic and self-serving community were meant to provide were 'A law court competent to scourge, a prison, a charity fund, a synagogue and a public bath, a public latrine, a doctor and an artisan, a scribe, a slaughterer, and a teacher of children'.[30] The inhabitants of the town were called *bene ha-ir* (sons, or children, of the city), and institutions like the bath-house were deemed common property. The local law courts, the size of which ranged from three persons to 23 in more populous centres, worked as secondary satellites to the main court of Great Sanhedrin in Jerusalem to which major cases were referred. Jewish women, unlike Greek women, could appear in court without representation by a guardian, but they could not act as witnesses in a case despite the rabbinic statement that 'scripture equalised woman and man for all legal actions mentioned in the law'.[31] They could not serve as guardians for minors or act as agents for others, both of which men could do.[32] Married women were not liable for any damage caused to another's person or property, because they usually had no independent means with which to pay the plaintiff. In general, women laboured under various legal disabilities which I do not have the space to go into here.[33] Suffice it to say that in the rabbinic discussions of legal responsibility, women are usually bracketed with slaves, imbeciles, minors, deaf-mutes, and persons of double or doubtful sex, all of whom were the passive recipients of the 'community's' law and not its active administrators or litigants. It is in this sense only, that is, that of passive recipient, that the statement of equality may be read.

In their introduction to a chapter on Jewish private law, Safrai *et al.*, in a nice piece of gender-blind prose which precisely highlights what I have been arguing in this chapter, write that

Talmudic law is based on the principle of personality, i.e. rights and duties depend on the traditional law of a man's father rather than upon the norms of the state in which he lives. *The law is part of the divine covenant with the People of Israel and stress is put upon the distinction between the 'sons of the covenant' and gentiles.* Therefore, personal law is particularly important in the Jewish legal system. *Rights and duties are*

generally limited to men. However, by way of personification, certain
rules are applied also to non-human beings. (my italics)[34]

That last sentence deserves a scree of exclamation marks! The same authors
close their discussion of the Jewish legal system with a paragraph on
women's legal disabilities, which they dismiss, in line with the ancients, in
terms of Psalm 45:13, where it says 'All glorious is the King's daughter
within', a descriptive passage which was taken as prescriptive of the modest
retirement of women from all matters to do with the public life of the
community. And with that, discussion of the Jewish community in both the
primary and secondary literature ends.

It is patently clear, however, that the story cannot end there. What we are
dealing with is both a gendered and hierarchical or exclusionary notion of
community. It comes as no surprise when looking at a rigidly patriarchal
society that all I have described so far by way of office and responsibility
pertains to the male. In line with the sources, both ancient and modern, I
have been reviewing aspects of only one notion of community, that is the
public and by definition, male one. But is that where the story ends? Were
women just spots on the canvas of the male community, without connection
to each other or to men? From cursory reading of the primary and particularly the secondary literature, one would think so. Their definition of community as public male activity denies the possibility of other terms of
reference or activity; it excludes other histories, perpetuates a bias, and
prevents us getting a fuller, more rounded picture of life in ancient Palestine. Women were a part of the picture. They undoubtedly saw themselves
as belonging to a people. They self-identified as Jews.

What can be done? First, present-day researchers can take care with their
language. We are dealing with a patriarchal society and with sources written
by, about and largely for men, but that does not mean that we should adopt
wholesale their terms of reference and present them as definitive, inclusive
and all-embracing. Secondly, we can comb the primary sources for evidence of possible female communities. This would be done in addition to
looking at the actual degree of female involvement in the supposedly total
male domain, and at the question of mixed communal activity as, for
example, in the economic arena. Careful scrutiny of the primary sources
does reveal women holding and disposing of property, engaging in the
business life of 'the community', and wielding some degree of power in
matters of private law as, for example, in the case of whether and whom to
marry. As stated at the start of this chapter, the ancients in many respects
were far less gender-blind than modern tellers of their story. In other words,
we have to be careful to avoid not only presenting male activity as the

totality of (male and female) Jewish activity but also community activity as totally male activity.

With regard to the search for possible female communities, we have, for example, the repeated biblical and rabbinic references to the magic and sorcery of women, which ran counter to the dictates of the official religion.[35] We know from one fleeting reference that eighty witches were hanged by a rabbi in the town of Ascalon in the first century AD.[36] We may ask, what was going on here? Given the male-stream orientation of our sources and the fact that they were trying to hush up such non-official religious practices, we may not get an answer. But it is possible that these women, and others like them with shared interests, were working together in some kind of association, were in a sense a 'community' with activities additional to but also a part of (if only by negative definition) the 'main community'. The possibility of such associations should, at the very least, be noted, and noted with a somewhat more scholarly appreciation of the broad reality of life and complexities of human organisation than, for example, Baron who on this subject simply followed his sources and wrote

> Women, generally more illiterate and superstitious than men, were irresistibly attracted to the magical arts . . . . Official Judaism protested vainly. Not even R. Simeon ben Shetah's fanatical execution of 80 women in Ascalon . . . could stop a practice rooted in the conditions of the age.[37]

No further attempt is made at appreciating these 'alternative' communities or seeing them as other than simply deviations from the mainstream religion.

In a similar vein and within the sphere of 'official' religious practice, we might wonder at the possible discussions and shared interests which doubtless were engaged in within the Temple Court of Women or in those synagogue areas occupied by women. Or alternately, we might muse on what lay behind the highly enigmatic rabbinic statement that women were sometimes allowed to take part in Temple sacrifice 'in order to appease them' (quoted above, pp. 59–60), a highly intriguing quotation which offers a tantalising glimpse of a reality different from what the sources might wish us to believe.

Similarly, we should be looking at the possibility of associations of urban women with shared interests, as, for example, professional midwives, funeral-keeners or simply widows dwelling in the same town. These would be additional to the public male functionaries and institutions noted above in the rabbinic listings of urban organisation. Or again, great play is made in the ancient and modern histories of the political, military and religious intrigues of men, both as individuals and as groups, but what of the 'intrigues' of women as, for example, in the biblical story of Ruth and Naomi?[38] What, apart from the culturally constructed fear of women, lies behind the constant male-to-male warnings in our sources about their power-mad, conniving and ever-gossiping wives? What about city prostitutes, an area which has hardly been touched on in Jewish scholarship, despite the obvious concern in this regard of the sources, or the possibility of female community through the extended kinship network, as, for example, in the Gospel story of Mary travelling to see her cousin Elizabeth to discuss pregnancy and childbirth?

All of these, and many more (all I have been doing is brainstorming a few suggestions), need to be looked at, and looked at in their own right and not as satellites of the 'main' community or secondary spheres in a hierarchy of activity. They need to be looked at not only to uncover a history (or rather, histories), but also, on being put in the public arena of scholarship, to stop the perpetuation of a gender-blind and gender-bound (non-) understanding of the past. As noted earlier, we may never, given the nature of our sources, acquire any detailed description, or even proof, of their existence, but on the limited evidence available, logic dictates the likelihood of such female associations. Note should be taken and warning bells should be sounded. 'Community' is not some kind of homogeneous, monolithic entity. Like all human social structures and, one would hope, tools of analytical enquiry, it is complex and made up of many parts. A more considered appreciation of this, and of the problems which its usage has suffered (and generated) over the centuries, will be of benefit to the histories of both men and women.

NOTES

1.　For details of the enormous changes that took place in this period – the flourishing of extra-canonical literature, formation of new laws, radical shifts in social organisation, the final demise of polytheism and the establishment of rabbinic leadership – see Archer (1987).

2.　For the fruits of this research, see Archer (1990a) which presents a detailed survey of the life, from birth to death, of the 'average' Jewish woman and the attitudes towards her in Graeco-Roman Palestine.

3.　Although, technically, the Bible largely falls outside the period with which we are here concerned, it obviously formed the bedrock of Jewish society, a source of inspiration and the basis of subsequent rabbinic writings. Other ancient writings which will be referred to in the course of the chapter are the works of the first-century AD Jewish historian Josephus, and the Mishnah which is the oldest extant (post-biblical) code of Jewish law, essentially a record of decisions reached by rabbinic scholars and leaders on the basis of biblical law and narrative during the period AD 70–200. The Tosefta, a rabbinic collection which roughly parallels the Mishnah in date and content, will also be referred to, as will later talmudic commentary on both Bible and Mishnah. The Talmud, of which there are two versions (Babylonian and Jerusalem) is the collective title for both the Mishnah and its subsequent commentary, the Gemara. Unless otherwise indicated, talmudic references in this chapter will be to the Babylonian Talmud.

4. For details, see Archer (1990a), pp. 29–34; Archer (1990b), especially pp. 33–5, 40–1; Archer (1990c), especially pp. 46–7.

5. For the change in the significance and timing of the ritual – from an ancient rite of redemption or mark of fertility performed on adult males at the feast of Passover, to the ritualised entry of a boy-child into the Covenant, see Archer (1990a), pp. 30–4. See Archer (1990b and 1990c) for the close connection between the rite's final significance and performance on the child's eighth day of life and the mother's week-long period of post-natal impurity: circumcision was both a rite of purification and separation from the female as well as an initiation into the male covenant or community.

6. This passage from Genesis was in all probability written in or around the time of the Jews' exile to Babylon in the sixth century BC, an event which marked a watershed in the history of Judaism and the social ordering of the people. For the fact that the Bible is not some kind of monolithic whole, but a complex composite work spanning many centuries, see Archer (1987). See ibid. for details of the exilic context of this passage and the social and religious upheaval and consequent reordering of that period.

7. See Archer (1990a), p. 32, and Morgenstern (1966), Ch. 12. Note that Strabo is certainly incorrect in his view that the Jews circumcised both male and female children (*Geographica* 16. 2.37, 4.9; 17. 2.5)

8. Jacobs (1985). For other, more traditional, arguments regarding 'who is a Jew', see the several other articles in the same issue and also in Vol. 35 of the same journal.

9. Baron (1950), 1, pp. 6–7.

10. *berith achim*, Amos 1.9. For the way in which circumcision allowed the individual to enter the covenant and join with his fellow 'circumcisees' to form a community or brotherhood of blood (shedding of blood being an essential part of the ritual), see Archer (1990b). This brotherhood was seen as extending laterally across a generation, vertically to fathers and grandfathers, sons and grandsons, and ultimately to God. So, for example, Malachi 2:10; Ezekiel 18:4.

11. Before this 'new' Covenant was decreed in Genesis, with circumcision as its mark, there had been other covenants which were now superseded. On this, see 'covenant' in the *Jewish Encyclopaedia*. See Archer (1983), pp. 274–6, and Archer (1987), p. 6 for the gradual and historic rise to supremacy of the single male God in Israelite history. Until the sixth-century exile to Babylon, polytheistic beliefs and practices, with a pantheon of both gods and goddesses, had flourished in Palestine.

12. Original delivery of the Law, Exodus 35:1ff; subsequent national assembly,

Deut. 29:9f, 31:12–13.

13.   Neh. 10:29f. According to later Jewish thinkers, there were 613 command-ments: 365 negative and 248 positive (a somewhat artificial enumeration, but one that nevertheless indicates the large number involved). The all-pervasive-ness of the commandments in a Jewish man's life is shown by the rabbinic characterisation of God as the one 'who sanctified us with His command-ments and commanded us' (Tosefta, *Berakhoth* 7.9), and the Jerusalem Talmud's declaration that 'a man performs 10 precepts before he even eats a piece of bread' (*Hallah* 58a). See Urbach (1975), pp. 315ff for details of the domination of Jewish life by the commandments.

14.   For full rabbinic references to these and other exemptions, see Archer (1983), pp. 277–9.

15.   *Sotah* 21a.

16.   Vol. 1, p. 213.

17.   *Contra Apionem* 2.102f. Cf. also by Josephus, *Antiquitates Judaicae* 15.418f; *Bellum Judaicae* 5. 193f, especially 227, and, in the Mishnah, *Kelim* 1.6–9.

18.   *Kiddushin* 1.8.

19.   *Hagigah* 16b.

20.   Safrai *et al.* (1976) I, p. 203.

21.   For arguments for this dating, see Archer (1990a), pp. 74–5.

22.   For the history of the synagogue, evidence for it over the centuries, and details of its instructional and liturgical function, see idem and *Encyclopae-dia Judaica* 15, pp. 579–83; Schürer (1979) 2, pp. 424–47.

23.   For details of that exemption, or effective exclusion, from the period's pro-gramme of formal education in and knowledge of Torah, that is, the nation's history, traditions, customs and laws, through home instruction, primary and advanced schooling, and active participation in the annual round of feasts and festivals, see Archer (1990a), Ch. 1.

24.   *Megillah* 4.3, 23a. Cf. 1 Corinthians 14:34–6; 1 Timothy 2:11–14.

25.   Although, given the taboos, such segregation was very probable, it is unfor-tunately not possible to say what form it took in these centuries. Clear evidence for women's galleries or screened areas only arises in the post-mediaeval period. See Archer (1983), pp. 281–2. For the Graeco-Roman period, it is likely that women just gathered at the back of the synagogue or possibly in a porch area. Frequently domestic duties and the care of young children would have prevented women from enjoying even that limited degree of attendance. See Archer (1990a), p. 93.

26.   *Megillah* 23a.

27.   Loewe (1966), pp. 44–5.

28.   Details of population count and civil organisation can be found in Schürer (1973–87) and Safrai and Stern (1976).

29.   Safrai *et al.* (1976) 1, p. 378.

30.   *Sanhedrin* 17b; Jerusalem Talmud *Kiddushin* 4, 68b.

31.   *Kiddushin* 35a; not acting as witnesses, for example, *Shebuoth* 4.1 where, in clear contradistinction to *Kidd.* 35a, it states that '"an oath of testimony" applies to men but not to women'.

32.   Tosefta, *Terumoth* 1.11.

33. For details of the general legal disabilities endured by women throughout their lives, and also examples of little appreciated exceptions to the usually assumed total state of female passivity and dependence, see Archer (1990a), *passim*.
34. Safrai *et al.* (1976) 1, p. 505.
35. See, for example, Leviticus 19:26f; Deuteronomy 18:9–11; Ezekiel 13:17f; *Sanhedrin* 7.7, 11, 67a; *Aboth* 2:7. The examples could be multiplied almost endlessly.
36. *Sanhedrin* 6.4 in context of Jerusalem Talmud *Hagigah* 2.2, 77d and *Sanhedrin* 6.9, 23c.
37. Baron (1952) 2, p. 21.
38. The tale found in the book of Ruth is fascinating, complex, and open to many interpretations. It tells the story of how Ruth and Naomi – respectively daughter- and mother-in-law, and both widowed – strove to secure a husband for Ruth and a child for both of them. It is a tale of female solidarity, with intriguing – and in the modern sources, usually overlooked – references to institutions such as 'mother's houses' and events involving the women of the town.

4 The Problem of Women Philosophers in Ancient Greece

Richard Hawley

Oh! There I met those few congenial maids
Whom love hath warm'd, in philosophic shades;
There still Leontium, on her sage's breast,
Found lore and love, was tutor'd and caress'd;
And there the clasp of Pythia's gentle arms
Repaid the zeal which deified her charms.
The Attic Master, in Aspasia's eyes,
Forgot the yoke of less endearing ties,
While fair Theano, innocently fair,
Wreath'd playfully her Samian's flowing hair,
Whose soul now fix'd, its transmigrations past,
Found in those arms a resting-place at last;
And smiling own'd, whate'er his dreamy thought
In mystic numbers long had vainly sought,
The One that's form'd of Two whom love hath bound,
Is the best number gods or men e'er found.

Thomas Moore, *The Grecian Girl's Dream of the Blessed Islands*

Moore's romantic presentation of Greek women philosophers as 'those few congenial maids' encapsulates more vividly than perhaps he realised some of the most prevalent of the ancient Greek images of the woman philosopher that I shall examine in this chapter. Firstly these women are 'few', exceptions to the rule of antiquity. Secondly, and typical of the influential attitude of that time towards the women of Greek literature, Moore depicts them as charming, gentle, sensual. Their appeal is physical rather than intellectual; they are effectively mere appendages to their male mentors. In this chapter I wish to explore these images of intellectual women and to place them in their literary and philosophical context. I shall demonstrate how the theories of the male philosophers accommodate the possibility of female philosophers, while the number of actual cases of women who

70

philosophised is remarkably small. Furthermore, I shall draw attention to major methodological difficulties involved in the study of the literary sources for the lives of these women. A pattern will develop that informs these sources, a pattern of women philosophers as anomalies whose departure from recognised social behaviour requires special explanation. These explanations often resort to the familiar conceptual link between women and the world of the senses, the physical, rather than that of the rational, the intellectual. I shall confine my discussion to between the sixth century BC and the first century AD, thus avoiding Hypatia. The sources for Hypatia are late and bound up with the complexities involved in the study of any Christian literature of the period. As such she deserves to be studied separately. Nor shall I discuss the complex and already well-documented case of Aspasia. Instead, I shall turn my attention to 'forgotten' women.[1]

VIEWS OF THE MALE PHILOSOPHERS

It is possible that the first school to have encouraged the study of philosophy by women was that of the Pythagoreans in the mid-sixth century BC. The philosophical biographer Diogenes Laertius (third century AD) tells us that they believed Reason, which was the most important human characteristic, was unaffected by gender.[2] Indeed the *Life of Pythagoras* by Iamblichus (third to fourth century AD) actually records 17 women followers of Pythagoras, whom he describes as 'the most illustrious', perhaps implying that there were also others.[3] At Croton, where Pythagoras founded his school, he was said to have spoken to the women specially.

Pythagoras may also form the starting-point for our examination of the recurrent commonplaces in classical discussions of women philosophers. For he is reported to have said that virtue was a realistic goal for girls as well as boys, married women as well as the elderly. His assimilation of children and married women with the elderly, as recognisably weak groups, can be paralleled elsewhere among male writers; for example in Protagoras, Clement of Alexandria or Minucius Felix.[4] Pythagoras may believe women merit inclusion among the philosophers, but the expression of that belief implicitly reveals his acceptance of the common Greek view of women as a distinct, separable and weaker group of society.

The ascetic lifestyle led by the Pythagoreans was the butt of at least two ancient comedies, by comic writers of the fourth century BC, Cratinus the Younger and Alexis,[5] which bore the title *The Woman who Pythagorises* (*Pythagorizousa*). The titles refer to a woman Pythagorean, but this need not imply that they depicted a woman actually teaching philosophy. She may well have simply followed the curious dietary laws of the sect which seem to have been a more common focus of comic attention. But a woman is still chosen for her comic potential: she is therefore a double anomaly.

The biographical tradition records that Pythagoras himself studied philosophy under the Delphic priestess, Themistoclea.[6] Here we encounter another biographical commonplace: the image of the priestess as teacher. We naturally recall Socrates and Diotima, his 'teacher' in Plato's *Symposium* 208c (fourth century BC). Diotima herself may be a literary invention. The story about Pythagoras can be easily understood. As poets could speak with the divine authority of the Muses, so the priestess of Delphi could act as the mouthpiece for Apollo. By having her as his teacher (whether in reality or in legend), Pythagoras could partake of her authority. Ancient philosophy was often a competitive activity: one had to woo adherents to one's side and away from others. Themistoclea's importance in the story, therefore, lies in her role as the authoritative Delphic priestess, not in her gender. Apolline connections may also be felt in the tradition (perhaps local, perhaps Samian) which actually made Pythagoras the son of Apollo.[7]

Pythagoras' advocation of monogamy may well explain why tradition recorded that he had a wife who also studied philosophy, for friendship theories often advocated common interests within a partnership. Once again, as with so much of this type of material, the philosophy dictates the form of the biography.

The marriage between Theano and Pythagoras is in many ways an ideal Pythagorean marriage, for although the wife has her own importance, this is subordinated to the union as a whole in due accordance with Pythagorean teaching on marriage. But I shall discuss Theano in more detail in my next section.

Among the Sophists of the fifth century BC, only Aspasia is recorded as a 'woman sophist' (*sophistria*),[8] but she is altogether an exceptional character and I shall not discuss her here. For there are complex literary reasons that dictate her image in the anecdotal tradition, which make accurate assessment of her historical role impossible. In the eyes of the sophist Gorgias,[9] women could achieve virtue, but even these virtues were defined in terms of gender. It was not until Socrates that a woman was to be thought equally capable, by nature, of attaining wisdom.

The texts we possess, written by his pupils, reveal Socrates' interest in the position of women. But this interest is treated in different ways by these writers. Xenophon, for example, in his *Oeconomicus*, limits women's learning to domestic duties. Later, Theophrastus was also to allow women only enough knowledge of letters as was necessary for household management (*oikonomia*).[10]

Socrates' own wife, Xanthippe, was not recorded as a philosopher. Her purpose in later philosophic writings was to highlight the ideal Stoic patience of her husband. If Socrates could tolerate Xanthippe as the most difficult (*chalepotate*) of women that have been, are or ever will be, he can tolerate anything. Xanthippe therefore becomes an idealised extreme.

But it is to the texts by Plato (fourth century BC) that we must turn for more direct thought (whether genuinely Socratic or Platonic) on the question of women. Bluestone (1987) has shown how in past scholarship these texts have been misunderstood or just ignored. But Plato's message has at least clear outlines. Essentially, the soul is immaterial, eternal and non-sexual; only our bodies are different. The souls of men and women can equally study philosophy. The wise man or woman should try to separate body and soul, so removing sexual difference. For Plato, education is essential for the acquisition of virtue and ought to be the same for boys and girls.[11] But even Plato cannot escape from the deeply-rooted Greek view of the natural inferiority of women. This physical weakness requires them to work longer to achieve the same level as men: a woman cannot, for example, assume any civic office until she is 40, while a man may do so at 30.[12]

Nonetheless, we do hear of women connected with Plato's Academy. Firstly, there was a tradition that Plato's mother, Perictione, was a philosopher.[13] But we may explain this as Plato's literary conflation of Diotima with the metaphors of midwifery used by his Socrates, whose own mother, Phaenarete, was said to be a midwife.[14] Perictione's name is given as that of the author of a later Neopythagorean work, but this only tells us that the tradition was already established by the time of that later work. Secondly, Diogenes Laertius records two women, Axiothea and Lasthenia, who were pupils of Plato and of his successors. The notoriety of the discussion of the equality of the sexes in Plato's *Republic* may account for the story that Axiothea was inspired by that work to dress as a man to study at the Academy.[15]

The appeal to the male writers of anecdotal sources of a strange woman, dressing as a man to enter a male world, is of course irresistible. The story of the male dress is so convincing and conventional in these contexts that it may be an invention. We recall, for example, how much transvestism is a source of humour in the plays of the comic playwright of the fifth century BC, Aristophanes. This humorous and perhaps titillating notion is another of our recurrent patterns, for Hipparchia, the wife of the Cynic Crates, is also said to have studied philosophy in male dress.[16] The Stoic Zeno advocated one dress for both sexes, but we may again assume that the women were to assume male dress and not vice versa.[17]

According to Diogenes Laertius, these two women, Axiothea and
Lasthenia, also apparently studied under Plato's successor, Speusippus. The
historical likelihood of this story is supported (although not proved) by
more concrete evidence in a papyrus fragment of a philosophical biography,
which records a woman (whose name is lost) who studied under Plato,
Speusippus and Menedemus.[18]

I have already mentioned Crates' wife, Hipparchia. Many legends and
anecdotes surround her and hamper our interpretation of her life and reputation. I shall discuss her in more detail elsewhere. It is sufficient to note
here how these sources emphasise Hipparchia more as a curious 'accessory'
of Crates than as a positive woman philosopher in her own right. She is the
subject of the only biography of a woman in Diogenes Laertius' *Lives of the
Philosophers*, but Diogenes' focus, as that of most of the traditions about
her, is upon how unusual a phenomenon she was. Her *Life* and that of her
brother Metrocles (also a follower of Crates and through whom she probably met the philosopher) are just brief appendices to that of Crates. We
learn nothing of any special teaching advocated by Hipparchia: Diogenes
merely gives us a vivid and sensational story about how the two first met.

It is well-known that Aristotle (fourth century BC) adopted some of
Plato's theories, while arguing against others. Aristotle did not share Plato's
belief in the basic similarity of man and woman. His scientific, and especially his biological interests affected his views upon women and philosophy. He could not think of woman apart from her physical nature. As a
woman was physically weaker than a man, so her capacity to reason was
poorer. He thought that Reason lacked control in the soul of a woman; it
denied her the ability to acquire true knowledge; she could not, therefore, be
a philosopher.[19] Consequently it should come as no surprise that we have no
evidence for any female pupils of Aristotle.

The Epicureans of the early fourth century BC were more of a general
community than a limited philosophical school like Plato's Academy or
Aristotle's Peripatetics. The prominence of equality in Epicurean theory (of
slave and free, woman and man) may help to explain why Epicurus was said
to have had some women as pupils, most notably Leontium and Themista.[20]
Leontium was reputedly a courtesan. Other names of women were linked to
the Garden (as the Epicurean community was called) and they too are
courtesans. I shall address in my third section the problem of whether such
courtesans were really women philosophers. For now, let us simply note
their existence and continue our brief historical survey.

The revival of Pythagoreanism in the third and second centuries BC in
Athens, Alexandria and Italy produced several minor works on women and

philosophy.[21] A work *On Women's Modesty* (*peri gynaikos sophrosunas*) is attributed to a Phintys and there are several letters that purport to be written by women to women. The validity of these attributions and their date are subjects of debate. But the content of the works remain matters that had traditionally been linked with women: the education of children, choice of a nurse, control of slaves, manner of dress, coping with a husband's infidelities. But this is, of course, no proof of female authorship. The works could have been written by men and given women's names as authors because of their content and anticipated readership. However, the attribution of the names (which include relatives of Pythagoras himself) at least reveals that works on philosophy could be published with women's names and be accepted as such.

But we need not assume that times were changing, that there was a growing 'feminist' movement or equivalent at that time. Philosophical interest in women, as we have seen, was nothing new. Authors may say that certain occupations are particular to men, others to women, others to both men and women and that philosophy is a pursuit open to both sexes. But women are still linked to the household: that is still her particular (*idia*) care. It may not be her only possible activity, but the association is still there. Of course this is not chauvinism, but neither is it real equality. We shall encounter similar philosophical subtleties when we consider Musonius Rufus and the Stoics.

Among the pupils at the early Greek Stoic school under Zeno (third century BC) we have no record of any women, although he encouraged the same education for free and slaves, men and women.[22] According to Diogenes Laertius, Zeno's successor, Cleanthes wrote a work *On the Thesis that Virtue is the Same in Man and Woman*, and one of Cleanthes' fragments states how essential it is for 'wise people to be united from every language, condition, sex and age'.[23]

Among the Roman Stoics, Seneca (first century AD) wrote *Consolations* to Helvia and Marcia, advising them not to exclude themselves from the study of philosophy because of their sex. Study is offered as a healing refuge.[24] But the most important Stoic for this question was Musonius Rufus (first century AD). He encouraged all sections of society, from kings to women, to study philosophy for the practical goal of an easier life. Essays 3 (*That Women too should study Philosophy*) and 4 (*Should Daughters receive the same Education as Sons*) explicitly support the study of philosophy by women.[25]

But even Musonius is firmly rooted in a traditional society, which expected respectable women to remain discreet and at home for the most part.

When he answers potential critics of his call to women to participate in philosophy, he couches it in decidedly traditionalist terms: philosophy will make a woman a better housewife. In the second century AD, the moralist Plutarch will parallel this stance exactly. While Plutarch's *Advice to Bride and Groom* urges the wife to study philosophy with her husband, the true benefit of philosophy is said to be that it will prevent her falling prey to sensual 'depravities' such as dance or superstition. Musonius' view of the importance of the wife within the household and the respect due her is what we might call progressive. He is certainly an 'improvement' on many of his predecessors. But the traditional association of women and household remains.

The reasons for Musonius' arguments may be many. He is, of course, writing in the tradition of philosophical literature, one of whose common themes for discussion was, as we have seen, the position of women. But Musonius is also writing in a broader literary context, that of poetry and rhetoric, where arguments for and against a particular proposition were common exercises for the training of potential politicians. His treatment of women, like that of Plutarch after him, can only be assessed correctly when all the facets of the background are acknowledged. Nor need Musonius' argument for women's participation imply that he is attempting an apology for any contemporary 'movement' of women philosophers. The theme is too much of a commonplace to justify that assumption.[26]

Let us therefore review our philosophic texts. They are decidedly conventional. Women are discussed, but often as anomalous groups, along with the elderly or children. They are included for the sake of completeness. In practice, we know of only a few women who answered the call to philosophy. However, the dominant influence of Aristotelianism in subsequent centuries has led to the erroneous belief that the Greek philosophers as a whole discouraged women from entering philosophy. Aristotle is the exception, not the rule. He bars them, even in theory, from philosophic study.

From theory, we must now proceed to our evidence for the lives of these women philosophers. Almost all our evidence is embedded in literary and especially anecdotal sources, which at once render them susceptible to potential abuse and misrepresentation both by ancient and modern writers alike. It is essential to examine the texts in detail and in context, if we are to arrive at a more balanced picture of the image of the woman philosopher. As an example of methodology, I shall choose Theano. I shall then pass on to a more general reassessment of our evidence for other alleged women philosophers.

THE CASE OF THEANO

Clement of Alexandria (second century AD) records in his *Stromata* that 'Didymus in his writings on Pythagorean philosophy observes that Theano was the first woman to philosophize and to write poems'.[27] The quest for an inventor of something (the *protos heuretes*) is typical of Greek tradition. For example, the laws of a city are often attributed to one name (in Athens Solon, in Sparta Lycurgus), which in turn takes on a life of its own. Legend and history as we know it become one.

In antiquity, historical details about Theano were already confused on even simple matters. By the third century AD, Diogenes Laertius can record that some thought she was Pythagoras' pupil, others (Diogenes included) that she was his wife. Her father's identity and even her provenance are also unclear.[28] Even when the sources agree that she is Pythagoras' wife, they cannot agree on the number or names of their children. Some sources give only daughters, others two daughters and a son, others two daughters and two sons.[29] We do not know whether she remarried after Pythagoras' death. But mystery such as this seems almost a prerequisite for characters who develop 'mythical' personae.

Theano's name attracted its own tradition. The stories about her often depict her as an ideal wife and mother.[30] I shall look here at only two. Her ideal modesty is exemplified in a story reported in Plutarch, and the Christian Greek writers Theodoret and Clement.[31] Clement writes: 'Did not Theano the Pythagorean woman achieve such a level of philosophy that when someone casually glanced at her and remarked "what a beautiful forearm", she replied "but it's not for the public"'. Theano here paradigmatically states how true feminine beauty, when allied with virtue, is something to be proud of, but confined to private occasions. This awareness of public and private seems to be what can be called a woman's 'philosophy'. The Greek words *kalos ho pechus, all'ou demosios* ('what a beautiful forearm but not for the public'), preserved in all our versions of the story, probably derive from one of the common sources of quotations or *apophthegmata* that were popular in antiquity. The ancient biographical reference work known as the Suda (tenth century AD) credits Theano with such a collection herself. But, given the late source, we cannot be sure whether Theano was to be thought the author or merely the subject of the collection.

The second anecdote may well derive from the same source, for both Theodoret (fourth century AD) and Clement follow with it. A woman asks

Theano 'How long after intercourse with a man is a woman pure enough to attend a religious festival?' Theano replies, 'If it was your husband, at once; if it was someone else, never'.[32] The commonplace structure of the question and answer makes the anecdote brief and memorable. While the content does not actually demand that a woman make the reply, it is more appropriate if it comes from Theano. As the wife of Pythagoras, in an ideally harmonious Pythagorean marriage, Theano is best suited to offer herself as a paradigm of conjugal fidelity and to encourage it in other women. She rises above the satirists' image of woman. Satirists often depicted women as talking only about sex. Here, when one woman talks to another, it is indeed about sex, but it is advice which confirms the conventions and morals of respectable society, rather than undermining them. We may wonder whether remarks of a similar tone were included in the *Advice for Women* (in the Suda entry I) also attributed to Theano. Theano here, therefore, performs the role of an appropriate woman adviser, decent and respectably moral. But there were other possibilities.

Tradition generally made Theano the wife of Pythagoras. In the romanticising period of Alexandrian poetry in the third century BC, Hermesianax gives the relationship between Pythagoras and Theano as an example of a romantic attachment: 'Such was the madness for Theano that bound with its spell the Samian Pythagoras; yet he had discovered the refinements of geometric spirals, and had modelled in a small globe the mighty circuit of the enveloping ether'.[33] Here the game is a literary one: the poem as a whole is devoted to learned men who nonetheless fall victim to love. These lines may well have been the inspiration for those by Thomas Moore with which I opened this paper. Indeed the comparison with Moore is instructive. Hermesianax and Moore both modify, almost sanitise the relationship and reduce it to the level of pure physical attraction. This is, of course, central to Hermesianax's poetic purpose here. Theano is but one image of sensuality. It would spoil the picture if either Moore or Hermesianax were to depict Theano as a philosopher herself. We shall encounter this again later: a tendency to depict women philosophers in different lights dependent upon the author's literary purpose. The content of this poem, therefore, and its literary tradition, dictate Theano's portrayal. It is not a safe document for historical biography.

As Theano's past before Pythagoras was considered unimportant and was undiscussed by the sources interested in her, so what happened to her after his death is unclear. Theodoret says that Theano and her two sons, Telauges and Mnesarchus, ran the school.[34] But even this may be antiquarian guesswork. It is also interesting that although Theano was well enough respected to become her husband's successor, she does not do so alone, but with her sons.

Diogenes Laertius records a different tradition that seems to derive from the (fictitious) *Letters of the Pythagoreans.*[35] He notes that the dying Pythagoras entrusted his writings to his daughter, Damo, instructing her never to let them out of the house. Nothing could persuade Damo to part with them and 'although she could have sold the writings for a large sum of money, she would not, but rated poverty and her father's solemn injunctions more precious than gold, for all that she was a woman'. When we compare this text with the letter as we have it elsewhere, we find that the texts are identical except that Diogenes himself seems to have added the final remark 'for all that she was a woman' (*kai tauta guna*). Diogenes clearly could not resist making his own comment in praise of Damo, for it is added in the Doric dialect of the letter which is not Diogenes' own. The final remark therefore tells us more about Diogenes' attitude to woman and his treatment of his sources than it does about the successors of Pythagoras.[36] Here too the presentation of the woman is manipulated for a special purpose. But let us now proceed from the particular to the more general.

THE LOVES OF THE PHILOSOPHERS

Much of our data for the lives of the female followers of male philosophers takes the forms of anecdotes. Many come from a work of the second century AD, Athenaeus' *Experts at the Dinner-Table* (*Deipnosophistai*). The general context of the work is a drinking-party, a *symposion*, at which only men were present as participants. If women attended, they would do so as slaves or courtesans. It should not be surprising, given this atmosphere, that the stories told relate more to the loves than to the lives of the philosophers. This, in turn, renders difficult the task of distinguishing true female students of philosophy from simply courtesan companions.

Many philosophers were said to have loved courtesans: Plato and Archeanassa, for example, or Aristotle and Herpyllis, by whom he is said to have had a son and with whom he lived until his death, despite having a wife, Pythias.[37]

These stories developed, as with Hermesianax's poem above, as part of a traditional literary reaction of humorous deflation of the philosophers who might appear pompous or self-righteous.

Several women who bear courtesan names are connected with the Epicurean school of the fourth century BC, but not all seem to be students of philosophy.[38] The rumours of the presence of such women would lead to stories of a 'free love commune'. These rumours clustered around the courtesan name of Leontium. Leontium seems to have been a special case: her fame in part results from her reputation as not only the lover but also the pupil of Epicurus.[39] As the consort of the head of the school, it was quite predictable that any gossip would accrue to her personally. For example, Athenaeus tells us: 'Even when she began to be a philosopher, she did not cease her strumpet ways, but consorted with all the Epicureans in the Garden and even before the eyes of Epicurus . . . .'[40] As she was not Epicurus' wife, she was credited with the indiscriminate lust associated with the courtesan name she still bore. Her status is never clear in our sources. One of Epicurus' followers, Metrodorus, is also said to have loved her and to have taken her as his concubine; Seneca makes her the wife of Metrodorus, without mentioning her reputation as a woman philosopher.[41]

Leontium's reputation as a philosopher was partly preserved by her being such an unusual phenomenon. We have seen earlier how this preserved the figure of Hipparchia. Theon (first century AD) cites among his rhetorical examples of people who became great (*megas*) from humble beginnings 'the courtesan Leontium who philosophized'; the Elder Pliny records that she was painted by the artist Aristides Thebanus; and among the works of the fourth-century BC artist Theorus, he lists 'Epicurus' Leontium thinking' (*Leontium Epicuri cogitantem*).[42]

Leontium was said to have written a reply to a work by Theophrastus (fourth century BC).[43] Our source is Cicero (first century BC), who only uses this story to attack the weakness and hypocrisy of the Epicurean school. Leontium, described with a contemptuous diminutive (*meretricula*, a pretty little whore), dared (*ausa est*) to write such a work: so great was the licence of the Epicurean Garden (*tantum Epicuri hortus habuit licentiae*).[44] Leontium's own achievement is ignored in this attack on Epicurus.[45] Cicero here only develops selected elements of her personality to suit the rhetorical purpose of his text.

We may therefore wonder whether Leontium was really a courtesan, or, if she were, whether she always stayed one. Her name suggests it was at one time her profession, and this may in turn have coloured later sources. The picture is further clouded by the popular commonplace of 'the lover as teacher' in both erotic and indeed philosophic literature. Certainty is therefore impossible. Unfortunately the Epicureans' toleration of such women left them open to much speculation and criticism. The women become the tools of satire and invective.

In *How a Pleasant Life is Impossible According to Epicurus*, Plutarch openly exploits (in a work clearly related to the rhetorical exercise of the *controversia*, a speech against a certain proposition) the Epicurean fondness for fine foods and women which was notoriously inconsistent with their professed moderation. Here Epicurus is said to consort with Leontium and with another courtesan, Hedeia, whose name means Pleasure, and to share with Polyaenus a joint family with Hedeia.[46] Given my remarks above, it is easy to see how such stories could be taken and elaborated, or even invented, within the context of a satirical work. The commonplace of hypocrisy is again deployed in another of Plutarch's works against Epicureanism, *Whether it is Rightly Said that One Should Live Unknown*: one would want to live unknown, says the satirist, if one were living with Hedeia and spending one's days with Leontium.[47] We might be tempted to read this as distinguishing the two women, one as concubine, the other as pupil. But this might not take sufficient notice of the neat literary balance the conceit thus exploits. The two names are added for rhetorical variation and amplification. The women are moulded to Plutarch's purpose.

So, Leontium's reputation as a philosopher did not preclude her from being used, like any other courtesan, to highlight the hypocrisy of a philosophic school. She is presented as a typically jealous, but witty courtesan in Athenaeus, for example. Another courtesan, Gnathaena, is also recorded by Athenaeus in his sympotic context as the authoress of a work prescribing *Rules for Dining in Company* that parodied similar works by male philosophers. Athenaeus adds that Gnathaena herself was 'not without wit': here a woman plays the satirists' own game.[48]

Other philosophers were also open to such criticism, of course, for it is a fundamental weapon of invective and satire to show that people in power or people who are respected are really no better than the common man or woman. We may turn once again to Athenaeus. He tells us about the fourth-century BC courtesan, Lais, mistress of the philosopher Aristippus, the orator Demosthenes and Diogenes the Cynic.[49] While it is perfectly possible that she was the mistress of all three famous men (for she would move in their social circles), it seems more likely that her one name was attached to theirs to blacken their collective reputations. Here the depersonalised Lais could stand for any courtesan, but the anecdote gains more piquancy if it concerns a woman already notorious in their social set.

Speusippus, Plato's successor, was criticised for an alleged liaison with Lasthenia, who was his pupil. When criticising Speusippus, his contemporary Dionysius of Syracuse uses his liaison with Lasthenia as but one example among many of his hypocrisy.[50] Lasthenia, with no word about her academic status, is merely another commonplace of abuse, along with and even symbolising hedonism and avarice. Her name has also been chosen for a special further reason: Lasthenia may have a reputation as a philosopher, but while both pupil and mentor profess to study philosophy, they really study something else. The whole class of philosophers is therefore ridiculed.

It is precisely because these attacks on philosophers conform to such conventional patterns that we cannot distinguish pupils from mistresses. For example, Diogenes Laertius records that Stilpo had a wife and a mistress, Nicarete. But only Athenaeus, whose context would encourage erotic associations, records that she was a philosopher. To make matters worse, there may have been two Nicaretes.[51]

Unattached women, therefore, could be called courtesans, whether rightly or wrongly, and used as tools of satire or invective. However, if a woman philosopher were a wife, she might be sure of a better press, as with Theano or Hipparchia.[52] The same could apply if one were a mother or a daughter of a male philosopher: e.g. Plato's mother Perictione, or Arete of Cyrene, daughter of the Aristippus linked with Lais. Arete was a remarkable woman. She apparently studied under her father and succeeded him as head of his school in her own right, unlike Theano who needed her sons' support. (It may be, however, that her sons were at that time too young to help.) According to Diogenes Laertius, at the school, Arete taught natural science, moral and ethical philosophy. She apparently wrote about 40 books and had around 110 pupils. (Whatever value one places upon the figures, their order of magnitude indicates how important she was in the traditional literature.) Her epitaph describes her as the 'Splendour of Greece', with 'the beauty of Helen, the pen of Aristippus, the soul of Socrates and the tongue of Homer'. The description is wonderfully poetic, but it is noteworthy how, among all these great men and their virtues, reference is made to Arete's beauty and to Helen. A clever woman must also be beautiful (cf. Cleopatra, Aspasia, Hypatia). Furthermore, the mention of Helen cannot fail to remind us of how treacherous her knowledge made her. None of Arete's work survives. Her fame rests upon that of her son, also called Aristippus, whom she educated herself. The younger Aristippus was accordingly distinguished from his grandfather by the epithet 'educated by his mother' (*metrodidaktos*).[53] In this instance Arete becomes merely a means of differentiating two men.

CONCLUSIONS

It is now time to draw the disparate threads of my study together and to offer some general reflections and caveats for the examination of ancient women philosophers.

I have shown how, in the world of explicit philosophical theory, only Aristotle resolutely excludes women from the pursuit of philosophy. But our evidence reveals how theoretical this position really was. However much she may have been considered as a possibility in philosophic argument, in practice the woman philosopher had to be prepared to submit to male scrutiny and often criticism. She was always an oddity.[54] Special lists were compiled of them, separate from men.[55] Interest in their stories lay more in their sexual histories or in how they became this unusual phenomenon (e.g. Hipparchia) than in their intellectual achievement. Part of the explanation must lie, of course, in the different nature of modern and ancient ideas of biography. But the dominant, traditional association of woman and passion, nature, the sensual was hard to escape. Indeed it positively encourages our anecdotal sources, like Athenaeus, and the satirists, like Plutarch. The woman's personality was moulded to and dictated by the writer's purpose, rendering impossible even an approximate estimate of their intellectual abilities.

But we should not, therefore, resort to charges of male chauvinism and, in a fit of over-enthusiasm, posit great women philosophers whom a male literary tradition has deliberately sought to obliterate. Idolatory can be just as dangerous (cf. the case of Sappho). Our evidence was never designed to relay the information we so earnestly desire of it and we cannot blame it accordingly. Nor might it be wholly fair to lay the blame on the predominantly Christian environment in which manuscripts were transmitted. Of course it is possible that works by women writers were destroyed because they were by women, at a time when the Church was attempting to confirm its control of society. But many of our sources are, ironically, early Christian writers who preserve the memory of lost pagan ideas and lives. But, for example, while Clement preserves stories about Theano, he does so without discussing her work. The second century AD writer Tatian and Lactantius in the third century AD also preserve details about ancient women philosophers, but they too have a purpose.[56] These women philosophers are listed as supporting evidence for the participation of women in Christian ceremonies. The writers are not interested in telling us what these women believed or said: their mere existence is enough for their rhetorical purpose. Their interest is antiquarian rather than feminist or philosophical. Once again, our evidence was not designed to give us what we want. It may, indeed, be the case that the works by women followers of male philosophers were deemed inferior philosophically to their mentors' originals and were ignored for that reason. We cannot say. Similarly we are unable to estimate how seriously women like Leontium studied philosophy, or whether they merely took it up because of the influence of the men in their lives.

Two significant patterns can be observed in these texts. Firstly, the continued importance of male connections.[57] As in other spheres of the Arts, women did not study philosophy alone. Often they entered the world through male relations: Theano through her husband Pythagoras, Hipparchia through her brother Metrocles, Arete through her father Aristippus.[58] Secondly, the women philosophers are still treated primarily as women. Interest is expressed in their beauty, their sexual passions. They represent physical temptation: a temptation that can be presented sentimentally (as in Hermesianax), satirically (Plutarch), or humorously (Athenaeus). It is the prejudices and commonplaces of these authors, in turn dictated by the male domination of the literary tradition, that shape the treatment of these women in our evidence. The evidence is sadly selective. It can only be turned to certain, finite use. Moreover, it is ultimately ironic that just as the male connections and relatives were allowing women to become philosophers, the male sources that recorded various aspects of their lives were driving them back inexorably into the dangerous shadows of anecdotal sources, shadows Thomas Moore might prefer to call 'philosophic shades'.

NOTES

1. This paper is primarily written as a corrective to M. E. Waithe (1987). Thorough accounts may be found in Pomeroy (1977) and (1984), pp. 61–71. See too P. Allen (1985). English translations of Pythagorean documents are in K. S. Guthrie (1987).

2. Diogenes Laertius, *Lives of the Philosophers* (*DL*), 8.30.

3. *epiphanestatai*: *Life of Pythagoras* (*Life*), 36.267. Note particularly the 'wonderful deeds' of the heroic Spartan Timyche, when she is ten months pregnant (Iamblichus, *Life* 32.214; 31.193ff.).

4. Plato *Protagoras* 325a; Clement, *Stromata* (*Strom.*) 4.8.58.3; Minucius Felix, *Octavius* 16.5.

5. Cratinus Junior in Fragment (F) 6 of Kassel and Austin (1983–9). *DL* 8.37 and the tenth-century AD biographical work the Suda, 10.46 made fun of Pythagoras; cf. also Alexis, *Tarentines* F7 in Kassel and Austin, F196–9 and F219–25 in Kock (1880–8), 2, pp. 370, 377–80, cf. Naevius' *Tarentilla* (Ribbeck (1898), p. 21).

6. *DL* 8.8. For the difficulties of distinguishing myth from history in the life of Pythagoras, see Guthrie (1962), Ch. 4, esp. pp. 148–56.

7. Porphyry *Life of Pythagoras* (*VP*) 2, where his mother is also said to have been descended from the founder of Samos.

8. Suda s.v. Aspasia; Scholiast on Aristophanes, *Acharnians* 526.

9. Plato, *Meno* 71d.

10. Theophrastus L35 in Fortenbaugh (1984) = Stobaeus, a mediaeval compiler, *Anthol*, 2.31.31.

11. Education essential: *Republic* 452a, *Laws* 804e, *Timaeus* 18c; same for girls, *Laws* 770d.

12. *Laws* 785b.

13. See Walcot (1987). Bentley (1699), p. 384 notes that she is not in Iamblichus' list and thinks the Neopythagorean work a forgery with this well-known name added.

14. *Theaetetus* 149a, 150d, 161e, 184b, 210b.

15. *DL* 3.46; Clement, *Strom*. 4.19.122.2. Inspired by Plato, *Republic*: Themistius, *Oration* 33 in Dindorf (1832), p. 356 = Aristotle F64 in Rose (1886). Dressing as a man: Dicaearchus F44 in Wehrli (1944), p. 21 = *DL* 3.46; Olympiodorus 145 in Westerink (1976), p. 5.

16. I study Hipparchia in depth in my forthcoming paper, 'The Legend of Hipparchia'.

17. *DL* 7.34.

18. *DL* 3.46; 4.2. *Oxyrhynchus Papyri* 42.3656.

19. *Politics* 1259b f.

20. Leontium: see below. Themista: variously called Themiste (Lactantius, *Divine Institutes* 3.25.15); Themisto (Clement, *Strom*. 4.19.121.4); but is generally known as Themista (Cicero, *In Pisonem* 26.62; *De Finibus* 2.21.68). She is the wife of Leonteus of Lampsacus, whose son is called Epicurus (*DL* 10.27). She is one of the friends (*philoi*) whom Epicurus meets at Lampsacus F176, Usener [1887], p. 154). Lactantius cites her as the *one* woman who philosophised: this is partly demanded by his argument and structure (see Lausberg [1970], pp. 130–1) and is clearly untrue, as the lists in e.g. Clement show (see below).

21. See Thesleff (1961) and (1965). Translations in Guthrie (1987). Waithe (1987), pp. 59–74 believes the works are genuine and date from the fourth to the third centuries BC. See also Pomeroy (1984), pp. 61–71.

22. Von Arnim (1903), 1, p. 59, no. 250 = Sextus Empiricus, *Hypotyp*. 3.245 and *Adversus Mathematicos* 9.190. Cf. *DL* 7.12: he only uses a female slave to avoid appearing a misogynist! He diverts the attentions of a flutegirl to his companion (cf. his love for Chremonides, *DL* 7.17).

23. *DL* 7.175. For fragment see Von Arnim (1903), 3, p. 59, no. 253.

24. *confugiendum . . . illa sanabunt vulnus tuum*, Seneca, *Ad Helviam* 17.3.

25. Van Geytenbeek (1949), pp. 56–89; Lutz (1947); Jagu (1979).

26. Rhetoric: e.g. Russell (1979). Poetry: e.g. Menander F702, Koerte (1912); Hippolytus against the wise woman (*sophe*) in Euripides, *Hippolytus* 604ff; Juvenal, *Satire* 6. Democritus did not encourage women to develop their reason (F110).

27. *Strom* 1:16.80.4.

28. *DL* 7.42. Suda s.v. Theano 1.

29. For children, see Porphyry, *VP* 4: some say that she had only a son, Telauges, and a daughter, Muia, others that she also had another daughter, Arignote: Suda s.v. Theano 2: two sons, Telauges and Mnesarchus and two daughters, Muia and Arignote.

30. See Thesleff (1965), pp. 195 ff.

31.   Plutarch, *Moralia*, 142c; Theodoret, *Therapeutike* 12.73; Clement, *Strom.*
      4.19.121.12 and *Paidagogos* 2.114.2.

32.   Theodoret, ibid.; *DL* 8.43.

33.   Hermesianax, in Athenaeus 13.597a f., trans. Gulick (1927–41).

34.   Theodoret, ibid. 2.23, cf. Eusebius, *Praeparatio Evangelica* 10.14.14.

35.   *DL* 8.42. See Hercher (1873), pp. 601–8; Meunier (1932); Stadele (1980).

36.   The letter goes on to say that Damo passed on the writings with the same
      instructions to her own daughter, Bistala (Hercher [1873], p. 603, 8). Cf.
      Porphyry, *VP* 4 where he records that the children (daughters?) preserve the
      writings of Pythagoras. On Diogenes Laertius and women, see Von der
      Muehll (1965).

37.   Athenaeus 13.589c. Aristotle has a son by Herpyllis, *DL* 5.1. Aristotle's will
      devotes considerable space to arrangements for Herpyllis, little to Pythias,
      although he was buried with his wife Pythias, as she desired, *DL* 5.16. His
      concentration on Herpyllis did not mean that he loved her more than his wife,
      but that her status after his death would be uncertain.

38.   Castner (1981).

39.   *DL* 10.6: Epicurus wrote to many *hetairai*, but to Leontium in particular, cf.
      10.5 to 'dear little Leontium'. There is at least one letter from Leontium to
      Epicurus (Usener [1887], p. 147).

40.   Athenaeus 13.588b, trans. Gulick (1927–41).

41.   *DL* 10.6,23; Jerome, *Against Jovinian* 1.48. Leontium as a wise woman
      (*sophe*): Clement *Strom.* 2.23.138.6. Athenaeus 13.593bc notes that she had
      a daughter, Danae.

42.   *Progymnasmata* 8, Spengel (1853–6), 2.111–12; Pliny, *Natural History* 35.99.
      The reference to Leontium in terms of Epicurus applies not so much to the
      strength of their relationship, but serves rather to distinguish her from others
      who bore this courtesan name (e.g. the dedicant of Hermesianax's poem –
      Athenaeus 13.597af f.). The verb used, *cogito* (to consider something thor-
      oughly) might imply that she was depicted in a normally masculine pose of
      philosophic contemplation.

43.   The work is alluded to, without mentioning Leontium, in Pliny, *Natural
      History*, Preface 29. There may be a reference to a letter to her alleged friend,
      Lamia, the courtesan mistress of Demetius Poliorcetes. This friendship (itself
      open to scepticism) provides the background for Alciphron's fictional letter
      4.17 in Benner and Fobes (1949).

44.   *On the Nature of the Gods* 1.93.

45.   It is possible that Leontium did not write the work given her name (if it
      existed at all). It might have been penned by Epicurus and circulated under
      her name if, as is thought by some, it dealt with marriage. This seems to be
      the view of Usener (1887), pp. 101–2 and Index 411.

46.   Plutarch, *How a Pleasant Life is Impossible According to Epicurus* 1089c,
      1098b.

47.   *Whether it is Rightly Said . . .* 1129b.

48.   For Leontium, Athenaeus 13.585d; Gnathaena, *Rules for Dining* 13.585b.

49.   Interestingly, Thomas Moore wrote about the relationship between Lais and
      Aristippus in *The Philosopher Aristippus*. Lais was notoriously beautiful:
      painters came to admire her breasts (Athenaeus 13.588de).

50. *DL* 4.2; Athenaeus 7.279e.
51. *DL* 2.114; Athenaeus 13.596e. Pomeroy (1977), p. 58 thinks there were two: one respectable, renowned for temperance and who studied with Stilpo (cf. Cicero, *On Fate* 5.581), and another who was a courtesan.
52. Hipparchia: there is perhaps a hint of an accusation of prostitution in the series of insults and names in Plutarch, *How a Pleasant Life is Impossible According to Epicurus* 1086ef.
53. *Metrodidaktos*: *DL* 2.86; Aelian, *History of Animals* 3.40; Theodoret, *Therapeutike* 11.1; Clement, *Strom.* 4.19.122.1. Cf. Pericles called by Olympiodorus 136 (Westerink [1976] p. 89) 'Educated by his wife' (*gynaikodidaktos*).
54. Cf. Theodoret, *Therapeutike* 1.17: only those who are really dedicated to the pursuit of philosophy will go to any lengths for wisdom, such as visiting barbarians or women. Theodoret cites Socrates who 'was even proud of having learnt wisdom from women like Diotima and Aspasia'.
55. Iamblichus records the woman philosophers of Pythagoras in a special section (36.267); Sopater made a list of women who philosophised (Photius 161, p. 104a); Philochorus wrote a volume on them (Jacoby [1923–], IIIB, 328 T1 = Suda s.v. Philochorus, also nos 25–6, pp. 379–80).
56. Tatian, *To the Greeks*, 32.2f; Lactantius, *Divine Institutes* 3.25.
57. As noted by Pomeroy (1984), pp. 65–6.
58. Also Cleobulina (= Eumetis) through her father Cleobulus; Hypatia through her father Theon. With Hypatia, there is no evidence that Theon actually taught her (as noted by Waithe [1987], p. 170), but he at least opened the way for her.

5 An Ancient Theory of Gender: Plato and the Pythagorean Table

Sabina Lovibond

Many feminist writers of the 1970s and 1980s were preoccupied with the phenomenon of binary opposition – the tendency to construct conceptual systems in terms of hierarchically-ordered pairs. It has even been suggested that this tendency is ultimately due to the foundational role of a single, archetypal pair: male and female. Literary theorist Hélène Cixous writes,

> Always the same metaphor: it transports us, in all of its forms, wherever a discourse is organized . . . . Thought has always worked by opposition . . . . By dual, *hierarchized* oppositions . . . . Wherever an ordering intervenes, a law organizes the thinkable by (dual, irreconcilable; or mitigable, dialectical) oppositions. And all the couples of opposition are *couples*. Does this mean something? Is the fact that logocentrism subjects thought – all of the concepts, the codes, the values – to a two-term system, related to 'the' couple man/woman?[1]

In the present chapter I shall not enter upon any such speculative question; my aim will be simply to draw attention to some of the earliest manifestations of binary thinking in the European philosophical tradition, and to make a start on reconstructing the associated 'theory' of sexual difference. Accordingly, I shall consider the form in which that 'theory' appears (or lurks) in some Greek philosophical texts, with particular reference to the *Republic* of Plato (*Rep.*). In this way I hope to contribute to the – necessarily piecemeal – effort of enquiry which any ambitious historical generalisation invites.

The first book of Aristotle's *Metaphysics* (*Met.*), which contains a review of the theories of his predecessors, gives us an inkling of the meaning attributed to femaleness[2] in early Greek philosophy. In Ch. 5 (986a22ff.) Aristotle sets out a 'Table of Opposites' which, he says, was accepted by certain members of the Pythagorean school, and which lists ten pairs of principles arranged in two columns:

Limit	Unlimited
Odd	Even
One	Many
Right	Left
Male	Female
Resting	Moving
Straight	Curved
Light	Darkness
Good	Bad
Square	Oblong

Pythagoreanism was a philosophy which incorporated both scientific and ethico-religious elements. Pythagoras himself (late sixth-century BC) is traditionally supposed to have discovered the mathematical basis of the principal musical intervals; his followers, at all events, treated number as the ultimate reality, and interpreted qualitative differences in nature as grounded in different geometrical configurations of matter. But he was also an ascetic and mystic who believed that the soul was condemned to be reincarnated in a succession of human and other animal bodies until it won release through the pursuit of purity, and he founded a quasi-religious order in southern Italy dedicated to this idea. Plato (*Rep.* 600b) names Pythagoras as one who bequeathed a distinctive way of life to the human race, and the fact that the Table of Opposites is composed of a 'good' and a 'bad' column confirms the point that despite its mathematical orientation, this philosophy was permeated by moral concerns and made no claim to be 'value-free'.

It would be naive to feel surprise at the fact that femaleness is listed among the 'bad' attributes. The question is: can we learn something from the Pythagorean Table about the particular way in which female inferiority was represented theoretically in Greek thought? According to W. D. Ross in his commentary on the *Metaphysics*, 'It must have been because they were thought inferior, rather than because they were even or unlimited, that the left side and the female sex, at least, were put into the second column; the inference seems to have been that because they were bad and the bad was unlimited, they must be unlimited'.[3] There may well be some truth in this; but it does not follow that the symbolic equation of femaleness with the various mathematical features named in the second column was unimportant for Greek, or for subsequent European, representations of gender.

Ross also notes that not all of the ten pairs of opposites were equally essential to the Pythagorean system: the fundamental antitheses were definite and indefinite, odd and even.[4] That the definite should be a basic value is understandable, given that Pythagoreanism was 'primarily an ordered way of life',[5] a life designed to imitate the mathematical constitution of the universe; and Plato takes up this theme when he states that the philosopher, whose energies are devoted primarily to intelligible objects, 'has his eyes fixed on an unchanging order; the things he contemplates neither inflict injustice nor suffer wrong, but observe due proportion and order; and of these he studies to produce the likeness in himself as best he can' (*Rep.* 500b).

The connection between the definite and the odd is less intuitively obvious. Briefly, the idea is that if you add together all the *odd* numbers up to a certain point, the result is always a square number, i.e. it is the product of two numbers which stand to one another in a single definite ratio, namely 1/1 or unity (e.g. $1 + 3 + 5 + 7 = 16 = 4$ squared; $1 + 3 + 5 + 7 + 9 = 25 = 5$ squared); whereas if you add together all the even numbers up to a certain point, the result is always of the form $n(n + 1)$, i.e. it is the product of two numbers which stand to one another in a ratio that constantly changes (increases) as the first number increases (e.g. $2 + 4 + 6 + 8 = 20 = 4 \times 5 = 4(4 + 1)$; $2 + 4 + 6 + 8 + 10 = 30 = 5 \times 6 = 5(5 + 1)$; the ratio of n to $n + 1$ is in the first case 4/5, in the second case 5/6, and so on).[6]

What can be said about the connection between maleness and the odd numbers, femaleness and the even numbers? Two passages in Plutarch's *Moralia*, cited by Ross, seem in fact to cast doubt on his own suggestion that maleness and femaleness appear in the Table only as an afterthought – that this pair lacks organic connection with most of the others. Both these passages express much the same thought, but the fuller and more interesting occurs in the treatise 'On the Letter E at Delphi':[7]

> [The number five] has received the name of 'marriage' (*gamos*) because of the resemblance of the even number [namely, two] to the female and of the odd number [namely, three] to the male. For in the division of numbers into two equal factors, the even number separates completely and leaves a certain receptive opening and, as it were, a space within itself; but in the odd, when it undergoes this process, there is always left over from the division a generative middle part. Wherefore it is more generative than the other, and in combination it is always dominant and never dominated. For in no combination of these two numbers (even and odd) is there produced from the two an even number, but in all combinations an odd. Moreover, . . . no even number united with even

gives an odd number, nor does it ever show any departure from its own distinctive nature, being impotent through its weakness to produce the other number, and having no power of accomplishment; but odd numbers combined with odd produce a numerous progeny of even numbers because of their omnipresent generative function.

Odd and even numbers, then, are male and female respectively not just because of an interpretation of the male and female genitals in terms of unity and duality, but also because certain entrenched Greek views about sexual reproduction are being projected on to the behaviour of integers: just as the father is the *real* parent (the mother only providing a receptacle in which the foetus can grow and the matter to nourish it),[8] so the odd numbers are 'more generative' because they always, as it were, assert themselves when combined with the even, i.e. if you add an odd and an even number together the result is always an odd number. (Of course the parallel with sexual reproduction is not all that satisfactory, since not all children are male; and as for the 'impotence' of even numbers, you might just as well say that the odd numbers are reproductively incompetent because they cannot produce another one of their own kind without the help of an even number, whereas the even numbers are enviably autonomous in reproducing *their* kind. But this debate need not, I think, detain us.)

We have dealt with the connection between oddness and definiteness (and between their respective opposites in the Table), and again between oddness and maleness. It remains now to fill in the third side of the triangle by saying something about the reasons for associating maleness with the definite or limited (*peras*), femaleness with the indefinite or unlimited (*apeiron*).

One thought which may spring to mind is that this association is suggested by the contrast between female and male roles in sexual intercourse: the fact that there is on the male side, but not on the female side, a definite moment at which the episode comes to an end.[9] This fact may also be felt to have a bearing on the one/many opposition – though, as previously explained, the latter is independently linked with the definite/indefinite by way of the contrast between the series 1 + 3 + 5 . . . and the series 2 + 4 + 6 . . . (one constant ratio, that of a number to itself; many different ratios, that of each successive number to itself-plus-one). But in the absence of further evaluative assumptions, it does not seem to make any contribution to the theory of female *inferiority*.

A more illuminating reading of the Table might start from the observation that the 'unlimited' in Greek philosophy can mean not just that which is undetermined in a numerical sense – that to which no definite number has been assigned – but also that which is undetermined in the more general sense of being *formless*, of not possessing a definite character. Suppose we interpret the first pair of principles (limit/unlimited) in this way. Then what the Table seems to be telling us is that to be male is, generally, to be a bearer of form, order or structure; and that to be female is, generally, to be devoid of these things.

This doctrine captures certain facts of social experience which, arguably, span the gulf between the ancient and modern worlds. If we adopt the characteristic Greek conception of the educational process as one of *formation* (cf. German *Bildung*) – the imposition of order on the partly tractable, partly anarchic raw material of individual human nature – then the suggestion of the Table is that femininity is a negative condition, the indeterminate state from which a determinate human identity emerges. To be female, in other words, is to be (relatively) devoid of cultural specificity; it is to bear a (relatively) faint imprint of the 'form of life' of a particular time and place.

In the Platonic–Aristotelian tradition, virtue (or excellence of character) is represented as itself a *logos* or formal principle. Underlying this view is a conception of purposive action in general as the transference of form from mind into matter.[10] *Virtuous* action, then, will be purposive action which is such as it ought to be, and which is so because it expresses an enduring psychic structure of the kind appropriate to (civilised) humanity. This formal principle, though potentially common to all rational beings, needs to be established in the soul over time through the incorporation into one's individual nature of certain habits of feeling and choice – that is, through what would today be called 'socialisation'. Moral rationality thus emerges – in keeping with a pattern already noted by Heraclitus[11] – from the gradual exchange of a mental condition that is private for one that is shared.

With these assumptions in the background, the association of the female principle with formlessness indicates that female (or, to speak moralistically, 'womanish') souls do not fully exhibit the *logos* which is the ground of personality. And from the patriarchal point of view, this state of affairs is unsurprising. Because the setting of women's existence is not the public but the private sphere, there is not the same need for women to have installed in their souls that identical form whose presence in each male citizen makes him a fit person to participate in social and political life. That is why it is only to be expected that the female mind should be multiple, unstable (cf. 'resting/moving'), devious (cf. 'straight/curved'), obscure (cf. 'light/dark') . . . in short, that it should have all the qualities typical of those who have not been fully integrated into the cultural order, and whose behaviour is therefore not fully intelligible (to others or even to themselves) in terms of the current conceptual repertoire.

The remainder of this chapter will deal more specifically with the philosophy of Plato, described by Aristotle as 'in most respects a follower of the Pythagoreans'.[12] I assume that it is no longer necessary to stress the limitations of Plato's officially rationalist position on gender – the position represented by his arguments for the admission of women as rulers in the *Republic*:[13] his credibility on this score has already been severely dented by the work of Julia Annas, who has shown how widely the pursuit of collective well-being (Platonically conceived) diverges from the modern project of women's liberation.[14] What does, however, merit closer inspection is the continuing organisational role in Platonism of the Pythagorean conception of gender – the interpretation of 'limit' and 'unlimited' as male and female principles respectively. For it is only when this factor is appreciated that the tacit, or unexamined, sexual politics of Platonism can be understood.

Consider first some evidence from the *Timaeus (Tim.)* which offers a 'scientific' explanation of the origin of the universe. At *Tim.* 49–51 there are said to be three fundamental constituents of reality: the intelligible and unchanging model, the visible and changing copy modelled on it, and finally space, the 'receptacle and nurse of all becoming'. The first two elements (model and copy) are familiar from Plato's middle-period epistemology and metaphysics from his 'two worlds' doctrine of knowledge and belief as relating to different realms of objects. The introduction of space, however, varies the standard dualism with a triadic metaphor drawn from sexual reproduction: 'We may . . . compare the receptacle to the mother, the model [i.e. that which is imitated] to the father, and what they produce between them [i.e. the realm of becoming] to their offspring.'[15]

Why is it imaginatively appropriate for Plato to characterise the model (i.e. form in general) as masculine and the receptacle as feminine? The following lines from the *Timaeus* are helpful:

> [The receptacle] never alters its characteristics. For it continues to receive all things, and never itself takes a permanent impress from any of the things that enter it; it is a neutral plastic material on which changing impressions are stamped . . . , making it appear different at different times . . . and we may notice that, if an imprint is to present a very complex appearance, the material on which it is to be stamped will not have been properly prepared unless it is devoid of all the characters which it is to receive . . . anything that is to receive in itself every kind of character must be devoid of all character. (50b7 ff., d4 ff.)

Femininity is here equated with absence of subjectivity and hence absence of individuality. The thought then is that just as a girl or woman is a 'neutral plastic material on which changing impressions are stamped by the things

[men, male subjectivities] that enter it', so space, the receptacle of becoming, is female because it confronts the Platonic forms (the paradigms and
sources of determinate being) in a condition of perfect indeterminacy: it
'has no character of its own'. (This is the proper condition for a young
woman being offered in marriage: there must be nothing about her which
will make her unreceptive to the imprint of her husband's subjectivity in all
its fine detail.)[16]

We now have some sense of what constitutes, in Plato's scheme of
things, the *positive* aspect of indeterminacy. Along with form, indeterminate matter is a necessary condition of all becoming (just as the artist or
craftsman must have raw materials on which to work). Elsewhere, however,
Plato connects the female with the indeterminate or limitless in a way that
shows these principles to be located, for him as for his Pythagorean predecessors, in the 'bad' column of the Table of Opposites.

The connection is clearly visible in the *Republic*, where Plato's overt
attempt at sexual egalitarianism is undermined by a 'Pythagorean' sub-text
in which the menacing aspect of the limitless is repeatedly brought to the
fore. This sub-text develops in parallel with the dialogue's account of
education or culture, the aim of which in Plato's view is to bring the inferior
elements in the soul (the irresponsible appetites and emotions) under the
control of their natural superior, reason (the faculty of deliberation). As is
well known, the conceptual resources on which Plato draws in order to state
his moral and political programme are those of the aristocrat who believes
in a natural order of rank among human beings.[17] Less widely noticed, but
no less interesting, are his resources for thinking about *what it is that has to
be overcome* in the name of reason and order – whether in moral or political
undertakings or in the pursuit of knowledge. For in all these spheres there
is evidence that a successful outcome is equated in Plato's imagination with
a successful establishment of the *male* principle in its proper position of
command.

The *Republic* gives an organising role to one in particular of the Pythagorean oppositions: that of one and many. The importance of unity as a value-
principle in Plato's specifically political theory needs no emphasis, but in
fact the ideal of the centralised regime begins to emerge almost as soon as
he embarks on the exposition of his positive views in Books II–III. Here we
discover that the main moral characteristic to be aimed at in those children
or young people who are destined for the governing class
is *haplotes*: 'simplicity', 'singleness' or, more loosely, 'integrity'. Thus
(361b6–7) the just man is described as 'simple and noble', *haplous kai
gennaios*; while music is likened to cookery in that both benefit from
'simplicity', which is conducive to moderation in morals just as it is to

health (404e3–5). 'Simplicity' here is contrasted with embellishment, diversity, complexity or variegatedness (*poikilia*). In the second of the passages just cited it is *poikilia* which is said to breed intemperance.[18]

The ideas we have just been reviewing apply with equal force to ethics and to aesthetics. Because of his belief that our customary objects of attention influence not only our patterns of speech and gesture but also, through these, our thinking and our character (395d1–3), Plato feels obliged to shield his prospective rulers from whatever is 'variegated' in art and literature. For he has committed himself to the principle that each is to concentrate on one task only – 'there is no two-fold or many-fold man in our city, since each does a single thing' (397e1–2) – and exposure to a wide range of emotions through the medium of literature or music would conflict with this principle, since it would infect individual souls with ambiguity and contradiction.

Now, does the *Republic* maintain the Pythagorean identification of plurality – the negative term of the one/many opposition – with the negative (i.e. female) sexual principle? I believe that it does, and indeed that the dialogue can be read as Plato's statement of position on a question with which a good deal of Greek ethical theory is preoccupied: that of true masculinity, or manliness, and how to achieve it.[19] As Michel Foucault has written, 'In this morality made by men for men, the elaboration of oneself as a moral subject consists in the self-imposition of a structure of virility: it is by being a man in relation to yourself [i.e. by self-mastery] that you will be able to control and master the male activity that you undertake towards others in sexual practice'.[20] Although the concerns of ethics are obviously not exhausted by questions of sexual behaviour, the wider relevance of this analysis is indicated for example by the role of the word *anandria* ('unmanliness') in the *Gorgias*, where the moral sceptic Callicles claims that *real men* do not allow their appetites to be thwarted by the demands of morality (429bi; contrast *Theaetetus* 176c4 and context). In opposing the anti-moralism of the sophists, Plato is proposing a rival account of what it is to be a 'real man': he is arguing that such a man is one who successfully subordinates the multiple, fluid and contradictory demands of feeling to a single, centralised agency of control which will resolve the contradictions between them.

Misogynist remarks of a general kind are fairly numerous in Plato,[21] but the following texts from the *Republic* seem to bear witness to a train of thought inspired more particularly by the Table of Opposites.

(i) 395d5–e3 describes how almost every conceivable situation of potential dramatic interest involving a female character is judged unsuitable to feature in the literary education of the guardians. These young people, 'being men' (Plato has not yet introduced the idea of allowing women to govern), must not be allowed to 'take the part of a woman, whether young or old, abusing her husband, or quarrelling with the gods and vaunting her own imagined happiness, or when she is in misfortune or grief, or weeping; still less of one who is in sickness, love or childbirth'. In other words, the quality of *poikilia* which makes women's experience (and behaviour) a tempting subject for the dramatist makes it at the same time a dangerous moral example.

(ii) 431b9–c3 states that emotional diversity, instability or unpredictability is ignoble; it is associated with inferior types, e.g. *women*, slaves and 'the worthless mass of so-called free men'.

(iii) 557c4–9: Plato says of democracy, 'This, then, may well be the most attractive (*kallisten*: beautiful, pleasing; or, the *finest*) form of government: like an embroidered garment spangled (*pepoikilmene*) with every different dye, it would present the most pleasing appearance because it is spangled with every different way of life. And no doubt there are many (men) who, like *women and children* gazing at brilliant decorations (*ta poikila*), would indeed judge it to be the finest.'

(iv) 605c–607a: The most dangerous characteristic of poetry is the scope it gives for vicarious emotional indulgence. This indulgence is at odds with the rational conviction that in real life one must keep up one's guard (*phylake*, 606a8) against the solicitations of feeling, 'since that is the part of a man, while the other is the part of a woman' (605e1).

Plato's advocacy of restraint in aesthetic taste – both for its own sake and for the sake of the moral restraint it implies – could still be heard (and admired) in relatively recent times as a celebration of the masculine. The following lines are taken from the Victorian aesthetician Walter Pater:

What [Plato] would promote, then, is the art, the literature, of which among other things it may be said that it solicits a certain effort from the reader or spectator, who is promised a great expressiveness on the part of the writer, the artist, if he for his part will bring with him a great attentiveness. And how satisfying, how reassuring, how flattering to himself after all such work really is . . . Manliness in art, what can it be as distinct from that which in opposition to it must be called the feminine quality there – what but a full consciousness of what one does, of art itself in the work of art, tenacity of intuition and of consequent purpose, the

spirit of construction as opposed to what is incoherent or ready to fall to
pieces and, in opposition to what is hysteric or works at random, the
maintenance of a standard. Of such art *ethos* rather than *pathos* [character
rather than feeling] will be the predominant mood. To use Plato's own
expression there will be here no *paraleipomena*, no 'negligences', no
feminine forgetfulness of oneself, nothing in the work of art unconformed
to the leading intention of the artist . . . .[22]

If I have drawn deeply at this point from the well of sexist rhetoric, it is
not simply in order to raise a smile. It is because these lines seem to me to
contain a sensitive reconstruction of one element in Plato's thought; and
because they testify to the force and truth which a serious writer could
attribute, less than a century ago, to the Pythagorean–Platonic theory of
sexual difference. The reconstructed argument can be summed up as follows. Masculinity (in art; but of course there is also, in Platonist terms, an
'art' of life) expresses itself in coherence – a value which brings together
unity and *determinacy*, since to make a body of material coherent is (i) to
convert it into a single organised whole, and (ii) by virtue of the work of
organisation, to bestow determinate form on what was previously formless.
Femininity by contrast expresses itself in incoherence – that is, in *plurality*
and *indeterminacy*, which are understood not as positive characteristics but
as the negation (or absence) of their opposites. To be feminine is to lack the
formative power which, on its inward side, constructs a definite identity for
itself; and on its outward side, continually seeks to imprint this definite
identity on its surroundings.

But if *haplotes* (singleness, simplicity) is connected in this sort of way
with masculinity in Plato's ethics, then his epistemology too can be interpreted as an affirmation of the male principle; for it too centres on the
progression of the mind from diversity to unity. The genuinely philosophic
spirit is the one which is impelled to pass beyond appearances and to make
contact with the underlying reality. Hence the (masculine) virtue of the
philosopher consists in a discipline of 'doxastic self-mastery' corresponding to the practical self-mastery which is the mark of the virtuous man as
such. Doxastic self-mastery is a matter of not giving in to the solicitations
of any arbitrary *doxa* (opinion, judgement) that happens to occur to you: not
allowing yourself to judge that *x* is *F* until you have achieved a grasp of the
real essence of *F*-ness (which, in the case of those predicates that lead
intuitive judgement to contradict itself, will be something hidden and
unobvious). Conversely, *apaideusia* or 'lack of culture' is a condition in
which one is apt to be swept away by the latest impression to present itself.
In the moral case, this was an appetite or inclination; in the intellectual case,

it is a particular aspect of something which catches the observer's attention and gives rise to a judgement about that thing.

Plato's ideal in both these spheres is that we should accept only those mental determinations which are *absolutely valid*: those which we can endorse not just when we look at a thing from a single, partial point of view, but which will continue to seem well-founded when we have examined it from every side and arrived at a coherent conception of it. While Platonic justice or 'psychic harmony' ensures that you will not pursue any goal unless it has been pronounced good by the *logistikon* on behalf of your entire soul (*Rep.* 442c), Platonic *philosophia* ensures that you will not give your categorical assent to any judgement unless you are in a position to deduce it from a *logos* which has been thoroughly tested in dialectical discussion – that is, one which has been exposed to criticism from every possible point of view (*Rep.* 534bd).

We might say that just as the only truly admirable human being, for Plato, is one who exhibits 'singleness' of soul, so the only truly satisfying object of knowledge is a unitary, *undeceiving* object: one to which a certain predicate can be applied without qualification. For example, *auto to kalon* (the beautiful itself, the idea of beauty) is the one and only object of which we can say that it is beautiful without qualification – that there is no point of view from which it would appear not-beautiful. It alone is guaranteed not to contain any hidden element of non-beauty, as particular beautiful things always do.[23] So whereas particular things are, so to speak, cognitively devious (because they have an inherent tendency to deceive us when we make judgements about them), the ideas – once we have shown ourselves worthy, through the ordeal of dialectic, to have commerce with them in the first place – hold nothing back from our judgement. They are in fact credited with a quality which Plato and many of his contemporaries regard as typical of the 'better sort of person' (the nobly-born or *gennaioi*), namely that quality of truthfulness which comes from having *nothing to conceal*. In keeping with the long-familiar thesis that 'like is known by like',[24] the character of the perfect object of knowledge – which, *qua* perfect, is also the only object of *genuine* knowledge – is modelled on that of the perfect man: it shares in the 'manliness' of Plato's ideal human type.

Thus although the point is never explicitly stated, Plato evidently sees not just moral development, but cognitive development generally, as a process which emancipates the subject from a symbolically feminine condition. A man whose judgement does not take command of the phenomena and penetrate them, but passively awaits their suggestions, is in terms of the Platonic educational ideal *no better than a woman*. Beguiled as he is by the 'spangled garment' of appearance, such a man shares in the incoherent, fragmented character of the imperfectly real world which furnishes the content of his cognitive acts.

Others have already embarked on the interpretation of Plato's writings from the point of view of a feminist psychoanalysis.[25] I will conclude instead by asking what, if anything, feminist political theory stands to gain from historical enquiries such as this.

The question is not a straightforward one. A reply of maximum briskness would be that since theories of female inferiority are *false* (expressing as they do the self-serving fictions of the sexual ruling class), they are best consigned to oblivion: only through bad faith, or a failure of nerve, might we choose to spend time articulating them in detail. But to this one may retort that the patriarchal character of such theories cannot, given the cultural reality of patriarchy, debar the study of them from contributing to our self-understanding. Life does, after all, imitate ideology, just as it proverbially imitates art; where it ceases to do so, this shows that the relevant bit of ideology is defunct.

Yet the brisk reply (the one issuing from the standpoint of ethics) contains a germ of truth, for feminism cannot limit itself to the task of explicating patriarchal fantasy. Admittedly, in reading what our literary tradition has to offer on the subject of femininity and masculinity, we are dealing with texts which claim to describe – and in a secondary, consequential and partial way, do describe – *how things are* with respect to gender identity; but at the same time, the very existence of these texts is a component of the *political formation* which feminism is calling into question. The writings discussed in this chapter are a case in point. Once we raise the Pythagorean–Platonic theory of gender to full philosophical consciousness it will impress us, I believe, not by its strangeness but by its crushing familiarity. Everyone 'knows' that women are inscrutable, inconstant, closer to nature – that the female sex has a special relationship with the irrational. But to reconstruct the ideological tradition which has spawned this 'knowledge' must in the end be a gesture, not of affirmation, but of critique. In so far as feminism is a politics of change, it is an invitation *not* to recognise ourselves in the prevailing image of woman as excluded from reason and culture;[26] or better, to invent a cultural condition to which the image would no longer correspond.[27]

NOTES

1. Cixous (1981), pp. 90–1. In this context, as Cixous goes on to explain, 'always' means 'throughout the history of Western philosophy'. She acknowledges a debt here to Jacques Derrida's deconstructionist method of textual criticism; for bibliography and discussion cf. Norris (1987).

2. In deciding between the terms 'male/female' and 'masculine/feminine' at various points in this chapter, I have tried to keep in view the convention widely observed in feminist writing whereby the first pair denote biological categories, the second symbolic or culturally constructed ones (with 'gender' as an abstraction from the latter). Thus 'femininity' means something like 'biological femaleness as mediated by a culture or sign-system'. Even in the best of causes, though, one can hardly subdue the forces of metaphor altogether (cf. 'male principle', 'female principle'); and in any case the contrast between *reality* and *representation* raises difficulties which I mention briefly at the end of the chapter.

3. Ross (1924) p. 151.

4. Ibid., p. 150.

5. Ibid., p. 148.

6. For more detail, cf. Cornford (1939), pp. 1–28.

7. *Questiones Romanae*, 102, 288ce; *De E* 8, 388ae (I quote from the Loeb translation by F. C. Babbitt). *De E* is one of Plutarch's 'Pythian dialogues', which 'contain the greater part of [his] philosophical and religious speculation' according to D. A. Russell in *The Oxford Classical Dictionary*; the point at issue in it is the mystic significance of the letter E (*epsilon*), which was the fifth letter in the Greek alphabet.

8. Cf. Aeschylus, *Eumenides*, 658–61; Aristotle *De Generatione Animalium*, 716a20 ff. On Aristotle, cf. also Okin (1980) Ch. 4.

9. Cf. Hippocrates in Lefkowitz and Fant (1982), p. 86.

10. Cf. Stocks (1914), pp. 193–4.

11. Cf. Heraclitus, DK B2, B89.

12. *Met.* A 987a30. For a detailed study of Plato's *Philebus* from this point of view cf. Sayre (1983), Ch. 3. Nussbaum (1986), Ch. 4 sees Pythagorean motivation behind Plato's quest in an earlier work, the *Protagoras*, for a unitary standard of practical rationality.

13. Cf. *Rep.* V, esp. at 454de. The most striking 'limitation' is a clause to the effect that on average, men as a sex excel women as a sex in all pursuits (455ce). But Plato's conservatism on this point does not wipe out his achievement in distinguishing between those aspects of the sexual division of labour which are biologically determined and those which are (merely) socially determined. Misguided as it undoubtedly is to describe Plato as a 'feminist', this distinction was a necessary preliminary to the development of any feminist theory properly so called: cf. Okin (1980), p. 41.

14. Cf. Annas (1976) and (1981), pp. 181–5.

15. *Tim.* 50c7 ff. Translation by Lee (1965).

16. Cf. Hesiod, *Works and Days* 699; Xenophon, *Oeconomicus* VII, 4–5.

17. Cf. Wood and Wood (1978), Ch. 4; de Ste Croix (1981), pp. 411–14; Vlastos, 'Slavery in Plato's thought' in Vlastos (1981).

18. Other typical occurrences of the word in the *Republic* include 426a2 (politicians who try to achieve good government through a welter of detailed legislation are like doctors who only succeed in producing more complex, or 'fancy', illnesses); 558c4–5 (democracy is a 'pleasant form of government, anarchic and variegated'); 559d9 (a young man may be corrupted by unscrupulous types who contrive 'many and various/variegated pleasures' for him); 604e1 (fretful states of mind – *to aganaktetikon* – admit of a great variety of dramatic representation (*pollen mimesin kai poikilen ecnei*), unlike wisdom and serenity, which lack entertainment value: this is one reason for the problematic nature of imaginative literature from Plato's point of view).

19. The role of the masculine ideal in Plato's ethics has not been altogether overlooked in recent English-language commentaries: cf. Gosling (1973), Ch. 3. Yet the meaning of this ideal cannot be grasped unless we consider it in relation to its opposite, and Gosling's discussion fails in this respect since he never explicitly acknowledges that not all human beings are male: 'it seems that Plato thinks that *we all* have a tendency to admire and aspire after manly behaviour . . . a perfect *human being* will be one whose behaviour is in part determined by admiration for a correct ideal of manliness' (p. 50, my emphasis). The masculine ideal in its dialectical relation to the feminine anti-ideal is the theme of Lloyd (1984), a study which ironically confirms Whitehead's famous description of European philosophy as a series of footnotes to Plato.

20. Foucault (1984), p. 96.

21. For a selection cf. Irigaray (1974), pp. 188–99; Annas (1976), pp. 316–17, which draws attention to a rich vein in *Laws* VI. Note especially the statement at 781a that the female sex is 'more furtive and crafty [*lathraioteron . . . kai epiklopoteron*] by nature owing to its weakness'.

22. Pater (1893), pp. 256–7.

23. Cf. Collingwood (1945), p. 56; Annas (1981), p. 207; Vlastos (1981), p. 63.

24. Attributed by Aristotle to the pre-Socratic philosopher Empedocles: cf. Empedocles, DK B109.

25. Cf. Irigaray (1974), pp. 301 ff.; Flax (1983), pp. 255–8; duBois (1988), Ch. 8. For a very helpful short account of Irigaray, see Whitford (1988).

26. Cf. Le Doeuff (1987), p. 196.

27. This chapter developed out of one of my contributions to a class on 'Philosophical Theories of Sexual Difference' which Joanna Hodge and I gave at Oxford in 1986. I am grateful to Joanna for mental stimulation and encouragement. Thanks also to Margaret whitford for comments on an earlier draft.

6 Producing Woman: Hippocratic Gynaecology

Helen King

Every established order tends to produce . . . the naturalization of its own arbitrariness. (Bourdieu, 1977, p. 164)

The collection of medical writings associated with the name of Hippocrates has until recently been somewhat neglected as a source for women in the ancient world. In the past, scholars have vigorously debated which, if any, texts in the collection were written by Hippocrates (traditionally c.460–c.370 BC) himself and, consequently, which texts should be assigned to the 'school of Cnidos' and which to the 'school of Cos' with which the 'father of medicine' was associated. Current scholarship has moved away from these topics, accepting that there are wide variations in style and content between the medical texts which were first written down between the fifth and first centuries BC, then circulated widely in various compilations and summaries before being assembled under the name of Hippocrates at some unknown date; perhaps as late as the tenth century AD.[1]

Regardless of their authorship, these texts are important on a number of levels. Within the context of medical history and the treatment of women, they were to be highly influential; such diverse medical systems as those of the medieval Arabic world, the Renaissance and Victorian England made use of the therapies and theories originally expounded in the fifth and fourth centuries BC. Within the context of classical studies, the texts provide evidence not only for the reality of women's lives, but also for the extent to which particular images of woman dominated male perception and female experience of those lives.

Since the classical period, during which the major gynaecological treatises of the Hippocratic corpus were composed, the influence of Hippocratic medicine has varied widely. In the west, from the second century AD onwards, the theories of Soranus and Galen were in competition; however, the Hippocratic texts re-entered the medical tradition between the fifth and seventh centuries AD, when many of them were translated into Latin at Ravenna.[2] The motives for such translation went beyond any merely scholarly concern to produce an 'edition' of the Hippocratic corpus, as can be demonstrated by looking at the principles of selection governing which sections were translated. What is selected is the practical, rather than the theoretical: that regarded as having direct relevance for the practice of medicine in the late antique period, together with that which is of use in the instruction of medical practitioners. Thus recipes to promote conception are transmitted, while the theories underlying the recommendations are not. In keeping with these principles of selection, the sections translated were also adapted to make them better fit the social and moral context within which they were to be used, or were recast in new 'instructional' formats, the letter being a particularly popular one.[3]

Transmission also took place through the Arab world, where versions of Hippocratic texts, based on several manuscripts, were produced from the ninth century onwards. Where the Latin west used the texts to create manuals of practice or instruction, the Arabic world also used the more theoretical treatises, so that the 'Arabic Hippocrates' is more complete than the 'Latin Hippocrates'.[4]

After the rediscovery, translation and publication of many Hippocratic texts in the sixteenth century, Hippocratic medicine became established in the west as an important source for medical ethics and practice. Before the publication of the Hippocratic corpus in Latin in 1525, and in Greek in 1526, many of these texts were only available through the intermediary of Galen, whose commentaries on the Hippocratic texts survived even when the texts themselves were lost to the west. With the rapid proliferation of editions and commentaries, the 'divine Hippocrates' came to be so admired that any new development in medicine was traced back to an imagined Hippocratic antecedent, while in Victorian London it was still possible for a medical practitioner to defend aspects of his gynaecological work by claiming that 'Hippocrates himself' had done the same.[5]

But what of the texts upon which this long-lasting tradition, so influential for the medical treatment of many generations of women and men, was based? Traditional histories of medicine follow a teleological, Whiggish approach to history. The questions they ask concern the discovery of un-questionable 'facts' by a series of 'great men'; for example, Harvey's discovery of the circulation of the blood in the early seventeenth century. They assume that the human body is something which every society expe-riences in the same way; that it is historically constant, naturally given. If the body is a fixed point, then other societies and other historical periods can be marked out of 10 according to the closeness of their models of the body, disease and therapy to our 'correct' model. Such a position prevents us from appreciating the nature of any medical system as a cultural con-struct, rooted in its own context of production.[6] It also leads to a low valuation of the gynaecological material of the Hippocratic corpus. Its explanations of menstruation and conception score poorly when compared to modern knowledge; its models of the body may thus be demoted by being given such labels as 'early folk medicine', 'primitive' and 'naive'. Compared to the supposed riches of the rest of the Hippocratic corpus, the gynaecology gets a resounding 'fail' mark for medical accuracy, even though its images of the female body continue to pervade later medicine.[7]

However, there are other standards by which Hippocratic gynaecology can be judged. As I have argued elsewhere, it needs to be read as 'text'; despite its later uses, it is the product of a specific culture, the values of which it reflects and confirms. A powerful discourse, medicine takes the social and represents it as 'natural'.[8] It defines which behaviour is normal, which is 'sick'; who is normal, who needs treatment. This may be illustrated with some examples from the field of later sexual medicine. What causes epilepsy, blindness, imbecility, insanity, rheumatism, constipation, piles and finally death? According to Tissot, writing in 1770, masturbation. This practice also dries out the brain so that it can be heard rattling around in the skull.[9] What cures an 'idiot girl' and enables her to read her Bible and obtain a position in service – an interesting definition of 'health' if ever I read one – in a published and by no means unusual case history of the 1860s? Surgical excision of the clitoris.[10] What makes you sick? What restores health? These two examples from our own recent history show that medicine can use its privileged position as guardian of the boundary between nature and society to make assertions which we may reject, but which seemed self-evident in another time and another place.

An example from the Hippocratic corpus will both illustrate the dangers of judging ancient Greek medicine by later medical standards, and encourage a certain amount of scepticism concerning the extent to which these texts can be used to tell us about women's real state of health in classical Greece of the fifth and fourth centuries BC. This example, presented in the form of a case history, reads 'At Abdera, Phaethousa the wife and mistress of the house of Pytheas, had previously borne children; her husband having fled, her menses were suppressed for a long time. Then, pain and redness in the joints. Following these, her body became masculine, hairy all over; she grew a beard and her voice roughened. All that we did to draw down the menstrual blood, it did not come, and she died.'[11] It goes on to describe the 'one hope' of returning to female form as the return of the menses. A modern diagnosis of this unexplained masculinisation would probably be 'postpubertal virilism caused by the adrenogenital syndrome'. That is, it *can* happen. But just because it can happen, does it mean it is happening here? I would instead suggest reading the text by noting what the anonymous author wishes to draw to our attention. Any description involves selection, and we must try to understand both the points which the writer deliberately brings to our notice and those which are so obvious that they are unstated. Here, menstruation is presented as essential to 'being a woman' in a very concrete sense. Her menses stop – her body becomes male. This text calls menstruation *gynaikeia*, 'women's things', and *ta kata physin*, 'the natural things'. The absence of one 'natural thing' leads to other unnatural manifestations. Marriage is also regarded as important to a healthy female physiology. The problems start when her husband leaves her; the Greek *gyne* – as in gynaecology – means both 'wife' and 'woman', and here ceasing to be wife also threatens being woman. Many of these texts prescribe marriage as a cure for women's disorders; to be a woman physiologically it is necessary to be a wife socially. Finally, crossing the male/female boundary is fatal. One has to be entirely one thing, or entirely the other.

The above example shows something of the nature of these texts and the difficulties raised by any attempt to measure them against a later medical standard; it also shows how medicine can classify observed phenomena, defining the norm and discouraging variation from that norm.

Who wrote such texts as these? The case history of Phaethousa comes from the *Epidemics*, some books of which have traditionally been seen as the case notes of Hippocrates himself. It is not necessary here to ask detailed questions about whether Hippocrates was responsible for the gynaecological material in the corpus of texts which bears his name; Galen regarded the *Gynaikeia*, or *Diseases of Women*, as genuinely Hippocratic, but since the second century AD these works have not been regarded as 'genuine works of Hippocrates'.[12] Depending on your point of view, they represent either the accumulated tradition of centuries of wise-women, eventually written down by men, or the wild fantasies of a few male doctors, enthusiastically accepted by the male household heads who employed such doctors to treat their women.[13] There is very little one can do to test any of these suggestions; it all depends on how you choose to use the evidence. If, for example, you focus on the use of cantharid beetle and rat-shit pessaries, the emphasis on marriage and childbirth as the cures for virtually all ills, and the imagery of a mobile womb rushing through the body in a desperate search for moisture, you may well conclude that this is all a punitive manifestation of male fantasy. If, on the other hand, you emphasise the detailed knowledge a woman is expected to have of her own body and menstrual cycle, the way the male healer defers to women's opinions as to whether or not they are pregnant, or the very wide range of remedies used (wider than in the rest of the Hippocratic collection put together), you may think that this comes from a female tradition which medical men have taken over wholesale.

What are the central points about women made in Hippocratic medicine? Aristotle believed that women are inferior to men because their bodies are too cold to 'concoct' semen, that in conception women supply the raw material (blood) but men impose the shape, and that woman is 'as it were, an incomplete (elsewhere, a 'mutilated') male'.[14] The writers of the Hippocratic corpus agree in general, but disagree on specifics. The first point they make is that women are, indeed, profoundly 'different'. A famous passage in the *Gynaikeia* says that many doctors make the mistake of treating the diseases of women as if they were the diseases of men; but they are not, and they need a separate medicine.[15] This is not the only approach around at that time. Some texts explicitly say that the principles of medicine – such as the idea of critical days, which suggests that certain days in the course of a fever are especially dangerous – can be applied to both sexes, while the theory of using like substances to cure like disorders, or of using opposites, can be applied to any patient.[16] However, even a text like *Airs, Waters, Places*, which is based on the idea of climate, location, winds and so on affecting the prevalence of certain illnesses in all people, also makes remarks about 'women', 'old people' and 'the young' as separate groups with specific problems.

Why are women singled out? For the same reason as the old and the young. The writers of the Hippocratic corpus generally believe that you are born hot and wet, and as you age you dry out and cool down.[17] You will thus be affected in a different way by hot climates, dry winds, and so on. The majority opinion in the Hippocratics is that women are hot and wet, in contrast to Aristotle's view that they are cold and wet. The Hippocratics say that the normal quality of the menses is hot and wet; two opposed conclusions could follow from this, the first (accepted by the author of the Hippocratic treatise *Regimen*) that women purge the hot every month and so become cold, the second (accepted by the gynaecological treatises) that women obviously have more blood than men, or they would have no need to menstruate, thus women must be hotter and wetter than men.[18] They will therefore be particularly ill in hot, wet climates, because they are hot and wet from the outset.

Making use of opposites such as hot/cold to emphasise the difference between men and women may have further implications for the representation of woman. Since the ideal human form is, for classical Greek culture, that of the adult male, those features associated with him take on a strong positive value. In Aristotle, 'hot is good'; thus woman's coldness leads to her inability to concoct semen, and becomes the point from which her inferiority to man originates.[19] Bearing in mind that not all Hippocratic writers would agree that woman is cold, it is worth noting that the heat or coldness of woman lead to different theories of her physiological processes, but reach the same conclusion; whichever pole is positively valued, women are at the opposite and, at whichever pole the theory locates women, that pole will be negatively valued. The underlying message remains unchallenged: women are biologically different from, and thus in some way inferior to, men.

It is furthermore worth emphasising that neither the theory of the heat of woman, nor that of her coldness, is falsifiable. Hippocratic gynaecology is, according to our medical theories, 'wrong', but it is also coherent, systematised, and intellectually satisfying. It provides adequate explanations for all observed phenomena; it can answer any question put to it.

This can be illustrated by looking further at the heat and wetness of women. *Why* are women wet? The Hippocratics located the difference between men and women at the level of the flesh. Women's flesh is clearly softer, of a looser texture – in a word, spongier – than men's. They therefore absorb more moisture from their diet.[20] This is natural, part of being a woman, but it is also social. Women sit around more; their place is in the home, whereas men do more tiring work which dries out their bodies. This idea is popular in the seventeenth century; Fontanus in *The Woman's Doctor* of 1652 puts it that 'Women were made to stay at home, and to look after household employments', a role which 'is accompanied with much ease, without any vehement stirrings of the body'. Writers of the sixteenth and seventeenth centuries correspondingly believed that a woman who took too much exercise would stop menstruating. Soranus, who wrote his *Gynaecology* some five hundred years after the Hippocratics, saw menstruation as the result of a low level of exercise; too much exercise could stop it, but he claimed that even women who stopped menstruating for this reason could conceive if they changed to a more feminine way of life.[21] The Hippocratics believe in far less flexibility; to them the absence of menstruation is always serious. Even the robust, masculine woman who is unable to conceive will menstruate a little, although the blood-loss will be scanty and will not last for the usual number of days.[22] For the Hippocratics, all women menstruate, because this is tied not just to the level of activity, but also to the fundamental nature of the flesh.

All women menstruate, because all women are wet and spongy. There are three exceptions to this rule, all of which must be – and can be – explained within the parameters of Hippocratic theory. One is the pregnant woman. In her case, the excess blood being produced by her body goes to form and nourish the foetus. When the foetus is still small, some blood will be left over, and this is stored through pregnancy and released during childbirth and afterwards, as the lochia. Blood-loss during pregnancy weakens the woman and may cause the death of the child she carries.[23] The second is the older woman. The Hippocratic explanation of menopause follows logically from the belief that ageing is a process of drying-out. Even the wet and spongy body of a woman will eventually dry out to the point at which there is no longer any excess blood to lose. The third, the young girl, I will come to shortly.

The fundamental anatomical difference between the sexes is thus the texture of the flesh. The presence of the womb is secondary to this. Since women are wetter, they need a way of evacuating excess moisture. This is achieved by the blood moving to the womb and thence out of the body. This natural *katharsis*, purification, can be thwarted in a number of ways, in which case it will cause illness. The womb is like a jar, with its neck and mouth pointing downwards. It can, however, swivel round so that the blood is unable to get out, or is poured out the wrong way. Inside a woman is a tube, a road – *hodos* – from the mouth and nostrils to the vaginal opening. If blood is prevented from going down, it will by preference go up this tube, and emerge as a nosebleed or as vomit. Hence the Hippocratic aphorisms, 'A nosebleed is a good thing if the menses are suppressed' and 'Vomiting blood ceases when the menses flow'.[24] The point is that, because women *are* wet and spongy, blood must regularly come out of them in one way or another. In this system, it is not possible simply to miss a period – the blood must be in there somewhere, perhaps stuck on one or other of its possible ways out, perhaps causing a swelling which indicates its whereabouts, perhaps rotting and causing symptoms in that part of the body which it has reached. The consequence of this anatomy of the female – wet and spongy flesh, womb-jar and tube – is that regular and *heavy* menstruation is seen as utterly essential to female health.[25] Anything at all is justified if it draws out the blood before it causes fatal illness.

If blood is unable to get out, the male seed is unable to get in; absence of menstruation and failure to conceive are thus two sides of the same coin. The presence of menstruation indicates that the womb is correctly aligned, open and able to provide nourishment for a child, while its absence does not necessarily indicate pregnancy, but rather that pregnancy is impossible due to some obstruction.

What is done to restore the womb to its correct position and clear out the blood? Marriage is recommended as a cure because sex opens up the bottom of the tube and also agitates the body, causing blood to move around more enthusiastically. While women's wetness is exacerbated by sitting around at home, sex as exercise dries them out without making them masculine. Childbirth is even better because it forces open more of the tube, and clears out the womb most effectively. What we may want to see as 'social' cures involving a change in the woman's social status, to wife and mother, are therefore given a medical overlay.

The most typical of Hippocratic gynaecological interventions is the fumigation, in which hot vapours are passed through a reed into the womb. This can go on for several days, with short breaks for bathing, eating specified foods, or intercourse with one's husband. It is interesting that even in this procedure, where the woman would seem very much a passive object having things done *to* her, she is allowed one way of resuming control. At intervals during the fumigation she is instructed to touch the mouth of the womb (the texts helpfully add, 'if she can feel it') and report on its position. Since the purpose of the therapy is to restore the womb to its correct position so that blood can flow out and the male seed in, the answer, 'Yes, I can feel it, and it's not tilted any more' will end the treatment.[26]

This aspect of female self-knowledge, permitting a degree of control over the process of therapy, is illuminating, but should not be pushed too far. The juxtaposition of female patient and male doctor creates its own difficulties in the Hippocratic corpus. In the *Diseases of Women* it is noteworthy how often the doctor does not himself examine his patient, but instead leaves this to the patient herself or to a female assistant. For example, in the course of a long episode of treatment we read the following advice: 'Next day the woman examines herself to see whether the mouth of the womb is straighter.' If so, then therapy can proceed.[27] In contrast, in a later chapter the author gives the dominant role in determining the course of treatment to the doctor: 'But if it seems to *you* that she needs more purging . . .'.[28] As Lloyd puts it, 'There is a certain ambivalence in the relationship between the male doctor and the female patient.'[29] Does this indicate a reluctance on the part of the male to touch the sick female body, or a healthy respect for the greater knowledge of her own body which the woman must possess? Should we condemn the doctor for his fear of the female, or admire the patient for having a degree of familiarity with her own body which exceeds that of many of her modern sisters? Again we find two apparently opposed ways of understanding these texts; we may follow the interpretation of Rousselle, that these texts give us 'women's knowledge', to which male doctors defer, and upon which all the explanations given are based; or that of Manuli, which suggests that the explanations owe more to male ideologies than to women's experiences.

There is, however, a third option here. When reading the texts, it is of interest that they divide in another way; that is, according to a classification based on 'experience'. In the *Diseases of Women* we read that youth, inexperience and shame are the main obstacles which not only prevent women from knowing that something is wrong, but also prevent them from telling a doctor. The writer of this section says that 'time and necessity' teach women to overcome these obstacles.[30]

One example of the 'experienced' woman occurs in a therapy in which a tube is inserted into the womb, and milk poured in through it to cleanse the womb and aid conception. The patient is trusted to insert and correctly position the tube because, the writer says, she will know where it should be placed. How does this woman earn the right to participate in her own treatment? The text notes that she is married, has previously been able to conceive and has reported that her husband's seed does not fall out of her womb; her sterility is thus not the result of a womb which is too 'open'.[31] The 'experienced' woman is thus a social construct, parallel to the 'tamed' woman to whom I will come shortly; her status is earned by marriage, past conception and observation of her own body.

A further point in favour of this woman as 'experienced' is that she cooperates with the doctor rather than trying to treat herself. In another passage a condition is diagnosed as the result of a woman touching the mouth of her womb and finding that it is narrow and moist, while a further 'model' patient examines her vagina and reports her findings to the physician.[32] Self-treatment is condemned by these texts; not surprisingly, since their authors need to earn a living!

Women who have learned through 'time and necessity' can thus be trusted; 'the inexperienced' cannot be trusted, think that absence of menstruation and a swollen abdomen invariably signify pregnancy,[33] and must be examined in person or through a third party. General descriptions by ancient writers of the origin of medical science emphasise that this aspect of the breakthrough from savagery to civilisation needs the conjunction of the qualities of reason and experience;[34] here, these two qualities come together but are represented as deriving from the two sexes. Female experience must combine with male reason to produce health.

It is thus possible to summarise the main tenets of Hippocratic gynaecology as follows. Women are different from men; this difference is located at the level of the flesh, although women's wetness is exacerbated by their sedentary lives. Due to the texture of their flesh, they need to lose blood regularly through menstruation. In the absence of menstruation, various forms of intervention are used to evacuate the blood, and also to ensure that the womb will be sufficiently open to receive the male seed as a means to the *katharsis* of parturition. Within this system of medicine, women are permitted a certain level of involvement in their own diagnosis and treatment, provided that they cooperate with the male physician and match the socially-established standard of the 'experienced' woman.

It should be noted in passing that the concern for evacuating menstrual blood by various means does not mean that the blood itself is seen as 'impure', in contrast to Jewish and later classical thought, and indeed to some sixteenth- and seventeenth-century medical writers. In consequence, for the ancient Greeks, intercourse while menstruating is not thought to engender monsters. On the contrary, because menstruation indicates that the womb is open to let the blood out, it also suggests that the womb will let seed in. The best time for fruitful sex is therefore when the period is ending. When it is flowing heavily, the seed will probably fall out again, but when it is still in progress but ending the seed can enter the womb most easily. Quite the silliest time for sex is midway between periods, when the womb is closed.[35]

For the Hippocratic writers, the most critical time in the female life-cycle is puberty. As has already been mentioned, the emphasis on menstruation as the inevitable concomitant of womanhood has to cope with those categories of woman who do not bleed; and, whereas pregnancy and menopause are relatively easy to incorporate into the system, menarche creates some difficulties. A woman who has never previously bled begins to bleed; or, far worse in terms of the model of the female as wet and spongy, a woman who is apparently mature does not bleed. Most work on female maturation in ancient Greece concentrates on ritual and myth, and shows a number of images associated with the process by which *parthenos* becomes *gyne*. One of these, which is also found in the medical texts, is that of ripening fruit. Unmarried virgin girls of the age for marriage are 'ripe for marriage', 'tender ripe fruit'; innocent girls carried off in battle are 'plucked unripe'; an unmarried but deflowered girl (and note our word!) is 'rotted fruit', 'corrupted', 'gone off'.[36] Another image is that of taming. The young girl is called an 'untamed filly', 'unyoked by marriage/Aphrodite'.[37] Xenophon's *Oikonomikos* casually mentions that before the speaker was able to hold a conversation with his young wife, he had to tame her. The ancient sources suggest that the cooperation of the filly/girl is not necessary to the success of the process; of Poseidon and the daughter of Nereus we read that 'he broke her in, although she was not willing'.[38]

Puberty is therefore represented as both a natural process of ripening, and a man-directed process of taming. It is important here to remember that the Greeks classified ripening and taming in a different way from ourselves, considering some foods to be partly 'tamed' by nature, needing only a little human intervention to cook them and make them fully edible.[39] The imagery of puberty would suggest that it is seen in the same way – a natural process of change, but needing a little extra push from men to complete it.

This brings us back to the point that medicine exists at the point where the 'natural' meets the 'social', where what is obvious and universal – pregnancy, menstruation – meets what is far less obvious and specific – particular cultural models of the female and her place in the world.

The Hippocratic construction of female puberty too involves a part which is due to changes coming from within the body, and another part which has an external origin. Externally, the creation of a mature female body with its tube fully open and its womb in the right place depends on marriage when ripe for it, sexual intercourse, and childbirth. Internally, the body shows itself ready for these by menarche, which is the result of the process of growth gradually opening up the flesh so it acquires the characteristic female sponginess.[40] If menarche fails to happen at the right time, male intervention, medical or marital – if such a distinction has any validity in this context – may be necessary to complete the opening up of the flesh. As the writer of the Hippocratic treatise *Diseases of Young Girls* puts it, 'she is relieved of this complaint when nothing prevents the flow of menstrual blood. I order young girls to marry as quickly as possible if they suffer like this. For if they become pregnant, they become healthy. If not, then at puberty or a little later she will suffer from this or from some other disease.'[41] Young girls only bleed when their bodies have grown to that point when their flesh has started to retain excess blood, and when the way out has opened. When they have shown they are ripe, they should quickly be tamed in marriage so that the process can be completed by childbirth.

The Hippocratic woman thus stands balanced between experience and image, medicine and myth, nature and culture. Ripened, tamed, wet and spongy, both socially and physiologically 'woman', the daughters of Pandora learn from their medical care the extent of their difference.

NOTES

1. On the authorship of the Hippocratic texts, see Lloyd (1975); Smith (1979). The date of compilation of the 'Hippocratic corpus' is discussed by Irigoin (1973). Among recent work recovering and reassessing Hippocratic gynaecology, see: Rousselle (1980; 1988); Manuli (1980; 1983); Gourevitch (1984); King (1983; 1985); Sissa (1983; 1990); Hanson (1990); Dean-Jones (1989; 1992).

2. Green (1985), p. 142 and pp. 146–7; see Müller-Rohlfsen (1980).

3. Mazzini (1985), p. 385; Agrimi (1985), pp. 391–2.

4. Irigoin (1973); Lippi and Arieti (1985).

5.   Coturri (1968); Joly (1966), pp. 1–30; on the activities of the clitoridectomist
      Isaac Baker Brown, see Nichol (1969) and Scull and Favreau (1986), together
      with the report of the meeting of 3 April 1867 given in *British Medical
      Journal* (6 April 1867), pp. 395–410.
6.   King (1989). As Turner (1984), p. 28 puts it, 'Biological facts exist but they
      exist by virtue of classificatory practices'. Medicine, like the other natural
      sciences, is a system for ordering the world.
7.   E.g. Kudlien (1968), p. 321 and n. 67; p. 325.
8.   King (1989).
9.   Engelhardt (1974).
10.   Tanner (1867), p. 376.
11.   *Epidemics* 6.8.32 (Littré 5.236). Reference to Littré will hereafter be given as
      L. On the problems of case histories and the principles by which the author
      selects points to note down, see Lonie (1983) and King (1989). The case of
      Phaethousa presents some problems of translation. She is described as both
      gyne and *oikouros*, and could thus be 'a woman who was housekeeper to
      Pytheas'; this reading would suggest the use of *gyne* in the sense 'married
      woman'. A manuscript variant gives *he kouros*, the daughter, for *oikouros*!
      Oikouros can, however, be used of a wife, to emphasise her domestic virtues,
      and it is this translation which I prefer here. The Greek is also unclear on what
      happened to her husband, whether or not he is to be identified with Pytheas;
      he may have 'fled', but he could be 'exiled'. Nevertheless, whether Phaethousa
      is wife, daughter or housekeeper to Pytheas, the central point remains that she
      had a husband, and he is no longer with her.
12.   Smith (1979), p. 142.
13.   Empirical knowledge of wise-women, Rousselle (1980); male fantasies, Manuli
      (1983).
14.   Coldness of women preventing concoction of blood into semen: Aristotle *De
      Partibus Animalium* (*PA*) 650a8 ff.; *De Generatione Animalium* (*GA*) 774al;
      Sissa (1983), pp. 130–5. Men supply the form, women the raw material:
      Aristotle *GA* 729a25–35 and 729b12–21. Woman as incomplete/mutilated
      male: Aristotle *GA* 728a17 ff. and 737a; Clark (1975), p. 29 and pp. 207–10.
15.   *Diseases of Women* (hereafter *DW*) 1.62 (L 8.126).
16.   *Seven month child* 9 (L 7.446) says that the same principles apply to concep-
      tion, miscarriage and childbirth as to 'diseases and healthy states and deaths
      in all human beings'.
17.   See *Regimen* 1.33 (L 6.510–12); *Nature of man* 12 (L 6.64); *DW* 2.111
      (L 8.238–40).
18.   Menses as hot and wet: *DW* 3.217 (L 8.418). In the Renaissance, when
      Aristotle's view that women were cold was dominant, such references were
      regarded as interpolations; see Maclean (1980), p. 34. The other passages
      discussed here are *Regimen* 1.34 (L 6.512) and *DW* 1.1 (L 8.12–14).
19.   Aristotle *PA* 650a8 ff.; *GA* 775a14–20. For the later history of this idea, see
      Maclean (1980), Ch. 3.
20.   *DW* 1.1 (L 8.12–14); Dean-Jones (1989); King (1989), pp. 26–7.
21.   *DW* 1.1 (L 8.14); cf. Xenophon's use of the pattern man:woman::outside:inside
      in *Oikonomikos* 7.2–3 and 7.20–43. The relevant passages of Soranus are
      Gynaecology, 1.22–3, 1.27 and 3.9.
22.   *DW* 1.6 (L 8.30).

23. *DW* 1.25 (L 8.64–6); *Nature of the Child* 14 (L 7.492); *Aphorisms* 5.60 (L 4.554).
24. *Aphorisms* 5.32 and 33 (L 4.542–4); see King (1989), p. 24.
25. On the implications of the expectation of heavy and regular blood-loss, King (1987); Dean-Jones (1989).
26. *DW* 2.133 (L 8.284–6); discussed in King (1985), pp. 94–5.
27. *DW* 2.146 (L 8.322).
28. *DW* 2.157 (L 8.334).
29. Lloyd (1983), pp. 70–9.
30. *DW* 1.62 (L 8.126).
31. *DW* 3.222 (L 8.430). This brief discussion of 'experience' develops the argument I advanced in King (1990), pp. 10–12. See also Hanson (1987), p. 597.
32. *DW* 1.59 (L 8.118); cf. 2.155 (L 8.330); *DW* 1.40 (L 8.96–8).
33. *DW* 2.133 (L 8.280–2).
34. For discussion, see King (1985), pp. 68–71.
35. Parker (1982); see *Nature of woman* 8 (L 7.324); Aristotle *GA* 727b12–25.
36. *Diseases of young girls* (L 8.466); cf. King (1983). Aeschylus, *Suppliants* 995–1005; *Seven against Thebes* 333.
37. E.g. Sophocles, *Antigone* 477–8; Aristophanes, *Lysistrata* 1308; *Thesmophoriazousae* 1136–42; Euripides, *Hippolytus* 546–7.
38. Xenophon, *Oikonomikos* 7.10; Oppian *Halieutica* 1.390.
39. Vernant (1979).
40. *On Generation* 2 (L 7.472–4); King (1989), pp. 26–7.
41. L 8.468–70; on this text see King (1983).

7 Social Stereotypes and Historical Analysis: The Case of the Imperial Women at Rome[1]

Susan Fischler

> From this moment it was a changed state, and all things moved at the fiat of a woman – but not a woman who, as Messalina, wantonly treated the Roman empire as a toy. It was a tight-drawn, almost masculine tyranny: in public, there was austerity and, often as not, arrogance; at home, no trace of unchastity, unless it might contribute to power.[2]

The image of the domineering and power-hungry imperial woman at the heart of Roman political affairs is familiar to anyone who has read, or seen the television adaptation of, Robert Graves' work, *I. Claudius*. But as this extract from the *Annals* of Tacitus (c. AD 56–c.115), decrying the rise of Agrippina II shows, Graves had no need to use his creative energies to devise these characters: such depictions of Roman imperial women can be found throughout ancient historical writing on the imperial period. The portrayals of these women tell us more about Roman social attitudes than how elite women lived: they enable us to understand more fully gender relationships and their bearing on power structures at Rome, as well as how male attitudes toward gender and power influenced the depiction of women within ancient literary texts.

In my analysis of these images, their purpose and their meaning, I will focus on the period of the foundation of the Roman monarchy, known as the Principate, from the start of Augustus' sole rule in 31 BC to the death of Nero in AD 68 (the Julio-Claudian dynasty). Before turning to discuss the depictions of the imperial women, it is importance to consider first some basic premises which underlie the approach this chapter will take, and help to explain why women throughout history who are seen as powerful tend to be regarded with suspicion in contemporary, or near-contemporary, accounts of their times.

The first of these premises is that dominant groups within societies tend to develop their own sets of images or beliefs.[3] These images, or social constructs, are always derived from relationships between those who hold power within a clearly-defined area of society and those who do not. They help to describe and justify power relationships. A primary example of such social structuring can be seen in the way in which gender is defined and represented: images of gender reinforce and explain the power-relationship between men and women. Despite their wealth and status, imperial women could not escape being constrained and defined by the Roman social construct of Woman (capital letters will be used throughout this chapter to denote constructed types or ideals).

In most pre-industrial societies, the socially-constructed role for women excludes access to positions of authority, by which I mean publicly-recognised offices which grant the holder the right to take independent action. Certainly, this was true at Rome, where women were legally restricted from holding constitutional office, and therefore, they were denied access to authority within the state. In certain circumstances, the socially-constructed role even excludes women from exercising influence, which I am defining here as being power exercised through informal channels.[4]

As the next logical step in this sequence, women who are perceived as having gained access to power are seen as having failed to conform to the accepted social construct for their gender in their given society.[5] This often (though not universally) makes the position of these women highly problematic and the source of tension. In the case of Rome, this tension can be seen in the sources, which are solely the product of that elite, dominant group whose position was most threatened by such women, i.e. the male members of the upper classes. It is not surprising, therefore, that in these works, the imperial women as individuals are often subsumed by their symbolic importance as Imperial Women.

The way in which a society deals with these 'problem' women, how it attempts to reconcile their position to the accepted image of women and resolve this dichotomy, can shed light on the socially-constructed role for women, at least among the elite classes. Moreover, it serves to illustrate the importance and the nature of gender definitions in that society, as well as the relationship between gender and power. Finally, it is of great use in that by understanding the role gender plays in the socio-political structure of Roman society, we can gain a better understanding of the context of the literary sources and therefore achieve a more sophisticated analysis of the presentation of women within these texts.

Before turning to look specifically at the evidence for the imperial women, we need to return to the first premise, that all societies construct images of groups which they define according to the values and interests of the dominant group, and briefly present a picture of the socially constructed image of the Roman elite woman.

THE SOCIALLY CONSTRUCTED ROMAN WOMAN

The first category of the socially constructed woman I will examine is the ideal Roman Matron, as seen, for example, in the following epitaph, which dates to the late second century BC:

> Stranger, my message is short: stop and read. Here is the unlovely tomb of a lovely woman. Her parents named her Claudia. She loved her husband with all her heart. She bore two sons. Of these she leaves one on earth; under the earth she has placed the other. She was charming in converse, yet gentle in bearing. She kept house, she spun wool. That is all. You may go now.[6]

This epitaph describes the archetypal Roman Matron, and as such, should not be assumed to be an accurate or complete description of Claudia: as with tombstones today, the message should not be taken at its face value. Tombstones with this length of inscription were expensive items, designed to commemorate the bereaved family by displaying the traditional virtues of the deceased. This purpose was served by describing the dead woman as maintaining the highest standards expected by her social class. Thus the virtues listed here represent a common motif which exemplifies the Roman Matron. The ideal woman was noted for her beauty, fertility and faithfulness to her husband, as well as her ability to run the household. In short, the image is one of a refined woman whose life focused on the needs of her family and household.

Such ideal standards would have served as a means of judging women and instructing them on their social role. Yet, as was often the case, this ideal was based on another ideal image, that of Rome as a traditional, small rural community struggling to survive. This latter image was entirely inconsistent with Rome of the last century BC, which had long been a complex, cosmopolitan society at the centre of a massive empire. By this period, the elite woman's daily life bore little relation to that epitomised by the ideal, if only because the vast influx of slaves into the city had made it unnecessary for elite women to take responsibility for menial household tasks.[7] Therefore, the ideal conflicted with the historical reality of daily life. Yet, as in other societies, the disjunction between image and reality is not significant or problematic; the ideal continued to serve its purpose, while some modifications were made to take into account the needs of daily existence, and especially the difficulties of running the household in the conditions of civil war which prevailed in the last century of the Republic (c. 133–31 BC).

An example of this evolved, socially approved role for elite women which will be of particular value to later discussion, is provided by Plutarch, a Greek writer of the late first century/early second century AD. Plutarch draws the reader's attention to the behaviour of Octavia, who, despite her husband Mark Antony's rejection of her in favour of the Egyptian queen Cleopatra in the 30s BC, continued to act as the exemplary wife, staying at Rome and working for Antony's benefit in the traditionally prescribed fashion.

> She continued to live in her husband's house as if he were at home, and she looked after Antony's children, not only those whom she had borne him but also those of Fulvia [his previous wife], with a truly noble devotion and generosity of spirit. Moreover, she entertained any friends of Antony's who were sent to Rome either on business or to solicit posts of authority, and she did her best to help them to obtain whatever they wanted from Octavius [her brother]. But in this way she unintentionally did great harm to Antony's reputation, since he was naturally hated for wronging such a woman.[8]

Octavia's virtues here lie in the way she exemplified the behaviour of the Roman Matron, in contrast to the decadent, archetypally Eastern image of Cleopatra held by the Romans. She acted in a responsible fashion and continued to care for the household, as if her husband were still in Rome.[9] This role still included raising the children, but Plutarch makes it clear that she also looked after family clients and conducted household business.

This type of public activity was in no way atypical in the late Republic: that women were highly active in conducting family business has been well documented by others. Dixon (1983) has drawn together much evidence from the period of the late Republic which shows how elite women exercised patronage and used their influence with male members of their family to achieve what could be termed, by modern commentators, 'political' ends.[10] Such activities, while not conforming to the ideal, were nonetheless tolerated and even approved within the limited circumstances of tending to family concerns.

Just as there was an archetypal ideal role for elite women in this later period, so there was an equally revealing opposite, the Wicked Woman. The classic example is provided by Sallust (approx. 86–35 BC), in his work on the Catilinarian conspiracy at Rome in 63 BC, where he describes the attributes of Catiline's fellow conspirator, Sempronia. He states that a number of disillusioned upper-class women joined the conspiracy to overthrow the government:

One of these women was Sempronia, who had often committed many crimes of masculine audacity. This woman was abundantly favoured by fortune in her birth and beauty, and in her husband and children. She was well read in the literature of Greece and Rome, played the lyre and danced more skilfully than was necessary for an honest woman, besides having many other accomplishments which ministered to voluptuousness. But she always held all things more dear than modesty and chastity. You could not easily judge whether she was less sparing of her money or her reputation. Her sexual desires were so inflamed that she sought men more often than she was sought by them . . . She often broke her promises, repudiated her debts and had been privy to murder; she was driven by her extravagance and poverty. Yet she was a woman of no little talent: she could write verses, bandy jests and use language which was modest, tender or shameless. In short, she possessed a great measure of wit and charm.[11]

Sallust's Sempronia is the classic transgressor of the female role. She has all the right attributes which she uses in all the wrong ways. Just like the ideal Roman Matron, she has beauty and wealth; fertility and charm. Sempronia is all the more worrying because Sallust has endowed her with traits of the ideal which she then threatens to use subversively. Sallust himself introduces the passage by saying she was typical of the *type* of woman attracted to Catiline's cause. Certainly, the inversion of the perfect Roman Matron image here suggests that is what she is meant to be: an example of the most wicked, immoral type of woman, who would undoubtedly wish to overthrow the state, and which Sallust's Roman readers would have no trouble recognising, just as we recognise within our own society the images of The Tart with a Heart or A Good Woman Gone Bad. The depiction here is so stereotypical that it begs the question of how useful it is to search for the historical woman behind the portrait, instead of simply accepting her as symbolic of the social disorder Sallust describes.[12]

The portraits of the imperial women must also be set in the context of those social ideals and expectations which were particularly applied to elite women. For example, the historian Tacitus wrote the following description of Poppaea Sabina, the wife of the emperor Nero:

She was a woman possessed of all advantages but a character. For her mother, after surpassing the beauties of her day, had endowed her alike with her fame and her looks: her wealth was adequate to the distinction of her birth. Her conversation was engaging, her wit not without point;

she paraded modesty and practised wantonness. In public she rarely appeared, and then with her face half-veiled, so as not quite to satiate the beholder, – or, possibly, because it so became her. She was never sparing of her reputation, and drew no distinctions between husbands and adulterers: vulnerable neither to her own nor to others' passion, where material advantage offered, there she transferred her desires.[13]

This depiction of an empress bears a remarkable similarity to that of Sempronia, so much so that some scholars have been tempted to suggest that Tacitus based his portrait upon Sallust's.[14] Yet both portraits describe an inversion of the standard attributes of the Roman Matron, suggesting that this image of an elite woman 'gone bad' was a common cultural construct, just as the Roman Matron was. Tacitus did not need to draw on Sallust, then, to derive his depiction of Poppaea: both she and Sempronia are classic portrayals of the Roman 'wicked' woman. The most threatening women are depicted in our texts as turning virtue and society upside-down.

Imperial women of the Julio-Claudian age are often portrayed as transgressive, violators of the established female role and ideal. These portrayals were in keeping with the attitude of the age in which the authors, such as Tacitus, lived. By the second century, the Julio-Claudian period was regarded as an aberration in Roman history, a time when emperors violated the privileges, and threatened the lives, of senators and other leading figures at Rome.

To place this attitude in its historical context, it must be remembered that the Julio-Claudian period was an age of transition. Before the advent of Augustus, Rome had been governed by male representatives of the wealthy elite families, who formed the Senate, and by the assemblies of all male citizens. This so-called Republican form of government was seen as ensuring the support of the gods and the success of the state; naturally, it also guaranteed the political dominance of leading members of the elite. To attempt to change this form of government was seen by the Roman upper classes as anathema, and over the centuries a number of rising politicians had been assassinated for what were perceived as attempts to establish monarchical rule.[15] Augustus succeeded in imposing a new political order only by masking his monarchy in the language of Republican government and senatorial tradition; thus he was never referred to as a king, but as a leading man or *princeps* (and hence his regime is the Principate). In order to survive, Augustus and his Julio-Claudian successors had to perform a balancing act between the reality of absolute rule and the maintenance of the image of Republican government.[16] This included according the Senate, and the senators as individuals, the respect and privileges they felt were due to them according to Roman tradition. Clashes between emperors and the senatorial order inevitably occurred in the first century, not only because individual emperors had difficulties maintaining this balance, but also because the elite themselves had yet to come to terms with their diminished status and their role within the regime. By the second century, some of these problems had been resolved, although the authors' depictions of themselves as living in a golden age of imperial and senatorial partnership and mutual respect may be attributed in part to a desire to stay in favour with the reigning emperor.

In contrast, these authors depicted the earlier period as one manifesting all the signs of great social and political disruption, into which they placed their chosen accounts of the lives of the imperial women. A literary tradition had already been established about the characters of each of the early imperial women, as well as the emperors and others close to the *princeps*. Many examples of violations committed by the imperial women which are found in the literary sources were derived from anecdotal evidence, much of which may have evolved years after events. Frequently the events described are said to have occurred in private, such as the imperial women's consultations with their various henchmen, casting some doubt on the historicity of the accounts. But the literary tradition is still of particular interest, for it suggests what needed to be recounted to justify the claim that imperial women had stepped out of line. It reveals what abuses were generally believed to be plausible and which were particularly reprehensible. In the tradition of imperial biography and character-drawing, those anecdotes which displayed reprehensible behaviour would have been chosen deliberately in order to illuminate the character of a 'bad' imperial woman for the reader, as seen in the case of Poppaea Sabina. Whatever their historicity (which is now unascertainable), lurid tales of intrigue were used by authors to illustrate the type of behaviour expected from such women, and were a response to the hostility which certain of these women had engendered in the governing classes.

This raises a number of questions about why certain imperial women warranted such a 'bad press', and thus returns us to our initial premises about the way societies react to women who might be seen to have untoward access to authority or power.

IMPERIAL WOMEN AS TRANSGRESSORS

Agrippina [the younger], indignant at this and other things, first attempted to admonish him [the emperor Nero, her son] . . . . But when she found herself achieving nothing, she took it greatly to heart and said to him, 'It was I who made you emperor' – just as if she had the power to take his authority away from him again.[17]

Senior imperial women are often portrayed in literary texts as having access to imperial power, as in this case where Agrippina seems to be claiming she has the power to create emperors (note that the incident, described by Cassius Dio, took place behind closed doors). Why were these women deemed to be so threatening to imperial control of the state?

Paradoxically, much of the answer to this question can be found in the socially accepted role of Roman Matron. Livia, Julia and the other imperial women were born into a society which demanded that they take part in activities outside the household in order to fulfil family responsibilities (this is one of a number of ways in which it can be seen that the classic distinction between the domestic and public domains was blurred in Roman society).[18] Hence the approval granted Octavia in the passage discussed above. They too, like many Roman elite woman before them, conducted family business and sought to influence any decisions taken by the head of the household in relation to the family and its concerns. However, the head of their household was the emperor and their family was Rome's ruling dynasty: thus the business of their family now included the running of the state. The proximity of the imperial women to the functioning of the state lent new meaning to normal family activities, and granted them the capacity for public acts of a new order. Furthermore, the access this apparently granted the women to the central authority within the Roman state was at odds with the constitutional settlements made between Augustus and the ruling classes at Rome in the early decades of the Principate, for only in a monarchy could women achieve such power within the state. As such, and consistent with my earlier premises, the position of the women was a source of tension, graphically revealing the contrast between Republican practice, in which women could never hold power within the state, and the new imperial order, which contained the threat that women might do so.[19]

There are a number of elements in the traditionally articulated role of the Roman matron which can be used to illustrate this phenomenon of the typical behaviour expected of elite women taking on connotations of political power in the case of the imperial women. I will only be discussing a few, pertinent examples here. The first examples will concern women as patrons. Patronage formed the cornerstone of Roman social relations: the passage regarding Octavia's activities shows its relevance for the public activities of elite women, as well as men. The second category of traditional female behaviour to be considered will be the influence which the senior women of the household (the *matresfamilias*) could bring to bear on the emperor. A number of recent studies have stressed that the right to proffer opinions on family affairs and to have these opinions respectfully received was a fundamental part of the role of the senior woman in a Roman household in all periods, and this has particular relevance to the development of the role of the imperial women.[20]

Before examining these two categories, it is important to stress that the texts which describe the activities of the imperial women are the same ones which depend on social constructs to convey interpretations of the characters of individual women. Therefore, there is a danger that any analysis will merely be confusing aspects of these constructs with 'historical reality'. However, certain types of elite female behaviour are depicted in sources for the Republican period, as well as the imperial, in both positive and negative contexts, suggesting that to ascribe all descriptions of imperial women's conduct simply to the domain of the literary construct of the Imperial Woman would be too simplistic. It is clear that certain activities were, in themselves, a common and accepted part of elite female behaviour. In the case of the imperial women, these two categories of activity, patronage and influencing male relatives, are also attested in inscriptions, suggesting that, historically, the imperial women did engage in such activities.[21] However, the 'ordinariness' of such behaviour was altered by the circumstances in which it occurred. In response to these changed circumstances, literary depictions of the imperial women often portray the women's actions as transgressive, the unacceptable behaviour of the Wicked Woman.

The imperial women's role as patrons was a traditional one for the elite class which took on a new, political twist in meaning under the Principate. As with the example of Octavia, imperial women acted either directly themselves as patrons in aid of clients, or by interceding with male family members on behalf of clients (this last form of action is directly derived from the second category of behaviour we shall be looking at, i.e. the influence which women have with their male relatives). The combination of the imperial women's wealth and their close relationship to the emperor made them formidable patrons indeed, able to contribute greatly to their clients' needs in both these categories.

Firstly, both Livia and Antonia the younger, in their capacity as *matresfamilias* of the imperial family, were renowned for looking after the children not only of their own extended family, but of other senatorial families and foreign monarchs as well. That this resulted in certain bonds of obligation on both sides can be seen in a few notable examples. Suetonius, the imperial biographer writing in the early second century AD, noted the following in his *Life of the Emperor Otho*:

His grandfather M. Salvius Otho, whose father was a Roman knight, while his mother was of humble birth, perhaps not even freeborn, became a senator through the influence (*per gratiam*) of Livia Augusta, in whose house he was raised, but he did not progress beyond the rank of praetor.[22]

In raising the boy, Livia replaced his mother, even to the extent of promoting his career beyond that which his parentage might suggest he could achieve.

Antonia could also act *in loco parentis* with regard to the children she raised. The best-documented example relates to a Judaean prince, Agrippa, son of Berenice, who was raised by Antonia with her son Claudius and whom she subsequently protected when he returned to Rome.[23] Both these examples provide noteworthy evidence for the superior, patronal relationships both Livia and Antonia maintained, all the more striking because one of the individuals was a senator and the other a foreign prince. These were typical examples of Livia's extensive patronage, as shown by Dio's record of the Senate's actions upon her death; they voted her an arch because 'she had saved the lives of so many, reared so many senatorial children and provided so many dowries for senators' daughters'.[24]

Within the household, women traditionally oversaw the operation of family affairs, owned slaves and were patrons of those slaves they emancipated from the household. At a time when the emperor's household staff were being used in imperial administration, the imperial women could conceivably be patrons of freedmen who were in some position of authority, for example, both Messalina and Agrippina the younger were said to be patrons of Claudius' influential freedmen Narcissus.[25] The family also had close contact with the praetorian guard, who acted as the protectors of the imperial household. For example, Livia and Tiberius jointly owned property in Gallia Narbonensis, over which Afranius Burrus was made procurator. This same Burrus later became praetorian prefect under Nero.[26] According to Tacitus, he owed his position to his proven loyalty to Agrippina the younger. Another example of the close relationship between an imperial woman and the prefect may be seen in Tacitus' account of the removal from office of the joint prefects Lucius Geta and Rufrius Crispinus because Agrippina believed they were still loyal to Messalina's memory; it was in their place that Burrus was appointed.[27]

The impression given by Tacitus' stories is that the women were in a position to control imperial appointments. The basis for this premise can be found in the closeness of the women to the emperor's household staff and the household's development into an imperial institution, with associated power. Female influence over household appointments would have been acceptable to Roman elite men but not in the context of the imperial household. Whether or not the women dictated the choice of prefect, many people in a position to be personally affected by the women's presumed power might well have feared that the devotion of the praetorians to the imperial family enabled the women to have access to, and even influence with, the major military power in the city. In the case of both the imperial freedmen and the praetorian prefects, it becomes apparent that as household affairs became imperial business, the women may have had and, as importantly, were feared to have greater access to power than many who could hold constitutional office.

A similar attitude can also be discerned in accounts of these women influencing the emperor in his decision-making, my second category of traditional female behaviour. The women's effectiveness as patrons depended on this influence, which also engendered great anxiety in the literary sources about the proper role of women within the imperial family. Not surprisingly, their close proximity to the emperor, coupled with this traditional role, was seen as a threat to the established order of the state. Claudius' reign provides the best examples of such fears. As a prelude to an anecdote, Dio casually notes, 'people were annoyed at seeing him a slave to his wife and freedmen'.[28] Suetonius also stresses the failure of an emperor who allows the affairs of state to drift out of his hands and into the control of his entourage:

> Completely under the control of [his freedmen] and his wives . . . , he acted the part not of a *princeps*, but of a servant, bestowing honours, army commands, pardons or punishments according to their interests or simply their desire or whim, and even that mostly in ignorance and naively.[29]

The fear was that if an imperial woman so chose, she might actually take over control of the state. The quotation from Tacitus at the head of this chapter more than illustrates such a concern over female domination.

The anxiety reached its greatest height when the imperial women violated what were seen as the primary functions of the emperor, thereby infringing upon his duty to the state and suggesting that power lay outside the emperor himself. Fundamental to the role of the emperor was his position as administrator of justice. As Millar (1977) and Talbert (1984), among others, have shown, the emperor had the right to hear cases as he saw fit, and he could exercise whatever amount of leniency he decided was appropriate.[30] Moreover, he was regarded as free to make his decisions in an arbitrary fashion, if he so chose, providing he was not seen to be overly-influenced by those outside the constitutionally defined political arena.

Consequently, the popular conception of the ideal emperor was the *princeps* who could be relied upon to exercise clemency and justice, two virtues which became central to imperial ideology. Thus, it became essential from the start of the principate that the emperor be seen to be acting in these areas as he chose, not as the imperial women dictated.

The examples of imperial women overstepping the bounds of acceptable influence in cases of jurisdiction permeate the literary sources, so I have chosen only a few to illustrate my point. The first is an early example: the Urgulania affair described by Tacitus.[31] Tiberius was sensitive to the risk of judicial abuse in his assessment of how to handle this case, which involved a friend of his mother, on whose behalf Livia had requested his intervention. He avoided a potentially embarrassing situation by arriving late at the trial. Asking for the support of the head of household in a court-case was not in any sense unusual or abnormal: as a friend and client, Urgulania deserved the family's protection. But all parties knew that if Tiberius had become involved, the imperial presence would have been tantamount to declaring Urgulania free from legal liability.

The crucial turning-point in judicial interference appears to take place under Claudius' reign, at a time when the emperor took a personal interest in a number of judicial cases and was involved in many prosecutions. The literary sources abound with examples of Messalina's and Agrippina's infamous abuses of the judicial system. Julia Livilla, Julia Drusi, Statilius Taurus, Domitia Lepida and many others, according to the senatorial tradition, all met their ends by the disgraceful manipulations of one or the other of these imperial consorts of the day.[32] Much of the hostility expressed toward Claudius' reign can be attributed to his alleged susceptibility to the influence of his wives and freedmen, specifically with regard to his judicial decisions. Cassius Dio pointedly upholds this tradition. For example, he notes Claudius' fondness for gladiatorial games and observes,

> After he had grown used to feasting his fill on blood and gore, he turned more readily to other kinds of murder. The imperial freedmen and Messalina were responsible for this: whenever they desired someone's death, they would terrify Claudius and as a result would be allowed to do anything they chose.[33]

Many of these accusations can be readily dismissed by sceptical modern readers, but their importance lies in what the authors (and presumably their ancient audience) thought *could* happen behind the closed doors of the imperial household. Through their household influence, the imperial women were believed to be able to dictate the judicial decisions of the court which most often dealt with senatorial cases.

Taking care of family clients and using private influence with the head of household for the benefit of those clients or others: these were the common pursuits of the traditional Roman Matron of the late Republic. At the core of most of the tales of female court intrigue is the presentation of behaviour which, in a politically different context, would have been expected from the women of such distinguished Roman families as the Julii and the Claudii. It was the change in the nature of the government which put the women in the position of being close to the centre of the state and laid them open both to the charges and to the actuality of being able to influence state affairs for personal gain: when the reins of the state were in the hands of only one man, then it became far easier for those without a constitutional office to have an effect on state decisions. As I suggested at the outset, it was this access to power, contrary to the social construct of the Roman Matron, which engendered the tension and anxiety seen in the senatorial sources. The portrayals of the imperial women, both the descriptions of their public behaviour as well as the anecdotes about their private lives, must be placed in the context of this conflict between approved roles for women and the threateningly powerful position of the imperial woman. Not all imperial women could achieve this power in reality, but due to the nature of the monarchy, they were all seen as having the potential to develop it.

THE IMPERIAL WOMEN AND THE STATE OF THE NATION

Thus the depictions of imperial women must be seen as more than simple historical presentations of individuals and their actions. The image of imperial women became weighed down by the expectations and fears of the male elite and so acquired added significance and symbolic meaning. Within the genre of history-writing (*historia*), these symbolic images became a standard motif, in part due to the nature of *historia* as a literary form in the imperial period. The aim of such literature had evolved under the Principate, so that its major concern was to explore relations between the emperor and the ruling classes (as seen by historians who were themselves members of that elite). The activities of the imperial women became a standard category which authors used to evaluate the quality of emperors. Thus, their consideration in historical literature was most often as one of a number of factors which depicted the quality and nature of a 'bad' ruler. By definition, 'good' emperors had wives and mothers they could control, who never overstepped boundaries set by convention. Yet, as shown above, even traditional behaviour was subject to reinterpretation when practised by an imperial woman: conventional or not, these women were now inherently a part of the Roman state, and a threat to good government as defined by Roman elite men. Like the wicked Sempronia examined at the start of this chapter, imperial women were often depicted as embodying all the attributes of the Roman Matron which they used to turn the world of the elite upside-down and to threaten the running of the state. In this way, historians such as Tacitus and Cassius Dio, writing after the Julio-Claudian dynasty, used 'bad' imperial women as symbols of a state in disorder.

The presentation of the imperial women as symbolic of the state of the nation occurred in contexts other than that of literature written more than forty years after the events described. There are clear signs that in the contemporary political scene, the images of the imperial women could hold a potent message for those concerned about the nature of central government and therefore there were careful attempts by those in power to control these images.

Suetonius credited Augustus with a recognition of the importance of manipulating the picture presented by his household and especially by his female relatives. The emperor was depicted as seeking to promote their image as conforming to the most traditional ideals, strikingly reminiscent of those proclaimed in epitaphs, like the one described above:

> In raising his daughter and granddaughters, he even had them taught spinning and weaving, and he prohibited them from saying or doing anything unless they did so openly and it was such as might be recorded in the household diary.[34]

Obviously the aim was to emphasise the traditional nature of Augustus' household and, by extension, his regime. Yet, just as Augustus' government was in reality a revolutionary new order, so was the women's behaviour seen as undermining the conservative ideal. Suetonius followed up this observation by reminding his readers of the fate of Augustus' daughter Julia and her daughter, both of whom were exiled for adultery.[35]

Other emperors strove to limit public displays which were suggestive of female power within the imperial order. Tiberius sought to constrain the public life of his mother Livia by refusing honours voted to her by the Senate and by preventing her from playing a prominent role on state occasions.[36] Claudius was also said to have prohibited the awarding of state honours to women of his household.[37] He thus promoted an image of himself as having Republican leanings.

Yet, at the same time, the imperial government also promoted the image of these women as symbols of the new political order. To ensure the survival of his new regime and the unrivalled position of the imperial family within the state, Augustus needed the concept of dynastic descent to be commonly accepted at Rome. The imperial women were used to symbolise the dynasty, an effective image because of their primary roles as mothers and consorts of emperors: it was, after all, their progeny who were to follow in Augustus' footsteps. Also, although the Roman elite may have feared the women's access to imperial power, the emperors must have felt that the women posed less of a threat than their male relatives, as women could not hold posts of authority, and therefore could not challenge the emperors directly for control of the Principate. In any case, it was clear from the outset that the prominent role of the Roman matron in the elite family meant that the imperial women could not simply be ignored, and so their public persona needed to be moulded into an image which would benefit the regime.

Within the confines of this chapter, I shall offer only a few examples. The first is the depiction of the women on state coinage, which was allowed not only by Augustus but also all subsequent emperors. These portraits were probably not intended to be seen as a new and strikingly innovative means of honouring the imperial women (few women had ever appeared on Roman coinage previously). For one thing, they were rarely depicted as themselves, but more usually, in the guise of Roman goddesses, such as Diana or Ceres.[38] Similarly, senior women of the family were depicted in relief sculptures on altars dedicated to the worship of the gods of the crossroads (the *lares*) and the spirit (*genius*) of Augustus throughout the city of Rome. Here they appear in an almost priestly capacity, helping their husbands perform rituals frequently associated with family events, such as the worship of the deified (deceased) emperor or even the appointment of a young prince as priest (*augur*). Thus, family occasions were elevated to the status of state affairs and celebrated within the state cult.[39]

Instead of being straightforward tributes to the women themselves, both coin and altar portraits present a complex picture of dynastic and religious significance. Although it is unclear who was responsible for these depictions, the images contained therein are consistent with other honours extended to the imperial women.[40] This suggests not only imperial acquiescence, but also the creation of a consistent ideology associated with their public persona. In allowing the use of portraits of these women in the context of state ideology, the emperors firmly bound the images of the female members of their family to the image of the Roman state and to themselves as dynastic rulers.

The promotion of these women as the embodiments of two ideals, as women and as symbols of the imperial order, encouraged the development of the concept of linking the imperial women with the state and helps to explain their appearance in the historical literature as symbolic of the nature of individual emperor's reigns. Not surprisingly, the reverse of the ideal was also used by ancient historians, so that the wives and mothers of discredited emperors were represented as Ideal Women Gone Bad (the Sempronia Syndrome).

At the heart of these representations lay the tension generated within Roman society by the imperial women's unusual status and the struggle to find a socially acceptable image and role for them. It is too simplistic to present the overall picture as being part of a conflict between the emperors, who were trying to promote dynastic government from above, and the Roman elite, who saw the women at the centre of the dynastic order as a threat to their own predominance. If this were the case, then few emperors would have permitted any public representations of their female relatives, as this would have damaged their own position with the senatorial order. In any case, such a picture is undermined by the fact that it was the Senate who voted honours to the women, while many emperors remained unsure of how prominent a role the women should be allowed in Roman society and the state. The various examples cited above of the symbolic importance of the imperial women suggest that both emperors and the elite felt highly ambivalent about the ideal place for imperial women within Roman society. Ultimately, no role could adequately rationalise their position within Roman power structures without there also being a change in elite perceptions of the Roman state and the place of women within its political structures. Therefore, the portrayal of these women in literary sources must be understood as a reaction to this tension and a product of the contradictory nature of the public role of the imperial women, which allowed the ideal matron access to the highest authority in the state.

NOTES

1. This article is substantially based on work presented in my doctoral thesis, see Fischler (1989). I wish to thank my colleagues Chris Wickham and Simon Esmond-Cleary for their help with the drafting of this paper, and especially Maria Wyke and Léonie Archer for their guidance, patience and editorial advice.
2. Tacitus, *Annales* (Tac., *Ann.*) 12.7.
3. For a recent, highly informative introduction to the social construction of gender, see Lorber and Farrell (1991). Also useful is Rosaldo and Lamphere (1974). Also see Spender (1989).

4.   For discussion of the significance to women of the differences between power and authority, see Rosaldo (1974), pp. 20–1.
5.   Sanday (1974) postulates that sexual antagonism develops or increases in societies in which there is a change in the sphere of activities of women resulting in an increase in their power or authority, without a belief system which legitimised or sanctioned power held by women, pp. 203–4.
6.   *Inscriptiones Latinae Selectae (ILS)* 8403 = Lefkowitz and Fant (1982), p. 133, no. 134.
7.   For the increase of wealth and slaves in Rome, see especially Hopkins (1978), pp. 8–56.
8.   Plutarch, *Life of Antony* (Plut., *Ant.*) 54.3–5.
9.   Another example from this period of an individual woman being praised for similar activities on behalf of her family during her husband's absence can be seen in the eulogy to Turia which was supposedly written by her husband (the so-called *Laudatio Turiae*), *Corpus Inscriptionum Latinarum (CIL)* 6.1527: her husband also commends her for her courageous intervention on his behalf with Lepidus, one of the generals who dominated Roman affairs during the proscriptions of 43 BC.
10. For example, Cicero appealed to Mucia Tertia, wife of the great general, Pompey, for her help in gaining Pompey's support, Cicero, *ad familiares* 5. 2; the people of Rome appealed to Caecilia Metella to intervene with Sulla, Plutarch, *Life of Sulla* 6.14–18; and Praecia was said to exercise such influence over Cornelius Cethegus that she could secure Lucullus' command in Cilicia, Plut., *Life of Lucullus* 6. See also Dixon (1988), esp. chapter 7.
11. Sallust, *The Catilinarian Conspiracy* (Sall., *Cat.*) 25.
12. As some scholars have attempted to do, see esp. R. Syme (1964), pp. 132–3, and, more recently, Boyd (1987). Both scholars, despite accepting that she has a symbolic importance within the text, nonetheless accept her existence as an historical personage. For further analysis of the ways Roman texts depicted 'aberrant' women as symbolic of social disorder, see Edwards (forthcoming).
13. Tac., *Ann.* 13.45
14. Syme (1958), p. 353.
15. A dominant theme of late Republican history, for example, note the assassination of Ti. Gracchus (133 BC) and other rebellious tribunes, as well as Julius Caesar (44 BC).
16. Augustus himself claimed to have restored the Republic *Res Gestae Divi Augusti (RG)* 34.1. Most introductions to the Principate discuss the so-called 'Republican facade'; for example, see Dudley (1962), pp. 124–7. For discussion of the imagery associated with maintaining this balancing act, see Zanker (1988).
17. Cassius Dio, *History of Rome* (Dio) 61.7.1–3.
18. The two case studies of the activities of Republican women provided by Carp (1986) support this scenario. Dixon (1983), pp. 91 ff., discusses the significance for gender roles of 'the absence of a clear distinction between the political and social areas of Roman life . . .'.
19. Thus the women's position was problematic regardless of their own person-

alities or activities. Nor was it simply a matter of the women progressing along a graduated scale from the private sphere to the public, *pace* Purcell (1986), pp. 87f. The honours which the women received were an attempt to legitimise their (unavoidable) access to central authority, see Fischler 1989), Ch. 11.

20. E.g. Dixon (1988), pp. 41–70, on the influence of mothers, primarily owing to their economic independence, cf. Dixon (1986) for the influence and support which Cicero's wife, Terentia, wielded within the family; Hallett (1984), less convincingly attributes the influence of women within Roman society overall to their familial role as daughters. For further elaboration of the argument presented here, see Fischler (1989), Chs 4, 9–10.

21. For epigraphic evidence of female patronage, see e.g. *ILS 8897* (Livia and Julia the Elder commemorated with their husbands as benefactors of two wealthy freedmen of Ephesus); *Inscriptiones Graecae ad res Romanas pertinentes* (*IGR*) 4.73 (the *demos* at Mytilene honoured Antonia Minor as patron); *IGR* 1.835 A and B (the demos of Thasos similarly honoured Livia and Julia the Elder). Epigraphic attestation of female intervention is much rarer (and would be unusual subject matter for a public inscription): Reynolds (1982), no. 13, records a letter of Augustus to the Samians, noting that Livia had requested that he grant them special honours. For more examples and further discussion, see Fischler (1989), pp. 58 ff.

22. Suetonius (Suet.), *Life of Otho* I.1.

23. Recounted by Josephus (b. AD 37/8), *Jewish Antiquities* 18.143; 156; 164–7; 179–86; 202–3; 236.

24. Dio 58.2.3.

25. For Messalina and Narcissus, see e.g. Suet., *Life of Claudius* 37 and Dio 60.14.3. Examples of Agrippina's association with him: Dio 60.33.3a; Tac., *Ann.* 12.57. Antonia Minor died before her freedman Pallas achieved his later standing under her son Claudius, but the younger Agrippina worked closely with him, Tac. *Ann.* 12.2; 3; 25; Dio *loc. cit.*

26. For evidence of Afranius Burrus' position as Livia's procurator, see Pflaum (1960/1), no. 13.

27. Burrus' loyalty to Agrippina, and his promotion over Geta and Rufrius Crispinus, Tac., *Ann.* 12.42.

28. Dio 60.28.2.

29. Suet., *Life of Claudius* 29.1.

30. Millar (1977), pp. 507 ff.; Talbert (1984), pp. 460–87.

31. Tac., *Ann.* 2.34.

32. For Messalina's instigation of Julia Livilla's death, see Dio 60.8.5. Julia Drusi's death was said to be due to Messalina's jealousy, Dio 60.18.4. Statilius Taurus was supposedly driven to suicide by Agrippina, Tac., *Ann.* 12.59. For further analysis, see Fischler (1989), pp. 346f.

33. Dio 60.14.1.

34. Suet., *Life of Augustus* 64.2.

35. Ibid., 65.1.

36. Tiberius rejected honours voted to her by the Senate, Suet., *Life of Tiberius* 26.2; 50.2–3; Tac., *Ann.* 1.14.1; Dio 57.12.4. For an example of Tiberius' attempts to limit her public prominence, see Dio 57.12.5.

37. Dio 60.12.5.

38. For example, for Julia as Diana, see Mattingly (1976), pp. 104–5, plate 4.2. For discussion of Diana as a patron-goddess of Augustus, see Zanker (1988), pp. 50–1; 66–7. For Livia as Ceres, see Mattingly (1976) I, p. 544, plate 14.8; 30–3, plate 22.20; pp. 34–43; 46–60.

39 Ryburg (1955), especially pp. 49–61 for iconographical analysis of altar reliefs depicting imperial women.

40. The overall picture is a complicated one associated with the development of the private household cult of the emperor into a new form of state worship. For greater detail, see Fischler (1989), pp. 251 ff. and for imperial ideology in general see Zanker (1988). Talbert (1984), pp. 379–82 provides a summary of the debate concerning who was responsible for choosing coin types.

8 Woman in the Mirror: The Rhetoric of Adornment in the Roman World*

Maria Wyke

The modern study of the female body in the ancient world is largely a study of reflections. In the metaphors of modern criticism, we do not gaze directly upon women of flesh and blood, instead we see women only indirectly in the mirror of discourses composed almost exclusively by men.[1] Thus two recent collections of essays on women in antiquity have stressed our confrontation with male constructions of the female by employing the terms 'reflections' or 'images' in their titles.[2] In this chapter I wish to survey some literary and visual texts of the Roman world which themselves articulate the female form as an image constructed in a mirror. For the Roman texts which describe the practice of female adornment, whether in a philosophical, medical, historical, comic or satiric context, hold up a mirror to the ancient world in which we see a woman who, before her own mirror, displays a body that has been 'made-up'.

In the Roman rhetoric of adornment the mirror is not, as in modern criticism, an evident metaphor for male constructions of the female. Instead the mirror is often treated literally as an actual instrument employed by women in the process of constructing *their own* body-image. Nevertheless, I would argue not only that the male rhetoric of female adornment belongs within the larger representational system that constructs the Roman concept of 'woman' but also that an exploration of that rhetoric helps elucidate the strategies of the larger system. The narratives of female adornment belong to many differing and historically bounded contexts which generate often inconsistent evaluations of the practice of painting and adorning the body. Yet a synchronic survey demonstrates that those narratives are all variously engaged with the female body as a prime site for the ideological struggle to construct a social and sexual identity for Roman women.

BEFORE THE MIRROR

The surface of the body is a site for the display of difference. Stylised adornment distinguishes human from animal, and civilised from savage.[3] In the Roman rhetoric of adornment, *cultus* or care of the body is necessary for the citizen. Although women were of citizen status, they could neither vote nor hold public office,[4] so the discourses of adornment centre on the male when defining the associated categories of humanity and citizenship. The Roman citizen must wash, cut his hair and beard, and eat adequately, otherwise he is no longer a citizen but a savage.[5] Thus, according to the Roman historian Livy, a man's unkempt beard and hair gave to his face the appearance of a wild beast.[6] The grooming of the *male* body defines visually the difference between cultured and brutish, and between city and country. To be physically groomed is to be urbane.[7]

By virtue of its direct contact with the outside world, the body is a necessary feature of social identity.[8] The Romans marked differences in age, status, class, sex, and religious or political role visibly with the colour-coding and decorative bands of their dress.[9] The Roman male citizen was defined through his body: the dignity and authority of a senator being constituted by his gait, his manner of wearing the toga, his oratorical delivery, his gestures.[10] In the practices of the Roman world, the surface of the male body is thus fully implicated in definitions of power and civic responsibility.

The surface of the body also operates importantly and paradoxically as a marker of the difference between male and female.[11] In the discourses of the Graeco-Roman world, the male is articulated as both human and citizen partly by virtue of his bodily appearance. The female, however, is denied full status as both human and citizen precisely through her portrayal as *essentially* a bodily being. In the Platonic dialogues, woman's nature is conventionally associated with bodily rather than mental functions, within a hierarchically-ordered distinction between the body and the soul. To have more concern for your body than your soul is, in Platonic philosophy, to act just like a woman and beneath the dignity of Man.[12]

In the Roman rhetoric of adornment, the mirror has a central role to play in the articulation of woman as essentially a bodily being and, constrained within the domain of the body, her self-image is constructed as the object of male sexual desire. The courtesan of Roman comedy, a character type inherited from the Greek dramatic tradition, is quintessentially a physical appearance. In a scene from a play by Plautus written for performance in the second century BC, the courtesan Philematium prepares her toilet on stage.[13] The conventions of the Roman stage require a male actor to play the part of the Greek 'woman' who attends to her appearance before a mirror. Any humour attached to such a scene is enhanced by a verbal play with the philosophical distinction between the value of externals (dress and adorn-

ment) and internals (soul or character). The maid is reluctant to assist in the
process of adornment because, she claims, a girl is sufficiently adorned
when dressed 'in charming behaviour'. When, however, she also claims
that it is not the clothing that lovers love, but its stuffing, the audience is
encouraged to think of naked female flesh as much as of naked female
character. Man as the subject observes woman as the erotic object, for the
girl's lover Philolaches is 'secretly' present on stage throughout the scene
as voyeur of and commentator on the process of adorning and is constantly
referred to as the person for whom that process is undertaken. Furthermore,
when the girl completes her toilet by kissing the mirror, she has joined with
the spectators (both lover and audience) in viewing herself as object. She
has identified herself both as an object of seduction and as happy critic of
that seductive object.[14]

Through descriptions of women's bodily adornment, a constellation of
negative values is attached to the female sex. Placed before her mirror,
woman is defined and recognised as less than a male citizen and disruptive
of his pursuits, irresponsibly frivolous and dangerously seductive. In another Plautine play of the second century BC, for example, humorous
generalisations about the labours undertaken by women to make themselves
a pleasing sight for men are placed in the mouths of two female characters.
The courtesan Adelphasium claims with some exasperation, and much
comic accumulation of activities, that as much effort or 'industry' is ex-
pended on the decking-out of a woman as on a ship: 'a whole community
could be kept more than busy by two women with their nightly, daily,
lifelong, and eternal need of being bedecked, bathed, dried, and prinked'.
The courtesan's companion Anterastilis, although she comes to the defence
of the female sex, effectively exposes even further the triviality of such
labours with the argument that women are like 'pickled fish' rather than
ships – requiring much preparation if they are to be rendered palatable for
male consumption.[15]

Thus, in the rhetorical strategies of Roman comedy, women's expendi-
ture of time in the cosmetic arts helps define the female gender as time-
wasting, frivolous, unconcerned with true civic life,[16] and as an inherently
sexual being, since female self-construction is read as part of a precise
seductive strategy to appeal to men.[17] Not only courtesans, however, but
also supposedly respectable and wealthy wives are felt to adhere to this
definition of womankind. In an early-second-century AD satire on the
whole monstrous race of women, the poet Juvenal includes among his
numerous examples of Roman women's evident lack of chastity the adulterous wife whose 'noxious preparations', whose 'sticky breadpacks' and
'heavy scents', cling to her poor husband as they sleep at night, so that an

apparently beautiful appearance may be offered to her lovers the next day. The entire process leading to her adulterous behaviour is seen as 'ridiculous' and 'disfiguring', the treatments leaving her not with a 'face' but a 'sore'.[18]

The surface of the body and its adornment also operate in these discourses as a site for articulating the constantly shifting and problematic boundaries of gender.[19] In an essay of the first century AD on the subject of consolation, the Stoic philosopher Seneca addresses his mother Helvia in her sorrow at his exile as one to whom the excuse of being a woman does not apply, because she has lacked 'all female flaws'. Among the vices which she does not possess, defiling the face with paints and cosmetics, and wearing jewellery or flimsy dresses, are ranked alongside unchastity and abortions. Modesty is instead Helvia's metaphoric adornment.[20] The cosmetic arts are thus expressly associated with aberrant sexual behaviour and with the rejection of the role of wife and mother. The woman who remains unadorned is permitted, in this moralising male discourse, to transcend the boundaries of her gender. If she cannot become an honorary man, she is at least raised above the massed ranks of women.

While the unpainted female may be raised above her sex and lauded, the painted male is reduced to a level below that of 'real' men and derided. In the Roman rhetoric of adornment a significant polarity is evident between male and female regarding the practice of caring for the body and its supposed purpose. Roman men are located within a much more limited category of acceptable practice than women, and those who stray beyond those limits are treated as transgressing the boundaries of their gender. Where Ovid deals with male *cultus* in his elegiac poem the *Ars Amatoria*, composed at the end of the first century BC, he confines male grooming to a smart toga, close-fitting shoes, well-cut hair and beard, neat nails and nostril hair, and sweet-smelling breath. All else, he claims, should be done by 'sexy girls' or the 'doubtful man' who seeks sex with another male.[21]

The wrong sort of attention to his appearance thus undermines a man's status as male and exposes him to the charges of effeminacy and sexual passivity and, consequently, of deliberately renouncing the privileges and powers of the masculine role.[22] Roman texts pay frequent and close scrutiny to details of male bodily appearance when in search of examples of lack of virility or male civic responsibility.[23] Seneca, for example, raises the question 'Who, among the effeminate youth of today, is sufficiently a man?', given that young men now 'compete with women in the softness of their bodies and cultivate themselves with sordid fineries'.[24] Such activities, Seneca argues, preclude these young men from engaging in any honest pursuit, and least of all in the celebrated practice of oratory.

In the Roman rhetoric of adornment, the mirror is thus employed in the process of constructing a female bodily and sexual identity, while, for men, the mirror can or ought to have a 'higher', intellectual purpose. Seneca writes, in a treatise of the first century AD, that the mirror used to be called the ornament of woman and condemns its current presence even in the baggage of soldiers. When attending to their *bodies*, he regards its use by the men of his day as appropriate for the production of 'good grooming' alone, rather than the erotic pleasures of physical self-observation. Otherwise, he claims, the mirror should be more appropriately used to care for and improve the male *mind*. When Seneca argues that the mirror was invented to observe the sun indirectly without harm to one's eyes, to know oneself, and to learn moral behaviour suited to one's self-observation, he employs the word *homo* which, as a gender-inclusive term meaning 'human', might seem to allow women access to the domain of these intellectual pursuits. The example which immediately follows, however, suggests that he is concerned only with men, for it is clearly gender-specific – it is the handsome *man* (*formosus*) who should look in the mirror to learn how to avoid infamy. The mirror is here an instrument for scientific observation, self-knowledge and moral improvement, but only in the hands of men. A contrast with the mirror as appropriate instrument for the improvement of the female *body* is implied in the claim that reflections surely do not exist in order that 'we men (*uiri*) may pluck out our whiskers in front of a mirror or make our faces smooth'.[25]

For men, the mirror can also aid a civic profession. In a first-century AD work on the education of orators, Quintilian notes that the illustrious Athenian orator Demosthenes used to practise his delivery in front of a large mirror.[26] He gazed into a mirror not to become a pleasing sight for or in himself, but to learn how to sway a jury effectively.[27]

These narratives suggest that, for women, time spent in front of a mirror is the preparation of a male-directed sexual identity sited on the surface of her adorned body. Woman is constructed and constructs herself as a physical appearance, an object to be gazed upon by men.[28] When man stands before the mirror, however, the reflection he sees is a self that can transcend the body. The mirror is supposed to aid male self-knowledge or the development of male civic authority, but not be an instrument for the production of his own or another's pleasure in his body.

DISFIGURING THE STATE

Many other Roman texts address the issue of female adornment in the terms of a supposedly 'natural' and 'traditional' difference between the sexes.

From early in Rome's history, a major category of legislation imposed constraints on the physical appearance and comportment of women. In 215 BC the Oppian law stated that no woman may carry on her person more than half an ounce of gold, wear garments with purple trim, or ride in carriages within one mile of the city of Rome except when participating in public ritual. Since the law had been instated as an emergency measure during wartime, its repeal was proposed in 195 BC by Marcus Fundanius and Lucius Valerius, although Marcus Porcius Cato advocated its retention.[29] More than 150 years later, in his history of Rome, Livy reconstructed the debate that was said to have taken place while the women of the city besieged the Forum.[30] Both those who defend the continued existence of the law and those who argue for its repeal make an appeal to a social definition of woman as a body surface, more animal than human, more child than adult, and treat constraints on female display as bound up with general issues of the limitations on female social freedoms and civic roles.[31] Thus, while the bodies of men may be used to mark their humanity and full citizenship, in the paradoxical rhetoric of adornment, the bodies of women are employed to mark their relative lack of these same qualities.

In Livy's reconstruction, Cato argues in defence of the law that female collective action against state legislation is a danger to the freedom of Rome's citizens – woman is by implication not a proper citizen, and is unable to comprehend civic responsibility. Woman is both 'uncontrollable nature' and 'untamed animal'. She initiates insurrection against the state for trivial, material reasons – to glitter in gold and purple. In Cato's rhetorical ploys, her obsession with adorning her body and displaying her wealth signals the entire state's submission to avarice and luxury. In reply, Valerius argues that women have had a beneficial public role to play in the state, as mediators, as contributors of their personal wealth to the state treasury, and in religious ritual. The sumptuary legislation, however, he describes as concerned with an issue which is peculiarly women's own. Women are little creatures – he uses the diminutive *mulierculae* – who are disturbed by small matters. Women can possess neither offices, priesthoods, military triumphs, decorations, nor the gifts and spoils of war. It is, therefore, 'elegance, adornment and finery' which are 'women's badges of honour'. The adornment of her body and its public display is thus treated as woman's social equivalent of public office. This is what constitutes the world of the woman and, because of her 'natural frailty', she asks that her world be ordered by her father or her husband.

In Livy's narrative, the two speakers agree that Roman women are traditionally and by nature different from and inferior to Roman men, and through their discussion of the Oppian law, they further disclose that woman's difference and inferiority is expressed visibly on the surface of her body. Woman's adorned body is thus a site of her social definition, and it is only in their relative evaluations of the role women can play in the Roman state that the speakers differ. Women are defined in a more visual, material and outward way than men.[32] In the context of narratives which explicitly construct gender difference, men are seen to create their social identity by extending out from their bodies to control a public domain. When contrasted with women, their civic, religious and military offices are viewed as higher-status, mental functions.[33] Women work with and within their bodies, gaining a limited and lower social status through physical self-cultivation.[34]

Writing in the first century AD on Italian agricultural practice, Columella offers an historical context for this definition of woman as non-citizen, or not fully citizen.[35] He places the sexual division of labour at the very origin of Roman culture, arguing that it is only right that the female sex has been provided for the care of the home, the male for out-of-doors and open-air activities, for the hardiness of the male has equipped him for the acquisition of food, the timidity of the female for its conservation and preparation. In the past, Columella continues, domestic duties were usually accomplished by the married woman, the fathers of families resting by the fireside from their public activities. Nowadays, however, women wallow in luxury and idleness to such an extent that they no longer supervise wool-work and spend their husbands' income on purchased dresses. The Roman woman's adorned body thus marks both her separation from full civic employment (to which she was, in fact, denied access) and her hindrance to male citizens who pursue it.[36] The frivolity of today's adorned wife is opposed to the dignity of her citizen husband, and her concern for luxury is opposed to the work ethic of the state.[37]

Columella circumscribes the adorned body of women within the temporal confines of 'today'. Many other Roman discourses also ascribe a history to woman's adorned body within a larger narrative of social decline, such that the woman's progressively more adorned body symbolises the progressively more degenerate state. Thus women are given access to the political system as symbols rather than agents. A well-known theme of Latin literature locates the initiation of the state's supposed moral ruin in the second century BC, around the time of the wars against Carthage, and attributes that decline to the influx of wealth from the East.[38] Much of Rome's culture (*cultus* in the broadest sense) was of Eastern, especially Greek, derivation. Linen, silk, Tyrian purple, perfumes, spices and jewellery were all imported from the East. Greek fashions in dress and coiffure were imitated at Rome. Practitioners of the cosmetic arts and the vocabulary of their practice were also of Greek extraction.[39]

Following a conceptual pattern in which the regimen of the body is thought to parallel the regimen of the state,[40] excessive care for the body is treated as symptomatic of the softening of the state's moral fibre. Seneca, for example, observes that when good fortune has spread luxury far and wide, people first take great pains with their personal appearance.[41] Since excessive care for the body, however nebulously and inconsistently defined for each of the sexes, is viewed as almost exclusively a feminine domain, woman's adorned body becomes, in this moralising discourse, the visible emblem of a whole network of social vices: luxury, extravagance, corruption and Orientalism. Thus while Seneca includes, in a list of the trophies of luxury, the tortoise-shell, precious tables, crystal and jewelled cups which men buy to decorate their houses, it is the women who adorn their own bodies, with pearls which consume men's fortunes, and expensive imported silks which, he claims, scarcely cover their wanton nakedness.[42] Similarly, Pliny the Elder, when recording in the first century AD that it costs the state 100 million sesterces every year to import perfumes from India, China and the Arabian peninsula, declares, 'so great a sum do our pleasures and our women cost us'. Woman as passive consumer of luxury goods is thus assimilated to the pleasures afforded by the foreign products she consumes.[43] Adorned in imported luxuries, the woman whose image is constructed in the mirror becomes herself a foreign commodity, and is defined through her body as all that is alien and pernicious to the traditionally-minded Roman male.

ADORNING THE COMMUNITY

No unifying logic attends the Roman rhetoric of adornment. Just as the body surface could be used inconsistently as a marker both of male humanity and citizenship and of the female lack of those qualities, so, within the realm of 'the woman's world', the body surface could act both as a symbol for the personal excesses thought to accompany social decline and as a site for the display of social status. For, as Valerius suggests in Livy's rendition of the debate concerning the Oppian law, the adornment and display of the surface of the body could be read as the exercise by women of some limited personal power and self-expression in the public domain of the Roman world.

In the visual arts, on funerary monuments for example, depictions of the process of being adorned operate iconographically to signify women of high social rank. The domestic realm within which women of leisure attended to their prescribed self-construction was put on public display as a tribute to their wealth or that of their husbands. A relief on a monument from the Roman province of Gallia Belgica dated to the third century AD represents the toilet of a matron (Plate 1). She sits on a delicately-worked wicker chair, her feet resting on a stool. Four servants stand in attendance, one of whom dresses her hair, while two of the others proffer perfumes and a mirror.[44] Gender interacts with status to determine the meaning of this representation. Although all the figures are implicated in a definition of woman as domestic and body-oriented, the labour of the maids is subordinated to the social status of the woman they serve.[45] The primary distinction displayed is not between male and female, but between slave and free.[46] Consumption rather than production defines the work of the free woman, and she becomes a luxury object in herself.[47]

Depictions on funerary monuments of the process of being adorned might signify women of high social rank, while depictions of the instruments of adornment might signify a lower-class woman's public profession. On a sepulchre found at Pisa and dedicated at the beginning of the second century AD by the mason P. Ferrarius to his wives Cecinia Digna and Numeria Massimilla, and to his son, are represented objects which visually differentiate the lives of male and female (Plate 2). On the right appear the tools of a mason's trade: ruler, plumb line, square and axe. On the left appear objects that define a woman's world: hairpin, mirror, comb, perfume bottle, curling iron and sandals.[48] Such monuments delimit women's social identity to the domain of the body, yet they may also honour the public profession of the dead, if they had been, for example, a commercial hairdresser or a dealer in perfumes.[49]

Thus, beyond the constraining narrative frame of discourses about the moral decline of the body politic, some visual space seems to have been allocated to the female toilet as an honorific, although limited, summation of Roman women's lives and social status. Furthermore, there are other specific contexts within which the process of female adornment was also viewed – however limitingly – as a marker of women's incorporation into the civic community rather than their exclusion from it. An element of the sacred could be attached to the care of the female, as well as the male, body. When a young man's beard was first cut by the barber, it was the occasion for a solemn religious ceremony. Similarly, a public ritual attended the preparation of a young girl for marriage, the unique occasion being put on visual display with a distinctive form of bridal dress and coiffure.[50] Thus both the young Roman male and the young Roman female performed a rite of passage through a unique act of grooming. For the male, however, this unique act of grooming signalled his passage to the status of adult citizen, while, for the female, it signalled her passage to marriage and a less direct connection with citizen status.

A story in Livy's history of Rome, however, demonstrates that a careful distinction was observed in the rhetoric of female adornment between unique practices of ceremonial adornment and the daily cultivation of the female form before a mirror. Livy tells the cautionary tale of Postumia, a Vestal Virgin, who was tried on a charge of sexual aberration in 420 BC. Suspicion had been aroused by her manner of speech and dress. On her acquittal, she was ordered by the High Priest to abstain from jokes and to cultivate an appearance which was holy rather than smart.[51] For the sacred status of the priestesses of Vesta was displayed visually in their costume, which consisted of the dress and hairstyle otherwise adopted by Roman women only on the day of their wedding,[52] and any departure by a Vestal from this special costume suggested a departure from her sacred, virginal status into the domain of sexual misconduct regularly associated, in moralising discourse, with Roman women's close attention to their physical appearance.

CRAFTING A WORK OF ART

Cultus is clearly an ambiguous term. Care for the body softens Roman citizens or civilises them, and marks the women of the city as excluded from or included in the civic community according to the social context and narrative framework within which adornment is viewed.[53] Thus disparagement of care for the female body and, therefore, of the woman who practises it, is least in evidence where the discourses of adornment associate woman with art.

The toiletry articles, in particular, of the Roman world – caskets, mirrors, and women's ornaments – literally display the adorned female body as a crafted object. A collection of 61 luxurious pieces from the fourth century AD, found on the Esquiline, includes the jewels and toiletry objects of a wealthy Roman family. A large bridal casket displays on a lid decorated with work in sheet silver the portrait busts of a husband and wife, Secundus and Projecta (Plate 3). On the front of the lid is shown the adornment of a semi-naked Venus, who combs her hair while small Cupids hold out offerings which include a mirror. Directly below, on the body of the casket, the clothed bride is displayed seated under a central arch and flanked by two servants holding a casket and a mirror. Around the remaining sides are seen other servants who assist the bride's toiletries with dishes, jugs, rich clothing, mirrors, torches and boxes.[54] Although the adornment of the unclothed Venus matches the adornment of the bride, and therefore suggests the bride's erotic possibilities, the process of adornment is safely contained within the sacred ritual of preparation for marriage. Moreover, the elaboration of the casket, designed to serve the aristocratic elite, associates the represented adornment and toiletry objects of the female body with the opulence and craftsmanship of the actual toiletry object on which that body is displayed.

Similarly, the bronze cover of a case which once held a mirror depicts in high relief an erotic scene. On a richly decorated bed, complete with four little figures carved on its back and floral motifs on its side, a woman and a man are seen in a sexual embrace (Plate 4). Whereas the male body is represented entirely unadorned, the female body is decked in a long necklace, armlets, bracelets, and anklets, and wears the elaborate hairstyle associated with the end of the first century AD.[55] Woman and bed are assimilated and displayed as the decorative furnishings on which man takes his pleasure.

Even the objects which adorned women's bodies were themselves crafted as, or decorated by, representations of an adorned female. The end of a hairpin dated to the Constantine era of the fourth century AD, for example, is delicately crafted in the shape of a woman (Plate 5). As both a material work of art and an instrument in the art of adornment, the tiny female bust is itself adorned with both a highly elaborate hair-style and a bronze necklace.[56]

Held in women's hands or displayed on women's bodies, these caskets, mirror-cases and hairpins all connect the adorned female body intimately with craftmanship. Through the toiletry objects that are handled, the ornaments that are worn and the cosmetics that are applied, the bodies of Roman women are visibly rendered luxury objects that are crafted ultimately for man's possession and pleasure.

In the Roman rhetoric of adornment, when the female body is literally connected with or incorporated into visual works of art (themselves usually crafted by and owned by men), it may become a welcome luxury object for the male viewer. Similarly, less disparagement may be attached to adornment when the bodies of women are associated metaphorically with verbal works of art, that is when the terms employed to describe the embellishment of female flesh are transferred to the embellishment of male texts. In the domain of ancient literary criticism, for example, the vocabulary of cosmetics – such as 'ornamentation' – was traditionally appropriated to define male styles of writing. By association with the moralising discourses that argue against any virtue in the practice of female adornment, these terms may take on a resonance of disapproval. In particular the absence of *fucus* or *fucatio* (the paints and powders of make-up) could signify the purity and veracity of a plain style of writing or speaking. So Cicero, in a treatise on oratory of the first century BC, praises the speeches of the consul Crassus as possessing 'a natural complexion' unmarred by the deceit of the paint-box[57] and Aulus Gellius, in the second century AD, argues that some types of prose and poetry can be made more resplendent with chaste and modest adornment, but become deceitful if painted and caked by the cosmetic arts.[58] Yet Cicero also describes his own writing-style without disparagement as one which utilizes the 'scent-box' of his Greek literary model Isocrates, all the 'rouge' of his pupils and some of Aristotle's 'paints'.[59] Thus, *cultus* either civilises or softens not only the Roman citizen and the body politic but also the written word.

It is perhaps Ovid, in two of his elegiac works composed at the end of the first century BC, who most provocatively and persistently removes the *cultus* and *ornatus* of the female body from the realm of moral disapproval. Drawing on the traditions of ancient literary criticism, both the *Medicamina Faciei Femineae* and *Ars Amatoria* Book 3 use the adorned body of women as a paradigm and extensive metaphor for the male creative process. Although these Ovidian texts are constructed explicitly as practical guides for women in the art of attracting men, the predominantly male audience at whom the poems would have been directed is provided with many opportunities to interpret the eulogies of bodily *cultus* addressed to the narrator's supposed female pupils as an implicit and witty eulogy of the *cultus* of the male poetic text. In the vocabulary employed by the narrative – such as 'raw materials', 'product', 'art', 'cultivation' or 'elegance', and 'decorum' – Ovid's readers are continually reminded of the simultaneous existence of these distinct levels of bodily and literary artistry. Since the adorned woman constructs herself as a work of art to which aesthetic categories may be applied and, within the author's elegiac narrative, is herself the poet's own artistic fiction, approval of her bodily *ars* may be read as approval of the elegiac text's *ars*.[60]

It is in such a context that the poet praises female *cultus* through the humorous inversion of the diatribes of the moralists. Here 'nature' does not demonstrate by contrast the artificiality and futility of women's self-cultivation and its supposed deceptiveness. 'Nature', instead, demonstrates by analogy the legitimacy of the *cultus* of the female body; by cultivation, sterile ground produces a harvest, grapes wine, and trees fruit. The unadorned Sabine women of Rome's rustic beginnings are made to embody the quality of boorishness rather than to display the purity and simplicity of the past over the immorality of the present. The cosmetic arts of women are presented humorously as the outcome of an uninterrupted progression from the primitivism of archaic Rome to the sophistication and modernity of the Augustan city.[61]

If we should ask why the poet produces such an apparently determined and unusual advocacy of cosmetics (and one which is to be immediately renounced in the *Remedia Amoris*), we will discover that the terms of female bodily *cultus* are being appropriated playfully and momentarily for the advocacy of male textual *cultus*. When appropriated to describe male creativity, the adorned woman takes on positive value and her body becomes a surface on which the male artist displays his literary skills.

THE ADORNED BODY'S DANGERS

In the more traditional discourses of adornment, men are given the power to paint gender definitions on to the bodies of women and then to erase the potential dangers which those definitions articulate. Women put on appearances and thus pose for men the problem of the relationship between reality and image, truth and falsehood. Thus, in the second century AD, following in the Greek tradition of diatribes against the deceptive artifice of cosmetics,[62] the doctor Galen distinguishes between good and bad cosmetic arts. As part of male-instigated medical practice, cosmetics preserve the body's natural beauty, but as part of women's bag of tricks, cosmetics attempt to bestow an unnatural, acquired beauty, by such procedures as whitening the face, and dyeing or curling the hair.[63]

In the *Remedia Amoris*, the final work of Ovid's cycle of erotic poems, where the first person narrator addresses himself explicitly to a male readership on the subject of curing oneself of love for a woman, the narrative reverts to this more traditional discursive pattern. The male poet demonstrates a capacity to deconstruct the contrivances of women for the apparent benefit of deluded male lovers. Thus, the Ovidian narrator portrays himself as a public champion of men, as a kind of medical practitioner who offers cures for love such as arriving early in the morning at the beloved's boudoir to catch her as yet unprotected by her cosmetic weapons or in the act of smearing herself with noxious substances whose powers are only transitory – for the constructed woman is described as falling apart when her cosmetic grease melts and 'flows into her warm lap'.[64] If a lover can be won over by a woman's *cultus*, the poet has the power to expose and undermine the female instruments of victory in his poetic narrative.

Here female adornment marks the women who are the subjects of the elegiac text disparagingly, as 'made-up'. The male writer locates on the surface of the woman's adorned body her gender definition as a construct designed to deceive men – 'the real girl', therefore, is the 'least part of herself'.[65] The male narrator and his male readership, however, are differentiated as 'real', for the elegiac text's express purpose is to take apart the construction of the female and to disclose to male lovers the attempted deceit. Similarly, some years earlier in the first century BC, the Epicurean poet Lucretius expresses the view that male love consists of an obsession with the image not the reality of women, and that to rationalise the male obsession with stage-managed Venuses is to be rid of it.[66] In recognising female constructedness, narrators and their addressees rise above it.[67] Men are neutral. Women are always the defined sex.[68]

Roman satirists frequently construct their diatribes as a direct assault on the credibility of the female sex, rather than as a warning to their male audience. This type of narrator, however, operates as a hyperbolically normative male who has the power to dismantle the mask that constitutes the deceitful female.[69] For example, Martial, a satirist of the first century AD, depicts his authorial role as that of a true mirror which exposes Maximina's three black teeth to full view.[70] Man thus becomes *explicitly* woman's mirror, telling her directly how to compose herself as physical object of the critical male gaze.[71] More dramatically still, this satirist also reduces the male act of seeing the true nature of the illusory, painted female to the level of a powerful sexual rejection. In poem 9.37, the old woman Galla possesses almost none of her original physical features. She is almost entirely a cosmetic construct. Her hair, her teeth, her clothes, her face are laid aside at night hidden in a hundred caskets.[72] Even the old woman's name 'Galla' suggests her lack of any real identity, since wigs were customarily made from hair imported from Gaul. By employing such cosmetic artifice, this creature is said to evince no respect for her worn-out body – symbolised here only by her cunt. But the poet, equipped with his 'one-eyed' prick, sees what she truly is and can therefore reject her sexual advances. Woman here is all sexual orifice wrapped in deceitful trappings, but man is pure phallus that recognises and escapes the bait.

As with his satires on painted women, the poet Martial places himself as narrator in a position of sexual power over the painted 'man'. In the hierarchical oppositions of one such satire, Martial is presented as Western, stiff, hairy, strong, an eagle, a lion and most importantly a man or 'brother', while his victim Charmenion is Eastern, sleek, smooth, feeble, a dove, a doe and most importantly almost a woman or 'sister'.[73] Satire once again clearly exposes the role of the body and its adornment in locating the boundaries of gender and its associated hierarchies of sexual and social power. Masculinity is both the unadorned face and the norm, and both the female and the 'doubtful' male are defined and subjugated by their visual difference from the unadorned male body.[74]

The Roman rhetoric of adornment thus uses the surface of the female body to define the social and sexual identity of woman as non-male, non-citizen and seductive trap. But interlinked with these issues of gender is the issue of power, for these texts effectively sustain a gender hierarchy and enact male control over the female, when the male narrative voice purports to expose to his readership the 'true' nature of woman, and suggests methods of exercising authority over her or avoiding her dangers.[75]

Thus while, from our perspective in the twentieth century, we search out a distinction between the representations and the realities of women's lives in antiquity, the Roman discourses of adornment already articulate the female as always unreal, as an image constructed in a mirror, and as the opposite and the inferior of the male. Furthermore, the narratives of adornment and their associated definitions of Roman women's social and sexual identities clearly 'paint' femininity on to the female form as a social 'tarnish' with a relatively arbitrary relation to real Roman women. A survey of the Roman rhetoric of adornment thus focuses attention on the superficiality and arbitrariness of the definitions of women displayed on the bodies with which male texts provide them.[76]

In these Roman discourses, the regulation of the adorned female body is bound up with the recognition of its otherness and its power to disrupt. Yet the narratives do not always leave their readers with a sense of male control successfully achieved over the adorned woman's latent dangers. One history of Rome imagines that when the head of Cicero was placed in the forum on the orders of Antony, in 43 BC, Antony's wife Fulvia tore out the tongue that had declaimed against her cause and pierced it laughingly with the pins she had used to decorate her hair.[77]

NOTES

I am very grateful to the co-editors of this volume, and to Duncan Kennedy, John Henderson and Jonathan Walters, for their comments on and criticisms of this chapter. I would also like to thank Roy Gibson for drawing my attention to some of the source material, and Maria Pia Malvezzi of the British School at Rome for her help in tracing the photographs reproduced here. I am grateful to the Faculty of Classics, Cambridge, for assistance towards the costs of the photographic reproductions.

1. See, for example, DuBois (1988), p. 36 on Greek texts and Wyke (1989), p. 25 on Roman.
2. Foley (1981); Cameron and Kuhrt (1983).
3. Lakoff and Scherr (1984), p. 158.
4. Gardner (1986), p. 262.
5. Dupont (1989), pp. 270–1.
6. Livy 2.23.4.
7. Dupont (1989), p. 295.
8. Turner (1984), p. 8.
9. Culham (1986), p. 239 and compare Dupont (1989), pp. 290–3.
10. Dupont (1989), pp. 269–70.
11. Lakoff and Scherr (1984), p. 161 and compare Chapkis (1986), p. 129.
12. Spelman (1982), pp. 109–27.
13. Plautus, *Mostellaria* 157–294.
14. Compare Barthel (1988), p. 60.
15. Plautus, *Poenulus* 203–31, and see Rosati (1985), pp. 12–13.
16. Rosati (1985), p. 10.
17. Rosati (1985), p. 12 and compare Virgili (1990), p. 20.
18. Juvenal 6.461–74, for which see Rosati (1985), p. 19 and Balsdon (1962), p. 262.
19. Compare Wilson (1985), p. 116 on modern fashion.
20. Seneca, *de consolatione* 16, and see Lefkowitz and Fant (1982), no. 148 for an English translation.
21. Ovid, *Ars Amatoria* 1.505–24.
22. Foucault (1985), pp. 18–19.
23. Veyne (1985), p. 30.
24. Seneca, *controversiae* 1, preface 8–9. For which see Richlin (1983), p. 3.
25. Seneca, *Naturales Quaestiones* 1.16–17.
26. Quintilian, *Institutio Oratoria* 11.3.68.
27. Compare Callahan (1964), p. 9 note 22.
28. Compare, on modern literature and art, La Belle (1988), p. 15 and p. 53; Berger (1972), p. 47.
29. On the significance of the *lex Oppia* see Culham (1982) and Culham (1986).
30. Livy 34.1–8. For an English version of the passage see Lefkowitz and Fant (1982), no. 191.
31. See Culham (1986), p. 235 and p. 238; Culham (1982), p. 791; Balsdon (1962), p. 33.
32. As, more generally, La Belle (1988), p. 14.
33. Compare Turner (1984), pp. 115–16 and Spelman (1981), pp. 120–1.
34. Compare Barthel (1988), p. 8 on Berger (1972), pp. 45–6.
35. In the preface to Columella, *de re rustica* 12. See also Maurin (1983), pp. 140–1.
36. Compare Rosati (1985), p. 10 on Greek views.
37. Maurin (1983), pp. 150–1.
38. See Maurin (1983), pp. 139–40.
39. Griffin (1976), especially pp. 92–4.
40. Turner (1984), p. 2.
41. Seneca, *epistulae* 114.9, on which see Rosati (1985), pp. 14–16 and Virgili (1990), p. 20.

42. Seneca, *de beneficiis* 7.9.
43. Pliny, *Historia Naturalis* 12.84. Compare Juvenal, *Satire* 6 and see Rosati (1985), p. 16.
44. Rheinisches Landesmuseum, reproduction in Museo della Civiltà, Romana inventory no. 2245. For a description of the relief, see Rome (1990), no. 40.
45. Kampen (1982), p. 73.
46. Compare Maurin (1983), pp. 147–8.
47. Compare the comments of Barthel (1988), p. 67 and p. 87, and Wilson (1985), pp. 50–2 on Thorstein Veblen's account of the leisured women of the late nineteenth century.
48. Florence, Galleria degli Uffizi, reproduction in Museo della Civiltà Romana, inventory no. 3416. See Rome (1990), no. 39.
49. For inscriptions commemorating women working in such trades see Treggiari (1979), pp. 65–86.
50. See Carcopino (1956), pp. 160–73 and Virgili (1990), p. 58.
51. Livy 4.44.11–12, on which see Balsdon (1962), p. 261.
52. See Beard (1980), especially p. 16 and p. 21.
53. Compare Dupont (1989), pp. 300–1.
54. London, British Museum, reproduction in Museo della Civiltà Romana inventory no. 2610. See Rome (1990), no. 223/1 and fig. 48, and Bandinelli (1971), pp. 98–102.
55. Rome, Antiquarium Comunale, inventory no. 13694 and see Rome (1990), no. 145.
56. Rome, Antiquarium Comunale inventory no. 18522 and see Rome (1990), no. 200.
57. Cicero, *Brutus* 162.
58. Aulus Gellius, *Noctes Atticae* 6.14.11. For further discussion of these and other texts which employ the terminology of cosmetics to describe stylistic adornment see especially Wiseman (1979), pp. 3–8.
59. Cicero, *epistulae ad Atticum* 2.1.1–2.
60. Compare Myerowitz (1985) and Ramage (1973), pp. 87–8.
61. See, for example, Rosati (1985), pp. 21–7; Virgili (1990), p. 28; Watson (1982).
62. For which see Foucault (1985), pp. 160–3 and Rosati (1985), p. 11.
63. Galen, *de compositione medicamentorum secundum locos*, Book 1, in *Opera omnia*, (ed.) C. G. Kuhn, 12.434–5. See also Rosati (1985), p. 20 and compare Virgili (1990), p. 22.
64. Ovid, *Remedia Amoris (RA)* 354 and see the commentary of Henderson (1979).
65. Ovid, *RA* 344.
66. Brown (1987), pp. 61–82.
67. Compare Henderson (1989), p. 55 and p. 62 on, respectively, Lucilius 1039–40 and Horace, *Sermones* 1.8.48–50.
68. Coward (1984), p. 30.
69. Richlin (1983), pp. 67–9 and Richlin (1984).
70. Martial 2.41.8.
71. Compare La Belle (1988), p. 27.
72. For a discussion of this poem see also Carcopino (1956), p. 172 and Rosati (1985), p. 14.

73.   Martial 10.65, and see Richlin (1983), pp. 136–8.
74.   Compare Chapkis (1986), p. 130.
75.   For the hierarchy of gendered values incorporated into the male narrative voice see Henderson (1989), p. 53.
76.   Compare on more recent discourses of adornment Chapkis (1986), p. 130 and Barthel (1988), p. 170.
77.   Dio Cassius 47.8.4.

9 Early Christianity and the Discourse of Female Desire
Averil Cameron

The most cursory reading of early Christian literature demonstrates that the representation of women presented major difficulties. They attracted attention from Christian writers – almost exclusively male – both as members of the Christian community and as the subject of discourse. Much of the latter was negative in character, expressing suspicion of the female and denying women a place equal to that of men in the Christian dispensation. Yet it coexisted not merely with a glorification of female virgins in general, and especially of the virgin mother of Jesus, but also with the description of the relation of the soul and God in explicitly sexual and bridal imagery. This chapter explores some of these tensions within the context of early Christian texts and asks what they mean in relation to early Christian attitudes to women. I use the term 'early Christian' rather broadly, since I shall be concerned not primarily with the New Testament period but with the centuries during which Christianity became the majority religion in the empire, and especially the period from Constantine (AD 306–37) to the sixth century.

The actual role of women in the first Christian communities, especially as seen in the New Testament ('earliest', or 'primitive' Christianity, in the specialist parlance), has been discussed at enormous length.[1] The focus lies especially on what can be deduced from the Gospels about Jesus's attitude to women, the passages in the Acts of the Apostles and, for example, the Epistle to the Romans, Chapter 16, which show women as playing an apparently influential role in the first Christian communities, and the various statements made by Paul about the proper place of women and about male/female relationships, especially the injunctions on female behaviour in church in I Corinthians 11, the prescriptions about sexual relationships in I Corinthians 7, and the famous statement of Galatians 3:28 ('there is neither male nor female; for ye are all one in Christ Jesus'). Whereas the genuine Pauline epistles are extremely early in the development of Christian thinking, even earlier than the Gospels,[2] the so-called Pastoral Epistles (I and II Timothy, Titus) represent a second stage, when Paul's still somewhat ambiguous position has crystallised into a much more developed set of negative attitudes. A large volume of scholarly literature has attempted to square the circle, and to recapture a lost Eden of early Christianity in which women were both active and prominent. No need to emphasise that the purpose behind such enquiries is not completely innocent, even when it is not actually presented in the forthright language of feminist theology; the search cannot be separated from a real and pressing practical issue in the church today, and indeed is sometimes explicitly expressed within the terms of those discussions. Christian feminist writers in particular are placed in a dilemma by the undoubted fact that so much of the later Christian tradition is so negative towards women, or even downright misogynistic, and have been at pains to justify their own agenda by appealing to an earliest phase that was much more positive. The American feminist theologian Elizabeth Schussler Fiorenza, in particular, does so by adopting an explicit methodology of 'remembering' this lost stage of female acceptance which lies buried under centuries of male rejection.

It is obvious that the project of studying the origins of a text-based religion to which many scholars are still committed, and in which the place of women is a highly sensitive issue today, is liable to import all kinds of preconceptions. Moreover, it implies the constant reexamination of the same, often ambiguous, texts. Indeed, it seems very doubtful whether further reexamination at this stage can produce any new results. But we can and should separate the search for the 'real' position of women in the early church from that of the way in which women are represented in early Christian discourse, which is where this chapter takes its starting point.[3] Leaving aside altogether the question of the role of women in the earliest church, I shall argue here that the concept of woman, in all its aspects, not only constituted a peculiarly problematic area within early Christian discourse but also provided certain convenient polarities round which other ideas could be expressed. This in its turn may help us to understand better the actual role of women in the first centuries of Christianity.

As we have seen, they had become problematic for Christian writers at a very early stage – certainly by the second century AD, when Tertullian was already writing in luridly misogynistic terms.[4] Both Tertullian at the end of the second century and Cyprian of Carthage in the third composed treatises in which women's dress, makeup and jewellery stood for concealment and deception, with the clear implication that women as such were liable to lead men into temptation.[5] Thus begins an overtly misogynistic strain in ancient and medieval Christian writing that lent itself readily to rhetorical play on real, as distinct from superficial, beauty, and which presented woman in the role of temptress originally associated with Eve.[6] Indeed, the latter theme is also to be found in second-century Christian texts, which already present the Incarnation of Christ as a reversal of the fall of Adam and Eve; for this

Eve is given the chief responsibility and, after her, women in general.[7] In this scenario, however, just as Christ was to be the second Adam, so Mary the mother of Jesus took on the role of the second Eve, that is, as Christ redeemed Adam, so Mary's purity was held to have cancelled out the sin of Eve.[8]

Thus even while presenting women in negative terms as the daughters of Eve, the early church also seemed to develop a more positive view, which it expressed in the concept of the Virgin Mary. Whether this was actually the case, we shall see later, after we have considered another apparent contradiction in early Christian representation of woman, namely its use of explicit bridal and even sexual imagery juxtaposed with the strong condemnation of female sexuality and promotion of the virginal ideal.

The area of textuality, often neglected in this regard, is of fundamental importance in understanding the development both of early Christian thought and practice. I wish to begin by considering the contrasting modes in which women are presented in early Christian writing. We may start with the condemnation of sexuality which formed such an important part of the strong ascetic ideal in the early church from at least the late first century onwards.[9]

It was not simply female sexuality that was to be abjured; nevertheless, temptation inevitably presented itself in the guise of a female. The classic text is the *Life of Antony* (an ascetic who died in AD 356), perhaps composed by the great fourth-century Father, Athanasius, but in any case one of the most influential of all Christian literary works. This text not only described the life of the man usually considered as the founder of monastic asceticism, but also laid down the parameters of an ascetic ideal for lay Christians of both sexes. Among those deeply influenced by it were Jerome, who brought it to ascetic circles in Rome in an early Latin translation, and Augustine, on whom it had a profound effect, featuring in the account of his conversion which he gives in the *Confessions*; it is interesting that the latter simply assumed that conversion entailed chastity henceforth. However, the influence exerted by the *Life of Antony* also went much wider, and its ideals percolated further than ecclesiastical circles as such.[10] Its vivid descriptions of Antony's struggles against the Devil can be read as representing the soul's desire for God, following on from the teachings of Origen in the third century. But Origen himself had advocated virginity as fundamental to the ascetic life, and Antony's temptations are seen in sharply physical terms.[11] It is striking that Antony's earliest experience of temptation at once presents him with the image of a seductress: 'The wretched Devil even dared to masquerade as a woman by night, merely in order to deceive Antony.' Ousted on this occasion, the Devil reappears to him in the form of a black boy, who is described as 'the lover of fornication'. It is explained that this first victory of Antony over the Devil represents the New Testament teaching of the primacy of spirit over flesh: thus through his Son, God is said to have 'condemned sin in the flesh'.[12] The conquest of lust for women thus comes early in the stages of Antony's ascetic progress, seen as belonging to the lowest level of the ascetic ascent. In his address to his followers he dismisses it out of hand as merely a preliminary:

> as to lusting after women or other sordid pleasure, we shall not entertain such at all, but turn our backs upon it as something transitory – ever fighting on and looking forward to the Day of Judgement. For the fear of greater things involved and the anxiety over torments invariably dissipate the fascination of pleasure and steady the wavering spirit.[13]

It is taken for granted that virginity is a mark of Christian virtue, and virgins are ranked together with martyrs as proofs of the faith: 'no one doubts when he sees the martyrs despising death for Christ's sake, or sees the virgins of the Church who for Christ's sake keep their bodies pure and undefiled'.[14]

To judge, however, from the collections of stories about the desert fathers who followed in Antony's footsteps in the late fourth and fifth centuries, it must be said that many seem to have been less successful than he was himself in rising above their susceptibility to the temptations of the female form. Take, for instance, the following passage about a certain John of Lycopolis:

> There was a monk, who lived in a cave in the nearest desert and had given proof of the strongest ascetic discipline . . . then the Tempter asked for him, as he did with Job, and in the evening presented him the image of a beautiful woman lost in the desert.[15]

They talk, and the ascetic is won over:

> He was frantic by now, like an excited stallion eager to mount a mare. But suddenly she gave a loud cry and vanished from his clutches, slipping away like a shadow. And the air resounded with a great peal of laughter.'

The moral is clear: 'Therefore, my children, it is not in our interest to have our dwellings near inhabited places, nor to associate with women.'

The forbidden sexuality, we see, is inextricably identified with the idea of women, who are seen as the bearers of temptation for unwary monks and hermits, and who must therefore be kept away from the places where the latter have made their home. It is a highly coloured view of the relations between the sexes, and one in which women – unless they have adopted the ascetic life themselves, and sometimes even then – occupy the roles of temptress and seductress.

Woman was seen, therefore, in terms of sexual allure, both as the object of male desire and as the subject, luring men astray. To insist on virginity was to control the dangers to which men felt themselves exposed. Of the responses of women themselves, we have little direct evidence, since nearly all the literature, including the fourth-century treatises on virginity and the works which praise women ascetics, is written by men,[16] but it is not surprising to find Christian women internalising this strong message and taking it over into their own lives. Thus in the later fourth century, when the ascetic ideal had taken firm root, we find many examples of Christian women enacting its precepts in their own lives. Significantly, many of those best-known to us (that is, most written-about) are the relatives or associates of the male writers who have recorded their lives. Macrina (d. AD 379), the sister of St Gregory of Nyssa and St Basil, and known to us through the *Life* composed by Gregory himself, is one of the most striking and best-known of these.[17]

It is very clear that as the theme of asceticism itself had allowed the author of the *Life of Antony* to develop certain textual ploys, that of female asceticism gives Gregory still more opportunities for underlining the polarities of gender. Unlike her many brothers, Macrina was of course not sent away from the family estates to be educated; her training, which she received from her mother, was in the Scriptures and the Psalms, her occupation sharing in the domestic work of the house (evidently, however, a very rich one). Thus Gregory can play on the idea that it was she who converted her intellectual and educated brother Basil (by dramatic irony one of the central figures in the development of an eastern monastic rule) to the 'true philosophy' of asceticism. Macrina, as a woman, stands for simplicity, the home rather than the world, the private rather than the public sphere, and the lack of (male) education. The *Life* is heavily indebted to Plato, especially to the *Phaedo*, in its description of Macrina's death, and like Diotima in the *Symposium*, it is Macrina who has the true philosophy of love, which is of course the love of God.[18] Gregory draws on a deep and familiar nexus of Platonic themes and imagery to give us a presentation of his sister which is idealised in every sense; nevertheless, whereas the discourse on love in the *Symposium* takes in the possibility of human and physical love as an allegory of spiritual union, the *Life of Macrina*, assuming from the beginning the rejection of human sexuality as a prerequisite of the spiritual life, finds an added dimension to the by-now familiar theme in that its central character, the model of spiritual knowledge and union with God, is not merely an ascetic but also, and piquantly, a woman.

Since women were inevitably associated with the idea of sex Macrina

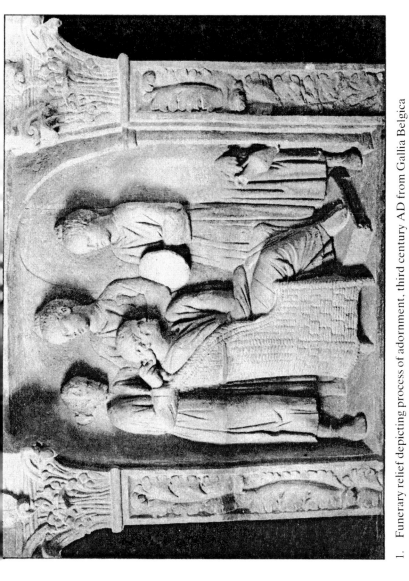

1. Funerary relief depicting process of adornment, third century AD from Gallia Belgica

2. Funerary relief depicting instruments of adornment, second century AD from Pisa

3. Bridal casket of Secundus and Projecta, depicting adornment of Venus and the bride, fourth century AD from Esquiline, Rome

4. (*above*) Bronze mirror case depicting erotic scene, first century AD

5. (*left*) Ivory female bust from end of a hairpin, fourth century AD

had to be virginal in order to represent the spiritual ideal. The thinking was not confined to Christianity; the late third-century Neoplatonist Porphyry, for example, addressed a lengthy treatise commending celibacy to his wife Marcella – we do not know how she reacted on receiving it.[19] Macrina is also presented in the context of an earlier and longstanding tradition of Christian virginity: Gregory explicitly recalls Thecla, the virgin heroine of the third-century apocryphal *Acts of Paul and Thecla*, set in apostolic times but reflecting a second and third-century enthusiasm for virginity. By now, the unhistorical Thecla had metamorphosed into a saint with an important local cult at Seleucia, but the context of the text in which her story was told was that of a real world of early Christian communities in which virgins, like widows, occupied a special and privileged place.[20] Thus the figure of Macrina as described for us by her brother Gregory draws at one and the same time on a real background of Christian practice, on the common ground of Christian and Neoplatonic thought, and on the textual field of gender and sexuality sharply drawn by previous Christian writers.

The latter in its turn exploited a discourse of love and desire for which the fundamental text was the Scriptural Song of Songs, on which Origen had already written a commentary in the third century. In apparently total contrast to the renunciation implied in the texts so far described, we here encounter an erotic imagery which is very explicit: 'Let him kiss me with the kisses of his mouth; for thy love is better than wine . . . his left hand is under my head, and his right hand doth embrace me.'[21]

The Song of Songs was to become one of the most commented on and most influential texts in the early Christian period.[22] It is a poem about love in a very physical sense, and perhaps on first sight a surprising model for ascetic writers to have chosen. In Origen's exegesis, the soul is the lover (the subject) and God the object of desire;[23] thus the roles are reversed, and the (female) soul is given the burden of desire. In later adaptations the Christian virgin is the subject, and Christ both the Beloved and the Lover. Woman is defined as the desirous subject, and the relation between subject and God as a relation of desire between female and male; the (female) soul desires union with God.

The Greek word *eros*, translated both as 'desire' and as 'love', allows for a reciprocal relation: God's love draws the soul towards union. But the detailed application of the imagery of the Song could produce surprising results, with the virgin envisaged as a nubile young girl, and her relation with Christ, the bridegroom, presented in openly erotic terms. Jerome quotes the very verse cited above in his notorious letter commending virginity; Christ is imagined as approaching the young daughter of Jerome's friend Paula through a crack in her wall.[24] In Jerome's application, the desirous subject manifests itself, as in the original Song, as a young female. But now, paradoxically, the girl must be virginal, while the object of desire is not a human being, but Christ the bridegroom, who nevertheless takes on the attributes and behaviour of a human lover. Although Jerome's own motives may sometimes seem somewhat suspect,[25] he writes within a well-established mode within the field of Christian textuality, according to which the desirous subject is female, while the object is the male God of Christianity or the male person in which He became incarnate.[26] But not only is the erotic imagery of the Bible utilised, exploited and allegorized in patristic writings; it is stood on its head and made to justify an ethic in which any real sexuality, let alone any actual eroticism, is denied and in which an erotic poem becomes a hymn to virginal spirituality.

The very theme of the Incarnation of Christ, implying physical birth from a woman, ensured that the issue of male–female relations would be enshrined in Christian texts. It was to a young woman that the angel announced the Incarnation, and to a young woman presented as the type of docility and submissiveness. At a very early stage the virtue of Mary, the mother of Jesus, was contrasted with Eve's role as temptress of Adam; as Christ came to save men, represented by the fallen Adam, so Mary quickly became the antithesis of Eve. Already in the second century the nexus is clear, but the logic had been implicit as soon as Paul had linked Christ with Adam; once expressed overtly, the balancing of Christ and Mary with Adam and Eve ran throughout early Christian and patristic writing.[27] It would be hard to exaggerate the implications for the Christian presentation of the female, but several obvious consequences spring to mind at once. In the first place, it is implied that women are normally to be associated with sin, and specifically with sexual temptation; thus abstinence becomes the logical way of neutralising this situation. Among others, Elaine Pagels has well described the crystallising of interpretation of the story of the fall in Genesis around the issue of sexuality, and the baroque excesses to which some Christian thinkers were led.[28] Thus the 'clothes of skins' which God gave to the fallen Adam and Eve could be seen as representing sexuality, or even marriage, while the related topics of whether or not they had enjoyed sexual relations in the Garden of Eden, and whether gender would be a part of the resurrection life in Paradise assumed at various times a burning importance. It was also assumed that Christ and Mary must both be virgins par excellence, with the corollary that the virginal life therefore also became the highest to which mere humans could aspire. It is striking that this ideal is thus defined from the beginning in negative terms.

We have so far identified both the negative view of woman in early Christianity, and the way in which erotic discourse could be put to use in reinforcing the ideal of abstinence. But there was yet another Christian presentation of woman, which came eventually to be enshrined in the figure of the Virgin Mary but which also appears in other connections; it is itself the reverse of the negative mode and, since it derives from it and is secondary to it, is correspondingly less common. This is what we may call the image of the saving female, woman as the saviour of man. Found in conjunction with a deep male suspicion of women as temptresses and whores, this too can take different forms, as is clearly apparent in the case of early Christianity. Though it is by no means confined to the discourse about the Virgin Mary, a highly ambivalent figure,[29] it is certainly immediately recognisable in that connection, especially in the later part of our period. Thus if the Devil was wont to appear in the form of a seductress, the Virgin was wont by that stage to appear as the virtuous woman who saved men from themselves. A young protégé of St Dositheus of Gaza in the sixth century, terrified by a picture of the torments of hell, was visited by a lady, who explained to him what he must do to avoid them: 'you must take up fasting, eat no meat and pray continually'.[30] Similar properties of help and consolation were attributed in the sixth century and later to the Virgin's pictures; in visions she was not usually so recognisable, and tended to appear as a mysterious but always beautiful lady.[31] A slightly different approach is found in a story from a seventh-century work, John Moschus' *Spiritual Meadow*, cited with approval by the supporters of icons during the Iconoclastic controversy, according to which a hermit on the Mount of Olives was tormented by a demon of lust who demanded that he stop bowing down to the icon of 'our Lady the Holy Theotokos Mary'; with the help of his abbot, the hermit was able to defy the demon and retain his loyalty to the picture. These stories are comparatively late in date, for the compassionate and maternal aspect of Mary with which we are familiar from so many later representations seems to have developed only gradually alongside the greater emphasis in the early literature on her virginity and her role as 'vessel of the Incarnation'. It is not an exaggeration to say that Thecla, the young virgin who never did become a mother, provided more of a female gender-model for Christianity in the early stages than did Mary. Significantly, the conception of Mary as the saving woman coincides both with the proliferation of icons and other images of Virgin and child which can be found in Byzantine art from the sixth century onwards and with the western collections of 'Mary miracles'.[32]

Nonetheless, it was not the only manifestation of an idealised male view of womanhood. We find another version in the immediately popular stories of female saints who had once been prostitutes. Mary Magdalene was the prototype for this group, which included Pelagia and Thais and in particular

Mary of Egypt; their popularity is demonstrated by the large number of versions of their stories.[33] They are typically repentant prostitutes who have become holy women and thus neutralised the dangers inherent in being female by complete renunciation of their sexual side. In doing so, they free the image of woman for safe adoption by male ascetics and by society at large, which is why such stories can and typically do coexist with a prevailing discourse which is profoundly negative. Since suspicion of women cannot after all be absolute, or there would be no procreation, it also tends to generate a supporting discourse which legitimates a more favourable view. Here too we may find the Virgin Mary intervening – thus we are told that St Mary of Egypt struggled with temptation for seventeen years, before she was helped by the Mother of God to change her ways and became so holy that she could walk across the waters of the River Jordan. Again, in these stories, the presumed reality of gender is concealed; the woman denies her sex and becomes like a man, sometimes literally so. Thus we often encounter female saints like the prostitute Pelagia who disguised themselves as men – Pelagia did so in order to become a desert hermit. But again, the very existence of such stories and indeed such practices only makes sense in the context of a prevailingly negative context. Like the type of the saving mother, they are secondary to a predominantly misogynistic view. Moreover, unlike the stories about the Virgin in which she appears as consoling and maternal, and thus at least presents a positive female image, having exploited their sexuality in their former lives, these repentant prostitutes henceforth typically attain holiness by denying it as completely as possible, thus attempting to attain the status of ascetic men. That the image of the 'honorary man' is also encountered frequently in the literature about the prominent Christian woman of the fourth and fifth-century aristocracy[34] in fact suggests that the image of the saving female, at least as interpreted in a positive sense, is after all less common than we might have thought. Alternatively it might be confined to the special case of the Virgin Mary, and even then is not obvious in the earlier stages of Christian writing about her. In general, we should perhaps conclude that even while individual Christian women, especially if they belonged to aristocratic circles, could find for themselves an active and honoured role, they must expect as the highest praise possible the statement that they had overcome their sex, or even that they were 'like a man'. The very textual advantages, which as we have seen a writer like Gregory of Nyssa could derive from having chosen a female subject, were themselves premised on the very fact that the general supposition about woman was so negative.

The central figure of the Virgin Mary displays features both typical and atypical of this situation. A male God with a virgin mother, attached to a creation story which laid blame for the sin of the whole human race on the first created woman, pointed in certain obvious directions. Women were at once the destroyers and the saviours of men; the latter role however was only to be realised through denial of their sexual side, which alone rendered them safe. There was nothing new about virgin mothers as such in the ancient world, where they appear in several other contexts.[35] But the linkage of the creation story of Adam and Eve, with its emphasis on the role of Eve, to the idea of redemption through the Incarnation meant that the Christian story imported a newly-compelling problematic to the familiar ingredients. This problematic, while it had already showed itself soon enough in certain quarters, became truly acute with the spreading vogue for asceticism which by the later fourth century was affecting the highest levels of church and society.[36] It was precisely at this time that the Virgin Mary began to attract serious attention in Christian writing and doctrinal discussion, and when in many cases the very same writers addressed themselves to new analyses of the Adam and Eve story in Genesis.[37]

Thus the now intense problems of gender and sexuality in Christian belief and practice were objectified in the figure of Mary, who also began to absorb the softer and safer aspects of womanhood that the desert fathers so roundly disallowed in real women.[38] However, if one can be permitted to differentiate chronologically between the texts of the late fourth and early fifth centuries and the miracle stories and Marian legends of the sixth and later, the objectification of the Virgin owed most in its first stages to the fact that she above all was held to have achieved the sublime state of sinlessness defined as non-sexuality. In contrast, we begin to see the domesticated Virgin in the familiar figure in the hagiography of the fifth, sixth and seventh centuries, who is also the prototype of the medieval *mater dolorosa* and of the blue-robed statues of Our Lady familiar in the Catholic tradition.[39] For the men who wrote the stories, it was highly congenial to sanitise the dangerous female element into a saving maternal figure, not only motherly but also safely virginal. By the sixth century the Virgin may have taken on these aspects even in the eyes of Christian women themselves, some of whom seem to have made her the special object of private devotion,[40] but she had not often been evoked in this way in connection with Paula, Melania, Olympias or the other rich ladies of the late fourth and early fifth centuries.[41]

The overall presentation of woman in early Christian texts is therefore a negative one, which is also a textual strategy. We can also see the importance of this textuality in the formation of Christian attitudes and practice in several other areas, some of which have already been explored. Thus the well-known early Christian rhetoric of misogyny can plausibly also be related to a rhetoric of power.[42] As yet, though, there are fewer analyses of this type of the many treatises on virginity produced especially in the course of the fourth century, though this would be a profitable line to follow.[43] More serious attention could also be given to the treatises on the subject of female dress, make-up and adornment, which expound the familiar idea of woman as alluring and deceitful; the traditional theme provided much scope for rhetorical play on the subject of what constituted real, as opposed to superficial, adornment; in the late fourth century Jerome and others, in conscious reversal, seriously expected their ascetic female circle to dress in sackcloth and regarded washing as a sign of undue attachment to sexual allure. Show of all kinds, except religious show, was to be eschewed; similarly the comforts of life – the model was to be Mary, not Martha. We should not underestimate the sheer pull of the rhetorical possibilities offered to a highly-skilled writer by the themes of asceticism and virginity, or, in turn, the powerful influence which this rhetoric exerted on actual behaviour.

Study of the rhetorical strategies of early Christian writing about the Virgin would also repay the effort. Like many of his predecessors, Jerome also links Eve and Mary in relation to discussion of the practice of virginity; as he puts it, 'death comes through Eve, life through Mary'.[44] But while there is a plentiful amount of literature on the figure and cult of the Virgin Mary, much of it has been produced by Catholic scholars with a technical interest in the subject. Useful studies do exist of the various social uses which the cult might serve at different times, and of its diachronic development, but again they tend not to unite psychological and social explanations with consideration of doctrinal and ideological factors; still less do they consider the very striking rhetorical strategies employed in these texts.[45] In general, again, the subject of the Virgin Mary is not given nearly enough prominence in the majority of the many discussions either of Christian asceticism or of women in early Christianity. On the other hand, we are now witnessing a considerable focusing of interest on the mechanics of charity and renunciation as practised by the wealthy Christian women of the late fourth century which is producing useful results in terms of the relation of theory and practice; however, though valuable, this discussion again does not usually address the issue as a whole.[46]

There is some danger in the fragmentation of the approaches which we have surveyed that we may lose sight of some of the basic issues which need to be highlighted in any consideration of the place of the discourse of female desire within early Christianity. I want therefore to return now to some fundamental features in Christian thought which help to explain why such a discourse became central and why gender itself seemed so problematic.

Whatever its origin, and leaving aside the contentious area of Christian origins and the relation of Jewish and Hellenistic elements in Christian thinking, the developed doctrine of the Incarnation rests on the notion of the tension between splitting and union, in Platonic language the problem of the one and the many.[47] How God could be divided into two natures, how the divine could relate to the human, and what was to be their relation, henceforth are questions at its heart. We have therefore a set of philosophical problems which are essentially Platonic in nature.[48] But the union/division was in the case of the doctrine of the Incarnation achieved through the primeval means of birth and motherhood. Mary therefore represented the means of separation; yet as Christian theology strove to emphasise the indivisibility of God in Christ, in time Mary herself came to stand for the image of maternal union. The title 'Mother of God' given to her at the Council of Ephesus (AD 431) set the seal on two paradoxes, namely that God could be both divine and human, and that Mary, as his mother, was to be thought of as both fully virgin and fully mother. At the heart of Christianity on this reading are the notions not only of the one and the many but also of the essential splitting that takes place in the process of birth, and which is irrevocably associated with female sexuality. Furthermore, Mary as mother represents reproductive desire, the desire to bear the child of the father; as we have seen, however, the eroticism of motherhood is muted into the paradoxical image of the Virgin as the Mother. The central problems of Christian doctrine focused in this way on the details of human parturition. Thus while it may seem odd or even distasteful to us, it is perfectly logical within the system that the same leading churchmen who debated the story of the fall in Genesis should also have argued over whether or not Mary's hymen remained intact during and after the birth of Jesus. In the same period a whole repertoire of images of marginality – door, ladder, dwelling, vessel, ark, sealed garden – was evolving in order to express the central paradox which she represented, and was fully in place by the time of the Council of Ephesus.

There was also a more philosophical dimension to the discussion expressed in a complex of ideas including those of union with God as the soul's aspiration and desire, love as a joining, putting back together what has been split, sexuality as an indicator of man's fallen condition, with asexuality as the heavenly or paradisal state and androgyny as nearer to that state than male or female sexuality. Like Christ and the church, so, according to the letter to the Ephesians, husband and wife become 'one flesh', 'a great mystery'.[49] But more commonly as time went on, this ideal of marriage as union gave way to the view that the only way to cancel out the disadvantages of male and female natures was through the virginal state itself, the 'life of the angels'. The notion of the virgin birth of Christ reinforced the notion of gender-difference as indicative of man's fall from grace; from the view that sexuality was part of man's fallen nature, it was only a small step to the conclusion that virginity was a necessary condition of success in the soul's desire for union with God. I would argue indeed that the Platonic language in which Christian theology was couched, together with its metaphysical arguments, was at least as important as any social factor in formulating early Christian attitudes to virginity and to women.[50]

The concept of union in terms of love and desire is basic to this Platonising Christian discourse, and indeed the fact that the dialogue where Plato's theory of love is most fully expressed is the *Symposium* was, as we have seen, not lost on Christian authors. At the turn of the third and fourth centuries, Bishop Methodius of Olympus produced his own version – a bizarre literary symposium on the theme of virginity at which the speakers are all female virgins.[51] Two generations later, Gregory of Nyssa describes the dying Macrina's imminent union with the divine in terms of erotic and bridal imagery: she made plain to those present the 'pure and divine desire (*eros*) for her invisible husband which she had nurtured hidden in the secret places of her soul, and revealed her heart's desire to be free of the chains of the body and hasten to be with the loved one';[52] the 'race' which she was running was 'truly towards her lover'. The description of the union of the soul with God is couched in the language of the Song of Songs, as Gregory himself expounded it in his commentary; but it is also the Platonic language of desire and union, based on the idea of the approach towards divine beauty.[53] We can begin to see how it is that early Christian discourse attaches so much importance to the concept of desire, *eros*, for it is desire which effects unification between human and divine, as between male and female, and which unites the world of man with that of the angels, and it is desire again which impels God to create the world, as it is desire which leads human souls to aspire to reach the higher beings on the hierarchy. We can also see why the Song of Songs, in particular with Origen's commentary, assumed such importance in fourth-century ideas of Christian love and marriage, for while the model of the bride in the Song of Songs, as representative of the soul in its aspiration towards God, placed the love relation at the heart of Christian understanding, the neutralisation of the erotic imagery of the Song into an understanding of the virginal state ensured that a positive Christian theory of marriage would be extremely difficult to formulate. Nearly all the elements in later Christian thinking on the subject are already present in Origen, especially the central idea that religious experience is to be read in terms of a mystic marriage of soul and God.[54] He was not afraid to adopt the language of the Song in all its physical implications, and to use it of mystical experience in a manner which leads directly to Ps. Dionysius the Areopagite and Maximus Confessor, two founders of orthodox mysticism.[55] Thus the erotic language of the Song of Songs passed into a profound religious understanding; at the same time, the complex of ideas of which it was a part, and the language in which they were expressed, had immediate consequences for early Christian attitudes towards the real relations between the sexes.

What we have then in early Christianity is a highly complex set of ideas, language and assumptions which together tended to focus suspicious attention on women as sexual beings. It is not just that early Christianity was misogynistic, or that women did or did not play a leadership role in the early church. Rather, we should be looking at the plasticity of the discourse itself as it developed over a long period, in different places and in different hands. All in all, it does not seem unfair to say that women did occupy a special place in the Christian discourse of desire, very little if any of which of course came from women themselves. The story of Eve, taken over by Christians, encapsulated male suspicion of women, and was far from completely neutralised by the attempts to rehabilitate Eve through Mary. Women continued to be seen both as being particularly desirous and as the objects of men's desire, and the denial of their sexuality as offering the best hopes of rendering them harmless in both guises.

Christianity is a religion heavily dependent on textuality, and I have tried here to emphasise the fundamental role played by Christian discourse in forming social attitudes, in contrast with the more usual scholarly strategy of marginalising theological writing and claiming that it had little impact outside a closed circle. Such a view both fails to do justice to the importance of the fact that all forms of Christianity presented a coherent and powerful world-view, understood on intellectual, emotional and practical levels, and forgets that this world-view was passed on orally, above all by preaching, as well as in written form. We have seen that in the case of the Virgin Mary, cult and piety followed on from christological issues; in the same way perceptions of woman too were shaped by theoretical considerations.

We have seen that gender did become problematic in early Christianity, and for several reasons. The male/female division is a paradigm of the problem of separation/difference implicit in the idea of God being born as man, and the assimilation of a Platonic philosophical vocabulary in which to describe it; the story of Adam and Eve, taken over by Christians from the Old Testament, strongly reinforced the idea of gender separation and all that goes with it, while at an early stage the language of *eros*, and the analogy of sexual love, was applied to spiritual experience. In turn, the increasingly emphasised ideal of asceticism, in which virginity was always a paramount ingredient, provided both a theoretical and a practical objectification of this difference. As a part of the textual basis of early Christianity, asceticism required its own discourse too which, given the social conditions of the time, was inevitably a discourse made by men. It was, in a paradoxical sense, a discourse of non-desire, neutralising and deflecting real sexual desire into safer outlets, and serving as a useful diversionary tactic against the actual subversive and revolutionary potential of Christian teaching. The actual discourse of *eros*/desire was reserved for God.

By these means, it became safe to describe religious experience, even the religious experience of young virgin girls, in explicitly erotic language. The relation between this erotic language, the advocacy of renunciation and the psychological influences in individual cases very much needs to be further investigated. Among other things, *eros* used in this way always implies an asymmetrical relation. The (female) soul ascends to knowledge of God. Women were placed low down on the ladder and had few spokesmen ready to promote them. Only with the greatest difficulty did Augustine manage to reach the conclusion that marriage was not actually intrinsically sinful. Not for nothing did the ladder become a symbol of the climb to divine knowledge. For a statement of *eros* in its highest and most intellectual form, but with profound implications for human relations, we may end with a quotation from the sixth-century mystical writer known as Ps. Dionysius the Areopagite:

> By *eros*, by which we mean the love which belongs to God, or to the angels or the intelligences, or to souls or natures, we understand a power of unification and connection, which impels higher beings to exercise their providence in relation to those below them, those of equal rank to maintain mutual relations and those who are at the bottom of the ladder to turn towards those who have more strength and who are placed above them.[56]

NOTES

1.   See e.g. Fiorenza (1983); Ruether (1979); Witherington III (1984, 1988) (the best recent discussion of the evidence).
2.   Thus it becomes a critical question to ask just what was Paul's own contribution to this set of ideas, as to Christian interpretation generally.
3.   See also Cameron (1990).
4.   See Clark (1983) for a very useful collection of texts.
5.   For these and later examples, see Bloch (1987).

6. See Ruether (1974); Bloch (1987); Pagels (1988).
7. Clark (1983).
8. Pagels (1988) brings out very well the political implications of this nexus of ideas.
9. Brown (1988) is the fullest and most vivid discussion. See also Brown (1986) and for the broader background, Veyne (1978, 1986); Dodds (1983), p. 34; Rousselle (1983); Lane Fox (1986), referring to Christian ascetics as 'over-achievers'.
10. See Harpham (1987); for a good introduction to the work, see Young (1983), pp. 81–3. The *Life of Antony* is the only non-Scriptural work recommended in a prescription for Christian reading laid down by St John Chrysostom.
11. For Origen, see Crouzel (1989).
12. *Life of Antony (Ant.)* 5–7; Rom. 8:3 f. (cited at *Ant.* 7); cf. Rom. 8:6; 'to be carnally minded is death, but to be spiritually minded is life and peace' and see Brown (1988), pp. 213 ff.
13. *Ant.* 19.
14. *Ant.* 79; Antony's sister was given over to nuns by her brother and remained a virgin (3, 54).
15. Ward and Russell (1980), pp. 56–7.
16. For an attempt to recapture early Christian women writers, see Wilson-Kastner *et al.* (1981), and see Clark (1986), pp. 124–71.
17. For the *Life* see Maraval (1983); see Momigliano (1985).
18. See Maraval (1983) intro., pp. 92 ff., esp. p. 98; cf. *Symposium (Symp.)* 204D; for Diotima, see Halperin (1990).
19. See Wicker (1987); other Neoplatonists also advocated ascetic practices, see e.g. Iamblichus, *On the Pythagorean Life* (Clark, 1989).
20. Thecla, see Brown (1988), pp. 156–9; apocryphal Acts and virgins in early Christian communities, Davies (1980).
21 Song of Songs 1:2; 2:6
22. See Clark (1986e); Consolino (1984); Cox (1986). Gregory of Nyssa and Jerome were among those who wrote commentaries on the Song. For bridal imagery in the Bible, Frye (1982).
23. Nevertheless, the erotic language is retained, extending to the use of the *topos* 'wounded by love' (cf. Isaiah 49:2, Song 2:5), so reminiscent of the classical Eros with his bow (see Crouzel [1989], p. 123). Crouzel (1989), p. 118 rightly argues against attempts to explain such language away.
24. *Epistles (Ep.)* 22.19.
25. Cf. Kelly (1975), who attributes much to his 'obsession with sex' and 'his troubled awareness of his sensual nature'.
26. Brown (1988), p. 274.
27. See Pagels (1988), xxi f., p. 62 f.; Clark (1986d). For Christ/Adam, see Rom. 5:14. The second-century writer Irenaeus develops the Eve–Mary theme, see the passages cited in Clark (1983), Ch. 1, esp. p. 38 ff.
28. Pagels (1988).
29. Warner (1976), and see Graef (1985); Brown *et al.* (1978) (with wider coverage than its title suggests).
30. Dorotheus of Gaza, *Discourses and Sayings*, trans. Wheeler (1977), p. 37.
31. Cameron (1991), Ch. 6.
32. See further, ibid.

33.	See Ward (1987); Brock and Harvey (1987).

34.	See Giannarelli (1980); Consolino (1986).

35.	For the Greek background and for discussion see Sissa (1987), pp. 97 ff. For the problems of the Gospel birth narratives and the Greek word *parthenos*, see Brown *et al.* (1978), pp 84 f., pp. 111f.; Sissa (1987), pp. 100f.

36.	Christian asceticism: Rousselle (1983); Brown (1988); see also Harpham (1987).

37.	Clark (1986d); Pagels (1988); Cameron, (1989). Origen had also written a *Commentary on Genesis* (see Crouzel [1989] p. 218).

38.	Carroll (1986) and others see the origins of the importance of the Virgin in the psychological need for the inclusion of a female element in the concept of Christian divinity. The two explanations are not mutually exclusive, but the earlier texts do not in fact lay stress on the maternal aspect.

39.	See Kristeva (1982) with (1986) pp. 164–5 (Mary as 'the prototype of love relationships' – based, however, on the later developments in Marian tradition).

40.	Herrin (1983).

41.	For whom see Giannarelli (1980); Consolino (1986); Clark (1984); Brown (1988), pp. 280ff.

42.	Pagels (1988); cf. Mann (1986).

43.	See Rousselle (1983), pp. 171ff. Among those who wrote on the subject were Gregory of Nyssa, Jerome and Ambrose; it was an easy step from praise of virginity to denigration of marriage (for which see also Jerome, *Ep.* 22.22, citing Tertullian, Cyprian, Damasus and Ambrose).

44.	*Ep.* 22.21.

45.	See especially Warner (1976).

46.	E.g. Brown (1982); Giardina (1988).

47.	Kristeva (1982), pp. 237, 250–1.

48.	See Mortley (1981, 1988).

49.	Ephesians 5:30–3.

50.	So also Mortley (1981), p. 77.

51.	Musurillo (1963); see Rousselle, (1983), p. 171; Brown (1988), pp. 183–8 (cf. p. 184 'a bare-faced pastiche of Plato's great work' – a strange judgement).

52.	Maraval (1983), 22.31ff., p. 215.

53.	Above, n. 18.

54.	See Crouzel (1989), pp. 141f., 118ff., 219f.

55.	See Lossky (1957), p. 192 and generally. Gregory of Nyssa is also a key author in this tradition.

56.	Ps. Dionys. Areop., *Divine Names*, 713 A–B.

10 Reading Between the Lines: Sarah and the Sacrifice of Isaac (Genesis, Chapter 22)

Sebastian Brock

The episode of the near-sacrifice of Isaac at the hands of his father Abraham, as recorded in Genesis 22, has elicited an immense variety of responses from readers and commentators over the centuries. Modern reactions to the biblical narrative are for the most part very different from those of the past, and indeed one can almost use the exegesis of this chapter as a mirror in which to discover the differing sensibilities of different ages reflected. This is possible largely thanks to the laconic starkness of the biblical narrative, admirably brought out in a famous passage by Erich Auerbach in his *Mimesis*,[1] where he contrasts the technique of the biblical narrator with that of Homer in the recognition scene in Book 19 of the *Odyssey*: in Homer we have 'externalised, uniformly illuminated phenomena . . . connected together, . . . thoughts and feelings completely expressed, events taking place in leisurely fashion, and with very little of suspense'. By contrast in Genesis we find 'the externalisation of only so much of the phenomena as is necessary for the purpose of the narrative . . . all else is left in obscurity; . . . thoughts and feelings remain unexpressed, are only suggested by the silence and the fragmentary speeches; the whole . . . remains mysterious and fraught with background'.

In such a passage, then, silence may well be significant. Does this also apply to the narrator's complete silence concerning Isaac's mother? This question, very rarely asked by modern commentators, was one in which both Jewish and (especially) Christian writers of the fourth, fifth and sixth centuries AD took a considerable interest, coming up in a few cases with a remarkably feminist interpretation.

The sources for the fourth to sixth centuries with which we shall be concerned are written in three different languages and they all come from the eastern Mediterranean littoral, modern Syria, Lebanon and Israel. All the texts are homiletic in character, and witness to a lively tradition of preaching in both synagogues and churches at that time;[2] those of Jewish provenance are written in Hebrew, while the Christian ones are either in Greek or in Syriac.[3] Several of the Christian texts are in verse, but it is probable that they were all used in a liturgical context. In the course of their homiletic retelling of the dramatic narrative they may introduce Sarah either at the departure of Abraham and Isaac, or at their return. Christian tradition tends to be more interested in the former, and Jewish in the latter. Reference to Sarah may also be made by Isaac at the site of the sacrifice. Why, during this particular period, there should have been a particular interest in the role of Sarah, is unclear, although once the topic had been introduced it clearly caught the imagination of preachers of both faiths (especially in fourth-century Syria there seems to have been considerable interaction between Synagogue and Church in matters of biblical interpretation).

The narrative of Genesis 22 hangs in the air, not obviously connected either with the events of Genesis 21 (the birth of Isaac), or with those of Genesis 23, which opens with the death of Sarah. Jewish exegetical tradition normally saw a close connection in time – and sometimes a causal connection as well – between the 'binding' (*Akedah*) of Isaac and the death of Sarah, and this explains why the Jewish homilists who introduce Sarah do so at the moment of Abraham and Isaac's return home. Connecting Sarah's death chronologically with the *Akedah* has a further exegetical consequence, for it allows the reader to deduce (by combining the data in Genesis 17:17 and 23:1) that Isaac was no child at the time of the *Akedah*, but was aged 37. On this understanding, no particular problem is raised about his leaving home with his father without his mother's notice, a matter which exercised the imagination of the many Christian (and a few Jewish) homilists who preferred to link the events of Genesis 22 with those of the preceding chapter (the birth of Isaac), and for whom, consequently, Isaac was still a young child.

THE DEPARTURE SCENE[4]

How then do these homilists portray Sarah? As far as the departure of Abraham and Isaac is concerned, the younger that Isaac is envisaged, the greater the problem posed: how did Abraham manage to extract him from his mother's care without the latter realising what he was about to do? A variety of different possibilities were envisaged:

– Abraham tells Sarah nothing, and the reason for this is given by the fourth-century Syriac poet Ephrem as follows: 'he did not reveal it to Sarah since he had not been ordered to reveal it'.[5]

– Abraham again tells Sarah nothing, but the reasons for this are put into

Abraham's own mouth. Thus an anonymous Syriac prose homily[6] from about the end of the fourth century has:

> So Abraham rose early and took his only-begotten son to set off, whither he did not know. He hid the secret from Sarah his wife. And why did he hide it from her, if not because he saw that God, who had told him, had not told her? Thus he perceived, discerning man that he was, that 'What God has kept hidden from her, it is not proper that I should reveal to her, lest I become someone who discloses his master's secrets. If God had known that it would have been advantageous to her to hear, then he would have told her in the same way as he told me; for he who revealed the matter to her when Isaac was given to us would have known to tell her now as well when he is being taken away from us. If God has not done anything about her now, then I am not going to cast vexation into her mind; for if I should reveal it while my Lord hides it, then I would be acting contrary to his will.

– Abraham once again tells Sarah nothing, but this time the homilist puts hypothetical words into Sarah's mouth in order to illustrate what she might have said, had her husband told her. This was a favourite device of the Greek homilists of the fourth and fifth centuries AD, and it is often linked with hypothetical speeches which the homilist also introduces so as to indicate what Abraham might have replied to God's seemingly outrageous command, had his faith and love of God not been so strong. In the unknown Greek author (fifth century?) designated today as Ephrem Graecus, Abraham considers it best not to tell Sarah since she would only raise a hullabaloo and try to hide her son; this writer then goes on to give the lament that Sarah might have uttered, if Abraham had told her:[7]

> Do not cut off this single bunch of grapes
> the only fruit that we have produced . . .
> do not harvest the single sheaf that we have borne . . .
> do not break the staff
> upon which we support ourselves . . . .

More often the homilist explains Abraham's action by attributing to him considerations such as in the following by Basil, bishop of Seleucia in Syria, who died c.459:[8] 'Though she is god-fearing, she is a mother: she might hide the child, or spoil the offering with her lamentations and tears. I'll comfort her afterwards.' Some writers of course cannot resist the opportunity to attribute to the patriarch a display of typical male chauvinism, alleging female weakness, and so on.

– A conversation between Sarah and Abraham may be introduced. Where
this is the case, there are two radically different ways in which the scenario
was handled: either Abraham resolutely conceals from Sarah his real intentions, or Sarah manages to extract from her husband his true purpose in
taking off her child. The first of these scenarios is the more common, and
is found in both Jewish and Christian sources, though handled in different
ways. Thus in a number of medieval Jewish writings (*Midrash ha-Gadhol*,
Sepher ha-Yashar, etc., perhaps based on older sources) Abraham tells
Sarah that he is taking Isaac off to school, to study with Melkizedek, who
is identified as Shem. Isaac's education is at stake, Abraham tells Sarah:[9]

> How long is your son going to be tied to your apron strings? He is already
> thirty seven years old and he has not been to school yet. Let him go off
> with me, and do you get together some provisions for the journey.

In the Christian homiletic tradition of the fifth and sixth centuries the
emphasis is rather different. An anonymous Syriac Dialogue Poem (*Soghitha*)
from this period introduces a lively altercation between husband and wife,
with Sarah suspicious from the outset:[10]

> Sarah says, 'What are you doing there,
> splitting that wood which you have in your hands?
> Might it be that you are going to sacrifice our son
> with that knife which you are sharpening?'

> Abram says, 'Sarah, be quiet,
> you are already upset, and you are vexing me;
> this is a hidden mystery
> which those who love only human kind cannot perceive.'

> [Sarah] 'You are not aware of how much I bore –
> the pains and birth pangs that accompanied his birth.
> Swear to me on him that he will not come to any harm,
> for he is my hope. Then take him and go.'

> [Abraham] 'The mighty God, in whom I believe,
> will act as a pledge to you for me, if you will believe it,
> that Isaac your son will quickly return
> and you will be comforted by his youthfulness.'

In the first of two anonymous verse homilies on Genesis 22 in Syriac,[11] the
long exchange between Sarah and Abraham at this point takes up over a
fifth of the entire poem. As Sarah sees Abraham and Isaac set off

terror seized her, and she spoke as follows:

'Where are you taking my only-begotten? Where is the child of my vows
 going?

Reveal to me the secret of your intention, and show me the journey on
 which you are both going . . . .

Why are you not revealing your secret to Sarah your faithful wife

who in all the hardships of exile has borne trials along with you?'

(lines 14–17).

Abraham tries to fob her off with an evasive reply,

'I wish to slaughter a lamb and offer a sacrifice to God.

At the fleece[12] which will come back with us you will give praise to God
 all the more . . .'.

(lines 28–9).

If it is just a sheep that Abraham wants to sacrifice, Sarah retorts, then why
does he have to take off Isaac:

'. . . Leave the child behind, lest something happen, and untimely death
 meet him,

for I am being unjustly deprived of the single son to whom I have given
 birth.

Let not the eye of his mother be darkened, seeing that after one hundred
 years light has shone out for me.

You are drunk with the love of God – who is your God and my God – and
 if he so bids you concerning the child, you would kill him without
 hesitation.'

(lines 34–38).

Abraham's final speech eventually manages to persuade Sarah to let Isaac
go, despite all her forebodings.

The only text of Greek origin to adopt this scenario is a homily of
uncertain date which survives only in Coptic translation, where it is attributed to Amphilochius, bishop of Iconium (died c.395).[13] Here Sarah over-
hears Abraham's instructions to the two young men who are to accompany
him. Unaware of the intended victim, Sarah begs to be allowed to join in
with the sacrifice. Abraham is put into a quandary: he imagines what Sarah
would say if he told her the truth, and so decides to keep his mouth shut.
Sarah then turns to Isaac and utters the following words, loaded with
prophetic irony:

Go, my beloved son, go with your father who has begotten you, and learn
to make offerings to God in this way . . . . Forthwith, you will bend your
knees to him and will throw yourself down on your face to the ground;

put your hands behind you, be as one who is bound, until the Good One may see you from heaven. And you will utter cries to God like a sheep that is to be led to the slaughter . . . . And now greet your mother and give a kiss on my mouth. Go with your father and return also with him in peace. For I trust that God will guard you and will also bring you both to me again. He who has given you to me as a present in hope, and who has called you in hope, will also return you to me. (lines 87–107)

In this homily Sarah remains to the last ignorant of Abraham's true intentions, but great emphasis is given to her own profound faith in God. Sarah's faith is brought out even more dramatically in the rare texts where she is portrayed as both aware of, and consenting to, God's bidding to Abraham. The seeds for this particular development were in fact sown in Ephrem's Commentary where he adds to the passage quoted above the following words:[14] '(Had Abraham told her) she would have been beseeching him that she might go and share in his sacrifice, just as he had made her share in the promise of his birth'. The possibilities raised by such an approach were taken up in the second of the two Syriac verse homilies on Genesis 22;[15] this is intriguingly a work for which there is some evidence, unfortunately ambiguous, that its author was a woman.[16] The writer, who clearly draws in places on the first verse homily (*Memra* I) and probably knows the *Soghitha* or dialogue poem, has Sarah question her husband suspiciously as he makes preparations:

Why are you sharpening your knife? What do you intend to slaughter with it?
This secret today – why have you hidden it from me?

(lines 15–16).

To which Abraham replies with characteristic male condescension:

This secret today – women cannot be aware of.

(line 18).

Sarah's reply is at first heavily dependent on *Memra* I but towards the end it develops in an entirely different way:

You are drunk with the love of God, who is the God of gods,
and if he so bids you concerning the child, you will kill him without hesitation:
let me go up with you to the burnt offering, and let me see my only child being sacrificed;
if you are going to bury him in the ground, I will dig the hole with my own hands,

and if you are going to build up stones, I will carry them on my
   shoulders;
the lock of my white hairs in old age will I provide for his bonds.
But if I cannot go up to see my only son being sacrificed
I will remain at the foot of the mountain until you have sacrificed him
   and come back.

(lines 23–30)

Sarah then proceeds to instruct Isaac how to act as the victim; unlike the
situation in the homily attributed to Amphilochius, she is perfectly aware of
what is to happen:

And if Abraham should actually sacrifice you, stretch out your neck
   before his knife;
stretch out your neck like a lamb, like a kid before the shearer.

(lines 35–6)

Having embraced her son, Sarah hands him over to Abraham, and the pair
set out on their awesome journey.

In the homiletic tradition as described thus far we have two antithetical
attitudes towards Sarah, the one (characteristic of most of the Greek sources)
portraying her in an entirely unsympathetic way and from a purely male
perspective, while the other (found notably in some of the Syriac texts)
shows much more sympathy for her, depicting her faith as at least on a par
with that of Abraham. A single Greek text, the hymn (*kontakion*) on Abraham
and Isaac by the great Byzantine poet Romanos (early sixth century),
remarkably combines both approaches.[17] First Romanos puts into Abraham's
mouth a hypothetical speech to illustrate what Abraham might have said,
had he not acted immediately in obedience to God's command; in the
course of this he introduces a second hypothetical speech, to illustrate how
Sarah, as a loving mother, might have reacted if she were told of Abraham's
true intentions. Then, in the middle of the poem, imagined speeches dramatically turn into reality, as Abraham suddenly rebukes Sarah:

Do not use words like that, woman, or you will anger God:
he is not asking us for anything that does not belong to him,
for he is simply taking what he earlier gave us.
Do not spoil the sacrificial offering with your lamentations;
do not weep, otherwise you will put a blemish on my sacrifice.

(verse 12)

Sarah's subsequent reply, addressed to Isaac rather than to her husband, is
in a vein which shows that all the imaginary speeches which have previ-

ously been put in her mouth are entirely unjustified: she assents to the sacrifice and thereby demonstrates that her faith in God and love for God are equal to Abraham's:

> If God desires you for life, he will give orders that you live;
> he who is the immortal Lord will not kill you.
> Now I shall boast: having offered you as a gift
> from my womb to him who gave you to me, I shall be blessed.[18]
> Go then, my child, and be a sacrifice to God,
> go with your father – or rather your slayer.
> But I have faith that your father will not become your slayer,
> for the Saviour of our souls alone is good.
>
> (verse 14)

ON THE MOUNTAIN

The second point in the narrative of Genesis 22 at which Sarah sometimes receives (indirect) mention is at the scene of the sacrifice itself. Here the homily attributed to Amphilochius is the only Greek text to introduce her, and this comes in God's words to Abraham: 'You indeed have brought the boy to me here; for her part, Sarah has not ceased to beseech me about him. So it is you whom I have honoured, and as for her, I have listened to her, I have saved the boy in order to return him to both of you as a gift' (lines 277–81). Some of the Syriac texts, however, have Isaac speak of his mother. Thus in the extended dialogue between Isaac and Abraham at the site of the sacrifice in the *Soghitha*, Isaac is made to introduce Sarah four separate times; first Isaac demands,

> Show me and explain – if that is possible –
> why you did not reveal to Sarah my mother
> the secret between you and the Lord,
> and why did you not take a lamb with us?
>
> (verse 19)

Then six stanzas later he comes back to this theme:

> If a miracle is about to be accomplished
> one at which angels and men will be amazed,
> what wrong did my aged mother do you,
> seeing that you did not tell her what you were going to do?
>
> (verse 25)

A little further on he stresses that he has come with Abraham only because Sarah's compassion has entrusted him to the Lord, and he returns to the thought of her again near the end of his long dialogue with Abraham:

> For three days now Sarah has been sitting
> in grief, looking out for us;
> offer up the sacrifice as you have been bidden:
> why are you doing nothing, but are gazing at me?
>
> (verse 33)

In the second Syriac verse homily (*Memra* II), by contrast, Isaac reminds his father:

> Sarah was wanting to see me when I was bound like a lamb,
> and she would have wept beside me with laments, and by her tears I
> would have received comfort.
> O my mother Sarah, I wish I could see you, and then be sacrificed!
>
> (lines 68–70)

THE RETURN HOME

The third place where Sarah may be introduced is at the homecoming. Once again the biblical narrative is entirely silent on this point, and the majority of the Christian homilists show no interest in remedying this silence. It is only some Jewish texts belonging to our general period of the fourth to sixth centuries, and the two Syriac *Memre* that take up this challenge. Jewish interest in this episode is readily explainable, given the connection in time which was seen between it and the death of Sarah. In some sources Sammael (Satan) arrives at Sarah's door before father and son can get there, and he maliciously informs Sarah that her husband has sacrificed her only son – whereupon she expires from shock.[19] In another account, in the Jewish homiletic collection known as *Pesikta de-Rab Kahana,* Sarah also dies from shock, but this time as a result of Isaac relating to her what had happened:

> When Isaac got back to his mother, she asked him: 'My son, what did your father do to you?' He replied, 'My father took me and led me up mountains and down the hills below them until he brought me finally to the top of one mountain where he built an altar, set up a pile of wood, arranged the kindling, bound me upon the altar, and took the knife into his hand to slay me. Had not the Holy One said to him "Lay not your hand upon the lad", I would have been slain.' His mother then said: 'Alas for

you, son of a mother so hapless that if the Holy One had not said "Lay not your hand upon the lad", you would have been slain.' Scarcely had she finished speaking when her soul left her. (26:3)[20]

A remarkably similar scenario appears in the Syriac *Memra* I, where Isaac replies to Sarah's questions about what had occurred as follows:

Why does your mind trouble you?
God indeed sent the lamb, and Abraham offered it to God in my place.
He stretched out his hand to the knife, and it reached the very neck of your darling
and had there not been the voice saying 'Abraham, raise your hand from the child',
I would yesterday have been killed, and they would have been looking for my bones in the fire.
So come now, give glory to him who kept your only son alive for you.
(lines 166–71)

In *Memra* I Sarah only faints from shock at what her son tells her. Eventually she recovers herself and gives Isaac a proper welcome home.

Memra II introduces a quite extraordinary new twist to the episode of the homecoming whereby Sarah's faith is tested a second time in a horrific way. The highly-charged passage deserves quoting at length:

Once he had arrived and reached home Abraham said to his son:
'O my son, please stay back for a little: I will go in and return to your mother,
and I will see how she receives me; I will spy out her mind and her thought.'
The old man returned and entered in peace: Sarah rose up to receive him,
she brought him a bowl to wash his feet and she began to say as follows:
'Welcome, blessed old man, husband who has loved God;
welcome, O happy one, who has sacrificed my child on the pyre;
welcome, O slaughterer, who did not spare the body of my only child
. . .
May the soul of my only child be accepted, for he hearkened to the words of his mother.
If only I were an eagle, or had the speed of a turtle-dove,
so that I might go and behold that place where my only child, my beloved, was sacrificed,
that I might see the place of his ashes, and see the site of his binding,
and bring back a little of his blood to be comforted by its smell.

I had some of his hair to place somewhere inside my clothes, and when
    grief overcame me I placed it over my eyes.
I had some of his clothes, so that I might imagine him, putting them in
    front of my eyes,
and when suffering sorrow overcame me I gained relief through gazing
    upon them.
If only I could behold his pyre, and the place where his bones were burnt,
and could bring a little of his ashes, and gaze on them always and be
    comforted.'
And as she stood, her heart mourning, her mind and thought intent,
    greatly upset with emotion, her mind dazed as she grieved,
the child suddenly returned, entering safe and sound. Sarah arose to
    receive him,
she embraced him and kissed him amid tears, and began to address him
    as follows:
'Welcome, my son, my beloved, welcome, child of my vows,
welcome, o corpse come to life . . . .'

(lines 94–128)

The author of this remarkable verse homily has, through her or his highly
imaginative treatment of the theme, successfully made Sarah – who never
receives a single mention in the biblical account – the true heroine of the
Akedah. Abraham's faith is indeed tested, but Sarah's is tested twice over,
and each time she emerges from the ordeal with immense dignity. Although
the person of Sarah is introduced into a number of much later literary
treatments of this biblical episode,[21] none of them, to my knowledge,
depicts her with such boldness, insight and sympathy.

    The primary concern of this essay has been simply to present some
unusual perceptions of a prominent biblical figure, taken from a little-
known area of early Jewish and Christian literature. Their interest lies in the
sharp contrast we discover here between the essentially male-oriented portrayal of Sarah that is found in the Jewish and the early Greek Christian
homiletic traditions and the much more sensitive handling of her character
in the Syriac writers (and above all in second of the two verse homilies,
Memra II). Do these unusual perceptions reflect a more affirmative attitude
to women within the early Syriac Christian society? Certainly there are
some indications that women may have played a more prominent role in
church life in the earliest (but alas extremely obscure) period, and in some
early Syriac literature we encounter an astonishing profusion of feminine
imagery, but by the fifth century (from when the texts presented here
probably date), the situation had changed, and women had become largely

marginalised in this society[22] – which makes the treatment of Sarah in *Memra* II all the more remarkable.

NOTES

1. Auerbach (1953), p. 9.
2. For the Jewish interpretation of Genesis 22, Spiegel (1969) provides an excellent introduction. For early Christian authors writing in Greek and Latin, the standard work is Lerch (1950); for Syriac writers, besides the references given below, see Brock (1981).
3. A detailed list of early Greek and Syriac texts can be found in Brock (1986), pp. 66–7.
4. Some of the materials presented here can also be found in Brock (1974), written without knowledge of the two Syriac verse homilies, and in Brock (1984, 1986).
5. Tonneau (1955), Section XX.
6. Edition and English translation in *Orientalia Lovanensia Periodica* 12 (1981), pp. 225–60.
7. Ed. S. I. Mercati (1915), verses 78, 80.
8. *Patrologia Graeca* 85, cols 107–8.
9. I borrow this delightful translation from J. Goldin's English translation of Spiegel (1969), pp. 48–9 (originally written in Hebrew).
10. Verses 5–8. Edition and German translation by B. Kirschner (1906), pp. 44–69.
11. This is *Memra* (= Verse Homily) I, edited and translated in Brock (1986).
12. The fleece is a feature confined to the two Syriac *memre*: perhaps the motif represents a distant reflection of the Greek legend of the Golden Fleece.
13. Edition and English translation by Van Rompay (1978), pp. 274–303.
14. For Ephrem's sympathy for Biblical women, see Brock (1985), pp. 140–4.
15. This is *Memra* II, edited and translated in Brock (1986).
16. For the technical evidence (which concerns a particular grammatical feature which, in its unvocalised form in the unique manuscript, is capable of being taken as either the normal feminine, or a rather rare masculine form), see Brock (1986), pp. 98–9.
17. It is likely that Romanos (who was from Homs in Syria) was bilingual in Greek and Syriac, and there are some indications that he may actually have known *Memra* II: see Brock (1986), pp. 91–6, and (1989).
18. The poet deliberately has Sarah anticipate Mary's words in Luke 1:48.
19. *Genesis Rabbah* 56:11; English translation in Freeman and Simon (1951), Vol. I.
20. English translation in Braude and Kapstein (1975).
21. E.g. in some Renaissance plays on the biblical theme (some references are given in Brock (1986), p. 99). For the role of Sarah in the Cretan play of that period entitled 'The Sacrifice of Abraham', see Alexiou (1989).
22. See Harvey (1983).

11 Public and Private Forms of Religious Commitment among Byzantine Women

Judith Herrin

The purpose of this chapter is to examine the development of the different forms of religious commitment expressed by women who lived in the Byzantine Empire between the sixth and eleventh centuries AD – a development predicated on their gradual exclusion from displays of public religiosity. Over this long period, as the Church consolidated its organisation through an administration grafted on to Roman imperial government, the ecclesiastical hierarchy of male bishops effectively excluded women from prominent public positions. This development can be traced through canonical rulings laid down at oecumenical and local church councils, which defined the Christian practice appropriate for women. It is also documented by women's participation in religious activities as recorded in a variety of sources, especially hagiographical.

In this process of exclusion, the seventh century marks an important stage. At the Council *in Trullo* held in 691/2 in Constantinople, restrictions additional to those that already existed on the public behaviour of women were decreed. The long-term consequences of these measures can be seen in the more private forms of devotion adopted by Byzantine women in the following mediaeval centuries.

In order to investigate this process, it is necessary to examine the legacy of early Christian practice and the models of female religious commitment inherited by Byzantine women. This forms the first section. It is also essential to establish the pattern of female life structures in the Byzantine period, within which women expressed their religiosity. These two sections precede the analysis of the gradual restriction of public roles for women and the growth of private forms of worship. It must be said, however, that a central problem exists in analysing the inheritance from the early Christian period. It is preserved in the generally misogynistic terms of male authors, who reveal their assumptions and self-consciousness clearly.[1] Unfortunately, very little written by women survives to reveal female self-consciousness. The account by Perpetua of her arrest and prison-stay as she awaited death is a notable exception. In the main, early Christian writings must be interpreted within the context of the then-prevailing patriarchal mentality which displays distinctly deprecating distrust of women.[2]

LEGACY AND MODELS

From earliest Christian times, women held a prominent place among those who followed Jesus and believed in him. He in turn accepted the service of Mary Magdalene, the reformed prostitute, and praised the faith of women, a faith which might procure miraculous cures. In addition to those women mentioned in the Gospel stories, St Paul recommended certain women to his correspondents, again in terms of their exemplary faith and value to the new religion. Through these New Testament stories women in later centuries learned of the importance attached to certain women by the founding fathers of their faith.

In both East and West, women devoted themselves to Christian practices even to the point of courting death, as did the slave girl Blandina at Lyon in 170, Febronia in fourth-century Nisibis, or Serena who incurred the antagonism of pagan senators in fifth-century Rome.[3] Through this commitment to the faith, four distinct roles for women developed in the early Christian period: that of martyr, dedicated virgin, women who served as *ministrae*, and those who acted as patrons of the faith. Of these, the martyrs occupied a very special place as women who suffered, like men, for their belief. Only under persecution could women realise an equality with men; neither the imperial authorities nor Christians themselves recognised any difference of sex in this context of suffering. Their stories were familiar and are known to have inspired Christian women of later centuries.

As persecution declined during the fourth century, this glorious aspect of equality was removed, although martyrdom remained a significant concept. It continued to inspire young women in fourth- and fifth-century Persia, or early-sixth-century Najran, who expressed an intense desire to embrace the same fate, going joyfully to Roman, Magian or Jewish tortures of the most humiliating and overtly sexual variety.[4] Their steadfastness in the face of a depraved cruelty, while shocking to onlookers of most religious persuasions, deeply impressed other Christians. The female martyr had become a model for later generations of Christian women.

Similarly, women who dedicated themselves to Christ, often at a young age, established a model of virginity which was to inspire women throughout the Byzantine period. Saint Thecla was an oft-cited case, an example of dedication to Christ overriding patriarchal family pressure to marry and to produce children. Another was St Macrina who at thirteen years, the age of marriage, insisted on a celibate vocation.[5] As an alternative to marriage, virginity was presented as a denial of the normal role of women. Others, such as Melania, sought to maintain their commitment to a chaste life after fulfilling the demands of marriage. Once children were grown, couples regularly agreed to separate in order to devote themselves to a celibate existence. Therasia and St Paulinus of Nola or Anastasia and the silver merchant, Andronikos, observed marriages based on virginity from the beginning and merely institutionalised their avoidance of sexual relations when they adopted separate celibate lives. Women who dedicated themselves to a celibate existence before marriage or without getting married often lived together in special houses under the care of bishops. Their presence increased the aura of holiness of such houses, but their vulnerability and dependence provoked problems associated with the *parthenoi syneisaktoi* or *subintroductae*, virgins who lived with celibate monks in spiritual relationships. Their existence is sparsely documented, for instance in the writings of St John Chrysostom, who condemned the practice while devoting considerable resources to support of virgins in Constantinople.[6]

Whatever the qualities displayed by women, even the most devout were denied priestly functions. Only in some of the unorthodox sects did women emerge as leaders; they taught, prophesied and spoke with tongues.[7] Yet references to women as *ministrae* seem to indicate at least some sort of official position within the early Christian communities. Some appear to have served as the female equivalent of presbyters in the guise of *presbytides*, or as female presidents, *prokathemenai*.[8]

Yet from the fourth century onward, as the Christian churches took control of their community of believers, the male hierarchy carefully restricted the public roles of women. It established that only elderly women at least over the age of 40 (originally over 60) and of known Christian character could ever hold office. Canons decreed at the council of Laodicaea banned women from any priestly role, and therefore from the sanctuary of the church. But some female officials were necessary to organise and induct other women converts, especially at their baptism. At the admission of adult women to the Christian community, decency required the presence of a female deacon who could guide the new believers through the ceremony of triple immersion. However, the gradual increase in the practice of infant baptism steadily reduced the need for deaconesses.

In addition to this activity in the world, deaconesses held positions of responsibility in nunneries; for example, the deaconesses Platonia and Bryene who ruled over 50 nuns in Nisibis.[9] They also on occasion were placed in charge of the young women who had dedicated their lives to

Christ, as for example, was the case for Justina in Antioch.[10] Sometimes a deaconess was also abbess. While monastic deaconesses might assist in running nunneries, their role as female leaders often remained limited. As deaconesses, they had very little public presence, although as individuals they evidently inspired others to adopt the monastic life as, for instance, with Febronia's reading aloud in Nisibis which made her the talk of the town.[11] As we shall discuss in the final section, the use of the title deaconess in the monastic context gradually eroded the public dimensions of the office and title.

The only other established order for women in the early Christian period was that of widows, a rank of righteous women who assisted the bishop and other clergy in their ecclesiastical duties. In contrast to deaconesses, they were not ordained and their precise roles are not closely defined. Nevertheless they occupied a special place in the church and appear to have devoted themselves to social work, probably undertaking charitable and funerary tasks connected with the care of sick women, laying out and mourning the dead. Before the rise of charitable associations linked with *diakoniai*, they may also have looked after the destitute, those suffering from leprosy and madness, or shipwrecked sailors and travellers who traditionally had a claim on ecclesiastical assistance. In the early Christian period, widows were supported by the church in special homes, *cherotropheia*, often associated with the houses for girls and young women who dedicated themselves to Christ.[12]

The public activity of female officials, deaconesses, widows and virgins, recognised and sustained by the official church, remained exceedingly limited and was not available to the great mass of women. For some, celibate communities provided an area of Christian devotion considered safer and more suitable. But even nunneries catered for only a very small number of Christian women. In the nunneries, however, those few women found an established tradition that went back to the earliest days of organised ascetic practice. From at least the third century onwards, perhaps earlier, celibate communities for women existed, often to accommodate female relatives of the founding fathers of eastern monasticism. St Antony placed his sister with such a community of pious women before he retired into the desert; Pachom's mother, who deplored his retreat, was similarly comforted by joining a group of women established close by. These early communities had produced great champions among the saints, martyrs and patrons of the early church, especially Thecla and Melania.[13]

The nunnery constituted one obvious outlet for female religious expression that was in some sense public. It provided a disciplined routine of communal religious life run by a female leader with the assistance of a priest who would bring in the eucharist. While it required outside intervention and could not function completely autonomously, it was not necessarily dominated by the secular clergy.

However, the most significant model for Byzantine women developed during the fifth century. This was the cult of the Virgin Mary, declared *Theotokos*, She who bore God, at the Council of Ephesus in 431. This accumulation of the highest honour ever accorded to a Christian woman, which combined an elevated public image with the more usual private and personal role of mother, forged a unique model. While the fact of the virgin birth remained an unresolved paradox, the Gospel depiction of Mary as an indisputably good woman as well as a mother added a novel dimension to the early Christian inheritance. It created a specific role for the Christian family. The cult was deepened by the 'miraculous' discovery of an icon of the Virgin and Child, allegedly painted by St Luke in Jerusalem and found by Empress Eudokia, wife of Theodosios II, between 443 and 461.

In due course, the theology established by the assembled bishops at the Third Oecumenical Council was integrated with relics associated with the Virgin, which further stimulated the new cult. Once identified as such, her veil and girdle were housed in special shrines, like the one constructed by Emperor Leo I and his wife Verina at Blachernai just outside the walls of Constantinople.[14] Similarly, icons commemorating the holy family commanded new chapels and even new ecclesiastical foundations; the church of the Virgin at Jerusalem had a beautiful icon which was held to be responsible for the conversion of St Mary the Egyptian.[15]

This zeal for the holy family of Christ in turn associated holiness with the everyday context of family circumstances, well known to the majority of women.[16] It encouraged a saintly role for women within a purely domestic context. It strengthened a particular aspect of holiness, which male ecclesiastics enjoined on every Christian family. So, behind the outpouring of praise in honour of the *Theotokos*, it seems that the church promoted the cult in part because it inspired a model of maternal and familial Christian dedication. Even when they married and became mothers, women were assured that they could aspire to a truly Christian life.

Note should be taken, however, of the fact that men in general considered their 'sisters in the Lord' as essentially unreliable, prone to impulsive action and therefore not to be trusted with serious responsibilities. Although mothers were encouraged to attend to their children's education, they were simultaneously enjoined always to love and support their husbands.[17] Their subordination to their male relations was uniformly presumed and was an essential characteristic of the holy Christian family.

Within this context, the most women could aspire to, even when they

were of irreproachable orthodoxy, was to command respect as very pious
followers of Christ, or to protect and patronise the new faith with their
private wealth.[18] This becomes even more evident after the acknowledge-
ment of the Christian God by Constantine I (sole emperor, 324–37), when
the establishment of Christianity as a state religion was achieved by a male
hierarchy, which marginalised the official roles of female believers. As
Ashbrook Harvey (1983) has shown, female symbols and models of feminine power were gradually corrupted and adapted to conform to male
ideas.[19] Biblical misogyny and Roman patriarchy in combination with early
Christian male distrust of women proved too powerful for women to assert
any equivalence with their Christian brothers.

So however exemplary their devotions, Christian women were characterised as inferior to their male relatives. Yet there is considerable evidence
that many families were converted by their womenfolk, and that imperial
society was won for Christianity partly through the activity of female
adherents.[20] Similarly, women privileged by personal riches continued to
'lead' by virtue of their social prominence and relative independence. The
example of Helena, Constantine I's mother, who 'discovered' the True
Cross during a pilgrimage to Jerusalem and founded the Church of the Holy
Sepulchre over Christ's grave, was followed by other women. Helena's
patronage also established another model for women, for she was later
recognised as a saint and elevated to a status comparable to that of the
earlier martyrs.

In this way, an exclusively male Christian hierarchy celebrated two types
of good woman, martyr and saint. These women's lives were commemorated and their behaviour was recalled in annual liturgies and both public
and private devotions. Christian women also inherited a tradition of service
dedicated towards the relief of poverty and illness, creating forms of a more
private religious expression that were open to all. Yet their religious experience remained lowly, conforming more to the pattern of serving and
obedient women than to that of Mary Magdalene, the reformed prostitute,
or Mary, the virgin mother. The all-male structure of authority which thus
excluded women from leadership roles, also confined them to familiar,
often domestic, activities.[21]

FEMALE LIFE-STRUCTURES

The majority of women could avoid neither the biological nor the social
role of motherhood. It is particularly important, therefore, in this survey of
female life-structures to investigate the religious commitment of married

women as well as that of the usually more closely-scrutinised celibate virgins.

For most women the family setting of Christian devotion was a necessity. Unlike St Febronia, who allegedly was dedicated to a nunnery at the age of two in early-fourth-century Nisibis, very few Christian women were shielded from the world and conventional lifestyles.[22] Most were born into families that sought to provide them with a modicum of education and training in domestic tasks as a suitable preparation for marriage. Mothers regularly taught their children, a duty stressed by Polycarp as early as the second century, and practised by women like Euphemia, who instructed her daughter Mary in 'psalmody, the Scriptures and writing . . . since her early youth'.[23]

Mothers also initiated the girls to women's work, usually defined as spinning and weaving, though in a rural context it could include agricultural tasks.[24] In some cases, they also imparted a professional training, for instance, as an entertainer, innkeeper or prostitute. The categories obviously overlapped in the upbringing of Theodora, wife of Emperor Justinian.[25] Similarly, Elpidia, grandmother of St Theodore of Sykeon, instructed her daughter (his mother) in the running of an inn.[26] Despite the emphasis on education, the ultimate aim of Byzantine parents was to marry off their daughters, without consulting them too closely, on the most favourable terms available. Female relatives, particularly grandmothers, often played a vital role in marriage arrangements.

At her marriage a Byzantine woman acquired her own property in the form of her dowry and gifts from her husband. Even if they were in fact controlled by him, legally they belonged to her and could not be alienated without her express permission. She also had the right to bequeath them as she wished. Normally, her children would benefit, for children were the chief aim of every marriage and failure to procreate was deplored and lamented.[27] Of course, husbands regularly abused female ownership and the legal records are full of women defrauded of their own possessions.[28] But the fact that women officially controlled some property, however exiguous, granted them a certain security. For instance, if they were widowed, it enabled them to negotiate a second marriage of their own choice.

Within this traditional life-structure there were therefore two points at which a woman could try to impose the dictates of her own religious feelings, and both were occasioned by the prospect of marriage. Since girls were often betrothed very young (at any age over seven) and could be married at 13, it was unusual for them to resist parental and social pressures. Saint Macrina, however, used the fact that she had been engaged from the age of 12 to a young man who subsequently died as a reason for not entering another marriage alliance. She considered the dead fiancé as someone away on a voyage and persisted in devoting herself to God.[29] The threat of marriage and ensuring procreation frequently prompted women to assert their spiritual vocation. Since celibacy was still held to be superior to the exercise of sexuality, they continued to commit their virginity to Christ in a ceremony that established the spiritual equivalent of marriage. It was accompanied by all the actions and vocabulary of a secular wedding, including the ritual washing, anointing with oil, dressing, wearing both wedding rings and crowns, with even the notion of marriage feasts and celestial bedchambers. The *Lives* of the Persian martyr Martha and of St Febronia provide telling examples of this vocabulary.[30]

Denial of marriage constituted the most serious disruption of what was normally expected of women. By their choice of singleness rather than family, they insisted upon the legitimate alternative of religious commitment. Their relatives sometimes objected and tried to prevent it, especially when a young heiress proposed to distribute her wealth to the poor or donate it to the church. But since self-dedication to God was always recognised as a worthy Christian act, there were also social pressures in support of women taking this step, however unacceptable it seemed to the immediate family.[31]

Once widowed or divorced for one of the causes that carried no ecclesiastical penalty, for example, proven infertility, women could – and often did – refuse to remarry. At this stage, particularly well-documented among women later commemorated as saints, the expression of a strong religious commitment could transform the regular pattern of female existence. The determination to retire from the world into a nunnery and pursue Christian devotion could be sustained even against serious objections. Those who successfully did so might also persuade their families to embrace the Christian life. Saint Matrona, however, simply entrusted her young daughter Theodote to a friend, Susanna, and went off to practise *ascesis*.[32]

The first of these disruptions (refusal to marry) is widely documented in hagiographic sources, which also record an identical process among devout young men. Even girls below the age at which they were expected to agree to be married are supposed to have declared themselves already betrothed to Christ and therefore not free to contract a regular marriage.[33] At their official entry to a nunnery they also became brides of Christ in ceremonies that symbolised spiritual marriage. The process of cutting their hair and putting on black robes (the equivalent to monastic tonsure and habit) marked this new stage in their lives.

For those young women who were unable to avoid the arrangements made for their marriage, there was an outside chance but only a very slight possibility, that their husbands had also been through a similar process.

Melania the Younger hoped in vain that this would save her from the dynastic union forced upon her by her parents.[34] For young men also experienced the desire to commit themselves to Christ and to adopt ascetic practices that 'tamed the demons of sexuality'.[35] When arranged marriages denied them this possibility, and then they found their marriage partners similarly inclined, it was, to judge from our sources, indeed a happy coincidence! Such a discovery was accompanied by great thanksgiving on the wedding night and an agreement to observe continued virginity. But the parents, who expected and desired grandchildren from the union, strenuously condemned this type of opposition.[36]

Generally, however, Byzantine women had to follow the prescribed life-structure of marriage, childbearing and (if they survived the process) old age, when they might adopt a celibate existence. As wives and mothers they could still perform the recommended Christian acts of charity and good works, as did Irene, mother of the author of the *Life* of Theophano; she devoted herself to good works with such vigour that she fell down as if dead and had to be cured by the saint's ring dipped in holy water.[37] Couples often decided to end their lives in separate monasteries, or to live as brother and sister in an entirely spiritual relationship, in the manner of the parents of St Theodore of Stoudios.[38]

As mentioned, the second stage at which women had a chance to disrupt this established life-structure was at widowhood. On the death of her husband, a woman regained her dowry and often increased her wealth by inheritance. She might thus acquire sufficient means to remain independent, and although most would usually employ this to negotiate a second marriage, a woman could legitimately embrace celibacy, for remarriage especially if undertaken before the required year of mourning, carried a general stigma of disrespect for her first husband.[39] Third marriages entailed more severe ecclesiastical penance and fourth marriages were eventually prohibited altogether.[40] Ecclesiastical approval of widowhood created an additional pressure for widows to revert to singleness, whether in a monastic context or in the world.

In Byzantine society at large, men expressed a variety of views on widows. Some held that nunneries existed as havens to enable women to avoid having to remarry. Thus, in the tenth to twelfth centuries, St Neilos of Rossano urged the men of his village to restore and maintain its nunnery, so that their widows would find shelter there and would not dishonour them by being forced to remarry. Others, however, urged women to remarry on the grounds that widowhood was insupportable, and some recommended against ever marrying a widow.[41] Despite the differing views, however, men nonetheless paid court to women with extensive means, sizeable dowries and significant inheritance in land or property, and remarriage appears to have been a very common event.

Young widows of high social rank regularly found themselves the object of renewed marriage proposals, occasionally backed by imperial decrees, for instance, St Athanasia of Aegina who was ordered to remarry by an imperial decree, enforced by her parents. She was, however, able to counteract the decree by converting her second husband to the pursuit of Christian excellence and eventually he retired into a monastery, leaving her free to do the same.[42] To those who were most at risk, entering a nunnery was perhaps the safest way to avoid such pressures. Like older women, they were thus assured of retirement to a *gerokomeion*, old people's home, attached to a monastery. But elderly widows often expected their children to support them, and went to live with their married children; those who were childless sometimes sought to adopt suitable sons and daughters to look after them in their old age, while others remained as heads of households.[43]

Together with the possibility of a religious commitment, therefore, other forms of secular activity were more easily realised by widows. Thus, many women exercised choice only after the deaths of their husbands, for becoming a widow presented the most radical potential for independence. In their reestablished singleness, they could pursue independent Christian devotions without restraint, attending to the needs of the poor and sick in charitable activities, founding and running nunneries, or simply spending their days in prayer, like Theodora, the elderly servant of Constantine the barbarian, whose visions of Paradise were interpreted as a sign of her great faith.[44]

Recently Jack Goody has claimed that the church's motive in sustaining widows was thoroughly selfish, in that it hoped to benefit from increased endowments.[45] The evidence from Byzantium suggests that this was indeed the result, but the women who bequeathed their land, buildings, material possessions and revenues to the church might well have done so in any case. Remission of sins and concern for the soul weighed heavily in their decision. An example may be found in the case of Zoe, long widowed, who decided in 1152 to become a nun. She donated an area of vineyard, olives, mulberries and other fruit trees, which formed part of her dowry, as well as other fields, a church with its buildings, and her freed slaves, to the church of St John Theristes, in which she requested to be buried. The gifts were made on the understanding that prayers would be said for herself, her husband and King Roger II of Sicily, and that alms would be distributed to the poor from the vineyards and fields donated. Since there was only a monastery for men attached to the church of St John, Zoe's commitment to the monastic life was probably pursued at her home until her death, when she knew that she would be buried in the church.[46]

PUBLIC AND PRIVATE EXPRESSIONS OF RELIGIOUS COMMITMENT

In light of the previous sections, this concluding section will aim to document the decline of recognised, public roles for women and the concomitant growth of more personal, private forms of Christian devotion. In this process the late-seventh-century Council *in Trullo*, held in Constantinople under Justinian II (685–95), marks a watershed. It was the first meeting to address disciplinary matters since the mid-fifth century and therefore had to consider a wide range of activities. From these, it is clear that both the behaviour of women in public and the roles of Christian women in the church gave the assembled bishops cause for anxiety.[47] Several canons were issued to curtail these public roles, or to correct aspects of them considered unsuitable, and others were intended to restrict the public activities of women.

By the end of the seventh century, there were only two official ecclesiastical positions open to women, those of deaconess and widow, which were limited to suitably Christian females over the age of 40.[48] In many cases sisters and daughters of male leaders were chosen to fill these roles, like the deaconess Elizabeth, sister of the bishop Paul, who was martyred after him at Najran.[49] While the council agreed to a reduction in the age at which a deaconess could be ordained, from 60 to 40, canon 60 does not relate to female ordination and the public role of deaconess, but deals rather with young men entering monasteries. So it's unclear whether the orders of widows and deaconesses continued to attract dedicated women.

As noted earlier, deaconesses held positions of responsibility within nunneries additional to their public roles in the baptism of adult women. The use of the title in a monastic context tended gradually to debase the public functions of the deaconess. By the ninth century, for instance, it seems to have become a merely formal attribute, as in the case of St Irene of Chrysobalanton, who was ordained deaconess of the Great Church by the Patriarch of Constantinople immediately before her election as abbess. Subsequently she never left her monastery to fulfil the public role of deaconess.[50]

This development may perhaps reflect a more general use of the title as one of respect for particularly saintly figures, or for women such as the ex-wives of bishops, who might be granted the title in compensation for the loss of their husbands (see below). The office was clearly subjected to pressures which rendered it more honorary, and reduced its potential for recognised female leadership. While monastic deaconesses might assist in running nunneries, their public presence might be very limited. It was as a very saintly and ascetic woman that St Irene inspired others to adopt a more Christian life, not because she was a deaconess.[51]

Similarly, the continued activity of an order of widows is not well-documented into the mediaeval period, and its functions may well have been taken over by charitable associations, such as the *diakoniai*.[52] An eleventh-century group, devoted to an icon of the Virgin based in the Naupaktiotissa nunnery in Thebes certainly included women, who participated publicly in the cult of the icon.[53] But there is no evidence that they also did any official work associated with widows. While it is possible that some of the duties of women in nunneries might be performed by widows, e.g. that of *thyroros*, the woman who guarded the door,[54] again there is no suggestion that these relate to an order of widows. So for neither deaconesses or widows, as an order, is there any specific evidence; both are better documented acting in a personal capacity (for instance, Theodora, mentioned above). Similarly, what had been a specific and separate order of virgins seems to have suffered a demise in the mediaeval period, no doubt due to an increasing social pressure to marry and the particular development of Byzantine nunneries. Those who succeeded in adopting virginity in the Byzantine empire normally did so under the aegis of a community of nuns or a particularly devout relative, although stray references to *parthenonas* being destroyed by the iconoclasts in eighth-century Constantinople indicate that institutions for virgins were maintained.[55] Included in the various restrictive canons of the Council *in Trullo* was a ruling on the mode of entry to the nunneries. The bishops particularly criticised the way parents dressed their daughters in fine silks and gold and jewels for the ceremony and ordered candidates henceforth to take their vows in plain attire.[56] This regulation stressed the intention of the future nun to leave the world, including its finery, which might have the opposite effect by recalling worldly things. And while the bishops admitted that a few tears might be shed on such an occasion, they were most anxious to prevent such signs from being interpreted as regret at abandoning the world. So for a calm and firm entry to the nunnery they condemned any display of worldly wealth.

Thus, the public activity of deaconesses, widows and virgins, which had been recognised and sustained by the early Christian church, does not appear to have flourished in the Byzantine period. And one can only conclude that the orders gradually became redundant and were considered unnecessary both by the church hierarchy and by those women who might have sought a more public role through them.

Although now removed from the world, however, nunneries nevertheless created a possibility for female leadership that developed the inherent powers of holy women like St Irene of Chrysobalanton.[57] Although she did on one occasion manage to use her influence at the imperial court to clear the name of a kinsman who had been unjustly accused, in the main her overt power was not explicitly in the public domain. Her leadership derived more from examples of her private dedication to ascetic practices than through any manifest public role or activity. As a well-known figure in Constantinople, however, she inevitably fulfilled a recognised role, which set up a model for other women.

Other abbesses performed the same function. Occasionally, the public esteem in which they could be held could even reverse male presumptions about female inferiority. An otherwise unknown abbess from southern Italy, who exercised the role of spiritual adviser to young St Neilos of Rossano, was honoured by him despite his vociferous hatred of the female sex.[58] Other women headed foundations for both men and women, like Anthousa, sister of Constantine V, who founded a double monastery and presided over it during the iconoclast persecution directed by her brother.[59] Women who were directly related to holy men often achieved a comparable distinction; Catharine, the sister of St Luke of Demena, displayed Christian qualities that were as renowned as his.[60] Even if they were not associated with religious communities, such women revealed the capacity to inspire which was greatly appreciated by both men and women.

While nunneries established an important outlet for the piety of Byzantine women, such communities were not always peaceful havens from the world. From an early date, they were subjected, like monasteries, to a secondary and sometimes abusive use as prisons. This custom appears to have been introduced by emperors who regularly disposed of their rivals by forcing them to enter a monastery. At the end of the seventh century, Tiberios ordered that Leontios, his predecessor, should be mutilated and confined in the prison of the Dalmatou community.[61] A similar practice was used to remove ex-empresses and imperial mothers who were thought to scheme to extend their influence. Constantine VI, however, divorced his first wife and banished her to a nunnery solely in order that he might remarry.[62] At a less exalted level of society, women convicted of prostitution, adultery or such unnatural crimes as incest were condemned to nunneries, though they were not necessarily tonsured. The institutions then took on an ambiguous character and their leaders became in effect jailers.[63] In the late tenth century Emperor Leo VI extended this role to cover women suffering from madness; his law states that the local bishop must find places where the abbess will guarantee to take good care of them.[64] But female communities were inevitably disrupted when the insane were thrust into their midst.

The rationale for committing prostitutes and adulteresses to nunneries apparently stemmed from the hope that by good example they would gradually adopt better, i.e. more pious, ways. But when this failed, those who had entered the nunnery involuntarily would not be likely to remain quietly inside. Prostitutes confined to the Metanoia nunnery near Constantinople in Theodora's efforts to reform them showed every intention of escaping if possible.[65] Quite possibly Emperor Michael IV's eleventh-century initiative met with a similar fate, although Psellos assumed that all those fallen women remained 'a youthful band enrolled in the service of God, as soldiers of virtue'.[66] Whether ex-prostitutes were generally kept physically separated from committed virgins is unclear. Whatever, it seems safe to presume that women imprisoned against their will would not always share the spiritual dedication of nuns. In this respect, particular nunneries were identified publicly with prisons and at least some of the nuns served as prison officers, in novel and recognised roles.

Another aspect of the nunnery generated problems of a non-spiritual nature, viz. the different ranks of nuns. While the principle of not denying entry to anyone who displayed genuine commitment to the religious life was clearly established, social distinctions persisted within monasteries.[67] Those who brought considerable wealth, property and servants to the community were received with greater honour than their servants. Byzantine nunneries were often run by aristocratic women, whose upbringing and education accustomed them to the services of others.[68] Similarly, women who came from very poor backgrounds may have been used to working in a humbler capacity, however great their piety. So certain gradations divided both the group of committed nuns and those women who had been cloistered for non-religious reasons.

Apart from those imprisoned for serious crimes, women whose only sin was to have married a future bishop were also relegated to nunneries. This was also decreed at the Council *in Trullo*, when the bishops discussed the problem of married clergy. The problem arose because in the East, unlike the mediaeval West, clerics ordained to the lower ecclesiastical orders were specifically instructed to respect their marriage vows. So they continued to live with their wives. But bishops were expected to be celibate. Priests who were nominated to bishoprics, therefore, were ordered to try and persuade their wives to enter nunneries in far-distant regions.[69] This meant that the women had to agree to dissolve their marriages in order to free their husbands for the highest office of bishop. While the council took care not to presume their agreement, it clearly considered the nunnery a suitable place for these ex-wives in what became in effect confinement. It also stipulated that if they proved worthy they might attain the rank of deaconess, perhaps as a reward for good behaviour (see above).

With these multiple functions, nunneries might come to house women who had none of the strong personal dedication associated with the heroic female leaders of such institutions. Not only those convicted of adultery or incest, but girls who persisted in unsuitable liaisons; younger daughters for whom dowries could not be afforded; widows who had no close relatives to look after them in their old age; those who were physically handicapped, like Saint Martha of Monemvasia, or the mentally disturbed.[70] Given these varied terms of entry, not all nunneries can have functioned in the ideal manner described in the acts of St Thecla and other basic documents of female monasticism. Jealousies were generated that did nothing to improve spiritual conditions inside the nunnery.

The combination of this ambivalence with the insecurity associated with under-funded family foundations meant that many nunneries had only a transitory existence. They did not succeed in establishing a permanent presence in the manner of well-patronised male communities, and some may have been quite like private institutions, family-based and personally-run. There is a notable absence of records from celebrated female communities, even the better-endowed Late Byzantine imperial nunneries, which form the equivalent to the houses of Mount Athos.[71]

Perhaps it was partly in reaction to this history that women with exceptionally strong religious feelings persistently sought out the desert areas of the empire.[72] But another reason is evident from canon 70 issued by the Council *in Trullo* in the late seventh century. This is the regulation that quotes St Paul in order to prevent women participating in the liturgy, with the famous words: 'let them be silent'.[73] Since in early Christian times this provision had not been observed, ordinary Byzantine women were effectively denied what had previously been one of their public roles, that of taking part in ecclesiastical services. Their attendance in church became that of observers.

In contrast, those who sought out the wilder areas of the empire desired a more rewarding spiritual experience in emulation of the original desert fathers. The fact that the literary tradition of holy women living alone in the wilderness was recreated in mediaeval instances leaves no doubt that *ascesis* was practised by individual women and gives the lie to recent attempts to dismiss the tradition as mere storytelling.[74] Although the *stylitissa* of the

Life of St Lazaros remains exceptional, there are other examples of feminine determination to pursue a solitary holy life.[75] Many had to adopt an element of disguise, for it was extremely hard for a woman to survive alone in the eleventh century.[76] But that some attempted the eremitical life cannot be doubted, even if they were not numerous. Their existence points to an ever-present possibility in Byzantine society, a potential that could occasionally be realised. It gainsays the fairytale interpretation of earlier stories, which continued to circulate widely and encouraged religious women to seek such an outlet for their fervour.

Although this manifestation of eremitical Christian devotion clearly involved an entirely private act of renunciation, it also created a public model of religious commitment. Such holy women inevitably became public models, however much they denied any desire for this role. Their commitment was recorded in hagiographic and narrative sources, and thus existed for other women, who might try to follow the same route.[77]

For the great mass of women, however, such a violent negation of the more usual life-structure was impossible. Their religious commitment had to be expressed within the bounds of family life. As married women and mothers, they nonetheless aspired to a truly Christian life. And notions of sanctity gradually adapted to this reality, moving from the context of virginity associated with early Christian martyrdom to that of the Byzantine family.[78] By the tenth century the case of St Mary the Younger provides a telling example of this new model of private commitment. Mary led a secluded family life; her public acts were restricted to generosity to the poor and other pious good works. Yet in this relatively modest contribution to holiness her biographer recognised the traits of an ideal piety. Her *Life* formed a tribute to this novel concept of sanctity.[79]

In this process Byzantine women expressed their familiarity with the Gospel stories that displayed an appreciation of individuals like Mary and Martha, or of Phoebe and others recommended by St Paul. These New Testament texts were regularly read in church and were learned by heart by many who could not read but who were inspired by them to greater devotion. Within their restricted family sphere, female commitment increasingly took on more private and personal forms.

As we have seen, one of the inheritances from the early Christian period included the attraction of married women to the Virgin. At the Council *in Trullo*, one canon in particular documents the involvement of lay women in her cult during the seventh century. This is the ruling that condemned people for preparing and eating a special dish of *semidalis* (a sort of sweet cereal mixture) in honour of the Virgin on the day after the feast of Christ's birth, a custom which had developed from the secular tradition of congratulating a mother after the successful delivery of a child and had been transplanted into the church. Although women were not specifically mentioned, it seems more than likely that they were responsible for the ritual in the church. The bishops forcefully denounced the practice as quite inappropriate. Since the Virgin had given birth miraculously and suffered no pain, She could not be celebrated as a normal mother.[80] In this way, an unofficial but rather public form of devotion to the *Theotokos* was banned.

Not long after, the famous icon of the Virgin at her shrine at Blachernai was visited by a mother, desperate to conceive a son. As she addressed her prayers to the virgin, she believed that the image responded, promising that she would bear a son. After his birth, she gratefully dedicated the child, the future St Stephen the Younger, to the Virgin at the same icon.[81] Such talking statues and imaginary conversations were not new, as the *Life* of St Mary the Egyptian shows, but this particular experience preserved and gave credence to a pious tradition that women could actually converse with the icon of the Virgin at Blachernai.

From these two instances it appears that the early life of Christ, in which His mother had played an important part, and the domestic history of his earthly existence, had a special appeal for married women who found themselves marginalised by both bishops and monks. The cult of the Virgin Mary perhaps offered a new avenue for their religious commitment.

Worship of the Virgin was not, of course, limited to lay women. In the ninth century a different form of homage to the Virgin was manifested by the nun Thecla, who composed a long hymn 'written by a woman, in honour of a woman, for and about women'.[82] This specifically feminine voice was directed towards the *Theotokos*, She who made the Incarnation possible, and to St Thecla, the first martyr, Anna, the mother of Mary, and even Eve, the first woman. In 198 verses, Thecla the nun devotes her skills as a hymnographer exclusively to the female sex in a highly-controlled and educated manner. Her achievement proves that it was not only men who wrote liturgies devoted to the *Theotokos*. On Her feast days, nuns in certain nunneries might be heard singing Her praises in hymns composed by a woman.[83]

Among women in general, one of the most striking instances of female expressions of religiosity involves the use of icons as intercessors, as in the tale related above of the woman interceding with the Virgin at Blachernai for the blessing of a child.[84] Approaching an icon is particularly well-documented for women denied their perceived and expected role of mothers by the curse of infertility. Those who failed to produce children, especially sons, often addressed their prayers to the Virgin, primary intercessor and chief role model for potential mothers. In one instance, we hear of an elderly couple turning instead to St Glykeria with a plea for a child, whom they promised to dedicate to her should the intercession be successful. The child who duly arrived, daughter, Elizabeth, was dedicated to the Saint and trained by an aunt, who was abbess of a nunnery.[85] Of course, such stories reflect ancient accounts of the miraculous birth to elderly parents of children marked out for particularly holy lives. But the additional evidence of female intercessors whose painted representations facilitated the miracles draws attention to the peculiarly private nature of icon veneration.

The domestic use of icons both in poor households and in the private chapels of the wealthy highlights a widespread satisfaction accorded to Christians through personal veneration. Even in public spaces where icons were displayed, such as churches and shrines attached to cult centres, people made their devotions alone, without the intervention of priest, liturgy or ecclesiastical ritual. In the case of women, such independent access to the holy, replete with the promise of relief from anxiety and resolution of problems, represented an extraordinary source of hope. The nature of icon-veneration appears to encourage a direct and individual relationship between the venerator and the holy person venerated. For women in particular, this quality seems to have been deeply appreciated, as imaginary conversations held with the saint represented confirm.

Through icons, mothers also instructed their children in the history of the holy family and other saints. Even the young could learn which saint was represented in a painting and could recognise the same figure in a different context, for instance, dreams. Children as well as adults identified figures as Christian saints coming to help them, rather than demonic temptations. Under iconoclast persecution, when possession of a single icon was prohibited, women of no great means sustained the cult and shared their precious images with other iconophiles.[86] Indeed, Emperor Theophilos, a stern persecutor of icon venerators, found that his wife and stepmother had arranged for his own children to make regular trips outside the palace for image-veneration.

In a period when medical science was fairly rudimentary and doctors often charged high fees, certain icons also offered women the hope of a cure. Miraculous powers were associated with the icons themselves (some exuded fluids that healed), or with oil from the lamps that burned in front of them. Many a cure was effected by the application of such blessed oil, not only for physical injuries but also for mental distress and apparent death. In addition to the problem of infertility, women with children regularly made their devotions in shrines where they implored the familiar holy images to cure cases considered medically hopeless. The combination of an already-established form of personal communication through the icon, with the high expectation of that saint's miraculous intervention, often proved successful. But it depended in large part on the private pattern of worship engendered by a familiar and much-loved image.

Icon-veneration appealed to a wide variety of people, male and female. It was particularly suitable for poor women who might never be able to own an icon, but who could spend hours in front of images in shrines and churches. For those with means, personal icons erected in their private chapels constituted a more secluded form of similar worship. Although the church endorsed and supported icon-veneration from the mid-ninth century onwards, it later came to appreciate the dangers posed by such an exclu- sively personal pattern of devotion. Ownership of icons might keep women from attending church; devotion to a particular icon in a church might become a pretext for unwarranted trips outside the home. However, the personal satisfaction gained from private contemplation and conversation with the saints through their icons continued right through the Byzantine period.

Whether it still remains as appealing to women in particular is hard to tell. But in Greece, lands of the late Soviet Union and other countries where orthodox practice is still observed, the association of women and icons appears deeply embedded.[87] Icon-veneration continues to provide an outlet for private devotion that is not met by regular ecclesiastical services.[88] In this respect, it preserves unchanged a tradition that can be traced back to the early church's fear and mistrust of women, which marginalised them and drove them to seek alternative outlets for their religious feelings. By allow- ing them no adequately satisfying public role, Christianity encouraged women to seek a more private one. And through the life-like representations of holy people, made in melted wax applied to wood, they found a means of expressing their intense commitment to the faith.[89]

NOTES

1.   See Cameron (1989).
2.   On the problem, see Cameron (1989), especially pp. 184–92.
3.   Clark (1984), pp. 13–15, and pp. 11–14 on Serena; in general, see Holum (1982).
4.   See Brock, Harvey (1987), especially the case of Febronia, the women martyrs of Najran and the Persian martyrs.
5.   *Vie de Ste Macrine*, 5. For St Basil, canon 18, see Ralles, Potles (1854) 4, pp. 140–2; also with the French trans. in Joannou (1962), pp. 118–21; and Eng. trans. in Percival (1900), p. 605.

6. See his two tracts against those who maintain the custom, St John Chrysostom, *Patrologia Graecae* (*PG*) 47, pp. 495–532.

7. Eusebius, *Ecclesiastical History* 5.14, 16; 18.13 on the Montanist prophetess, Maximilla, 'who pretended to prophesy' (for English translation, see Williamson (1989), pp. 158–63; 166–7. See also Pagels (1990), pp. 60–77 on the Gnostics.

8. *Canons of Laodicaea* 11; 44; Ralles, Potles (1853) 3, p. 181; 212; Joannou (1962) 1/2, p. 135; 148. For a useful discussion of the terms used, see Maclean (1919).

9. See Brock, Harvey (1987), p. 154.

10. See Wilson-Kastner (1981), pp. 142–3.

11. See Brock, Harvey (1987), p. 155.

12. Sozomenos, *Ecclesiastical History* 5. 15. 5. See Schroeder (1937), p. 54 and n. 124.

13. See Clark (1985), pp. 17–33 and Ruether (1979), pp. 71–98.

14. See Mango (1972), pp. 34–5.

15. *Life of St Mary the Egyptian* 23; *PG* 87. 3, 3713B–D.

16. See Mango (1972), p. 40.

17. See Wilson-Kastner *et al.* (1981), p. xi. See also Polycarp, *Letter to the Philippians* 4 and Lightfoot (1889), 2/3, p. 329.

18. There is considerable dispute over the precise nature of women's power in the early Christian period, see for example, the claims made by McNamara (1983); Fiorenza (1979). On leadership through personal wealth, see Clark (1985).

19. Pp. 290–3.

20. See Kyrtatas (1987), pp. 131–5; MacMullen (1984), pp. 39–41.

21. Witherington (1988), pp. 184–210.

22. Brock, Harvey (1987), p. 156.

23. Ibid, p. 126, cf. the mother of St Stephen, who ensured his Christian education to the age of six, *PG* 100. 1081A–B. The number of educated women among early Christians, such as St Thecla, indicates not only recruitment to Christianity from the upper classes but also a more widespread determination to acquire Christian learning.

24. Kazhdan, Constable (1982), p. 72; cf. Laiou (1986), pp. 111–22.

25. Most famously described by Procopius in the *Secret History* 9. esp. 9–26. See Dewing (1960) 6, pp. 104–11.

26. *Vie de Théodore de Sykéôn* 3–4. See also Festugière (1970) 1, pp. 3–4.

27. Trapp (1971), G 7, lines 180–8; 342 on childlessness.

28. Laiou (1981), pp. 233–60.

29. *Vie de Ste Macrine*, 4–5. See Maraval (1971), pp. 152–7.

30. Brock, Harvey (1987), pp. 70–1; 165.

31. Basil, *canon* 41, citing St. Paul, I Corinthians 7: 39. Also see Ralles, Potles (1854) 4, p. 188; Joannou (1962) 2, pp. 134–5 = Percival (1900), p. 607.

32. *Life of St Matrona* 3; *Acta Sanctorum* (*AASS*) NOV 3 (1910), p. 792.

33. See, for example, the case of Justa, who followed the example of Thecla and declared that 'Christ alone was her successful Suitor and Lord', see Wilson-Kastner (1981), p. 149.

34. See Clark (1984), pp. 1–8.
35. See Brown (1988).
36. For example, see the father of Theophanes Confessor, De Boor (1885) 2, pp. 5–6; 15–6.
37. See Kurtz (1898), 26. 18–19.
38. See Herrin (1983), esp. p. 181; Talbot (1985), esp. pp. 107–8.
39. See I. and P. Zepos (1931) 4: *Peira Eustathiou tou Romaiou*, for judgements imposing penance on women for marrying again within the period of mourning, 24.10, 13; 25.47.
40. See Beaucamp (1977), esp. pp. 159–61.
41. See *PG* 120.85C–D; Trapp (1971), G 8.135–41; 362, on remarriage better than widowhood. Cf. Kazhdan (1973), p. 509.
42. See Carras (1984), pp. 212–24.
43. See Trapp (1971), Z 8.5011–17, 399, on elderly mothers living with married children. For the case of an adopted son, see Guillou (1972), 30.12–18; and on female heads of households, Laiou-Thomadakis (1977), pp. 89–94.
44. See Vilinsky (1911–13), p. 20.
45. See Goody (1983).
46. Guillou, Vol 5 (1980), 21, esp. pp. 131–2.
47. See Herrin (1992).
48. For the Council of Chalcedon, canon 15, see Ralles, Potles (1852) 2, p. 254; Joannou (1962) 1, pp. 81–2 = Percival (1900), p. 279, cf. Schroeder (1937), pp. 107–11. For St Basil, canon 24, stipulating the age of 60 for widows, see Ralles, Potles (1854) 4, pp. 154–5; Joannou (1962) pp. 126 = Percival (1900), p. 606. For the Council *in Trullo*, canon 40, see Ralles, Potles (1852) 2, pp. 422–3; Joannou (1962) 1, pp. 175–7 = Percival (1990), p. 384. On the development of the deaconess, see Sr Teresa (1989) and A. G. Martimort (1986) *Deaconesses, An Historical Study*.
49. See Brock, Harvey (1987), pp. 105–7.
50. See Rosenqvist (1986), 7, 21 (28.3, with n. 8).
51. Ibid., 10, 35: '*gynaikon de kai parthenon ton periphaneia genous semnynomenon*' (44.9); cf. Ch. 23, 89 (108.26).
52. See Magdalino (1991).
53. See Nesbitt, Wiita (1975), pp. 360–84, esp. 367; 372 (signatures of the wife of Theodoros Kamateros, a representative of a famous local family, and three other women).
54. See Rosenqvist (1986), 13, 42; 15, 54; 21, 76 (54; 68; 94) in every case the feminine participle confirms that this is a female doorkeeper.
55. De Boor (1885) 1, p. 443.
56. For canon 45, see Ralles, Potles (1854) 4, pp. 411–12; Percival (1900), pp. 386–7; Joannou (1962), pp. 182–4.
57. See Rosenqvist (1986).
58. Abrahamse (1984), pp. 31–49, esp. 40. Many earlier examples could be cited, see Shirin, spiritual mother to many monks, Brock, Harvey (1987), pp. 179–81, or Susan guiding a monk tormented by demons, ibid., pp. 129–41.
59. Mango (1982), pp. 401–9.
60. *AASS* OCT 6, 15.341D.

61. De Boor (1885) 1, p. 371.

62. Empress Maria was forced to have her hair cut and to enter a nunnery, see De Boor (1885) 1, p. 469. The scandal caused by this improper divorce and adultery (*moicheia*) was to divide the church for many years.

63. Ralles, Potles (1855) 5, p. 57: judgement of Patriarch Eustratios (in fact, Eustathios, June 1023) ordering a woman illegally married to be tonsured in a monastery, cf. Grumel (1947), 933, corrected by Seibt (1973), pp. 103–15.

64. Noailles, Dain (1944), 111, 360–3. The law continued to be enforced into the fourteenth century, Talbot (1985), pp. 115–16.

65. Dewing (1935) 6:199 = Procopius, *Secret History* 17.5–6; Dewing (1940) 7:75–7 = *Buildings* 1.9.1–10 (where, however, the imperial provision of beautiful buildings and generous maintenance for the women is presumed to 'set virtue free').

66. Psellos, *Chronographia* 4.37; Sewter (1966), p. 108.

67. Access to monasteries for all who genuinely desired to adopt the spiritual life was reiterated at the Council *in Trullo*, canon 43, Ralles, Potles (1852) 2, p. 402; Joannou (1962) 1, p. 181 = Percival (1900), p. 386. On the social divisions that persisted within, see Laiou (1985), pp. 89–91.

68. Again the example of St Irene of Chrysobalanton is instructive, see Rosenqvist (1986), as above, note 51; Talbot (1983), pp. 604–18; Talbot (1985), pp. 103–17; Laiou (1985), esp. pp. 89–102.

69. Ralles, Potles (1852) 2, p. 419; Joannou (1962) 1, p. 186 = Percival (1900), p. 388. Cf. Schroeder (1937), p. 112. This regulation continued to be enforced in the fourteenth century, Talbot (1985), p. 112, n. 28.

70. Rosenqvist (1986), Ch. 13, documents the case of a Cappadocian noblewoman, whose ex-fiancé had recourse to a sorcerer to try to win her back from St Irene's foundation. While the text presents her as willingly renouncing the world and her fiancé, he certainly refused to accept her decision, cf. Herrin (1983), pp. 180–1.

71. See Laiou (1985).

72. For example, the case of Susan, cited in Brock, Harvey (1987), pp. 136–41, and the transvestites documented by Patlagean (1976); Delcourt (1961), esp. appendix, 'Female Saints in Masculine Clothing', pp. 84–102.

73. I Corinthians 14.28. Ralles, Potles (1852) 2, pp. 467–8; Joannou (1962) 1, p. 208 = Percival (1900), pp. 396–7.

74. See Anson (1974), pp. 1–32; Abrahamse 1984), esp. p. 39 on the legendary aspect of tranvestism in lives of holy women: 'a popular tradition of romantic fiction that dominated the biographies of women saints of the fifth and sixth centuries'.

75. For example, *AASS*, NOV 3, 59.528.

76. See, for instance, the sister of a monk who disguised herself in order to enter the shrine of Holy Elias, where she was cured of demonic possession, 'Life of St. Elias', *AASS*, SEPT 3, 82.881–2

77. An example of this emulation is found in a miraculous story recorded by Paul, tenth-century bishop of Monemvasia, see Wortley (1987), no. 12, pp. 96–103.

78. On the alternative domestic model of female sanctity, see Patlagean (1976), esp. pp. 597; 617–22.

79. *AASS*, NOV 4, 692–705; cf. Kazhdan, Constable (1982), pp. 72–5.
80. Canon 79, Ralles, Potles (1852) 2, pp. 486–7; also with French trans. in Joannou (1962) 1/1, pp. 215–16; and English trans. in Percival (1900), p. 399.
81. See his *Life*, PG 100:1076B–D (conversation), 1080A–B (dedication).
82. Topping (1982–3), p. 105.
83. Topping (1980), pp. 353–70.
84. On this issue of women and icons and for the whole discussion, see Herrin (1982), pp. 56–83.
85. See the instance of the mother of St Stephen the Younger (above) and Halkin (1973), 3–4, pp. 253–6.
86. For the courage of women in sustaining iconoclastic persecution, see De Boor (1885) 1, p. 452; Theophanes is of course a biased (i.e. iconophile) witness, but it is unusual for women to be singled out.
87. See, for instance, the observations on the relation of contemporary Greek women and icons in Kenna (1985), esp. pp. 364–5; Herzfeld (1990), pp. 109–21.
88. Huschon (1981).
89. Nelson (1989).

12 Women in Anglo-Saxon Poetry

Fiona Gameson

The study of mediaeval women has become fashionable in recent years, and the women of Anglo-Saxon England have received their share of scholarly attention.[1] Students of Anglo-Saxon society have used Old English poetry along with archaeology, art and legal documents as evidence for contemporary life. However, this application of literary material has certain inherent limitations since, unlike the other sources of information, we have little or no absolute knowledge about the date or authorship of the poems, the kind of audience for which they were intended or, indeed, the relationship of the extant texts – all in manuscripts dating from the end of the period – to the poems as first composed.

There are few poems in Old English for which a definite date of composition can be given. *Caedmon's Hymn*, according to the facts we have from Bede, must have been composed during Hild's abbacy at Whitby, AD 657–80, and *Bede's Death Song* would presumably date from around 735. The *Anglo-Saxon Chronicle* contains some poetic accounts of dated events which provide a form of chronology, like the *Battle of Brunanburh* (937); and the poem the *Battle of Maldon* records an encounter in 991 respectively. In all other cases there is no definite way of assigning a date and, for example, a poem like *Beowulf* has been attributed to every century of the Anglo-Saxon period. Even such apparently useful dating criteria as linguistic or metrical features cannot be relied upon since these may have been a result of scribal intervention at some point or even reflect a conscious archaising in an attempt to create a suitably poetic language. There is equal uncertainty about the authorship of most Old English poetry: though the name Cynewulf appears in a runic signature at the end of *Elene*, *Fates of the Apostles*, *Christ II*, and *Juliana*, we do not know who exactly this person might have been. The only other named Anglo-Saxon poet, Caedmon, for some time was held to be the author of not only the Hymn which bears his name, but the four poems *Genesis*, *Exodus*, *Daniel* and *Christ and Satan*, a view which is now rejected.

Our knowledge is little better with regard to the actual audience and we cannot necessarily deduce anything from the nature of the literature itself. The one codex of Old English poetry about whose early history we know something, the Exeter Book, belonged to Leofric, Bishop of Exeter, *d.* 1072, though it was written at an unknown centre at an unknown date anything up to a century before this.[2]

Furthermore, while all evidence from the Anglo-Saxon period has suffered the ravages of time to a greater or lesser extent, literature and especially poetry had already undergone a form of censorship before the close of the period itself. The preservation of this material relied upon scribes who were ecclesiastics, and so we would expect uplifting and improving religious texts or poetry of an elevated tone like heroic epics to have survived at the expense of drinking songs and bawdy tales, despite the fact that these probably appealed to a much wider cross-section of society. The latter may, in fact, have remained in an oral form and never have been committed to writing. Thus with almost no hard facts to use as landmarks it is very difficult to chart the chronological development of Old English poetry and impossible to extract from it evidence for perceptions changing with time. We cannot take the image of women provided by one poem and compare it with that found in another and use this to posit a development of social attitudes or literary approaches from one century to the next. All that can reasonably be achieved is to note in general terms how matters seem to have been during the five hundred years and more of developing Anglo-Saxon culture and how they appear in the poetry, and from the similarities or differences draw some cautious conclusions about the veracity and purpose of Old English poetic representations. With such limitations in mind, this chapter approaches the poetry primarily from the viewpoint of a literary critic and examines the depiction of women less in an attempt to contribute to a knowledge of social history, than in order to further an understanding of the art of a particular group of Old English poems.[3]

It is interesting to note that if only those poems in which women are main characters or speakers had survived to the present – *Genesis B*, *Elene*, *Juliana*, *Wulf and Eadwacer*, *Wife's Lament*, *Judith*, and some riddles – we would still have a fairly representative cross-section of Old English poetic genres and styles, though, of course, on a greatly reduced scale.[4] The absence of the religious elegies like the *Wanderer* and *Seafarer* would leave a regrettable gap in our knowledge; similarly the loss of the great secular epic, *Beowulf*, would have been a tragedy; yet *Judith* preserves a taste of the heroic style. The surviving Old English poetry, although conforming to the requirements of the various literary genres, provides a picture of women which seems to be neither pure fiction nor entirely idealisation. Therefore, before discussing the poetic representation of women, it is useful to examine briefly the position of women in Anglo-Saxon society, drawing upon the improved understanding which has resulted from recent studies.

I

It may surprise the reader of documentary sources to note the power, influence, wealth and educational opportunity that many women could enjoy in Anglo-Saxon England. It appears that social class was more important than sex in determining how the individual stood with regard to the law, and we find the value of a person's 'man price' (*wergild*), for example, determined according to social status – women being rated on an equal footing with men. Numerous wills and charters show that women could have equal rights with men to inherit, own and bequeath land and property[5] and a husband had no assured claims of inheritance upon that which belonged to his wife. Records also show joint benefactions being made and received by husband and wife together, and since at this period there was no law of primogeniture, matters of inheritance could be determined by personal preference for, or the ability of, the recipients rather than by their sex.[6] Domesday Book records that one woman, Eadgifu the Fair, owned land in seven counties, yet she was exceptional only for the extent of her property, for many Anglo-Saxon women enjoyed a position of financial independence on a smaller scale. Numerous female land-owners are mentioned, and there are a number of place-names – compounds of female personal names with a word for a settlement – which attest to a longstanding tradition of female ownership.[7] When a woman married she might bring property with her, but more important she received a 'morning-gift' (*morgengifu*) which was given by her husband and became hers to dispose of as she chose.[8] Although some women were forced into marriage by family pressure, some later law-codes record provisions designed to prevent unwelcome marriages. Thus V Æthelred, 21.1, of 1008, says that a widow should remain unmarried a year and then choose whom she likes; and II Cnut, 73, declares that a widow should not be consecrated a nun too hastily, and that neither a widow nor a maiden should be forced to marry a man she dislikes.[9]

From 597 Christianity played a dynamic role in determining the form of Anglo-Saxon society, and women played an important part in the shaping of the church. The reputation of Hild, abbess of Whitby,[10] was high in her own day, for as Bede says: 'So great was her prudence that not only ordinary people but also kings and princes sometimes sought and received her counsel when in difficulties.'[11] It was she who was responsible for encouraging the cowherd Caedmon's divinely-inspired poetic gifts.[12] The foundation at Whitby was a double minster and Hild was just one of a number of women who ruled both nuns and monks.[13] The extent of the influence of such women is suggested by the fact that five bishops came from among Hild's monks at Whitby.[14] Hild is an example of the important role Anglo-Saxon women could have in the Christian life of their own society; but we also find women involved in the missionary work of the early period – some actually going to the Continent, others supporting the cause by prayer and gifts, especially of books, as we can see from surviving correspondence.[15] The missionary Boniface wrote from Germany in AD 735–6 to Abbess Eadburh asking her: 'to write for me in gold the Epistles of my lord, St Peter the Apostle'.[16] Eadburh was the abbess of Minster, Thanet – not to our knowledge a double minster – suggesting that fine manuscript illumination was not carried out by monks alone.

These were not the only nuns whose intellectual powers and skills were rated highly by their contemporaries. Towards the end of the seventh century Aldhelm's treatise, *De virginitate*, was specifically addressed to the nuns at Barking and his introductory remarks about their intellectual pursuits, not to mention the complexity of his Latin, make clear he had great expectations concerning their abilities to appreciate his work. Complimenting them upon their endeavours, he pictures them

> roaming through the flowering fields of scriptures, . . . now energetically plumbing the divine oracles of the ancient prophets . . . scrutinising with careful application the hidden mysteries of the ancient laws, . . . now, exploring wisely the fourfold text of the evangelical story, . . . now, duly rummaging through the old stories of the historians and the entries of the chroniclers, . . . now, sagaciously enquiring into the rules of the grammarians and the teachings of experts on spelling and the rules of metrics.[17]

This grandiloquent catalogue may be more a reflection of Aldhelm's remarkable prose style than a guide to the studies of the nuns at Barking, since apart from the references to grammar, spelling and metrics, the remaining branches of study can be interpreted as merely circumlocutions for reading the Bible – 'prophets', 'laws', 'historians' and 'chroniclers' being the Old Testament, 'the fourfold text of the evangelical story' being the Gospels. Nevertheless, that the nuns were capable of reading his work is surely testimony to the fact that they were not educationally disadvantaged by being women.[18] Just as in legal matters it seems that class more than sex determined a person's standing with the law, so it was by being in a religious rather than a secular milieu which determined a person's literacy and education. Not that all lay people were necessarily without books or unable to read: to mention but two examples, Wynflaed left books to her daughter in her will,[19] and Asser records in his *Life of King Alfred* that it was the king's mother who introduced him to the delights of books – and what is more, of poetry.[20]

Finally, mention should be made of Æthelflaed, Lady of the Mercians, eldest daughter of Alfred the Great. For seven years after her husband's death in 911 she was acknowledged ruler of the Mercians, and was probably ruler in all but name from around 902. Between 910 and 916, working in collaboration with her brother Edward the Elder, she oversaw the building of ten fortresses, part of a chain that kept the Danes at bay, led her army to take the Danish strongholds of Derby and Leicester, and accepted the submission of the men of York.[21] There is no doubt that Æthelflaed was in every way the equal and more of the men of her time, and post-Conquest writers appear to have viewed her as remarkable for her sex,[22] but it is noteworthy that no Anglo-Saxon writer raised a proverbial eyebrow at such deeds being performed by a woman.[23]

II

Unsurprisingly, the females who are major dramatic characters in Old English poetry tend not to be the 'women in the street', but are rather the high-born lady and the saint. We do, however, have some references to less exalted women in a variety of roles – wife, mother, perhaps even prostitute,[24] as well as in the elevated position of partner in courtly gift-giving and bestower of drink (which seems to have been as much a ceremonial as a practical duty). Such glimpses of women at work or in the family setting form part of poems where women are not the main characters but merely incidental to the larger plot, or where the depiction is one in a series of short episodes. Such brief allusions perhaps tell us proportionately more about women in society than the poems where they are major protagonists and as such may be modelled to comply with the demands of a particular genre or other poetic criteria.

'It is proper for a woman to be at her embroidery' (*Maxims* I, 63b).[25] This line is not belittling, nor does it run at variance with what has been said about the position of Anglo-Saxon women. That 'embroidery' should not be equated with 'polite' young ladies doing needlework is made clear by works such as the monumental Bayeux Tapestry, the exquisite gold-worked stole and maniples found in St Cuthbert's tomb, and also, perhaps, the hanging given to the foundation of Ely by the widow of Ealdorman Byrhtnoth that commemorated his deeds.[26] The Anglo-Saxons put a high value upon such handiwork: many wills itemise rich hangings which are to be left to

particular individuals, and the inventories of numerous religious foundations list costly liturgical hangings and vestments donated by kings, nobles
and ecclesiastics.[27]

Another description of a woman's work is given in a riddle:

> I heard of a something-or-other rising in a corner, swelling and rising up,
> lifting its covering. The proud-hearted bride grasped at that boneless
> thing; the prince's daughter covered the swelling thing with her robe
> (*Riddle 45*).

This graphic description of a woman working with dough(!) is purposefully
suggestive, and is one of a number of riddles that are rich with *double
entendre*. References to sexuality are rare in Old English poetry; and even
in *Judith* where the poet presents his heroine as sexually attractive to
Holofernes, this is principally designed to underline the former's purity and
the latter's licentious evilness. Here, however, there is deliberate exploitation
of thinly-veiled sexual explicitness to amuse and titillate an audience while
they attempt to guess the innocent solution.[28] We should not overlook the
more 'earthy' side of Anglo-Saxon taste, for it contrasts markedly with the
elevated nature of much of the poetry which has survived and which forms
the basis for our conception of their heroic literature. One suspects that such
riddles were recited no less frequently than the epic tales which are recorded
in heroic verse, when, after feasting, time came for the entertainment in
which all were expected to participate.[29] That such poems might appeal to
popular taste is unremarkable, but that this riddle is to be found, along with
a large number of others – both serious and suggestive – in a codex of
poetry which was once the property of Bishop Leofric of Exeter, (*d*. 1072),
raises some questions.[30] Did some ecclesiastics of Anglo-Saxon England
enjoy a little harmless if bawdy amusement?[31] Or was this brief poem
transcribed into the manuscript by accident along with the other riddles?[32]
The latter solution seems unlikely.

A longer passage in *Maxims I* describes in tender terms the reunion of a
sailor with his wife:

> Dear is the welcome one to the Frisian's wife, when his ship is at anchor;
> his boat has come in and her man come home, her own husband. She calls
> him in, washes his sea-stained garments and gives him fresh clothes, and
> grants him on the land what his love asks. (*Maxims I*, 94b–9)

Such an evocation of tenderness in a loving relationship, unalloyed by any
sense of sorrow, is unique in Old English poetry. In passages like *Wanderer*
ll. 39–48, and *Wife's Lament* ll. 21–4, the speaker recalls moments of
intensely happy human contact, but such recollections are designed to be

poignant, not blissful – the happiness belongs to the past, while the speaker's present situation is utterly desolate and friendless. Yet even in *Maxims I* the poet does not allow us to become lost completely in this picture of conjugal bliss for, realistically, he also puts forward the alternative results of a long separation, immediately adding that women should be faithful – many are, but others dally with strange men while their husbands are away (100–6).

Another poem gives us a picture of the shared responsibility of parenthood:

It very often happens through the might of God that a man and wife bring forth a child by birth into the world, and deck him in colours, and encourage him and teach him until the time comes, arrives in the course of years, that the young body, the lively limbs become mature. Thus his father and mother carry him and walk with him, provide for him and clothe him – but only God knows what the years will bring as he grows up. (*Fortunes of Men*, 1–9)

Though both father and mother are here depicted as having a hand in the rearing of their child, when, in the following lines, the grown youth meets his death by wolves, it is the mother alone who is described as mourning. In 'The Father's Lament' (*Beowulf*, 2444–62a), we do have an example of a man grieving, but more usually if a male speaker utters a lament it is for a group of comrades gone or a way of life that has passed,[33] while it is women who seem associated with grieving for departed loved-ones. Whether this is purely a poetic convention, or an accurate reflection of the particular temperament of the Anglo-Saxons – allowing women to express emotion,[34] but preferring stoicism in men – one cannot say. Such a divergence in emotional response, however, would be in keeping with a warrior society where men were expected to go to battle, preferring death at the side of their lord to the shame of retreat, while women stayed at home and could mourn the fallen.[35] Indeed, the rarity of depictions of men giving expression to personal grief, taken in conjunction with certain more explicit passages elsewhere in the poetry, may suggest that there was felt to be an ideal of manly stoicism to be emulated. The poets expressed this by example in a way comparable to, if less direct than some gnomic statements upon behaviour.[36]

Man and wife are also seen as partners in an aristocratic setting, with lord and lady having shared responsibilities towards their retainers:

A king must procure a queen with a payment, with cups and with rings. It is proper for both to be very generous with gifts. The arts of war must flourish in the nobleman, and a woman must thrive, beloved of her people; be cheerful, preserve knowledge [keep a secret?], be open-hearted in the giving of horses and treasures. In deliberations over the mead, in the presence of the host of retainers, she must always and everywhere first of all greet the ruler of princes with the first cup, present it to the lord's hand; and teach him wisdom for them both together, as rulers of the hall. (*Maxims I*, 81–92)

This passage is interesting for several reasons. Here we see poetically expressed what has been mentioned before – that a man had to 'buy' his wife, or certainly give his prospective bride property, not just expect her to bring a dowry. The woman is seen not only as having a ceremonial role to play – serving mead to her husband and their retainers, giving gifts of her own accord and in conjunction with her husband – but also as being a positive influence for good government through wise counsel. We find women as 'gift-givers' elsewhere in poetry,[37] and that this indeed could be their role is confirmed by other evidence such as charters and, perhaps, the ring of queen Æthelswith. This is inscribed with her name and title, and it has reasonably been interpreted as a gift or a symbol of office bestowed upon a faithful retainer.[38] As to the matter of giving good advice, a notable historical example is provided by the wife of Raedwald, king of the East Angles, who wisely dissuaded her husband from betraying his guest, Edwin, when he was considering killing him or handing him back to his enemies for money.[39]

When we consider the character of Wealhtheow, the queen in *Beowulf*, we see put into practice the advice given in the passage from *Maxims I* just quoted. The scene is set largely in courtly surroundings, at some unspecified time in the past, but the values and mode of life it reflects may not have been alien to the experience of aristocratic Anglo-Saxons.[40] In such a tale of heroic deeds women are not amongst the major protagonists, but this is not because they were seen as second-class citizens, but rather, where a tale glorified the prowess of armed warriors, women were at a natural physical disadvantage. Their theatre of action was within the hall where their influence could be considerable – not only through the dispensing of material comforts, gifts, and good advice, but also by becoming involved in political manoeuvring.[41] Thus in several scenes of feasting, Wealhtheow, the gold-adorned and noble queen (614, 1163), serves drink to her husband first of all, and then passes it to all the retainers; she joins in giving gifts to the hero Beowulf, and to other warriors; and speaks courteous and encouraging words to the guest. She also gives her husband, Hrothgar, wise counsel – politely suggesting that rewarding a deliverer is only right and proper, but that wishing to adopt him as a son is going beyond the call of duty (*Beowulf*,

1170b–88).[42] The relationship between the lord and his retainers was two-sided: the lord gave gifts, which conferred honour, and provided a social focus, the hall, in which the pleasures of feasting and drinking could be enjoyed; in exchange he expected loyalty and service from his men. The queen, Wealhtheow, shares in the role of gift-giver and adds to the joys of the hall as mead-bearer, so she is able to expect reciprocal service from her thanes:

> Here every warrior is true to the other, gentle of spirit, and loyal to his lord; the thanes are in accord, a people in readiness, a band of men who, having drunk, will do as I command. (*Beowulf,* 1228–31)

The word *druncne* literally means 'drunken' or 'having drunk', and it is possible that Wealhtheow's words were chosen with care to signify that these men, having drunk mead given by her own hand, now might be expected to carry out their side of the relationship by providing loyal service upon her demand.

One other aspect of a woman's role that we see exemplified in *Beowulf* is that of 'pledge of peace of the people' (*friðusibb folca*) (2017), or 'peace-weaver' (*freoþuwebbe*) (1942) – where a woman is part of a marriage arranged to bring about a truce between two hostile peoples. Women did not fulfil this function in literature alone: historical examples are also to be found in the Anglo-Saxon period.[43] Whether Wealhtheow is such a 'peace-weaver' is not mentioned,[44] but we learn that her daughter, Freawaru, will play this part – unsuccessfully. We are also told in a sub-plot of queen Hildeburh who failed in this role, and after seeing her son, brother, and finally husband, fall victim to renewed feuding, was eventually taken back to her own nation (1069–1159a). The figure of Hildeburh functions as a poignant parallel to the main narrative, for in her tragic situation we see vividly portrayed what may well have been the ultimate fate of Wealhtheow, or any other queen caught in internal strife.[45] The position of queen might bring honour, wealth and power, but the vulnerability of a royal lady, victim of warring nations, does not go unnoticed by the poet.[46]

In this poem there is another character of considerable interest who, although female, is not exactly a woman – Grendel's mother. In her we have a fascinating synthesis of those elements most appropriate for, and utterly alien to a woman. She is a grieving mother – her most common epithet is 'Grendel's mother' (*Grend(e)les modor*)[47] – who has lost her only child, yet, at the same time she is an avenger and a dangerous adversary – both typically male roles. It should be noted that counterparts to such unfeminine behaviour also appear in Anglo-Saxon history.[48] Furthermore there are aspects of her character which are purely monstrous, and which make her a suitable oppone it for the hero Beowulf.[49] That we are meant to consider her both woman and monster is made clear by the variety of words used to describe her: 'lady' (*ides*) (1250, 1351), as well as 'monster woman' (*aglæcwif*) (1259), 'water woman' (*merewif*) (1519), and 'sea-wolf' (*brimwylf*) (1505). Similarly, the setting in which Beowulf meets with her is a fire-lit hall with weapons hanging on the wall (1512b–17, 1557–9) – this is no beast's lair, but neither is it a normal hall, being under water. As a woman she presents a very marked contrast with the figure of the courteous and gracious Wealhtheow; indeed, she is the inverse of all that the ideal Anglo-Saxon lady, according to the passage from *Maxims I* discussed earlier, should be, for she gives neither good counsel, nor gifts – unless it is 'fierce grappling' (1542) – and the only hospitality she offers is hostile and life-threatening. The poem underlines this grim irony with the words: 'she sat upon the hall-visitor' (1545). In addition to being shown as an anti-type of the noble Anglo-Saxon lady, she departs radically from the usual standards of female behaviour as portrayed elsewhere in poetry: rather she displays male traits which, by contemporary standards, may well have enhanced her unnatural and fearsome qualities, adding to her impact as a monster.[50] Firstly she carries out a vengeful attack against the warriors in Heorot which, though described as less fearful than the onslaught of a man (1282b–4), still causes total panic in the Danes and leaves one of their number dead. Secondly the actual encounter between her and the hero is no mean test of Beowulf's strength, and it gives rise to the only occasion in his Danish exploits where he is seen to feel fear for his safety, being 'despairing of life' (1565a). There is never any suggestion that the fight with Grendel's mother is just an interlude in the narration of the hero's adventures, nor is the outcome a foregone conclusion – Beowulf himself admits that it was thanks to God that he succeeded (1655–8). By uniting within her the two opposite yet individually credible sets of female and male characteristics, and by imbuing her with great strength and ferocity, the poet creates a figure of considerable interest who is more than a mere excuse for the hero to demonstrate his valour.

III

So far we have examined the women who are either minor characters in the poet's narrative, or are a small part of a wide-ranging description of the world at large, but now we turn to those poems where women are the central protagonists. A number of these Old English poems have sources still extant, and so here it is possible to see how the poet adapts and presents preexisting material for his Anglo-Saxon audience. A natural place to begin is with Eve in the Old English poem *Genesis*. The part which concerns us is the 600-line interpolation, *Genesis B*, which relates the rebellion and fall of the angels, and the consequent fall of man. The effect of linking the two Falls is psychologically powerful for the temptation of Adam and Eve is thus placed in a context that makes their actions both understandable and inevitable. The Old English version contrasts markedly with the biblical account in Genesis, 3:1–6. The beginning of the text where God establishes Adam and Eve in Paradise and gives the injunction against eating of the Tree of Knowledge is incomplete and consequently it is difficult to assess the Old English version at this point.[51] However, no sooner are the innocent couple installed in Eden than the poet focuses attention upon the creation of Lucifer, his over-reaching pride, and the consequent fall of the rebel angels (246–321). In hell the devils suffer bitterly – the greatest cause of grief for Satan is that mankind has been created to fill the realm of Paradise once his – and so he determines to make mankind lose God's favour. The scene is set for the temptation, and we know that all the malice of Satan, a mixture of hatred and outraged pride, is about to be unleashed upon unsuspecting mankind. Although 'more subtil than any beast of the field' (Genesis 3:1), the biblical serpent remains merely a reptile, but in the Old English *Genesis* we are shown the Devil's calculated plot against Adam and Eve, and are provided with the motive behind it.[52]

The Devil, who presents himself as an angelic messenger from God,[53] first tries his wiles upon Adam, with no success (523b–46), then turns to Eve, appealing to her in terms that are worthy of comment.[54] He first plays upon the fact that she is a woman: as she is a mother, he threatens that refusal will harm her children (549b–51a), and as she is a wife, he promises that upon her compliance he will overlook Adam's insulting treatment and distrust (578–82).[55] More interestingly, however, he also works upon her in terms of a heroic retainer, wishing to serve the Lord and gain his favour, and, along with this, he presents her with the possibility that she will have power over her husband (564–9). That the former of these two sentiments is laudable in itself is undeniable, but to play the part of a loyal retainer is not the normal role of a woman. The latter is, without doubt, an incitement to sin and this unsuitable desire (for a woman to control her husband) is the cause of the eventual yielding by Eve – the first step on the path which leads to the Fall.[56] In theological terms, Adam, who possessed reason, was the major transgressor, giving in to the persuasion of his wife, but as the story is presented in *Genesis B*, had the Devil not used all his wiles upon Eve and seduced her from God's command, Adam would never have been prevailed upon to eat the forbidden fruit. The poet, although not trying to present Eve as blameless, makes two extenuating comments:[57] the first is about Eve herself:[58]

> the ordaining Lord had marked out for her a frailer resolution.
> (*Genesis*, 590b–1a)

The second, even more unexpected, is a remark about God:[59]

> It is a great wonder that eternal God, the Prince, would ever suffer it, that so many a man should be led astray by lies, as came of those counsels. (*Genesis*, 595b–8)

Continually the poet stresses that it is the evil of the deceitful and hateful Devil, rather than the disobedience of Eve, which is the dominant factor, and even the enhanced perception that Eve experiences after eating the forbidden fruit – clarity of vision and an awareness of the mighty works of God – are merely 'lent' to her by the Devil. The outcome of her actions, in persuading Adam to take the apple, is unquestionably disastrous, but we are left in no doubt about her good intention – she is completely taken in by the Devil's deception:

> Yet she did it out of a loyal spirit; she did not know that there was to follow so much evil and distress for the race of men, because she took to heart what she heard in the counsellings of that loathsome messenger; but rather she thought that she was gaining the favour of the heavenly King by those words which she presented to the man as a sign, and promised her good faith . . . . (*Genesis*, 708–14)

There may be irony in the very phrase 'loyal intent' (*holdne hyge*) (708), used of Eve's action, because the Devil applies it to himself – not the best recommendation (586, 654).

The Demon returns jubilantly to hell, rejoicing in his work, which brings a double pleasure to the devils – he has caused humanity to share their suffering in hell, and has dealt a 'heart-felt grief' (755) to God: now they can bear their own torments more easily. This explicitly reminds us of the link between the two Falls and the motive behind the devilish temptation. Adam and Eve are immediately filled with remorse and in their turn suffer 'heart-felt sorrows' (776) – she is deeply repentant and admits her guilt fully when rebuked by Adam (791–826). It was believed that Eve, the direct creation of God, was more beautiful than any subsequent mortal woman apart from the Virgin Mary, and repeatedly the poet has stressed her loveliness (457, 527, 549, 626, 700), twice calling her 'most beautiful of women' (627, 701). Now, as she accepts Adam's angry outburst and is wracked by remorse, he again reminds us of her beauty, even though she has fallen:

> Then replied Eve, the fairest of ladies, most beautiful of women; she was God's handiwork, although she had by then been ruined through the Devil's cunning. (*Genesis*, 821–3)

This is a remarkably compassionate treatment of a subject which, throughout Christian history, has provoked wrath and indignation against Eve in particular, and women in general.[60] It has been postulated that some lost source, other than the Bible, lies behind the stance taken by the poet,[61] and it is certainly the case that, in contrast to the biblical narrative, he makes the Fall of Man a much more understandable event by raising Eve from a disobedient and sinful woman to a well-intentioned but misguided one, the victim of the Devil's machinations.

Rather than the sinful Eve, it was the victorious saint or 'soldier of Christ' (*miles Christ*), both native English and foreign, amongst whom were many women, who seems most often to have attracted the Anglo-Saxon writer's attention. Numerous homilies treating the lives of saints and martyrs, an Old English Martyrology, and, of course, several poems, bear witness to the prevalence of such improving tales.[62] A typical example of such a life is Cynewulf's *Juliana*. For the modern reader it is not gripping: a catalogue of ingenious but ineffective torments leading inevitably to martyrdom which brings an immediate entrance into heaven, is far from engaging, even if enlivened with some polemical debate between the heroine and an evil spirit. What we first learn about Juliana is typical of most female saints – she is dedicated to Christ and virginity, and is lusted after by a sinful heathen man, who persecutes Christians as a matter of course. Juliana is undismayed – she will only consent to marry him if he becomes a Christian, and she would gladly welcome all manner of tortures rather than recant. This is slightly different from the Latin version of the story which has come down to us in *Acta* (*Sanctae Iulianae*), as Cynewulf emphasises Juliana's sanctity and casts her opponents as irredeemable villains.[63] However, in both versions the final result is the same – fury upon the part of the rejected suitor, Juliana's father outraged, and tortures threatened and then executed with alacrity. Despite all, the virgin martyr remains divinely beautiful and physically unscathed, and, of course, her faith is unshaken.

Juliana may be too sweet and pure for modern taste, but she is undoubtedly the equal of both her human and her demonic adversaries. While she is imprisoned for one night the Devil comes to tempt her, only to have the tables turned upon him. Juliana forces him to confess, at enormous and didactically detailed length, what evil sins he has committed and how he causes the downfall of men (242–529). Having completely worsted him in argument, and reduced him to a whining and snivelling creature, she drags him in chains to her audience with her heathen persecutor, and it is then that the Devil, utterly demoralised and begging for mercy, pays the saint a compliment:

> I beg you, my lady Juliana, for the sake of God's peace, not to do me further insults and disgrace before men, than you have already done when you overpowered the cleverest one beneath the darkness of the prison, the king of the denizens of hell in the fortress of the fiends . . . . Look, you have punished me with a painful beating! I know for a truth that neither early nor late have I met any woman in the world your equal, bolder of purpose or more determined, among womankind. It is clear to me that you have come to be in all respects blameless and wise in spirit. (*Juliana*, 539–53a)

Faced by Juliana's saintly, steadfast demeanour, her human persecutors, who are depicted as utterly evil, are equally overwhelmed and resort to impotent raging and less than human behaviour:

> Then the judge grew wild and savage-minded, began to tear his robe, likewise he bared his teeth and ground them. He grew crazed in his wits like a wild beast. Black-spirited he railed at and abused the gods because they, with their power, could not withstand the will of a woman. (*Juliana*, 594b–600a)

Naturally the saint is unmoved, and when she hears that she is to be beheaded – the only way to despatch a martyr effectively – her reaction is predictable:

> Then hope was renewed for the saint, and the virgin's spirit was made very happy, when she heard the man devise that evil counsel. (*Juliana*, 607–10a)

Such contrasts in behaviour between the saint, strengthened and uplifted by faith, and the evil-minded persecutors might have furnished an opportunity for the poet to show by example how Christian faith is a desirable thing. Indeed we find this type of treatment in the story of St Guthlac in *Guthlac B*, where the saint is unperturbed by death, his servant distressed (1047–68). However, in *Juliana* the characterisation has degenerated into stock types of good and evil, so that Juliana is always 'blessed' and 'holy' (105, 130, 246, 315, 345, 607, 627), 'noble' (175, 209), and 'unafraid' (147, 209, 258); while the persecutors, her father and Eleusius, display unbridled passion, are 'enraged' (58, 90, 158), and are called 'furious', *gealgmod* (531, 598).[64] This depiction of Juliana and her opponents in terms of extremes of saint-liness and villainy is not a feature of the *Acta* and clearly the poet has chosen to exaggerate the contrast between his characters. We may wonder why he did so in such an apparently unimaginative and insensitive fashion. Yet perhaps it is to do Cynewulf an injustice to bring modern critical judgements to bear upon a mediaeval work and in particular to demand psychological subtlety from a saint's life which belongs to a genre with its own distinctive formulas – good triumphs over evil; that is sufficient. And these were probably not the only formulas which influenced his treatment of the subject, for the conventions of heroic literature can arguably also be seen to underlie it. The stark polarisation allows the heroine to demonstrate the key Anglo-Saxon virtues of bravery in the face of danger, loyalty to a lord, and repression of personal emotion; her qualities being thrown into relief by the sharply contrasting depiction of her villainous enemies who are characterised by their lack of these desirable traits.

Fortunately we have more promising material in *Elene*, another poem by Cynewulf for, whereas his handling of his source in *Juliana* strikes us as pedestrian, the approach to it in *Elene* is more imaginative and bears the stamp of the Anglo-Saxon author. This poem tells the story of St Helena's finding of the cross, and is based upon a Latin original, probably similar to the extant *Acta Quiriaci* in the *Acta Sanctorum*.[65] The outline of the story is such that, with a little skilled alteration, Cynewulf is able to shape it to suit Old English poetic conventions – he adds a dramatic battle-scene, a sea-voyage, and has Elene (Helena) make her triumphal progress into Jerusalem like a hero at the head of his band of retainers. True, she is given a conventional description as 'noble queen' (275, 662), and 'clad in gold' (331), but the word which the poet seems to have coined to describe her is 'warlike queen' (*guðcwen*) (254, 331), and this is in keeping with her character as we see it portrayed in the poem in contrast to the Latin. The description of the journey across Greece to Jerusalem of Elene and her companions is a notable example of heroic style and demonstrates how an Anglo-Saxon poet could elaborate a minor point in his source with a wealth of formulaic phrases and stock descriptive elements, to create a passage which conforms to the canons of contemporary poetry (so far as we can judge them), and yet is appropriate, both artistically in its context and psychologically for the character involved.

> There the linked mail-coat was clearly seen on a man, the tried sword, the ornamented armour, many a visored helmet and the matchless boar-crest. The spear-soldiers, the men about the victorious queen, were eager for

the expedition; the enthusiastic warriors, envoys of the emperor, soldiers clad in their battle-gear, set out with a will into Greece . . . .The blessed Helen, bold in thought, was mindful of the prince's wish, and eager in spirit that she should seek out the land of the Jews, over fields of battle, with her picked troop of shield-warriors, her company of men. So it came about then, within a short time, that the might of the nation, battle-famed heroes, entered the city of Jerusalem with the greatest of hosts, warriors renowned with the spear, together with the noble queen. (*Elene*, 256–75)

This picture of the full panoply of a band of warriors ready for battle quite eclipses the similar description of Beowulf and his retainers on the march (*Beowulf*, 321b–3a). The heroic tone of Elene's progress underlines the fact that she is simultaneously presented as a saint carrying out the work of God in finding the cross, and as a warrior engaged in a campaign. It should be added that the Latin version simply says: 'she entered the holy city of Jerusalem with a mighty army'[66] – there is no mention of her triumphal progress through Greece. Another alteration in keeping with this portrayal of Elene in heroic terms is that the Old English woman of action immediately heads for Jerusalem to cross-examine the Jews for information, whereas the Latin source shows her undertaking a great deal of preparatory reading before setting out.[67]

We saw earlier in the case of *Juliana* that a saintly and determined woman is more than a match for a sinful adversary, and similarly we find the Jews and their spokesman, Judas, later called Cyriacus, overwhelmed by Elene's rigorous enquiry into the whereabouts of the cross. Indeed, as with the demon in *Juliana*, Judas is helpless:

he could not escape that anguish, nor turn aside his regal adversary: he was in the queen's power – he answered her. (*Elene*, 609–10)

Judas eventually confesses all, the cross is found, he is immediately converted and becomes a bishop. Good once again triumphs over evil, but this time the story is packed with action: Elene is a dynamic figure, and we are hurried towards the final discovery of the holy relics. This saint is a forthright and capable woman, more reminiscent of Æthelflaed, Lady of the Mercians, discussed in the first section, or perhaps one of the dominant royal abbesses of the seventh century, like Hild of Whitby, than of the pure and pious Juliana.

Another striking depiction of a woman is that of the heroine in *Judith*, a poem based upon the apocryphal Book of Judith. The beginning of the text is incomplete,[68] so we join the story on the fourth day after Judith's arrival in the camp of Holofernes, the Assyrian chief. He is portrayed as all that is loathsome, lecherous and abhorrent. Again we see the poet altering his source for his own purposes: in the Bible Judith, although chaste, is a widow who, for the express purpose of attracting Holofernes, decks herself in all her finery; however in the Old English poem she is not only marvellously beautiful, 'the lady of elfin fairness' (14),[69] but repeatedly she is described in terms reminiscent of a virginal saint (35, 43, 56, 78). Although mention may have been made of her widowhood in the lost opening, the poet has clearly recast her in the mode of contemporary hagiographical writing; while simultaneously he manages to enhance interest in her sexuality which further underlines the contrast between virtue and evil. Virgins are more desirable fare for lecherous kings than widows! The poet stresses Judith's beauty and Holofernes' evil desires upon her:

> Then he, corrupted by wickedness, commanded the blessed virgin, decked with circlets and adorned with rings, to be fetched in haste to his bed. (*Judith*, 34b–7a)

Once alone with the insensible Holofernes, Judith prays for divine aid; then, showing great presence of mind, and a commonsense approach to her gory task – a point not elaborated with such care in the Bible,[70]

> she took the heathen man firmly by his hair, dragged him ignominiously towards her with her hands, and with care laid out the debauched and loathsome man, so that she could most easily and best manage the wretch. (*Judith*, 98b–103a)

The poet strengthens his portrayal of Holofernes as the lecherous lord, whose reputation is well-known, and feared by his men, by his graphic description of the dilemma of the terrified Assyrians the following morning: which is worse, to disturb Holofernes' debauched pleasure, or be massacred by the approaching Hebrews (246b–75)?

Judith is depicted by the poet both as the beautiful and virginal saint like Juliana, and the heroic woman of action like Elene. She is 'the glorious hand-maid of the Saviour' (73b–4a), and she had

> won outstanding glory in the battle, as God, the Lord of heaven had granted her and given the victory. (*Judith*, 122–4)

Whereas the previous poems have turned upon the inevitable assertion of the supremacy of Christianity over paganism, in this one we find a strong Christian sense of the triumph of good over evil forcefully blended with heroic excitement, as Judith despatches Holofernes and the Hebrews rout the Assyrians. An Anglo-Saxon parallel for this dual focus is provided by the work of the homilist Ælfric. Writing at the turn of the tenth century,

Ælfric presents Judith as an example of chastity conquering evil and the flesh, and also equates her with Ecclesia overcoming the devil – a reading well-grounded in the writings of the Fathers.[71] Furthermore, in his letter to Sigeweard, he suggests that the story of Judith could also be seen to represent, and encourage by example the English fighting against the Danish invaders.[72] Since moral laxity on the part of the English was seen by some contemporaries to have brought divine retribution in the form of the Vikings,[73] the two levels of meaning could co-exist easily.[74] Whether or not the Old English poet had similar interpretations in mind, it is clear that he has produced an exciting poem, where Old English heroic imagery and language are displayed to advantage, and where the heroine, Judith, is spiritually holy, femininely attractive, and humanly resourceful.

It may seem surprising that so far there has been no mention, among all these holy women, of the Virgin Mary. The Virgin was greatly revered in Anglo-Saxon England,[75] and her popularity is attested by the numerous churches dedicated to her, by artistic depictions, and by several extant homilies intended for various Marian feasts.[76] Perhaps Anglo-Saxon writers with their fondness for the genre of the heroic saint's life with its concentration upon the torments and struggles of martyrdom, were unable to provide a similar mould into which to fit the figure of the Virgin. In addition, the complicated patristic exegeses upon Mary's typological significance, and the mystical symbolism of much Latin writing which praised her, may have been restrictive to most Anglo-Saxon poetic imaginations.[77] Her one appearance in Old English poetry in *Christ I* (*The Advent Lyrics*), presents her more as a concept than a person. Here, in Lyric II (*Christ*, 18–49), she is mentioned in all her aspects – maiden, mother, bride, the chosen of God (35–8). In Lyric IV (71–103), it is the mystery of her co-existent virginity and motherhood which is marvelled at and expounded to the 'son and daughter of Jerusalem' who represent the expectant faithful in the Advent period. In Lyric IX (275–347), Mary is saluted as *Domina mundi*, her most exalted role, recognised as heavenly bride and queen, and mystically identified with the 'beautiful gate' of Ezekiel 14: 1–3. This last image has a double significance: not only does it focus attention upon the Virgin as intermediary, through whom God passed when descending to man, and who intercedes for humanity with God when petitioned, but also it suggests the 'golden gate' which gives entry into Paradise.[78] Mary appears at her most human in the interchange of Lyric VII (164–213), which is not based on one of the Advent antiphons, like the other lyrics, but is reminiscent of mediaeval liturgical drama. On one level it is a touching dialogue between the confused and hurt Joseph and the serenely assured Mary, while on another it explores the inadequacy of the Old Law of the

Old Testament, represented by Joseph, for understanding the mystery of the Word incarnate, Mary's child, which fulfils and supersedes it. These lyrics are moving and mystical, a blending of the various strands of meaning behind Advent, but as a clue to the Anglo-Saxon conception of the Virgin Mary they are far from enlightening.

IV

I have left till last discussion of two of the most unusual poems featuring women – *Wulf and Eadwacer*, and *Wife's Lament*. These are unique in Old English literature because they are both 'spoken' by women[79] and are expressions of a highly emotional and personal kind. Given their singularity, the cryptic and confusing nature of their language, and their position in the manuscript on either side of a group of riddles, it is unsurprising that the modern literature of interpretation devoted to these two poems is sizeable.[80]

Both poems are enigmatic, although *Wife's Lament* is perhaps slightly less obscure. It would seem that here we have a woman telling her own story of harsh existence and separation from her beloved. Her husband's kin alienated the two of them, and whether they turned him against her, causing her banishment, or, more plausibly, whether they are both victims of the plotting kindred, it is certain that they are now separated.[81] But whatever the background to the story – what might be termed the plot – the thoughts and language the poet gives to the woman, and the immediate environment within which she is set, are themselves sufficiently potent to evoke fully the pathos of her plight. The speaker is now living alone in miserable surroundings – a cave in the earth, under an oak tree, in a landscape of dark valleys, high hills, and bramble-covered buildings (*Wife's Lament*, 27–32a). Her wretched external conditions both reflect, and form a suitable setting for, her internal afflictions – inconsolable sorrow, a sense of isolation, and a longing for her lord. In a poem of 53 lines, words and phrases for melancholy states occur some 32 times. Among repeated expressions are simple forms and compounds of 'sad' (*geomor*) (1, 17, 19, 42); 'exile' (*wræc*) (5, 10, 38); 'to yearn after' (*langian*) (14, 29, 41, 52); and compounds formed with 'sorrow' (*cear*), or 'pain' (*sorg*) (7, 44, 45, 51). The emotive effect of such words and phrases is heightened by adverbs like 'always' (*a*) (5, 42), and 'never' (*æfre ne*) (39), and the phrase 'the summer-long day' (*sumorlangne dæg*) (37), which suggest the endlessness of her condition.[82] There is no escaping the sense of misery and the lack of any relief for her isolation:

There I must sit the summer-long day; there I may weep over my ways of exile, my many afflictions; for never may I find rest from my anxiety of mind, nor from all the longing which in my life overwhelms me. (*Wife's Lament*, 37–41)

Her 'paths of exile' (*wræcsiðas*) (5, 38) are cheerless enough, her isolation and separation from her beloved lord is insupportable, but her position is accentuated by a contrast with happier times:

Happy at heart, we two often vowed that nothing else at all, except death alone, should part us; that has all since changed, it is now * * * as if it had never been, our loving relationship. (*Wife's Lament*, 21–5a)

She also draws comparisons between her miserable and friendless condition and that of other lovers who are able to remain together:

Here very often my lord's departure has bitterly oppressed me. On the earth there are lovers, living dear to each other, they keep to their beds, while I pass alone at dawn under this oak tree, through this earth-cave. (*Wife's Lament*, 32b–6)

In the closing lines of the poem we also learn that her 'lover' (*freond*) (47), or 'friend' (*wine*) (49, 50), probably referring to her absent husband, is also in unpleasant surroundings – a poignant touch, for thus her own grief is made yet more intense by knowing, or imagining, her husband in distress. It seems fitting, therefore, that in the last part of the poem (42–53), she apparently utters a curse upon whoever was responsible for her, and presumably her lord's, plight, and wishes upon him a taste of what she has suffered – sorrow and anxiety, and the fate of an exile. The persona of the wife has much in common with other exile figures found in Old English poetry – her desolate surroundings, lack of friends and lord, solitary suffering with no one to hear the lament, no immediate hope of relief, and her dwelling upon happy times that have passed. However, the intensity of feeling revealed by the language employed, the poignant evocation of the past unity of a loving couple now irrevocably separated, and the unusual feature of this lament being uttered by a lonely woman, makes the poem more than a restating of a familiar and well-tried theme.

Whereas in *Wife's Lament* we were faced merely by uncertainty of plot, and doubt as to who does what to whom, in *Wulf and Eadwacer* we are tantalised by a plethora of ambiguities and interpretational problems. We may ask, how many characters are involved? Who is Wulf and who is Eadwacer? Is the fact that the names can be interpreted as common nouns, 'wolf' and 'guardian of happiness' a clue or a red herring? What is the exact meaning of words, like *lac* (1, 6), *apecgan* (2, 7), *dogode* (9)? Indeed, what is the exact meaning of the poem? The customary reading is that Wulf is the lover for whom the speaker yearns and fears; Eadwacer is her husband who is joined to her in body but not in spirit, and that at the end of the poem Wulf carries the speaker's child (the father is unidentified) off to the woods, possibly to destroy it.[83] Another more recent interpretation, that makes a coherent whole of the poem and offers some plausible readings for the ambiguous passages, would have but two characters – the speaker and Wulf, perhaps both suffering exile, and sees the 'whelp' (*hwelp*) (16) that Wulf carries off as a metaphor for the love between the two.[84] That the poem lends itself to many widely divergent readings is shown by yet another, less convincing, view which argues that Wulf is not the speaker's lover, but her son, about whom she is desperately worried.[85] Unlike *Wife's Lament*, where the very words are charged with pathos and grief, in this poem it is the allusive references to a drama of human passion which suggests a sense of underlying distress. This is reflected in the many alternative interpretations which are not merely scholarly differences of opinion with little real bearing upon an appreciation of the poem itself, but are attempts at providing a guide or frame of reference by which to understand the conflict. Such a line as 'Wulf is on one island, I on another' (4) must mean that she is separated from Wulf, but it may also mean more than that. Since the possessive adjective, 'my' (*min*) is used by her of Wulf (9, 13), and his absence makes her ill (14–15), she presumably must wish they were together and that this separation is a cause of pain to her. Similarly, we do not know who it is that embraces her:

> when the battle-bold man embraced me, that was some pleasure to me, but also pain. (*Wulf and Eadwacer*, 11–12)

However, that this physical contact is both pleasure and pain indicates the fact that she is suffering an emotional conflict.

It is true that, in literature before the twelfth century, sexual relationships and romantic passions were not the commonplace themes that we have grown to expect today.[86] Penelope is the epitome of a faithful wife, but it is Antikleia, Odysseus' mother, who died of grief over his non-return, as she tells him (*Odyssey*, XI, 166–72). Dido is passionately in love with Aeneas, but this brings ruin upon herself and the relationship is something from which he has to be rescued (*Aeneid*, IV). In Old English poetry it is the conflict of loyalties between the family and the relationship of lord and retainer, rather than the 'eternal triangle' that we find. However, the fact that these two poems express something rarely found in poetry of the period is hardly justification for interpreting them out of existence. After all, were it not for the survival of a vernacular translation of the Latin work *Apollonius of Tyre*,[87] we might mistakenly think that the equally atypical genre of romance was also unknown in Old English literature. Why, therefore, try to read into the *Wife's Lament* a riddle for the soul,[88] or into *Wulf and Eadwacer* a charm against wens?[89] There is no denying the emotional force and poignancy of these two poems, and the poet, who is not here following any model which dictated that the speaker of the poem was a woman, has made a conscious choice in the creation of this particular persona. As we read the words of a grieving and passionate Anglo-Saxon woman it would be appealing to think that here, at least, we might have also a female poet giving voice to her personal grief, not just a sympathetic man who empathises with the plight of some more or less fictional female character.

> My Wulf's far journeys I followed with hope. When it was rainy weather and I sat weeping, when the battle-bold man embraced me, that was some pleasure to me, but also pain. Wulf, my Wulf, hopes for you, and your rare coming, have made me ill – a sorrowing spirit, not hunger for food. (*Wulf and Eadwacer*, 9–15)

If we turn to Old English poetry in search of highly individualised characters like the heroines of Greek drama, or for realistic depictions of Anglo-Saxon society, we will be disappointed. This is to approach the material with the wrong preconceptions, for it is a literature which, though often expressive, functioned within pronounced conventions of genre, style and formulaic vocabulary. Elene is an empress – noble, wise, imperious and efficient – yet we learn little about her personality beyond these traits which are necessary for the story. But then the same is true of Beowulf, the greatest hero in extant Old English literature; though he is wise, brave, generous and self-sacrificing, as his exploits demand, we are shown relatively little of him as a man with thoughts and feelings. Such stylisation is a feature of Old English poetry, both describing and prescribing characters, yet not reducing the importance of the individual within the literary context. Thus Juliana is a stock figure of the virgin martyr, about whom it is unnecessary to know more than that she is faithful unto death to her God: character development is here irrelevant. When skilfully handled, stylisation can be put to good effect, as we see in the creation of Judith who, it will be recalled, is presented in terms of two conventions simultaneously – the heroic woman of action and the beautiful virgin saint – and is thus an unconventional and arresting figure. However, in neither case do we see the workings of the minds and hearts of these women, only their actions or occasional authorial comments upon their reactions to events.

This absence of three-dimensional characterisation does not mean that the women – and men, for that matter – of Old English poetry were unconnected with reality; and what is lacking in the realistic presentation of individuality is more than made up for by the resultant universality of the character-types portrayed. As has been seen, in the real world, noble Anglo-Saxon women gave gifts and shared with their husbands many social responsibilities, just as a queen should, according to the 'rules' laid down in *Maxims I* and as exemplified by Wealhtheow in *Beowulf.* Noble women were not alone in being able to find kindred spirits or role-models in the poetry: there are the mother and wife of *Maxims I* and the women of the *Riddles* performing mundane tasks, and there is Juliana, in her piety and fervour, rejecting worldly ties and attaining union with Christ which was the desire of all dedicated nuns. These two extremes suggest that the interrelationship of the actual and literary worlds varied from one poem to the next. Some acted as mirrors of reality, reflecting, with differing degrees of accuracy, images of society as it was at some point during the Anglo-Saxon period. Others, especially the *Lives* of saints and heroic tales, provided visions of an ideal to which many might aspire but few, if any, could hope to reach. It is not possible to say whether poetry or society had the dominant role in this two-way exchange, only that it appears to exist and we should consider art and the real world in conjunction for the insights thus given into the poetry and for the light correspondingly shed upon the lives and thoughts of the Anglo-Saxons.

It is, perhaps, only in the realm of interpersonal relations between the sexes that the poetry fails us both as a mirror of reality and as a model of perfection. True, we have the sorrowful women, like Hildeburh, the speakers in the *Wife's Lament, Wulf and Eadwacer,* and even Grendel's mother, who have been parted from their loved ones by circumstance or death; and the very different dominant women, like Elene, Judith and Juliana who have the upper hand in their dealings with men – but these encounters turn upon issues of religion, not sex. The growth and development of human relationships, the stuff of which so much subsequent literature was made, is not to be found in Old English poetry. Love and romantic intrigue were not the driving passions of Anglo-Saxon literature; these were rather adherence to heroic values, Christian faith and, in all its manifestations, a sense of displacement and loss.[90]

NOTES

1. General studies of mediaeval women are Baker (1978); Kirshner and Wemple (1985); Lucas (1983). An extensive survey of primary and secondary material relating to Anglo-Saxon women is Dietrich (1980). Studies dealing specifically with Anglo-Saxon women are: Stenton (1957); Page (1970), Ch. V; Fell (1984). Particularly useful is the collection of old and new essays in Damico and Hennessy Olsen (1990).

2. On dating of *Beowulf*, see Chase (1981); on Cynewulf, see Sisam (1953), pp. 1–28; for the Exeter Book, see notes 30–2. On Caedmon, see Greenfield and Calder (1986).

3. Chance (1986) discusses the female protagonists of Old English poetry. Many of her points have merit, but she tends to over-interpret the evidence to support her arguments.

4. These poems total c. 3100 lines, just over a tenth of the c. 30 000 surviving lines of Old English poetry. The extant corpus ranges from the heroic epic, through biblical paraphrase and religious verse of both a heroic, meditational and eschatalogical character, to shorter poems including riddles, charms and collections of gnomic wisdom.

5. For female land-ownership as evidenced in Domesday Book see Stafford (1989). On women as benefactors, particularly of religious foundations, see Meyer (1977).

6. Whitelock (1930); also Fell (1984), Chs 4–5, Meyer (1980), and Richards and Stanfield (1990).

7. Stenton (1970).

8. Though a *morgengifu* is not mentioned specifically, an informative document is 'concerning the betrothal of a woman', in Whitelock (1979), pp. 467–72. This sets down very particular regulations concerning the financial arrangements made by a suitor for his bride, both at the time of marriage and in the event of her outliving him. From this it appears that the woman need not bring any property into the marriage but could expect to be supported by her husband.

9. Robertson (1925), pp. 84, 210–12. See further Fell (1984), Ch. 3; Hill (1979). For changes in circumstances from the time of the Conquest, see Stafford (1989), p. 87.

10. For details of Hild, see Nicholson (1978); Fell (1981).

11. Colgrave and Mynors (1969), p. 409.

12. Colgrave and Mynors (1969), pp. 414–18.

13. On double minsters and the importance of aristocratic religious women, see Mayr-Harting (1972), pp. 148–52. For a broad survey of nunneries in Southern England throughout the period, see Yorke (1989).

14. Hunter Blair (1985).

15. On the role of women in missionary work, see Fell (1990); also Talbot (1954), pp. xii–xiii.

16. Whitelock (1979), p. 811.

17. Lapidge and Herren (1979), pp. 61–2.

18. Other evidence of the competence of religious women in Latin is given by Dronke (1984), pp. 30–3; Fell, (1990); and Talbot (1954), pp. 87–8. Whether the woman Berginda, whose name appears in a Latin letter in an Anglo-

Saxon manuscript, was the patroness for whom it was written, or the scribe herself, it presupposes no little degree of education, see Sims-Williams, (1979), esp. pp. 10ff.

19.   Whitelock (1930), no. III. The opposing views about Wynflaed's precise status at the time of making her will – whether a secular individual or a religious – are stated by Fell (1984), p. 102, and Owen (1979) pp. 197–9. On Anglo-Saxon lay literacy and why there seem to have been more literate lay women than men, see Wormald (1977).

20.   Stevenson (1904), pp. 20–1; trans. Keynes and Lapidge (1983), Ch. 23, p. 75.

21.   On Æthelflaed, see Wainwright (1959).

22.   For example, see William of Malmesbury in Stubbs (1887), p. 136, and Henry of Huntingdon in Arnold (1879), p. 158.

23.   Given its West Saxon bias it is unsurprising that the *Anglo-Saxon Chronicle* does not make much of Æthelflaed's achievements; that even the *Mercian Register*, recording the deeds of a Mercian ruler, seems unsurprised by her activities in the light of her sex is noteworthy; see Wainright (1959). See Bandel (1955) for a discussion of pre- and post-Conquest attitudes to Æthelflaed.

24.   Kiernan (1975).

25.   All translations are my own, based upon the texts of the poems as printed in Krapp and Dobbie (1931–42).

26.   Most recently reproduced in Wilson (1985); for the textiles in St Cuthbert's coffin see the sections by Plenderleith, Hohler and Freyhan, in Battiscombe (1956); see also Blake (1962) p. 136.

27.   On textiles and vestments in general see Dodwell (1982), Chs 5 and 6. On the continuous tradition of fine English embroidery, *opus Anglicanum*, see Christie (1938).

28.   An illuminating discussion of sexuality in some of the riddles, and how woman's sexuality is treated in an enthusiastic and non-denigrating fashion is in Williams (1975).

29.   See Colgrave and Mynors (1969), pp. 414–16.

30.   Exeter Cathedral Library, ms 3501; see Chambers *et al.* (1933). The popularity of riddles in learned circles is shown by a number of collections written by Anglo-Saxon scholars; see Mayr-Harting (1972), pp. 201–4. Aldhelm's riddles are translated in Lapidge and Rosier (1985), pp. 61–94; for texts of riddles known in Anglo-Saxon England see De Marco and Glorie (1968).

31.   The continuous flow of ecclesiastical comment and legislation designed to prevent the worst elements of secular literature from infecting church practices encourages one to reply in the affirmative. Documents supporting this view include: Councils of Clovesho, 746–7, Ch. 12 (Haddan and Stubbs [1871], pp. 366–7); Alcuin's letter of 797 to Higebald of Lindisfarne (Dummler [1895], 124, p. 183, trans. Allott (1974), pp. 154–6); Wulfstan's *Canons of Edgar*, 1004–8, (Fowler [1972], Ch. 59, p. 14); and the *Law of the Northumbrian Priests* (Whitelock [1979], p. 474).

32.   *Riddle 45* is only one of some nine 'obscene' riddles in the Exeter Book; in addition there are others with very explicit sexual imagery.

33.   'The Elegy of the Last Survivor', *Beowulf*, 2247–66; *Wanderer*, 92–100; *Seafarer*, 80b–8a.

34. The figure of Hildeburh in *Beowulf* is the epitome of the vulnerable woman, helpless except to mourn her fallen loved-ones. That women had an association with public expressions of grief is seen in the figure of the 'Geatish woman' of *Beowulf*, see Mustanoja (1967).

35. See the highly perceptive discussion of the stereotype of the grieving woman and her role in heroic literature by Hill (1990).

36. The manly reaction to grief is succinctly expressed in: 'Better it is for each man that he should avenge his friend, than he should mourn a lot.' (*Beowulf*, 1384b–5.) More expansive is the statement about the need to suffer silently in the *Wanderer*: 'I know for a truth that it is a noble virtue in a man, that he should bind fast his breast, and keep close the treasury of his thoughts, let him think as he pleases. A weary spirit cannot withstand fate, nor can troubled thought bring help. Therefore, those eager for repute often bind fast in their breasts a cause of sorrow.' (*Wanderer*, 11b–18)

37. Widsith praises the generosity of Queen Ealdhild (*Widsith*, 97–102); and in *Beowulf* Wealhtheow is partner with her husband in rewarding the hero.

38. On the ring of Æthelswith see Wilson (1964), cat. 1, p. 117; pl. XI, fig. 1. A recent alternative view is in Backhouse, Turner and Webster (1984), cat. 10, p. 30.

39. On Raedwald's wife, see Bede II. 12 (Colgrave and Mynors [1969], p. 180).

40. The exact dating of *Beowulf* has been much argued; see Chase (1981). On the appreciation of *Beowulf* by an eighth-century audience see Wormald (1978). However, Busse and Holtei (1981), argue for the poem being equally fitted for a tenth-century context.

41. On the political influence (and its limitations) of women in the later Anglo-Saxon period see Stafford (1981). Such ideas are discussed in relation to the poetry by Hill (1990).

42. Wealhtheow is not over-reacting on behalf of her sons, since during much of the Anglo-Saxon period the line of succession was chosen from the male members of a ruling house, not necessarily passed directly to the eldest son, and royal women laboured to ensure the success of their own sons' claims to rule; see Stafford (1978).

43. Political marriages in aristocratic families were common, though not always undertaken purely to stop family or national feuds. See, for example, Colgrave and Mynors [1969] p. 400, 564. On the 'peace-weaver' in Old English poetry, see Sklute (1970).

44. Robinson (1964).

45. Stanley (1966), p. 133.

46. Kliman (1977) contrasts Anglo-Saxon attitudes to women seen in *Beowulf* with those of later mediaeval writers.

47. Lines 1258, 1282, 1538, 2118, and 2139.

48. Ælfthryth, third wife of King Edgar, determined that her son, Æthelred, should come to the throne, even though his elder brother, Edward, had been crowned after the king's death in 975. In 979 she engineered Edward's death. She then beat her son, the new king, with a candlestick, because he was overcome by grief at his brother's sudden death; see Stafford (1978), pp. 79–80, but note Keynes (1980) pp. 167ff. About a century earlier Asser records the history of Eadburh, daughter of Offa of Mercia, who married the West

Saxon king and, having tyrannised her people and allegedly caused her husband's death, was forced to flee to the Continent, where she became abbess of a nunnery but does not seem to have mended her evil ways; see Keynes and Lapidge (1983), Chs 14–15; pp. 71–2.

49. A female monster as part of a pair to be dealt with by a hero is a recurrent feature in other northern heroic tales, see Chadwick (1959).

50. Chance (1986), Ch. 7, sees Grendel's mother as anti-type of the traditional queen like Wealhtheow or Hildeburh – refusing passively to accept the role of victim and actively seeking vengeance. Some interesting points are made, but the extent of the reversal of the female role and the adoption of male attributes is much over-emphasised in the discussion. The display of so-called male traits alone was not necessarily abhorrent in a woman, as was seen in the example of Æthelflaed, Lady of the Mercians, discussed earlier, and as we shall see with regard to Elene and Judith, but Grendel's mother is a threat to the 'heroes' and thus extremely alarming.

51. Doane (1978), pp. 8–11. The newest and most complete analysis of the make-up of the manuscript and the losses from it is Raw (1984).

52. Woolf (1963), p. 25, points out that Adam and Eve, rather than being presented as the sinful anti-types of Christ and the Virgin Mary, are the heroes of *Genesis B*, contrasted with the evil Devil, and this is made clear by the poet's comments. Also see Evans (1963).

53. This is based in Scripture, for St Paul says: 'And no marvel; for Satan himself is transformed into an angel of light' (2 Corinthians, 11:14).

54. For a perceptive and highly entertaining discussion of the Devil's temptation of Eve, see Renoir (1990).

55. Cherniss (1969), pp. 491–2, argues that Eve is being urged to act the role of a good wife, like Wealhtheow or Raedwald's wife, in giving her husband advice for his own good, and that she is not overstepping her place in the created order.

56. It is an over-statement to suggest that Eve, appealed to by the Devil to be 'peace-weaver' between God and Adam and herself, sins by over-stepping her role in Anglo-Saxon terms by taking on the guise of a retainer; see Chance (1986), p. 71. More convincing is that here we have a psychologically realistic presentation of the Fall: Eve's sin is not pride – wanting to be like God – but the human wish to be as good as her neighbour – equal to Adam; see Woolf (1963), p. 29.

57. How innocent, or otherwise, Eve may be considered, and whether the poet views her as culpable or not is a moot point. Finnegan (1976), argues that she is neither innocent nor guilty; Vickrey (1969), does not concur with the idea that the poet excuses Eve's actions.

58. This reference to the 'weaker resolution' (*wacran hyge*) of Eve may be a comment upon the unfair attack of the Devil who, contrary to Germanic concepts of matched adversaries, took on the weaker of the two mortals, see Woolf (1963), p. 25. Renoir (1990), p. 269, sees it as a comparison of Eve with the tempter himself.

59. The poet's wonder at God's motives in allowing mankind to be thus deceived is not new. Cf. Augustine, *De Genesi ad litteram*, 11.4. As a comment upon God's benevolence, not indifference, Vickrey (1971).

60. Patristic opinion on Eve and women is summarised in Tavard (1973), and Warner (1976), pp. 57–9. Also see the discussion of the progressively anti-feminist and misogynist mediaeval view of women in Kliman (1977), p. 39ff.
61. Woolf (1963), p. 16.
62. On Old English hagiography in general see Woolf (1966). The largest single collection of homilies is that in Skeat (1966). For an example of a martyrology, see Hertzfeld (1900). Other Old English poems not discussed here that deal with saints are *Andreas, Fates of the Apostles,* and *Guthlac A* and *B.*
63. Translated in Allen and Calder (1976), pp. 121–32, esp. p. 123. In the Latin she first agrees to marry Eleusius if he becomes a prefect and then, when he has obtained this office, she adds the clause about becoming a Christian. For his part, he is willing to be a Christian in theory, but only refuses baptism because he is afraid of losing the favour of the emperor.
64. *gealgmod* is a compound which may have had more significance to the Anglo-Saxon audience than is suggested by the translation 'furious'. The word *gealg/gealh* means 'sad' (see Bosworth and Toller [1898], p. 363) but it may also have been connected with *g(e)alga* (gallows) and so borne some association with death. See *Andreas,* 32, 563, and *Beowulf,* 1277.
65. The Latin sources and their transmission are discussed in Gradon (1977), pp. 15–18.
66. *The Acts of St Cyriacus,* Allen and Calder (1976), p. 61.
67. Both *Elene* and the Old English homily *In inventione sanctae crucis* omit the point of Helena's preparatory reading found in the Latin. It has been argued that the Old English versions of the story have this common feature because of 'the Anglo-Saxon clergy's attitude towards women engaging themselves in the study of the Scriptures', Bodden (1987), p. 45. As seen in Part I above, women do not seem to have been educationally disadvantaged in religious circles. The similarity between the poem and the later homily in no way detracts from the aptness of characterisation in the former, demonstrating Elene's preference for action over study.
68. Woolf (1955).
69. Swanton (1987), p. 160, sees the description of Judith as far from attractive. The word 'elfin fair' (*ælfscinu*), he holds, has unpleasant magical connotations, the Anglo-Saxons thinking no good came from elves. He suggests that Judith's brightness, like that of Eve, is provocative and likely to cause man's undoing. However, we may wonder if the word *ælf* would occur in so many Old English names if believed to be ill-omened. As for the brightness in the case of Eve, it was a sign of pre-lapsarian innocence and grace, while it seems to be misreading the whole poem to interpret Judith's appearance and behaviour as deceptive and ethically ambivalent.
70. Judith's wisdom is frequently stressed (ll. 13, 55, 125, 145, 148, 171), and she also shows her wisdom by her actions. According to Kaske (1982), this is one aspect of her character as 'hero'; the other, courage, is granted to her by God for her undertaking.
71. *Homily upon the Book of Judith,* Assmann (1964), pp. 102–16.
72. The letter to Sigeweard is printed as *Ælfric: On The Old and New Testament,* in Crawford (1969), pp. 15–75; see esp. p. 48.
73. See the denunciation of the English by Wulfstan in his *Sermo Lupi ad*

Anglos, Bethurum (1957), no. XX, pp. 267–75; and trans. Whitelock (1979), pp. 928–34.

74. Possible historical characters behind Judith are listed in Timmer (1978), pp. 7–8; see also Pringle (1975).

75. Clayton (1984), and in greater detail, eadem (1990).

76. Thorpe (1844), *On the Purification*, pp. 134–52; *On the Annunciation*, pp. 192–206; *On the Assumption*, pp. 436–54. Also *The Assumption of the Virgin*, in Grant (1982), pp. 13–41; *The Annunciation of St Mary*, and *The Assumption of the Virgin Mary*, in Morris (1967), pp. 2–13, pp. 136–59; *The Assumption of St Mary*, in Warner (1917), pp. 41–6. There are also entries for Marian feasts in Hertzfeld (1900), p. 146.

77. The complex of ideas and patristic debate focusing upon the Virgin is discussed in Warner (1976).

78. Burlin (1968), pp. 148–9.

79. Bambas (1963), and Stevens (1968), argue that the speaker of the *Wife's Lament* was a man; otherwise there is almost universal acceptance of a feminine speaker in these poems.

80. Apart from works on the Elegies in general, editions of the two poems and those articles mentioned in the notes, see also the works cited by Greenfield and Robinson (1980), pp. 285–8; the essays and bibliography in Green (1983); and the articles by Orton (1985), Schaefer (1986), and Klinck (1987).

81. This interpretation is elaborated by Ward (1960).

82. The repeated vocabulary of the poem is more than an expression of emotion but functions also as a formal device, see Stevick (1960).

83. Malone (1963).

84. Greenfield (1986).

85. Frese (1983), and Osborn (1983).

86. Women's love-songs are discussed in Davidson (1975).

87. Goolden (1956). With particular reference to the portrayal of women, see also Riedinger (1990).

88. Bradley (1982), pp. 382–3.

89. Fry (1970–1).

90. I would like to thank Dr Dorothy Horgan for her comments on an earlier draft of this paper. My debt of gratitude to my husband who has helped in countless ways at every stage of this paper cannot be adequately expressed.

13 Recycling Ancient Material: An Orthodox View of Hindu Women

Julia Leslie

INTRODUCTION

For countless traditional Hindu women in India today, the perfect woman is the *pativratā*, the devoted wife whose entire existence is dedicated to her husband. The word *pativratā* says it all: 'she whose vow (*vrata*) is to her husband (*pati*)'.[1] After a blameless life, such a woman ideally dies before her husband. If by some mischance she does not, she may put that wrong right by taking her own life on her husband's pyre;[2] she is then worshipped as a goddess, the perfect example of the self-sacrificing wife. During her lifetime, however, the good wife should regard her husband as her own personal God. For the man ordained to be a woman's husband is far more than a man: he is the incarnation of the supreme law in her life; the definition and summation of her religious duty.

This is the normative view of the orthodox Hindu tradition. It is expounded in a range of religious texts, both old and new; assumed in most of the ancient myths and traditional stories; and widely held by both women and men throughout India today.[3] So powerful is this ideology, and so deep-rooted its effect on women, that Indian feminists feel the need to tackle it head-on. Thus the first published collection of articles and letters from the outspoken feminist magazine, *Manushi*, contains the following editorial denouncement:

> The pervasive popular cultural ideal of womanhood has become a death trap for too many of us. It is woman as a selfless giver, someone who gives and gives endlessly, gracefully, smilingly, whatever the demand, however unreasonable and harmful to herself. She gives not just love, affection and ungrudging service but also, if need be, her health and ultimately her life at the altar of her duty to her husband, children and the rest of her family . . . This ideology of slavery and contempt for women in the family plays a more important part than even beatings or bullets in keeping women oppressed.[4]

But what exactly is this powerful ideology that is accepted without hesitation by some women, and yet rejected vehemently by others? Where may we find its ideals, aims and arguments clearly set out? Where are the great debates on the status and role of women? The answer is clear: sprinkled here and there in the greater and lesser texts of *dharmaśāstra*, the ancient discipline (*śāstra*) of Sanskrit religious law (*dharma*).[5]

This chapter focuses on one late text in this tradition: Tryambakayajvan's *Strīdharmapaddhati* or *Guide to the Religious Status and Duties of Women*.[6] This bizarre discussion of the proper behaviour of women was written in Sanskrit from within the discipline of Sanskrit religious law. Its author (or, more accurately, its compiler) was an orthodox pandit living in Thanjavur (Tanjore), in what is now the state of Tamil Nadu in southern India, in the eighteenth century.

But before I explain the origins of this text and detail its contents, it is important to put it into its religious and historical context.

RECYCLING RELIGIOUS IDEAS

First, what is meant by Sanskrit religious law (*dharmaśāstra*)? This is not the brisk world of legalities – the Sanskrit word for 'law' (*naya*) occurs only rarely – but the utopian realm of precepts. The key Sanskrit words are: *dharma*, *svadharma* and *strīdharma*. *Dharma* is cosmic law, the fundamental order of the universe. *Svadharma* is the reflection of cosmic law at the level of the individual (*sva*, meaning 'self' in a non-gendered sense but often taken to denote the male). *Strīdharma* covers the precepts relating specifically to women (*strī*).

At both cosmic and human level, *dharma* means 'what is right' or 'righteousness'. Derived from the root *dhṛ* meaning 'to bear, support, maintain', *dharma* means that which sustains creation, the eternal principle underlying the universe. The concept is both descriptive and prescriptive, indicating both what is and what should be. Indeed, in the realm of individual action (*strīdharma* for women, *svadharma* for men), it may be said that the real is the ideal. For it is believed that one's actions are impelled by one's inherent nature (*svabhāva*) which is itself ordained. Thus *dharma* denotes both what one does and what one ought to do, for ideally they are the same. One's action, impelled by one's nature and defined by circumstance, is also one's religious duty, for it was ordained to be so and is therefore right. In theory, at least, there is no conflict.[7]

The status and role in society of each individual, woman or man, thus not only reflects *dharma* but upholds it, and in doing so maintains the universe.

One's religious duty, therefore, is to conform to the moral precepts laid down by the specialists in and teachers of *dharma* in the vast literature of Sanskrit religious law. These precepts are based on the threefold 'source of *dharma*' (*dharmamūla*): (1) Most sacred of the three is the category of 'revealed' scripture (*śruti*): the *Vedas*, the oldest religious texts of Hinduism, composed in archaic Sanskrit, and brought to India by the *ārya* ('noble' or 'Aryan') people in approximately 1300 BC. (2) The second most sacred source of right behaviour is provided by 'tradition' (*smṛti*): that is, by the precepts of Sanskrit religious law (*dharmaśāstra*) and by the stories enshrined in the great epics of India (the *Mahābhārata* and the *Rāmāyaṇa*). Both these groups are said to derive in some sense from the most sacred source (*śruti*). The earliest religious–legal texts may be dated to about 600 BC; the most recent (both modern commentaries written in Sanskrit and new compilations in the form of Sanskrit digests) belong to the twentieth century. (3) The third source is 'accepted custom' (*śīla*), that is, the behaviour of respected members of the orthodox community. If (or, more accurately, when) there is a conflict between these three external authorities, some texts allow an internal guideline.

If we now narrow our focus to the treatises of Sanskrit religious law (*dharmaśāstra*, see group (2) above), we find a vast literature stretching from antiquity to the present day. As I have indicated, this entire corpus is said to derive in some sense from the tradition of 'revealed scripture'. This notion of sanctity and authority through antiquity is emphasised by quotations from and allusions to Vedic texts. The process of development within the literature of *dharmaśāstra* is more obviously self-perpetuating. Later texts quote or allude to earlier ones. Commentators quote earlier commentators as they expound upon and reinterpret the great authorities of the past. Compilers of digests rearrange ancient material in ever-new combinations for the edification of their contemporaries. This complex literature forever feeding upon itself may be divided into two main groups: primary texts, and secondary material.

The *primary texts* are presented in one of three forms: (i) The earliest and the most venerated are the treatises in verse: the *sūtras*, such as the *Āpastambadharmasūtra* and the *Baudhāyanadharmasūtra*, dating from approximately 600 to 300 BC. (ii) Next in both antiquity and sanctity are the collections of aphorisms: the *smṛtis*, such as the famous *Manusmṛti* and the *Yājñavalkyasmṛti*, dating from approximately 200 BC to 400 AD, some even as late as 900 AD. (iii) Finally, there are the collections of myths, teachings and folklore loosely grouped together in narrative form: the *purāṇas*, such as the *Skandapurāṇa* or the *Bhāgavatapurāṇa*, dating from about 300 to 900 AD.

The *secondary material* includes all Sanskrit commentaries and digests based directly on these primary texts. They fall into five main categories:[8] (i) straightforward commentaries; (ii) works of comparative scholarship; (iii) the more controversial treatises on special subjects, such as the rights and obligations of inheritance; (iv) the 'scissors-and-paste' type of digest; and (v) the superior type of digest that is more like a lecture with supporting quotations.

To return, then, to the text that is the focus of this chapter, Tryambakayajvan's *Strīdharmapaddhati*, as a religious–legal text belongs to group (2), 'tradition'. As an eighteenth-century recycling of ancient authorities, it belongs to the subgroup of secondary material. Placing it within that subgroup is more difficult. As a treatise on a special subject, the proper behaviour of wives, it obviously belongs to category (iii). Since it takes the form of a long lecture with supporting quotations, all converging to make one main basic point, it also belongs to the superior type of digest (v). In places, however, it shares the characteristics of the considerably inferior, scissors-and-paste composition (iv). Like all digests, it draws its evidence (and hence its authority) from every kind of ancient Sanskrit text: from the early *Vedas*, through the primary verse treatises of Sanskrit religious law, to the later (medieval but not modern) commentaries and digests, dropping the odd reference to drama, myth and poetry on the way.

While the *Strīdharmapaddhati* or *Guide to the Religious Status and Duties of Women* is clearly not in the same class as the great digests of Sanskrit religious law, its importance lies in the fact that it seems to be the only work of its kind. Although many texts, including those of *dharmaśāstra*, contain a section or even several sections pertaining to women, there is -- as far as I know – no other extant major work in Sanskrit devoted to this topic. This is not to say that the *Strīdharmapaddhati* is full of new material; it is not. Every piece of evidence brought to bear in this text, every quotation, every story, every allusion, is taken from some other, more ancient, more authoritative, and more sacred text. That is the point. For a treatise to be authoritative, it must invoke the authorities of the ancient and sacred past. Tryambaka's creativity in compiling the *Strīdharmapaddhati* lies in how, working in the eighteenth century he rearranges the familiar traditional material in a way that brings home his essential message to his audience: that a woman's most sacred duty is to serve her husband.

THE EIGHTEENTH-CENTURY CONTEXT

Two questions remain regarding the origins of this text. First, who was

Tryambakayajvan? Second, what was happening in eighteenth-century Thanjavur to prompt him to take the apparently unusual step of compiling a treatise on women?

It is almost certain that Tryambakayajvan was the famous Tryambakarāyamakhin (1665–1750), minister to two of the Maratha kings of Thanjavur (Śāhajī and Serfojī), and famous in his own right as a scholar of religious law. He is described in a contemporary text as a learned minister, the performer of Vedic sacrifices, and a patron of scholars. On the assumption that Tryambakayajvan and Tryambakarāyamakhin are one and the same individual, I shall refer to both as Tryambaka.[9]

Tryambaka was trained by Ekojī (c. 1630–86/7; the first of the Maratha kings of Thanjavur) to act as minister for his eldest son Śāhajī (who ruled 1683–1711/12). Ekojī himself was the half-brother of Śivājī (1627–80) of the even more famous Deccan (or Maharashtra) Marathas. When their father Śhāhjī (1594–1664) left Maharashtra on a military expedition to the south (on behalf of the Muslim Sultan of Bijapur), he left his first wife and son Śivājī behind and took his second wife and son Ekojī with him. By 1676, both sons had set themselves up as independent Hindu kings in an India dominated by Muslim overlords.

But their independence (such as it was) was shortlived. After Śivājī's death in 1680, Maratha opposition in the Deccan was at a low ebb. The Deccan Sultans were conquered in turn by the Mughals operating from Delhi, their power spreading slowly southwards. By 1691, Thanjavur was controlled by the Mughals who demanded and (eventually) received an annual tribute. The Maratha kings of Thanjavur were completely cut off from their Deccan homeland. This created what must have been a numbing sense of isolation: the cultural isolation of a ruling Maratha elite amidst a Tamil-speaking local population; and the political and psychological isolation of a Hindu kingdom struggling to retain both independence and identity in the face of Mughal might. The response of those who (like Tryambaka) were in positions of influence must surely have been to consider ways of reinforcing their own cultural ideals, perhaps by commissioning or writing relevant treatises.

Certainly, the reigns of Ekojī and his three sons (Śāhajī, Serfojī and Tukkojī; 1676–1736) have left an astonishing crop of literature in several languages: Telugu (inherited from their predecessors, the Nāyak kings), Tamil (the language of the region), Marathi (the language of the elite at court) and Sanskrit (the sacred language of Hinduism). For Marathi and Sanskrit in particular, this was a period of the most intensive scholarship under the patronage both of the royal family and of the family of pandit-ministers (including Tryambaka) who guided them. Śāhajī himself seems to have been proficient in Marathi, Telugu, Sanskrit, Persian and Hindi, and a remarkable number of works in several languages are attributed to him. These include some Marathi works relating to the religious role of women (*strīdharma*) and the model of the devoted wife (*patrivratā*). In 1693, Śāhajī dedicated an entire village to 45 named pandits to be a centre for traditional scholarship and the perpetual performance of sacrifices.

The only woman from this period who emerges as a distinct individual is Dīpāmbā, Ekojī's chief wife. She is mentioned in contemporary works, both for the part she played in effecting a reconciliation between the half-brothers Ekojī and Śivājī, and for being herself an example of the good wife and mother. She is also cited as the patron of several scholars. Her commissioned works include two Marathi treatises from a well-known pandit named Raghunātha on the subject of women. The colophon of one of these reads as follows:

> She [Dīpāmbā] feels that because of Muslim influence, people are turning away from Hindu principles; and that is why she has asked Raghunātha to write on the religious role of women (*strīdharma*).

Whether or not the *Strīdharmapaddhati* was also commissioned by Dīpāmbā,[10] it is safe to conclude that it was inspired by similar fears and aspirations.

To a man like Tryambaka, the conservative minister of an isolated Hindu kingdom, the attack on orthodox Hindu *dharma* must have seemed to come from many quarters at once: the constant threat of Muslim political domination and the encroachment of Islam; the insidious influence of Christian missionaries with their egalitarian ideas; the customs of the local Tamil population, whose women (especially those involved in the productive sphere) enjoyed a greater freedom than their northern sisters; and the increasing popularity of devotional religion which claimed that women and low-caste (or *śūdra*) men could reach heaven directly without even attending to their traditional duties.

Tryambaka's concern was to meet this challenge. He was interested in women not as individuals but as parts that fit into and therefore strengthen the whole. That whole is *dharma*. For the basic assumption of Sanskrit religious law is that, if every individual performs her or his allotted role (allotted, that is, by the precepts of *strīdharma* and *svadharma*), then universal harmony will result. Tryambaka's task (whether commissioned or self-imposed) was to persuade women to perform their ordained role. Following the example of those before him, therefore, he combed the ancient scriptures for rulings relating to women and rearranged them in such a way that all who read or heard the result would be encouraged to behave accordingly. He recycled the tradition once more.

THE PROPER BEHAVIOUR OF WOMEN

The *Strīdharmapaddhati* falls into five sections. The divisions of the text, and the order in which the individual topics are dealt with, follow those of the earliest available manuscript of Tryambaka's work. I shall comment briefly on each section in turn.

Tryambaka's Frame of Reference

Section I contains Tryambaka's introductory remarks and is extremely short. It is important, however, because it provides the first sketch of the framework into which the treatise will fit. It is here that some of the more important assumptions, tensions, even contradictions, inherent in the traditional image of the orthodox Hindu wife become apparent. I shall mention only two striking examples.

First, Tryambaka's concern is solely with the immigrant Maratha elite, that is, with the women of the prosperous Thanjavur court that originally came south on military expeditions from Maharashtra. There are no references to women agricultural labourers, market women, or any of the vast army of women who must have been living and working outside the context of the court. The few lower-class or outsider women who are mentioned are referred to fleetingly, with either indifference (such as female servants) or disapproval (such as courtesans, gambling women, washerwomen, female mendicants, and so on). The women in Tryambaka's scheme of things (as in Sanskrit religious law in general) are severely restricted – personally, socially, economically, sexually – and the most extreme standards of idealised behaviour are demanded of them. For, as we might expect, and as anthropological fieldwork increasingly shows, the more orthodox ideas concerning women tend to be held by elitist families; by high-ranking, landholding groups among whom patrilineage is strong and wives are economically dependent upon their husbands and their husbands' families.[11] Conversely, women who work outside the home wield their own economic power: they are far more likely to hold independent, even idiosyncratic, views about their social and religious role. Tryambaka follows the general pattern of Sanskrit religious law in making no allowance for women like these.

Second, one of the main points that Tryambaka makes in his introduction is that the rulings he is about to expound apply only to married women. He argues by analogy with the case for men. For religious law prescribes no rules for men until they have been invested with the sacred thread,[12] their initiation into the sphere of the sacred. In the case of women, marriage takes the place of initiation. The proof quotation is a famous one, taken from the *Manusmṛti*:

> For women, the marriage ritual is held to be the equivalent of initiation, serving one's husband that of residing in the teacher's house, and household duties that of the worship of the sacrificial fire. (2.67)

Tryambaka concludes that the sacred duties he is about to expound are therefore to be performed by women only after they are married. The analogy sounds both explicit and uplifting: an elevation of marriage and, with it, of the married woman.[13] For the implication is that a boy before initiation and a girl before marriage are ritually equivalent while afterwards they are both, in some sense, 'twice-born' (*dvija*). If this were really so, however, then religious–legal texts would group women of the three higher classes – the priestly or brahmin (*brāhmaṇa*) class, the warrior (*kṣatriya*) class, and the artisan (*vaiśya*) class – with their men, and not (as they invariably do) with the men of the lowest or serving class, the uninitiated *śūdra*. I shall return to this fundamental contradiction later.

The Daily Duties of Women

Section II represents less than a fifth of the text as a whole. But this compact and complex section on 'the daily duties of women' (*strīṇām āhnikam*) is unique. For while detailed descriptions of the daily practice of the orthodox Hindu male householder form a recurrent and important topic of Sanskrit religious law, it is unusual to find parallel rulings for women at any length. This rare attempt to map out a woman's day in detail therefore deserves careful consideration. For everything the good Hindu wife should do – from the moment she wakes in the morning to the moment she sleeps at night – is discussed from the point of view of the 'sacred norms' of religious law.

Section II is divided into four major subsections. (IIA) The first subsection concerns the ritual duties to be completed before dawn. It is further divided into three: (1) the importance of waking early, and the activities associated with waking; (2) household tasks, such as preparing the grain, cleaning the house, smearing it with cow-dung, worshipping the threshold, and so on; and (3) a variety of ablutions and related activities (urinating and defecating, cleansing oneself afterwards, sipping, teeth cleaning, bathing, and getting dressed for the day).[14]

(IIB) The second subsection concerns the ritual duties to be performed at dawn; primarily the fire ritual, and the precise part played in it by the chief wife (*patnī*).[15]

(IIC) This is the longest subsection and covers the ritual duties to be carried out during the day. It is further divided into four: (1) the requisite salutations and services to in-laws and husband; (2) more household tasks (in particular, how to manage the household accounts, and how to cope with tradesmen without breaking the strict code of proper behaviour); (3) the important midday rituals, including image worship, the *vaiśvadeva* ritual to all gods, and an extremely lengthy mini-treatise on paying homage to guests; and (4) the duty of the wife to serve her husband at meals, and afterwards to eat what he has left.

(IID) The final subsection is the shortest. It describes very briefly the duties of the wife in the evening, and includes a passage on how she should prepare herself for her husband's pleasure in bed.

Before comparing these duties for women with those usually ascribed to the initiated or twice-born man (about whom we have considerably more information), let us look briefly at the latter.

Early in the morning, between 4.30 and 6.00, a man should wake, perform the necessary ablutions and the sipping ritual, clean his teeth, bathe, and observe the twilight rituals. Between 6.00 and 7.30, he should worship his special deity and pay homage to his teacher. Between 7.30 and 9.00, he should study the *Vedas*. Between 9.00 and 10.30, he should work for the maintenance of his family, following only those professions permitted to his class.[16] Between 10.30 and 12.00 noon, he should bathe and perform the so-called 'twilight ritual' (*saṃdhyā*) appropriate at midday. Between 12.00 noon and 1.30 p.m., he should perform the 'five great sacrifices' (*pañca mahāyajñāḥ*): to the cosmic principle (*brahman*) by the study or recitation of the *Vedas*; to the gods, by ritual offerings into the fire; to the ancestors, by the offering of water; to all beings, by food offerings; and to humanity, by offering hospitality to guests. He should also take his midday meal. In the afternoon, between 1.30 and 4.30, he should study secular literature. Between 4.30 and 6.00, he may receive or visit friends, and should perform the evening twilight ritual. In the evening, between 6.00 and 9.00, he should attend to the duties omitted during the day and spend time with his family. From 9.00 p.m. until 4.30 the next morning, he may take rest.

In order to demonstrate the parallels between a woman's day as described by Tryambaka and that generally ascribed to men in *dharmaśāstra* texts, I have sketched out a rough timetable comparing the two.

Topics relating to women discussed by Tryambaka	Topics relating to men in dharmaśāstra
IIA *Before Dawn*	
waking	walking
housework	ablutions
ablutions	
IIB *At Dawn*	
assist at:	fire sacrifice
fire-worship	the 'twilight' ritual
offering to the sun	worship of special deity
IIC *Day*	
respects to elders	homage to one's teacher
housework	Vedic study
	work for the family
midday rituals:	midday rituals:
image worship	the ritual bath
the *vaiśvadeva* ritual	the 'twilight' ritual
homage to guests	'5 great sacrifices'
	(Vedic recitation to
	brahman; sacrifice to
	the gods; offerings
	to the ancestors, all
	beings, and humanity)
meal-time duties:	midday meal
serving at meals	
ritual offering	
own meal	
clearing away	study of epics and *purāṇas*
housework, etc.	visiting friends, etc.
IID *Evening*	
fire-worship, etc.	evening twilight ritual
going to bed	

Many of the rulings for women cover activities to be carried out before dawn. In addition to most of the duties prescribed for men, a woman must also prepare the day's quota of rice or millet, sweep the house and smear it with cow-dung, perform the ritual of threshold worship, and attend to the cows. At dawn, when her husband performs the morning fire-sacrifice, she assists him, and then makes an offering to the sun. In the morning, while her husband studies the *Vedas* and works at his profession, she attends to her household duties. At midday, when he performs the 'five great sacrifices', she assists him. When he eats, she serves him, eating what he leaves. After the meal, while he studies the epics and *purāṇas*, she clears away, washes, sweeps and cleans. In the evening, while he is visiting friends, she is still doing housework, for the food for the evening meal must be prepared afresh. At the evening sacrifice, she assists him again.

Now the crucial question in an analysis of these duties is how each ruling for women relates to its equivalent for men. The answer takes the form of four distinct categories.

The first group consists of rulings which are exactly the same for women as for men. In Tryambaka's scheme of things, these include the rulings concerning what one may or may not see first thing in the morning, urinating and defecating, cleaning the teeth, and so on. But this apparently straightforward group of rules in fact conceals a significant issue in the history of the religious status of women.

The question that is debated at length in both grammatical and philosophical texts is whether or not women should be excluded from initiation, from Vedic study, and from the performance of religious sacrifices.[17] The point at issue here is that virtually all ritual injunctions in the sacred texts are given in the masculine form. But is this masculine form to be taken as a superordinate (meaning 'person') or as a hyponym (meaning 'male' as opposed to 'female')? According to the early grammatical texts, the rules of modification applicable to such an injunction include that of gender. Later texts, however, redefine the rules of modification to exclude gender. The effect on the role of women in religious ritual is obvious: most injunctions are in the masculine; the modification of gender is not invoked; women are excluded. As a result, ritual texts are usually taken to apply only to men. What is interesting about Tryambaka's text is that he feels free to invoke the modification of gender when it suits him to do so without any fear of the logical consequences. Clearly, as far as Tryambaka is concerned, the question of whether or not ritual injunctions might apply to women is now too ludicrous to be considered.

The second category of rulings are the same in principle but different in detail. For example, when purifying oneself after urinating or defecating, the colour of the earth used and the number of lumps required are different for women and men. In the sipping ritual, the water should touch the heart, throat or palate of a twice-born man, but it need only touch the mouth of a woman or a *śūdra*. A man performs the bathing ritual with mantras or prayers, a woman and a *śūdra* without. Both men and women should wake around 4.30 a.m., but the wife should wake before her husband. Both should eat at the appropriate times, but the wife should serve her husband and eat only what he leaves. This is a large group of rulings and, in each case, the implications are interesting.

To take one example, why should a woman be barred from performing her ritual bath with mantras? This is in origin a historical problem. Before 500 BC, the initiation ceremony and the period of study and discipline that followed was deemed essential for girls as well as boys.[18] The reason is important: the initiation of women was vital to the continuation of the four-class system. Without it, all women would be reduced to the level of the *śūdra*, the lowest class, and (surely) *śūdras* cannot give birth to brahmins, *kṣatriyas* or *vaiśyas*. Although the actual practice of female students probably came to differ from that of males, the fact of initiation remained. But as language and culture developed away from those of Vedic texts, more extensive commentaries became necessary, and increasingly long periods of study were required to understand the accumulating literature. But whereas it was acceptable for boys to postpone marriage until their twenties or thirties, it was still thought essential for girls to marry in their teens. The effect was to divide women into two kinds: those who were initiated in the normal way, and those for whom the ceremony was a mere formality just before their marriage. By approximately 500 BC, the majority of girls came into the latter category. The lack of Vedic study and training for girls made nonsense of their use of mantras and so their initiation was performed without them. By the first or second century of the Christian era, the initiation of girls was prohibited altogether. Now at some point during this transition – in order to justify the marriage of uninitiated girls to twice-born men and thus to rescue the four-class system – there arose the compensatory theory that the marriage ritual took the place of initiation for girls. This in turn lent weight to the idea that girls should be married at a very early age. For it was felt that the girl's so-called 'initiation' (that is, her marriage) should take place at the same age as that appropriate for the boy's true initiation. In time, the argument turned full circle. Instead of the absence of initiation having as its consequence the status of *śūdra*, the *a priori śūdra* status of women came to be seen as the reason for their ineligibility in the first place. *Śūdra* status is now associated directly with the female state and only indirectly with the lack of initiation and Vedic education.

This creates an interesting problem for Tryambaka. In order to persuade women of the religious importance of their role, he expounds the view that the marriage ritual is their initiation on to the religious path. But again and again the ruling; he quotes carry the conviction that even married women are ritually equivalent to the uninitiated *śūdra*. Tryambaka uses the first view to inspire women to take their domestic existence seriously, at the level of religious ritual, and to discourage them from wasting their devotional energy on non-domestic forms of worship.[19] He uses the second view to remind women that being female is an awesome hurdle they must strive to overcome. The rulings on daily duties follow from the first view; the digression on the inherent nature of women (given in section III) follows from the second. Either way, the problem of how ritual *śūdras* can give birth to brahmins, *kṣatriyas* and *vaiśyas* remains.

The third category of rulings consists of those relating to the husband's ritual obligations and thus to the wife's corresponding duty to assist him in fulfilling them. In the early morning meditation, for example, the man is told to meditate with his wife. In the fire-sacrifice, although the wife has little to do, she must be present for the ritual to bear fruit. In the ceremony of paying homage and hospitality to guests, the wife must prepare the food and serve the guest on her husband's behalf. These rulings indicate the role and status of the wife in the joint ritual duties enjoined upon the married couple. There is a great deal that could be said here but I shall restrict myself to one point. Briefly, the main thrust of orthodox Hindu opposition is ranged against the independent *réligieuse* and not against the orthodox high-caste wife taking her legitimate part in religious ritual jointly with her husband. Here too, however, the role of the wife was gradually whittled away. By Tryambaka's day, all injunctions for the joint sacrifice not given specifically in the feminine form are taken to refer only to the male sacrificer, the husband. Even those expressed in the feminine are reinterpreted according to current notions of the religious inequality of women. This inequality is in turn justified by the insistence that women are not initiated into sacred learning and are not allowed to study the *Vedas*.

The fourth and final category of rulings consists of those which are peculiar to women. These are predominantly rulings concerning housework, such as grinding grain, cleaning the house, smearing it with cowdung, clearing away after the meal, and so on. As the parallel timetable shows, these duties are to be performed either when the husband is studying religious literature or when he is working for the family maintenance. They are thus part of both a woman's religious path and her contribution to the family. The parallel with the man's religious duties becomes more apparent in the context of the famous dictum on marriage for women quoted earlier: a wife serving her husband is like a student serving his teacher, and her household duties are equivalent to her husband's performance of the fire-sacrifice. Looked at from this point of view, household tasks become part of the powerful 'vow' (*vrata*) or religious observance of the wife. Hence the high tone in which these apparently mundane activities are described.

The Inherent Nature of Women

Section III of the *Strīdharmapaddhati* contains a brief but riveting digression on 'the inherent nature of women' (*strīsvabhāva*). Here Tryambaka bravely faces, and attempts to resolve, an apparently insuperable problem. If, as is widely acknowledged, women are inherently wicked, is there any point in instructing them on how to be virtuous? Is not the *Strīdharmapaddhati* itself a waste of time? Tryambaka's response to this question rests on a radical (if theoretically illogical) distinction between two crucial concepts relating to women: *strīsvabhāva* (the wicked nature of women) and *strīdharma* (the virtuous behaviour of women or, more properly, wives). This distinction underlies many of the extraordinary pronouncements concerning women that must strike anyone familiar with Indian literature. The physical aspects of being female – menstruation, female sexuality, childbirth, and so on – are taboo; women as biological creatures are condemned; the wild, untamed goddesses – their counterparts in myth and symbol – are feared and appeased. Respect, even reverence, is reserved for those women in whom the biological has been controlled: the obedient wife, the selfless mother, and the gentle goddesses of the Indian imagination.[20] This section is crucial for any real understanding of the complexities surrounding the position of women in Indian culture from ancient times until today. Both fascinating and terrifying, women as women are condemned. But if they allow themselves to be controlled by their ordained function as wives, the condemnation reserved for women no longer applies. By transforming themselves into devoted wives, women can annul the evil inherent in their natures. In ruling after ruling, Tryambaka's treatise describes precisely how this miracle may be wrought.[21]

General Rulings Applicable to Women

Section IV represents a third of the text. Under the general heading of 'duties common to all women' (*strīṇāṃ sādhāraṇā dharmāḥ*), Tryambaka groups together a variety of rulings to form nine extremely important topics.

(1) The general rulings on behaviour appropriate to women tend to repeat or rephrase notions of piety, modesty, service and so on that have already been covered.

(2) The 'things a woman should avoid' include roaming around on her own, sleeping in the daytime, reading sacred texts, performing austerities,

going on pilgrimages, the life of the renouncer–ascetic, chanting mantras, and worshipping deities (other than one's husband). All these activities may be deemed to distract the good wife from her domestic duties.

(3) The rulings on 'women's property' deal with the married woman's rights of ownership, inheritance, and the independent disposal of property. Not surprisingly, Tryambaka decides that the wife has no rights over her husband's property. With regard to the distribution of property owned jointly by wife and husband, she needs his permission but he does not need hers. With regard to the various kinds of 'women's property' (*strīdhana*; including gifts from her husband or her natal family), she still needs her husband's permission to exercise her right of ownership; but he has no right to use her property without her permission.

(4) The subsection in praise of the devoted wife (*pativratā*) consists almost entirely of quotations. These are mainly passages describing the meritorious behaviour of famous women or consort-goddesses taken verbatim and at great length from the epics and *purāṇas*.

(5) The rulings relating to the menstruating woman cover a number of important points: the polluting power of menstrual blood; the defects accruing to the unborn child if a woman defies the prohibitions applicable during menstruation; the ritual bath of purification after the crucial fourth day of bleeding; and the 'season' (*ṛtu*) or proper time to make love with one's husband.

(6) The rulings relating to the pregnant woman are mainly prohibitions, together with a description of the correct procedure for entering the lying-in chamber. There is also an intriguing discussion of the pregnant woman's cravings, their significance, and the importance of gratifying them.[22]

(7) The behaviour appropriate for a woman whose husband is away is described briefly: she should wear none of the marks of the happily-married woman whose husband is present (that is, no bright colours, jewellery, flowers, and so on).[23]

(8) The injunction to become a *satī* (that is, a supremely 'virtuous woman') by dying with one's husband on his funeral pyre is discussed at some length. In view of the official abolition of *satī* in India in 1829, and also in the context of the apparent increase in the number of *satī* cases in the 1980s, Tryambaka's rather laboured recommendation of the practice is of particular interest.[24]

(9) The subsection on widowhood describes the appropriate conduct for the wife to whom the injunction to die with her husband does not apply (because she is pregnant, perhaps, or nursing an infant). Tryambaka also discusses the ancient practice of temporary levirate 'marriage' (*niyoga*) for the purpose of providing offspring for a husband who has died childless.

Section IV ends with the statement that there are three kinds of devoted wife (*pativratā*): the wife who dies before her husband and patiently waits for him to join her; the wife who follows her husband on to his funeral pyre; and the wife who after her husband's death leads an ascetic and celibate life for the rest of her days.[25]

Tryambaka's Conclusion

Section V is the longest. While section II was probably intended as a kind of instruction manual for the chief wife of the head of the household together with her co-wives, section V seems to be more a collection of inspirational material directed primarily towards the new daughters-in-law coming as brides into the home. In essence, however, it contains only one point: that a woman's highest duty is service to her husband. Tryambaka's stark message is defined in three ways. First, she should have no regard for her own life. Second, she should even allow herself to be sold, if her husband should wish it. Third, obedience to her husband takes precedence over all other religious duties; if her husband requires it, she should even do what is wrong. These three sub-points are then illustrated at varying length with stories culled from the epics and *purāṇas*, often without added comment. It is this section that earns Tryambaka's text the dubious distinction of being to some degree a scissors-and-paste type of digest.

There follows a brief discussion of what is meant by 'service to one's husband' and 'obedience to his command', followed by the story of Sāvitrī – the most devoted wife of all – taken more or less verbatim from its source, the *Mahābhārata*. Tryambaka's summary, the closing verses, and the colophon finally bring this extraordinary document to an end.

CONCLUSIONS

The *Strīdharmapaddhati* does not describe how all Hindu women behave in India today; and yet, a surprising proportion of the behaviour described is praised or adhered to in traditional areas even now.[26] Nor does it tell us how all women behaved in Tryambaka's day; yet we can assume that high-caste women were expected and encouraged to conform. What it does tell us without any doubt is how an orthodox pandit in eighteenth-century Thanjavur thought women ought to behave. It also demonstrates precisely how such a pandit, steeped in the rulings of Sanskrit religious law, was able to recycle for his own time a religious and cultural tradition already over a thousand years old.

As always in religious law, the result is an odd mixture of reality and utopia, a heady brew created by the often confusing series of prohibitions and injunctions. For example, a prohibition is only necessary if someone is actually doing what is prohibited. Indeed, it is a basic principle of *mīmāṃsā* philosophy that something can only be prohibited if its occurrence is possible. Thus the prohibitions on wearing no blouse during the day, for instance, or on wearing heavy earrings during love-making, imply that some women were in fact doing these things. The injunctions, on the other hand, betray the ideals of a utopia: a woman should always wake before her husband; she should herself attend upon her husband instead of delegating such duties to servants; she should think only of her husband, worshipping him as her god; and so on. Whether they seem to us to be important or trivial, these ideals are the visible signs of the ancient Hindu culture that Tryambaka was trying to defend.

While advocating conformity, however, the *Strīdharmapaddhati* is itself an admission of the power of non-conformist women to wreck the entire edifice of Hindu orthodoxy. The *Bhagavadgītā*[27] explains:

> When wickedness triumphs, it is the women who are corrupted; and once the women are corrupted, there will be the mixing of castes and all the horrors of hell and destruction that that entails. (1.41–2)

Reinforcing the proper role of women in society was thus in ancient times – and is still to some extent today – the surest way to restore the orthodox Hindu moral code and, by extension, the perfect world. In the context of the recent revival of Hindu fundamentalism both within and outside India, it is important to understand the implications for women of pursuing this particular path.

NOTES

1. For a detailed account of one self-professed *pativratā*, see Jacobson's life-history of a high-caste brahmin woman in Madhya Pradesh in the 1970s (1978). For information on votive rites (*vrata*) for women in general, and the stress that all these rites lay on the welfare of husband and children, see McGee's study of women in Maharashtra in the 1980s (1991).
2. While the practice of satī ('suttee') is today both illegal and rare, the woman who dies in this way is still highly regarded in traditional circles. See also n. 24 below.

3.   Not all Hindu women subscribe equally to this view, of course. Different emphases are arrived at in the different regions of India, and as a result of the varying beliefs and assumptions of the many different religious sects. For an examination of how the theologies of Śaivism and Vaiṣṇavism affect the religious paths of women, for example, see Gupta (1991).
4.   Quoted in Kishwar and Vanita (1984), pp. 46–7.
5.   This chapter concentrates on the textual evidence of Sanskrit religious law. For a more general survey of women and religion in ancient Indian texts, see Leslie (1983). All translations from the Sanskrit are mine.
6.   All references to the *Strīdharmapaddhati* are to Leslie (1989).
7.   Unfortunately, this apparent harmony vanishes when the theory is applied to women (see my discussion of the inherent nature of women, below).
8.   See Derrett (1973).
9.   For a more detailed discussion of the identity of Tryambakayajvan, see Leslie (1989), pp. 10–13; 16–19.
10.   For a discussion of this possibility, see Leslie (1989), p. 32.
11.   A clear example is provided by a recent study of the women of a high-caste Hindu community in Nepal, see Bennett (1983).
12.   According to ancient tradition, all male members of the three higher classes (*varṇa*) were expected to spend a period of time in religious studentship, studying and performing rituals under the guidance of a teacher, serving him, and living in his home. A boy was initiated on to the path of the religious student in a ceremony involving the tying of a 'sacred thread' around his body. This ritual was normally performed at about the age of eight. There is evidence to suggest that both initiation with a sacred thread and religious studentship were once open to girls as well as boys (see below).
13.   For a detailed analysis of the changing marital expectations dramatised in marriage rituals from the *Vedas* to the present day, see Menski (1991). For the importance of marriage before death, or at least before cremation, see van den Bosch (1991).
14.   For a detailed discussion of the significance of the rulings on dress for women, including the requirement to wear the forehead marking (*tilaka*), see Leslie (1992).
15.   For a discussion of the role of the *patnī* in the fire ritual, and of the gradual suppression of that role, see Smith (1991).
16.   This is an intriguing ruling in any context. Even in the utopian world of *dharmaśāstra*, however, a satisfactory working day of an hour-and-a-half makes sense only in relation to men of a privileged elite, secure in the hierarchy established by wealth and class.
17.   See n. 12.
18.   See n. 12.
19.   The 'non-domestic' worship implicitly or explicitly excluded by Tryambaka includes all forms of the holy life for women, even those of acclaimed poetess–saints, see Ramanujan (1982); Gupta (1991), and women ascetics, see Denton (1991), let alone those of the oft-maligned temple-dancer (*devadāsī*), see Kersenboom-Story (1987); Kersenboom (1991); Marglin (1985).
20.   It is interesting to note that, while Tryambaka repeatedly instructs the good Hindu wife not to worship any god other than her husband, he does advise her

to worship two goddesses, Śrī and Jyeṣṭhā. Curiously, neither of these sister-goddesses fits the polarised schema implied by the *strīdharma/strīsvabhāva* dichotomy set out here. For an exploration of the peculiar ambivalences surrounding Śrī and Jyeṣṭhā, and of their significance as role models for Hindu women, see Leslie (1991b).

21. For a more detailed discussion of the problem of 'the inherent nature of women', and of Tryambaka's solution to it, see Leslie (1986).

22. Tryambaka devotes little attention to the pregnant wife, even less to the mother of young children. In the context of the pregnancy and mothering rituals evident in India today, see Stork (1991), this seems surprising.

23. See n. 14.

24. For an exploration of the contrast between the Sanskrit term glorifying the woman (*satī*) and the Anglicised term denigrating the act ('suttee'), see Leslie (1987/88). Tryambaka's traditional views regarding the act (*sahagamana*) are juxtaposed with current opinions on the widely publicised death of Roop Kanwar in Rajasthan in September 1987, and the ethical issues embedded in cross-cultural work of this kind are confronted.

25. For a discussion of widowhood as the necessary complement to sati, and an exploration of the parallels between the widow and the male renouncer/ascetic, see Leslie (1991d). Tryambaka is silent on the subject of remarriage as an alternative to either widowhood or divorce, see Lariviere (1991).

26. This is true in general terms about much of traditional India today. More specifically, however, while I was visiting south Indian temples and libraries in 1981 in search of manuscripts of the *Strīdharmapaddhati*, I came across copies of a bilingual (Sanskrit and Tamil) edition printed (I was informed) around 1920. I also met an old pandit attached to one of the major south Indian temples who knew and revered Tryambaka's text and who had, quite independently, copied the manuscript out for his own use. He explained to me how useful the treatise was because it brought together in one place all the ancient rulings and traditional stories relating to women. He also told me that he gave regular sermons based on the *Strīdharmapaddhati* to a mainly female audience, and he showed me the weekly pamphlets containing choice passages from Tryambaka's work that he had translated into Tamil for their benefit.

27. The *Bhagavadgītā* ('The Song of the Lord'), a self-contained episode in the *Mahābhārata*, and the most popular and influential of all the ancient Hindu scriptures, may be dated to just before the beginning of the Christian era.

14 The Witch and The Wife: A Comparative Study of Theocritus, *Idyll* 2, Simonides, *Idyll* 15 and *Fatal Attraction*[1]

Laura Gibbs-Wichrowska

While there are many different witch-images found in Western art, one that quickly comes to mind is the witch-hag with a prominent wart on her nose and a bearded chin who comes trick-or-treating on Halloween, prophesies to Macbeth, and causes Dorothy so much trouble in the Land of Oz. This chapter, however, deals with a different witch-image: the erotic enchantress, both scary and sexy. Many of today's erotic clichés derive from this ancient idea of witchcraft: an attractive woman may be 'enchanting' (from the Latin *incantare*, to chant or intone magic words); 'charming' (from the Latin *carmen*, song or incantation); 'fascinating' (from the Latin *fascinare*, to cast a spell); and, of course, 'bewitching' (from the Middle English *bewicchen*, to bewitch, to put a spell on). There are many illustrations of the erotic enchantress in both ancient and modern art. In this chapter, I will compare the representation of the enchantress in three very different works: Theocritus *Idyll* 2, from Hellenistic Greece, *circa* the third century BC; Simonides, *Idyll* 15, from Renaissance Poland, *circa* the early seventeenth century; and *Fatal Attraction*, an American film of the 1980s.

While different rules of representation operate in the different historical periods in which these art-works originate, as well as important differences in language and artistic medium, the rules for representing the erotic enchantress have not changed as much as the outward civilisations have. In Hellenistic Greece, in Renaissance Poland, and in modern America, the same witch-figure continues to haunt the popular imagination. In the case of Simonides, *Idyll* 15 we can call this 'the same witch-figure' because the poet Simonides explicitly set out to translate Theocritus, *Idyll* 2, copying the ancient Greek witch-figure in a Renaissance Polish poem. In the case of *Fatal Attraction* the ancient origins of the enchantress are not made explicit in the film, but critics have been quick to compare the film's female villain to prototypical witches of antiquity. There is, thus, a chain of representation stretching from antiquity to the present day.

In this chapter I will not be making a detailed analysis of the three individual texts, each of which has its unique and puzzling features, to be sure. Instead, I will be using the texts to illuminate one another, drawing attention to the similarities in representation which persist throughout the tradition. The crucial link between these three representations is not so much the specific witch-imagery itself, but the use to which it is put. While there is a feminist tradition that conceives of witchcraft as a rebellion against the patriarchal order or as a womanist counter-culture, witchcraft has also been used in a misogynistic cultural tradition which takes a derogatory attitude towards women and their desires (especially their sexual desires). The fictitious witches examined in this chapter are all frustrated, love-sick women seeking the domestic bliss of married life. In each case, the men have wronged the women by denying their fulfilment as housewives, causing them to turn to witchcraft as a desperate last resort. Hence, the witch and the wife.

THEOCRITUS, *IDYLL* 2

Two thousand years before Congreve declared that 'Heaven has no rage like love to hatred turned, nor hell a fury like a woman scorned', Theocritus wrote his *Idyll* 2, precisely the story of a woman scorned, enraged by her lover's faithlessness, summoning up the powers of darkness for revenge. This story of love and witchcraft is one of the most popular and accessible of ancient Greek poems. Theocritus, *Idyll* 2 is narrated by a woman, Simaetha, who is using witchcraft to try to bring back her lover, Delphis, who has left her, it seems, for another man. In the midst of casting spells, Simaetha tells the story of her ill-fated love affair, including an unusually explicit reference to the sexual satisfaction she experienced with Delphis. Although the poem has its linguistic obscurities, the story is simple, especially in comparison to other poems by Theocritus which are complicated by ancient Greek politics or intricate mythology. Unlike the now obscure ritual of Theocritean pastoral poetry, the ritual of witchcraft is still familiar. Simaetha's use of fire, magic potions and incantations makes sense to us because this general notion of witchcraft persists in popular culture. Although Theocritus is best-known as the inventor of European pastoral poetry, his witch, rather than any of his shepherds, is most accessible to readers today.

We know that Theocritus, *Idyll* 2 was popular in antiquity because it was closely imitated by Vergil in his *Eclogue* 8. For Vergil, however, the pastoral was such a vital and important form of ritual culture that he took the freestanding, first-person witch of Theocritus, *Idyll* 2 and integrated her into a pastoral framework. Instead of having the witch sing her own song (as in Theocritus, *Idyll* 2), Vergil subordinated her to the ritual of pastoral: a shepherd sings what had been Simaetha's song in a singing contest with another shepherd. In this pastoral adaptation of Theocritus, *Idyll* 2, Vergil also made numerous small alterations, three of which will be important for our understanding of Simonides, *Idyll* 15, the Renaissance adaptation of Theocritus, *Idyll* 2. First, Vergil changed the name of the witch's lover from Delphis to Daphnis (probably because Daphnis is a standard character in the pastoral tradition). Second, in Vergil, *Eclogue* 8 the marital status of the couple is more obscure than in Theocritus, *Idyll* 2, where the witch is clearly *un*married and complains specifically about that fact. Finally, Vergil changed the ending of the story. Originally, in Theocritus, *Idyll* 2, the witch simply bids farewell to the moon goddess, resigned to carry on with her life, despite her lack of fulfilment, both sexual (she is abandoned by her lover) and social (she is unmarried). In Vergil's adaptation, the witch believes she hears Daphnis coming home at last.

The difference in the endings of the poems is perhaps itself linked to the issue of marital status. Because Simaetha is not married to Delphis, she has no real claim on him. Thus, while her witchcraft seems to fulfil a particular purpose (what a psychologist might call 'ventilating' her frustration), it cannot change her social position nor give her power over a man. In Vergil's poem, the witch's spells are not different from or more powerful than Simaetha's spells but her relationship to the man is different. Because the man and woman are involved in a stable situation, and perhaps even married, the man eventually comes back to the woman, i.e. back to his own home. In Theocritus, *Idyll* 2, Simaetha's home is not Delphis's home. Thus, while the two versions of the story end differently, in both cases, the power (or powerlessness) of the woman with respect to the man is not altered by the use of witchcraft. Rather, the balance of power results from the established social situation in which the woman finds herself already.

Even though Theocritus, *Idyll* 2 is the 'origin' for the chain of representation which I wish to discuss, this is not the first depiction of the erotic enchantress in literature. Theocritus invokes earlier depictions of erotic witchcraft in *Idyll* 2 by having Simaetha appeal to the examples of Circe and Medea. Circe and Medea are mythological witches of antiquity who, unlike Simaetha, are 'real' witches, i.e. their personal exploits actually illustrate magical powers at work. Circe (in the story of Odysseus and his journey home) turned men into beasts and Medea (in the story of Jason and the Argonauts) performed assorted miraculous deeds. Medea is the most crucial subtext for Theocritus, *Idyll* 2 because, like Simaetha, Medea resorted to bizarre behaviour when ultimately betrayed by Jason. In the infamous version dramatised by Euripides, she killed her own children and, using magic powers, did away with Jason's bride-to-be as well.

As critics have often pointed out, the legendary figures of Circe and Medea are an ironic contrast to the undistinguished, simple Simaetha. Halperin refers to Simaetha as 'naive' and suggests that 'the reader is amused to hear a suburban teenager cite mythological precedent for her erotic entanglements'.[2] Theocritus did indeed take great pains to depict the details of Simaetha's 'suburban' existence as Halperin puts it, revealing the ordinariness of Simaetha's daily life. In addition to the information about her sex-life, she explains how she had borrowed a dress from a girlfriend to go to a festival, how she gossips with the old lady who lives down the street, how she purchased magic powders from an Assyrian travelling salesman, and so on. A great deal of the poem's effect comes, in fact, from this blend of the sinister and the everyday. On the one hand, Simaetha invokes the goddess Hecate and addresses herself to the moon goddess Selene but, on the other hand, Simaetha gossips with the goddesses as she might gossip with her next-door neighbour. Barriss Mills's excellent translation captures the tone of this ironic juxtaposition:

> And when I had gone halfway
> on the road, near Lykon's, I saw
> Delphis and Eudamippos walking
> together. Their beards were golden
> as helichryse and their breasts
> brighter far than you, o Selene,
> for they had just come from the manly
> work of the gymnasium.[3]

In *Idyll* 2, Theocritus has pioneered the technique of combining the imagery of witchcraft with a girl-next-door type of character, who is realistic to the very core, rather than supernatural. Critics still cannot agree on the ultimate significance of representing the supernatural and the quotidian side by side. Thus, in its own way, Theocritus *Idyll* 2 provokes a critical debate similar to the controversy which surrounded the film *Fatal Attraction* when it was released.

Some critics assert that Theocritus is calling into question or even satirising the tradition of witchcraft itself. This is the interpretation forwarded by Halperin, who concludes that the reader, having encountered Simaetha in Theocritus *Idyll* 2, might conclude that 'Medea in actuality may not have been a very different sort of person', i.e. that the *grand dames* of witchcraft

were also love-crazed, silly suburbanites.[4] Dover suggests something similar
when he speculates that the 'emotional predicament' of a realistic character
such as Simaetha and a mythical being such as Medea are not essentially
different from one another.[5] Rist likewise suggests that Theocritean idylls
often have as their point the deflating of high mythological images, bringing
them down to everyday size. She cites Theocritus's treatment of Hercules in
Idyll 24 as one example, and Simaetha as another. According to Rist,
Theocritus is not trying to satirise the high mythological tradition so much
as he is trying to give it human warmth and liveliness. As she writes of *Idyll*
2, 'In Simaetha, Theocritus accords women the tribute of being human
characters and intrinsically interesting.'[6]

Yet, at the same time that critics think the juxtaposition of the supernatural
witch and the everyday girl-next-door throws into question the nature of the
witch, other critics think that the juxtaposition throws into question the
nature of the girl-next-door. Maybe all women, this argument goes, are
Medeas waiting to explode, supernatural hysterical creatures with a very
short fuse. This is the argument advanced by Walker who insists on the
sinister nature of Simaetha (as implied by the sinister deeds of the dangerous
Circe and, most especially, the deadly Medea). As Walker sees it:

> [Simaetha] is willing to try anything, including murder, to see to it that
> she will not have to play the role of the helpless forsaken maiden . . . her
> magic incantations have put her in contact with the feminine powers of
> darkness, the surviving matriarchal forces of feminine strength and
> endurance.[7]

Thus, there is a real conflict in the interpretation of Theocritus's juxtaposition
of witchcraft with the everyday character of Simaetha. On the one hand,
Simaetha charms some readers with her down-to-earth everydayness; on
the other hand, she scares some readers with her dangerous audacity.

Regardless of the value-judgment critics read into the juxtaposition of the
high tradition of witchcraft and the realism of Simaetha's depiction, there is
a strong parallel between Simaetha and her mythological precedents: Medea,
Circe and Simaetha alike are associated with men whom they attempt to
subdue and possess by supernatural means but ultimately without success.
Circe thinks she can control Odysseus and all his men but is undone by the
greater magic of the moly plant and, once she and Odysseus have become
lovers, he leaves her; Medea, despite her best efforts, loses Jason to a Greek
princess; and even lowly Simaetha loses her Delphis to an anonymous rival.
Because Medea and Circe are archetypal abandoned women, Simaetha's
appeal to the stories of these women does not bode well for her own
success. Even professional witches like Medea and Circe were betrayed by

their men. Although Simaetha has armed herself with the trappings of supernatural power – magic knots, elaborate curses, evil potions, demon goddesses, and (she hints) poison – she is not able to alter the course of events. Her deeds take place at night, in private, but her public life by day remains the same. When we turn to Simonides, *Idyll* 15 we will see the same pattern of desperation and failure.

SIMONIDES, *IDYLL* 15

The first translations of poems by Theocritus into a European vernacular did not appear until the seventeenth century with the publication of the Polish pastorals of Szymon Szymonowic (who published under the name of Simon Simonides) in 1614. His Polish *Sielanki* (or pastorals) include translations and adaptations of both Theocritus and Vergil as well as more original works. His translation/adaptation of Theocritus, *Idyll* 2 appears as *Idyll* 15 in the collection. In order to discuss the specifics of Simonides' adaptation of Theocritus, *Idyll* 2, however, we need to be able to read the poem. Theocritus, *Idyll* 2 is already available in many English translations but Simonides, *Idyll* 15 has never been published (to my knowledge) in English translation. Accordingly, I have prepared a verse translation of the poem, relying on the Polish edition of Sielanka Pietnasta appearing in the recent edition of Simonides's selected idylls prepared by Sokolski (1985). To the right of the translation of Simonides, *Idyll* 15 are excerpts from Barris Mills' (1963) translation of Theocritus, *Idyll* 2 which helps define the derivative nature of Simonides's poem.

Simonides, Idyll 15: The Spells

1 Three nights and still my husband is not here;
   abandoned stands the house he once held dear.
   Anxiety and fears beset me while
   my stomach fills with bitter-tasting bile.
5 Bring, Thestylis, the things I set apart,
   and let me try to soothe my aching heart.
   If he meant to leave, why take a bride?
   By my distress his pain is multiplied.
   The woman who has ruined him will learn
10 that doing wrong brings sorrow in return.
   I swear, oh moon, grief makes me thus resolved:
   Let vengeance against evil be absolved.
   I gave him what was fitting, without shame:
   A dowry, and a noble family name.
15 Though I am mistress of the house, his wife
   and servant, still he mocks our married life.
   A curse on him! He sees not God above:
   No wonder he betrays my friendly love.
   He scorns the Lord, his conscience he forsakes:
20 The harsher lord of hell will make him quake!

Excerpts from Barris Mills's verse translation of Theocritus, *Idyll* 2 (see Acknowledgements, p. ix)

Where are my bay leaves? Bring them, Thestylis. And where are the love-charms? Crown the bowl with fine red wool. I'll weave a spell against my cruel lover, who for twelve days now hasn't come near, the unkind man, and doesn't know whether I'm alive or dead. Not once has he knocked at my door, the heartless fellow. Surely Eros and Aphrodite have turned his fickle attention elsewhere. Tomorrow I'm going to Timagetos' wrestling school to see him, and ask him why he treats me so badly. But now I'll put fire spells on him. Shine brightly, Selene, for I'll sing softly to you, goddess, and to Hekate underground.

I know that magic is a mortal sin,
  but rage is strong. Thus let the spells begin.
Why aren't you back yet, Thestylis? Make haste.
  Obey my words! We have no time to waste.
25 Pour millet in the pan above the fire
  and seize the bellows, fan the flames still higher.
Now say: As millet crackles, pops and burns,
  thus let my lady's husband soon return.
Bring my husband home, oh mighty spell;
30   My sorrow is so great no tongue can tell.

My heart's on fire for Daphnis. In his name,
  consign these leaves of autumn to the flame.
They burn entire, and leave no ash behind:
  Let burning passion seize his heart and mind.
35 Bring my husband home, oh mighty spell;
  My sorrow is so great no tongue can tell.

I melt this wax upon the fire. As rain
  in torrents melts the earth and floods the plain,
Let him be soaked with sweat from every pore,
40 and he will scorn his worthy wife no more.
Bring my husband home, oh mighty spell;
  My sorrow is so great no tongue can tell.

I spin the spindle: As the spindle spins
  so let my honest longing reel him in.
45 Anxiety will goad him to return;
  Awake, asleep, his wretched thoughts will churn.
Bring my husband home, oh mighty spell;
  My sorrow is so great no tongue can tell.

I tie my shawl with magic-binding knots
50 and braid my hair: Behold, I bind his thoughts.
I hold him trapped in this captivity
  till he returns, contrite, to honor me.
Bring my husband home, oh mighty spell;
  My sorrow is so great no tongue can tell.

55 A bat is sealed, alive, within this pot.
  Now scorched by flame it bakes and glows
  red hot.
My husband's heart thus bakes, and if I could
  I'd add the fires of hell to mortal wood.
Bring my husband home, oh mighty spell;
60   My sorrow is so great no tongue can tell.

My neighbour Baucys calls ghosts from the tomb
  with magic herbs and flies upon a broom.
Burn all the herbs she gave me on the flame:
  Together they are more than he can tame.
65 Bring my husband home, oh mighty spell;
  My sorrow is so great no tongue can tell.

His handkerchief, unwashed, from long ago:
  We danced and as the sweat began to flow
He wiped his brow. Thus let it now grow wet
70 again and drown him in a flood of sweat.
Bring my husband home, oh mighty spell;
  My sorrow is so great no tongue can tell.

Pour wheat into your apron, lift it higher:
  The wheat has boiled itself without a fire.
75 But someone's coming, is it him? I hear

before whom even the dogs shiver
as she passes over the graves of the dead
and the dark blood. Hail, awful Hekate!
Be my helper to the end.
And make these medicines of mine
as strong as Kirke's or Medeia's
or golden-haired Perimede's.
Magic wheel, draw the man to my house.

. . . As the bay leaves crackle loudly
and catch fire suddenly
and we don't even see the ashes,
so may Delphis' body burn.
Magic wheel, draw the man to my house.

. . . With help from the goddess, I melt
this wax, and so may Delphis
of Myndos quickly melt with love.

And as this wheel of brass turns,
so, by Aphrodite's power,
may he turn and turn about my door.
Magic wheel, draw the man to my house.

. . . Three times I pour libation, and three
times,
o mistress, I say whether he lies by a woman
or a man, may he forget them, as Theseus
they say, forgot blonde Ariadne in Dia.
Magic wheel, draw the man to my house.

. . . I'll grind up a lizard, and tomorrow
I'll bring you an evil drink . . .

. . . but if he still treats me badly,
by the Fates, he'll do his knocking
on the gates of Haides, I say –
such evil drugs I keep for him
in a box, taught me, o Queen,
by an Assyrian stranger . . .

. . . Delphis lost this fringe from his cloak.
I pull it to pieces and cast it
into the cruel flames . . .

Now I'll burn the husks, O Artemis,
you can move the gates of adamant
in Haides and all other

the dogs, now someone's at the gate, he's near.
Enough for now! The dogs no longer howl.
   They recognise his scent and do not growl.
He has come back, and we will greet him sweetly,
80   but keep our distance, hold him off discreetly.
He thinks it's right to run away, of course,
   but we will teach him to behave by force.
Don't damp the fire, not yet. Most potent charm:
   Avenge my grief with still more grievous harm.

85 First take these entrails, burn them, and proclaim:
   May she now shrivel up and writhe in pain.
My lady's heart thus writhed and shriveled while
   her husband was deceitfully beguiled.
Please help me, powerful and potent charm:
90   Avenge my grief with still more grievous harm.

Then drag these rags along the road and say:
   The hangman drags my lady's foe away.
He sinks his fiery pincers in her breast,
   and tosses to the dogs her putrid flesh.
95 Please help me, powerful and potent charm:
   Avenge my grief with still more grievous harm.

The owl hoots shrilly in the woods, in vain!
   Should she escape my agony and pain?
Let everyone begin to hoot and cluck,
100 proclaiming her true name out loud: The slut!
Please help me, powerful and potent charm:
   Avenge my grief with still more grievous harm.

Then spit three times and say: As this spit sprays
   the ground, let pimples fester on her face
105 And scabs and worms and ulcers dripping blood.
   She'll grovel with the beggars in the mud.
A ringing in my ears assures me: I have won.
   My enemy will pay for what she's done.
It sounds as if in haste he lost a shoe?
110 We'll go and greet him. What else can we do?
Though angry at him still, I am relieved:

   My ravished heart rejoices, though it bleeds.

---

immovable things. Thestylis,
the dogs howl in the town . . .

. . . the mother
of Philista, our flute-player,
and of Melixo came to me.
She told me many other things
and that Delphis was in love.
And she didn't know for certain
whether desire for a woman
or for a man possessed him,
but only this, that this pledge
was always to Eros, in unmixed wine,
and he went away at last in a hurry,
saying he was going to decorate
a certain house with garlands.
These things my visitor told me,
and she's right. For he used to come here
three or four times every day,
and often he'd leave his Dorian
oil-flask with me. But now
it's the twelfth day since I've even
seen him. Mustn't he have found
some other delight, and forgotten me?
Now I'll bind him with my love-charms . . .

. . . And I
will bear my longing as I've borne it
until now . . .

Simonides, *Idyll* 15 is intentionally identical to Theocritus, *Idyll* 2 in both poetic structure and much dramatic detail. It certainly causes a strange sense of literary vertigo for readers closely acquainted with Theocritus's original. Because the poem is told in first person by the witch herself (along with details such as the name of the maidservant Thestylis), it is obvious that Simonides set out to imitate Theocritus, *Idyll* 2 rather than Vergil's version, despite the fact that Vergil was the more popular poet at the time Simonides was writing. As discussed earlier, there are some elements of the poem taken from Vergil's adaptation, but Simonides, *Idyll* 15 is essentially Theocritean.

Simonides's poem is shorter than Theocritus *Idyll* 2, largely because he has omitted and altered much of the erotic material in the Greek original (Vergil's version was also much shorter, largely because of the structural necessity of fitting the poem into a pastoral frame). Simonides was adamant in his censorship of homosexuality in classical literature and may have been attracted to Theocritus, *Idyll* 2 because of its generally hetero-erotic character. Yet, it is also true that there is an element of homosexuality in Theocritus, *Idyll* 2; Simaetha is abandoned by her male lover who has left her for another *man*. Simonides, however, went out of his way to identify the witch's rival as female, having the witch resoundingly curse this rival woman in the final stanzas of the poem. (Recall the Medea prototype who brutally murdered her female rival.) In addition to changing homosexual references to heterosexual references, Simonides also carefully avoided explicit references to sexual activity itself. Thus, in place of Simaetha's bold seduction of Delphis and her sexual relations with him, Simonides substituted something far more acceptable: the witch's courtship with her fiancé prior to their marriage. While their sweaty dancing scene does not have the passion of Theocritus, *Idyll* 2, it is Simonides's best attempt to convey an acceptable sense of the erotic original.

The inclusion of this dancing scene is quite important for it shows that Simonides was not attempting to de-eroticise the witch by making her a wife. The images of sweat, fire and the rhetoric of passion in the poem are Simonides's attempt to convey the erotic nature of the witch-wife's dilemma without compromising the decorum of his poem. The fires of the domestic hearth itself become erotic symbols and, even though the witch is married, she is as much driven by burning lust as any unmarried woman might be. Like Theocritus, Simonides has not created a violent heroine. She does not actually kill her rival nor physically attack her husband. But she does have violent emotions and, on some level, the violent rhetoric of witchcraft is one big metaphor for the violent passion of female lust (traditionally understood).

Given the Renaissance audience for whom Simonides was writing, Simonides had to condemn the witch as being 'evil' on some level. In fact, this gave Simonides another reason to emphasise the woman's burning lust, as unbridled female sexual desire was an important part of the Christian understanding of witchcraft at the time. Lust and femininity were both gateways to the Devil. The authors of the widely-influential *Witches' Hammer* of 1486 argued that 'All witchcraft comes from carnal lust which is in women insatiable', which is 'why a greater number of witches is found in the fragile female sex than among men.'[8] The *Witches' Hammer* even asserted that the Latin word for woman, *femina*, 'comes from *fe* and *minus* since she is ever weaker to hold and preserve the faith.'[9] In keeping with the prevailing condemnation of witchcraft, Simonides eliminated references to pagan deities and made explicit the witch's own sense of religious guilt. She agonises over her 'mortal sin' and, instead of Hecate, she invokes the Devil, the 'darker Lord of hell'.

Yet, at the same time, Simonides has not created a full-blown European witch. He has borrowed little from the European stereotypes of witchcraft, relying more on his ancient Greek and Latin sources. The inclusion of the witch on the broomstick (actually a fire poker in the Polish original) is the only egregious example of European imagery mixed in with the images taken from ancient sources. Moreover, the Devil is referred to only indirectly, and there is no demonic epiphany. The witch neither summons the Devil into her presence, nor does she make a pact with him. Thus, like Theocritus, Simonides was not trying to depict a 'real' witch so much as he was trying to depict the real desperation of a passionate woman that would drive her to attempt witchcraft.

As in Theocritus, *Idyll* 2, Simonides, *Idyll* 15 juxtaposes the words and images from the supernatural realm of witchcraft with the everydayness of the girl-next-door. Both Theocritus's and Simonides's witches may act in the belief that they are able to summon up powerful, threatening forces, but they are actually powerless victims of their own sexual desires. Both poems thus end on a bittersweet note of failure rather than in actual magical mayhem. Simaetha prepares to keep on suffering from frustrated desire and the witch-wife in Simonides, *Idyll* 15 can feel only mixed pleasure at the return of her husband. Indeed, the Renaissance witch-wife is even more pathetic. Simaetha, at least, still dreams that if she could only marry a man, she would be satisfied and at peace both with him and with her own desires. Simonides's witch-wife shows how that married life may not be much of an improvement.

What, then, has Simonides accomplished by turning the witch into a wife, by taking Vergil's vaguest hint and making it central to the poem? As mentioned above, marriage was an important part of making eroticism appropriate. The woman can sympathetically discuss her desire for her husband without moral indiscretion. Like Simaetha, who insists Delphis had made a commitment to her, this witch-wife also maintains her illicit acts are justified, because she did all that was required. She brought her husband a good dowry, has been a good housewife, and has not brought him any shame. By making the witch into a wife, Simonides has given her, as much as possible, the moral high ground in the dispute. In *Fatal Attraction* we will find a different sort of attempt to give the witch a bit of moral high ground. Whereas in Simonides's Renaissance version the witch becomes a wife, in *Fatal Attraction* she gets pregnant.

FATAL ATTRACTION

The 1987 film *Fatal Attraction*, unlike Simonides's poem, is not obviously neo-classical. Yet it uses the same basic storyline of an otherwise everyday woman who makes very dangerous threats when crossed. Like the women in Theocritus, *Idyll* 2 and Simonides, *Idyll* 15, the heroine (or villainess) of the film is overwhelmed by sexual frustration and a kind of righteous anger. She persecutes her faithless lover in ways that become increasingly horrifying as the film progresses, far exceeding the verbal imagery found in the poems of Theocritus or Simonides. Like the poems of Theocritus and Simonides, *Fatal Attraction* assumes that women's erotic insanity can drive them to desperate, illicit attempts to control men and attack their female rivals. Even though the film is filled with up-to-date images of modern, American women, it is in many ways an altogether old-fashioned story like the stories told in Theocritus, *Idyll* 2 and Simonides, *Idyll* 15. Social opportunities for women may be quite different in modern America and the witch in *Fatal Attraction* is, we are told, a successful career-woman, unlike the housebound females of ancient Greece and Renaissance Poland. Nonetheless, her deepest fantasies are of domestic bliss and her deadly anger is unleashed when these domestic fantasies are frustrated.

Yet, as I mentioned at the outset of this chapter, *Fatal Attraction* is not linked to Theocritus, *Idyll* 2 in the same, direct fashion as Simonides, *Idyll* 15 is tied to the ancient original. Theocritus's Simaetha does, however, seem to have a namesake in modern culture: Samantha, from the popular American television series *Bewitched*. Samantha (Simaetha?) is an actual witch married to a mere mortal, Darrin (Daphnis?), whom Samantha's mother, Endora (the witch of Endor?), intensely dislikes. Darrin, like the Inquisition, thinks witchcraft is a bad thing, and the show's episodes revolve around Samantha's promise to Darrin not to use her witchcraft. Of course, this witch-wife secretly uses her powers, but only in order to preserve the suburban domestic order and her happy marriage to Darrin. Exactly as in the poems of Theocritus and Simonides, the powers of the witch are turned entirely toward domestic purposes, harnessing the heretical forces of magic for the good of the marriage.

While *Bewitched* gives us a witch-wife, *Fatal Attraction* returns to the roots of extra-marital witchcraft with a love-sick single woman casting spells in the hope of securing domestic bliss. Dan Gallagher, the film's hero, is a successful lawyer, and happily married husband and father, who has a two-night stand with a professional colleague, Alex Forest. Dan breaks off the affair but Alex persists: she attempts suicide, claims to be pregnant with Dan's child, pours corrosive acid on his car, attacks him with a knife, kidnaps his daughter, and even sneaks into the house and boils the Gallaghers' pet bunny rabbit to death. Finally, Alex appears in the Gallagher bathroom as Mrs Gallagher is preparing to take a bath. Alex has gone utterly mad and sees herself as the wife (the witch as wife) and Mrs Gallagher as the intruding adulteress. Alex insists that this is her home and she frantically attempts to stab Mrs Gallagher to death. Dan then runs in and drowns Alex quite thoroughly in the bathtub. But just when we think all is well, Alex sloshes ghoulishly out of the bathwater, rising from the dead, wielding a knife. Whereupon Mrs Gallagher, who has fetched a revolver, shoots Alex dead.

Alex thus plays a role like that of Theocritus's Simaetha, using witchcraft to take back by threat or force a man who is not her husband but on whom she feels she has some claim (sex and/or pregnancy). She thinks, in the depths of her insanity, that she is like the witch-wife of Simonides, *Idyll* 15, using witchcraft to keep her husband and kill the 'other woman'. When compiling Alex's credentials as a witch, the boiled rabbit is crucial. This bubbling pot with its gruesome stew is a powerful image of witchery, like the cauldrons from *Macbeth*, the baked bat in Simonides, or the horrifying feasts of the witches' Sabbat. But in addition to the boiled rabbit, there are other elements of witchcraft: Alex's 'magic potion' which destroys Dan's car; her 'flying through the air' (on a roller coaster); her apartment in the meat-packing district (witches were often associated with corpses and entrails); her haunting curses (cassette-recorded); her theft of a child; her 'insatiable carnal lust' (as cited above from *The Witches' Hammer*); and, finally, her last name, 'Forest', which is the antithesis of 'home' and the site of witches' Sabbats. Alex is even subjected to the ultimate witch-trial: immersion in water. Those who drowned, were innocent; those who did not drown, were guilty. Alex failed the test and did not drown, which is why Mrs Gallagher had to shoot her.

The 'fatal attraction' of the title is that same erotic force which wreaked havoc in the poems of Theocritus and Simonides. It is the fatal attraction of the woman for the man as a result of her lust, and the fatal attraction of the man for the woman resulting not from his lust so much as from her seductive powers, from her bewitching him. While Simonides had avoided the sexual plot of Theocritus, *Idyll* 2 (substituting courtship and marriage instead), *Fatal Attraction* returns to the ancient version: the erotic enchantress seduces the man. The fact that the woman takes the initiative is made explicit in Theocritus, *Idyll* 2 and has a humorous aspect: Delphis does not know exactly how to respond to such an aggressive woman, since he is used to making the first move himself. The same sequence of events unfolds in *Fatal Attraction*: it is Alex who first makes sexual overtures with Dan and he is both amused and taken aback by her aggressiveness. On the one hand, this masquerades as a kind of feminism in *Fatal Attraction*; women, at last, are able to take charge of their own sex-lives. On the other hand, it harkens back to a long misogynistic tradition, beginning with Adam and Eve in the Garden, where only bad girls make the first move.

This kind of aggressive female lust, because it is wild and untamed, can be characterised as bestial. This is the understanding of the director of *Fatal Attraction*, Adrian Lyne, who describes the film's plot as follows: 'A man has a brief affair and then the woman becomes a crazed beast. It could happen to anyone.'[10] The film's director, like Theocritus and Simonides, has adopted a girl-next-door ('it could happen to anyone') approach in his depiction of the witch. This woman is not one in a million, not a princess of Kolchis like Medea, but just someone you might meet at a party, on the street. Yet this girl-next-door is perverted by a bestial sexuality which becomes so bizarre and violent that critics also see supernatural, mythical dimensions to her character. As in the poems of both Theocritus and Simonides, this realistic girl-next-door is associated with terrifying images of witchcraft drawn from myth and legend.

Critics and audiences echo Lyne's description of Alex as a 'crazed beast'. Alex is 'a monster',[11] even a 'full-scale movie monster',[12] 'barely even human'[13] who 'hounds' Dan.[14] She is, specifically, a bitch (in heat?): 'At the end of the film you hear the audience in theatres screaming "Kill her! Kill the bitch!"'[15] Moreover, in addition to being subhuman in her sexuality, Alex is also supernaturally evil: she is a 'witch', a 'demon lady . . . from hell' or 'vengeful hellion'[16] with 'a witchy look',[17] a 'satanic schemer'[18] who is 'devilishly persistent' while Dan is 'an ordinary bedeviled man'.[19]

Yet, despite being a beast of supernatural evil, Alex does not lose her feminine charms. At one point Alex strikes a classic Marilyn Monroe pose: standing, back against the wall, her neckline low-cut and revealing, her expression half-dazed, half-inviting. 'Marilyn' is thus an icon of enchanting femininity invoked in much the same way that 'Ariadne' was invoked in Theocritus, *Idyll* 2: Ariadne abandoned by Theseus was a kind of 'Marilyn' in her day, a perfect picture of seductive feminine helplessness and a popular study for both literary and visual artists of antiquity. Although we are supposed to think of Alex as a successful, unhappy career woman, the film dwells entirely on her traditionally feminine emotions and erotic hysteria, ignoring her professional life. We see Alex spending time cooking dinner for Dan in her kitchen; we never see the office where she works.

This combination of bestiality, evil and femininity makes Alex difficult to characterise. Rather than a 'typical' American career-woman of the 1980s, Alex is best compared to implausible women-creatures from ancient myth who fuse bestiality and evil in feminine form. She is 'a ravening fury – the kind hell hath no like of'.[20] Furies, in antiquity, were depicted as monstrous bird-like women. She is 'a vicious knife-wielding gorgon'.[21] According to ancient tradition, these gorgons were monstrous women whose hair was composed of venomous snakes. She is also 'a film noire harpy'[22] or 'a knife-wielding harpy'.[23] Harpies, too, are part of the ancient tradition, winged women-creatures who were sometimes wreathed with snakes. In addition to ancient myth, critics cite two Hollywood monster-women: Alex is 'a woman whose sexuality makes her both super and subhuman. Vampire. Or in Hollywood's word, vamp',[24] and she is 'an electrified bride of Frankenstein with her taut face and her golden hair rising angrily from her head'.[25] Although both vampires and Frankenstein's monster have literary origins, critics here refer to Hollywood images which reconfigured these monster-men into monster-women for cinematic purposes.

Finally, there are two specific women of ancient myth used by critics to describe Alex: 'Circe',[26] the witch mentioned in Theocritus, *Idyll* 2 who could change men into beasts (bringing them down to her level, in a sense); and 'Medusa', one of the Gorgons. Of all the possible ways to characterise Alex, Medusa was clearly the critics's choice. They consistently comment on Alex's 'Medusa hair-do',[27] calling her a 'Medusa-coiffed temptress'[28] with 'Medusa tresses',[29] 'blond Medusa dreadlocks',[30] a 'Medusa tangle of blonde hair',[31] etc. Whether the director had Medusa in mind is not certain; what was clearly important, however, was the use of this 'wild hair-do' to distinguish Glenn Close's role in this film from the saintly, restrained women she had played in her previous films (including her probably best-known role at the time as the mother of Garp in *The World According to Garp* where her hair was kept bundled under her nurse's cap).

This catalog of critical reactions illustrates two important points. First, despite the fact that Alex is supposed to be a plausible career-woman-next-door, the film leads critics to see her in terms of extravagant mythical archetypes. Secondly, these archetypes are predominantly ancient. Modern imagination cannot compete with the ancient panoply of monster-women. Although *Fatal Attraction* does not explicitly invoke these monsters and women from antiquity, critics responding to the film do. These ancient subtexts implicitly underlie readings of the film even if they are not openly acknowledged in the way that Simonides openly acknowledged his use of Theocritus, *Idyll* 2.

In the end, *Fatal Attraction* is just another variation on the bloody triumph of domesticity over women's liberation, a deceitful kind of pseudo-feminism. As I suggested at the opening of this chapter, witchcraft can be seen as a symbol of feminist autonomy and matriarchal power, but it can also be used as a way to characterise a woman as bestial, desperate and grasping at imaginary power. This view is articulated by the film critic Pauline Kael who, alone of film critics in the popular press, seriously explored the implications of Alex's witch-like character:

> Alex parrots the aggressively angry self-righteous statements that have become commonplaces of feminist fiction, mouthing a modern career woman's jargon about wanting sex without responsibilities and then turning into a vengeful hellion all in the name of love. The horror subtext is the lawyer's developing dread of the crazy feminist who attacks his masculine role as protector of his prosperity and family. It's about men who see feminists as witches and, the way the facts are presented here, the woman is a witch. . . .[32]

Without discussing witches, David Denby makes much the same point:

> [the screenwriter] uses feminist perceptions and arguments as a way of creating Alex and then he gives way to male paranoia and betrays her altogether.[33]

According to *Fatal Attraction* feminists recklessly choose careers over marriage, and the consequences are disastrous. Because Alex is unmarried, she, like Simaetha, is overwhelmed by unsatisfied sexual desires. Moreover, because Alex is not successfully confined to the home of a husband or father (the death of Alex's father is the one detail about her past mentioned in the film), she becomes a sexual predator, free to prowl Manhattan, where the opportunity for dangerous erotic stimulation, 'fatal attraction', is unlimited. Alex first met Dan at a business cocktail party and later at a Saturday business meeting. Similarly, Simaetha met Delphis when attending a public religious festival. If only they had been good girls and stayed home. . . . And, as Simonides's poem shows, even otherwise good girls can get into trouble if they are left at home alone.

Without exception, the men in Theocritus, *Idyll* 2, Simonides, *Idyll* 15 and *Fatal Attraction* are weak, ridiculous characters. Like Delphis, Daphnis and Dan, Darrin in *Bewitched* was similarly fallible and hardly heroic. (The 'D's' just keep on piling up and I can't help but thinking that on some level they add up to the ultimate D-man, the Devil.) Delphis, Daphnis and Dan are each partly to blame for the emergence of the 'witch' because they cannot face up to the implicit or explicit commitments they have made to the women: Simaetha's affair with Delphis had been going on for some time and she had not expected it to end; Daphnis, in Simonides, had made vows of matrimony he could not fulfil; and Dan could not cope with the consequence of his affair with Alex (her pregnancy). Because they are cowards, the men run away: Delphis doesn't come back to see Simaetha, Daphnis has run away from home, and Dan moves out of the city.

Moreover, Delphis, Daphnis and Dan are all erotically clumsy, despite their Don Juan ambitions. Delphis is taken aback by Simaetha's forthright seduction, and protests much too loudly that he was just on the verge of breaking her door down and forcing himself upon her, if she hadn't asked him in first. Likewise Dan, in *Fatal Attraction*, was surprised by Alex's sexual self-assertion. Daphnis does not actually appear in Simonides's poem but we know he is clumsy: he apparently left a shoe behind at his lover's, or lost it on the way home, and is limping loudly. Dan, in *Fatal Attraction*, is similarly clumsy: at one point when he is making love to Alex his pants fall down around his ankles and he stumbles around awkwardly, limping (like Daphnis) and looking thoroughly ridiculous.

In the case of *Fatal Attraction*, the absence of a strong male hero has led critics to perpetuate a further feminist fallacy: because there is not a male hero, the film is feminist. Once again, I hope to have shown that the literary tradition leads us to a different interpretation of the male's role in this story. Just as in the case of Theocritus, *Idyll* 2, Dan's weakness is a foil to Alex's powerful lust. Instead of being under Dan's control, Alex is overwhelmed by her own sexual desires. Neither Alex or Simaetha are liberated women, despite their seeming independence from men. The point is not that they have been set free, but that they have been abandoned. This is what allows Simonides to fit his Renaissance housewife into the same pattern, for the witch-wife has been likewise abandoned by her husband. In all three versions of the story, the woman is abandoned by a man and, overwhelmed by lust, resorts to witchcraft as a desperate attempt to take control, both of her desire and its object.

CONCLUSION

Theocritus, *Idyll* 2 depicts an unmarried woman in ancient Alexandria who turns to witchcraft. Simonides, *Idyll* 15 depicts a married woman in Renaissance Poland who turns to witchcraft. *Fatal Attraction* depicts a swinging single career woman in modern Manhattan who turns to witchcraft. The possibilities, of course, are endless. Realistic, believable characters are used to make the witch-myth contemporary, perpetuating the pernicious belief that any woman, the girl-next-door, is secretly a monster of supernatural, insatiable desires ready to resort to violence when frustrated. Although the particular cultures have changed, and the roles of women are quite different, the same misogynistic myth from antiquity persists.

NOTES

1. The research for this paper was completed at St Antony's College, Oxford University, and the paper was first presented at the Oxford 'Women in Antiquity' seminar in 1988. I would like to thank the editors of this volume for their valuable assistance in preparing the paper for publication.
2. Halperin (1983), pp. 221–2.
3. Mills (1963), p. 9.
4. Halperin (1983), p. 222.
5. Dover (1971), p. 95.
6. Rist (1978), p. 38.
7. Walker (1980), pp. 97–8.
8. Cited in Kors and Peters (1972), pp. 114 and 227.
9. Cited in Kors and Peters (1972), p. 121.
10. Interview in *Rolling Stone Magazine*, Hirschberg (1987), p. 34.
11. Kael (1987), p. 106.
12. Ansen (1987), p. 76.
13. Stone (1987), p. 79.
14. Simon (1987), p. 57 and also McGuigan (1987), p. 76.
15. Corliss (1987), p. 74.
16. Kael (1987), p. 106.
17. Denby (1987), p. 116.
18. Corliss (1987), p. 76.
19. Simon (1987), p. 57.
20. Simon (1987), p. 57.
21. Denby (1987), p. 118.
22. Corliss (1987), p. 79.
23. Ansen (1987), p. 76.
24. Corliss (1987), p. 79.
25. Denby (1987), p. 116.
26. Corliss (1987), p. 72.
27. Kael (1987), p. 106.
28. Stone (1987), p. 78.
29. Corliss (1987), p. 72.
30. McGuigan (1987), p. 76.
31. Ansen (1987), p. 76.
32. Kael (1987), p. 106.
33. Denby (1987), p. 118.

General Bibliography

Anderson, Bonnie S., Zinsser, Judith P. (1988), *A History of their Own. Women in Europe from Prehistory to the Present*, 1–2, New York.

Ardener, Shirley (ed.), (1978) *Defining Females: The Nature of Women in Society*, London.

Bluestone, Natalie Harris (1987), *Women and the Ideal Society: Plato's Republic and Modern Myths of Gender*, Oxford.

Bynum, C., Harrell, S., Richman, P. (eds) (1986), *Gender and Religion: on the Complexity of Symbols*, Boston.

Cameron, Averil, Kuhrt, Amelie (1983), *Images of Women in Antiquity*, London.

Douglas, M. (1966), *Purity and Danger. An Analysis of the Concepts of Pollution and Taboo*, London.

DuBois, Page (1988), *Sowing the Body: Psychoanalysis and Ancient Representations of Women*, Chicago.

Fiorenza, E. Schussler (1983), *In Memory of Her: A Feminist Theological Reconstruction of Christian Origins*, New York.

Foucault, Michel (1984), *The History of Sexuality 3: The Care of the Self*, London.

—— (1985), *The History of Sexuality 2: The Use of Pleasure*, London.

Gaines, Jane, Herzog, Charlotte (1990), *Fabrications: Costume and the Female Body*, New York.

Gero, J., Conkey, M. W. (1991), *Engendering Archaeology. Women and Prehistory*, Oxford.

Greene, Gayle, Kahn, Coppelia (1985), *Making a Difference: Feminist Literary Criticism*, London.

Jacobus, Mary (ed.) (1979), *Women Writing and Writing about Women*, London.

Kaplan, E. Ann (ed.) (1980), *Women in Film Noir*, London.

Lipshitz, Susan (ed.) (1978), *Tearing the Veil: Essays on Femininity*, London.

Lloyd, Genevieve (1984), *The Man of Reason: 'Male' and 'Female' in Western Philosophy*, London.

Lorber, Judith, Farrell, Susan A. (eds) (1991), *The Social Construction of Gender*, London.

MacCormack, C., Strathern, M. (eds) (1980), *Nature, Culture and Gender*, Cambridge.

Moi, Toril (1985), *Sexual/Textual Politics: Feminist Literary Theory*, London.

Okin, Susan (1980), *Women in Western Political Thought*, London.

Ortner, S., Whitehead, H. (eds) (1981), *Sexual Meanings. The Cultural Construction of Gender and Sexuality*, Cambridge.

Polity, Susanne Kappeler (1986), *The Pornography of Representation*, Cambridge.

Rosaldo, Michelle, Lamphere, Louise (eds) (1974), *Women, Culture and Society*, Stanford.

Ruether, R. (ed.) (1974), *Religion and Sexism: Images of Women in the Jewish and Christian Traditions*, New York.

Sayers, Janet (1982), *Biological Politics*, London.

Scott, Joan W. (1988), *Gender and the Politics of History*, New York.

Warner, M. (1985), *Monuments and Maidens: The Allegory of the Female Form*, London.

Bibliography of Works Cited

De F. Abrahamse, D. (1984), 'Byzantine Asceticism and Women's Monasteries in early medieval Italy', in Nichols, J., Shank, L. T. (eds), *Medieval Religious Women I: Distant Echoes*, Kalamazoo, pp. 31–49.

Agrimi, J. (1985), 'L'*Hippocrates Latinus* nella tradizione manoscritta e nella cultura altomedievali', in Mazzini, Fusco (1985), pp. 388–98.

Aldred, C. (1968), *Old Kingdom Art in Ancient Egypt*, London.

Alexiou, M. (1989), 'Women, marriage and death in the drama of Renaissance Crete', in Mackenzie, M. M., Roueché, C. (eds), *Images of Authority: Papers Presented to Joyce Reynolds*, Cambridge, pp. 1–23 (Cambridge Philological Society Supplement 16).

Allam, S. (1981), 'Quelques aspects du mariage dans l'Égypte ancienne', *Journal of Egyptian Archaeology* 67, pp. 116–35.

—— (1989a), 'Women as owners of immovables in Pharaonic Egypt', in Lesko (1989a), pp. 123–35.

—— (1989b), 'Women as Holders of Rights in Ancient Egypt (during the Later Period)', *Journal of the Economic and Social History of the Orient* 32, pp. 1–34.

Allen, M. J. B., Calder, D. G. (eds) (1976), *Sources and Analogues of Old English Poetry*, Cambridge.

Allen, P. (1985), *The Concept of Woman*, Quebec.

Allott, S. (ed.) (1974), *Alcuin of York: His Life and Letters*, York.

Annas, J. (1976), 'Plato's *Republic* and Feminism', *Philosophy* 51, pp. 307–21.

—— (1981), *An Introduction to Plato's Republic*, Oxford.

Ansen, D. (film review) (28 September 1987), *Newsweek* 110, p. 76 (US edition).

Anson, J. (1974), 'The Female Transvestite in early Monasticism: the origin and development of a motive', *Viator* 5, pp. 1–32.

Archer, L. J. (1983), 'The Role of Jewish Women in the Religion, Ritual and Cult of Graeco-Roman Palestine', in Cameron, Kuhrt (1983), pp. 273–87.

—— (1987), 'The Virgin and the Harlot in the Writings of Formative Judaism', *History Workshop. A Journal of Socialist and Feminist Historians* 24, pp. 1–16.

—— (1990a), *Her Price is Beyond Rubies. The Jewish Woman in Graeco-Roman Palestine*, Sheffield.

—— (1990b), 'Bound by Blood: Circumcision and Menstrual Taboo in Post-exilic Judaism', in Martin Soskice, J. (ed.), *After Eve. Women, Theology and the Christian Tradition* (London), pp. 38–61.

—— (1990c), '"In thy blood live": Gender and Ritual in the Judeo-Christian Tradition', in Joseph, A. (ed.), *Through the Devil's Gateway. Women, Religion and Taboo*, London, pp. 22–49.

Ardener, S. (ed.) (1981), *Women and Space*, London.

Ariès, P., Duby, G. (eds) (1986/1987), *Histoire de la vie privée* I, Paris/*A History of Private Life from Pagan Rome to Byzantium* I, Cambridge, Massachusetts (trans. Goldhammer, C. A.).

Arnold, T. (ed.) (1879), *Henrici Archidiaconi Huntendonensis Historia Anglorum*, London (Roll Series 199).

Arwill-Nordbladh, E. (1989), 'Oscar Montelius and the Liberation of Women. An Example of Archaeology, Ideology and the Early Swedish Women's Movement', in Larsson, T. B., Lundmark, H. (eds), *Approaches to Swedish Prehistory. A Spectrum of Problems and Perspectives in Contemporary Research*, Oxford, pp. 131–42 (British Archaeological Reports International Series No. 500).

Assman, B. (ed.) (1964), *Angelsachsische Homilien und Heiligenleben*, Darmstadt.

Auel, J. (1980), *Clan of the Cave Bear*, New York.

Auerbach, E. (1953), *Mimesis. The Representation of Reality in Western Literature*, New York.

Backhouse, J., Turner, D. H., Webster, L. (eds) (1984), *The Golden Age of Anglo-Saxon Art*, London (British Museum Exhibition Catalogue).

Badawy, A. (1961), 'Miszellen', Zeitschrift für Ägyptische Sprache 86, pp. 144–5.

Baines, J. (1985), *Fecundity Figures. Egyptian personification and the iconography of gender*, Warminster.

——, Eyre, C. (1983), 'Four notes on literacy', *Göttingen Miszellen* 61, pp. 65–96.

Baker, D. (ed.) (1978), *Medieval Women*, Oxford.

Balsdon, J. P. V. D. (1962), *Roman Women: their History and Habits*, London.

Bambas, R. C. (1963), 'Another View of the Old English Wife's Lament', *Journal of English and Germanic Philology* 62, pp. 303–9.

Bandel, B. (1955), 'The English Chroniclers' Attitude Towards Women', *Journal of the History of Ideas* 10, pp. 113–18.

Bandinelli, R. B. (1971), *Rome: the Late Empire. Roman Art AD 200–400*, London.

Baron, S. (1952), *A Social and Religious History of the Jews*, 1–2, London.

Barthel, D. (1988), *Putting on Appearances: Gender and Advertising*, Philadelphia.

Battiscombe, C. F. (ed.) (1956), *The Relics of St. Cuthbert*, Oxford.

Beard, M. (1980), 'The Sexual Status of Vestal Virgins', *Journal of Roman Studies* 70, pp. 12–27.

Beaucamp, J. (1977), 'La situation juridique de la femme à Byzance', *Cahiers de civilisation médiévale* 20, pp. 145–76.

Benner, A. R., Fobes, F. H. (1949), *Alciphron, Aelian and Philostratus*, Boston.

Bennett, L. (1983), *Dangerous Wives and Sacred Sisters: Social and Symbolic Roles of High-Caste Women in Nepal*, New York.

Bentley, R. (1699, repr. 1816), *Dissertation Upon the Epistles of Phalaris*, London.

Berger, J. (1972), *Ways of Seeing*, London.

Bernard, J. (1972), *The Future of Marriage*, New York.

Bethurum, D. (ed.) (1957), *The Homilies of Wulfstan*, Oxford.

Billigmeier, J.-C., Turner, J. A. (1981), 'The Socio-Economic Roles of Women in Mycenaean Greece: A Brief Survey from the Linear B Tablets', in Foley, H. (ed.), *Reflections of Women in Antiquity*, London, pp. 1–18.

Binford, L. R. (1981), *Bones. Ancient Men and Modern Myths*, New York.

Blake, E. O. (ed.) (1962), *Liber Eliensis*, London (Camden Society, third series, 92).

Bleeker, C. J. (1929), *De Beteekenis van de Egyptische Godin Ma-a-t*, Leiden.

—— (1973), *Hathor and Thoth*, Leiden (*Studies in the History of Religions: Supplement to Numen* 26).

Bloch, R. H. (1987), 'Medieval Misogyny. Woman as Riot', *Representations* 20, pp. 1–24.

Bluestone, N. H. (1987), *Women and the Ideal Society*, Oxford.

Bodden, M. C. (ed.) (1987), *The Old English Finding of the True Cross*, Cambridge.

Bosworth, J., Toller, T. N. (eds) (1898), *An Anglo-Saxon Dictionary*, Oxford.

Bourdieu, P. (1977), *Outline of a Theory of Practice*, Cambridge.

Boyd, B. W. (1987), *Virtus Effeminata* and Sallust's Sempronia', *Classical Quarterly* 117, pp. 183–201.

Boylan, P. (1922), *Thoth the Hermes of Egypt*, London.

Bradley, S. A. J. (1982), *Anglo-Saxon Poetry*, London.

Braidwood, R. J. (1948, repr. 1975), *Prehistoric Men*, Chicago.

Braude, W. G., Kapstein, I. J. (1975), *Pesikta de-Rab Kahana*, London.

274   *Bibliography of Works Cited*

Brock, S. P. (1974), 'Sarah and the Aqedah', *Le Muséon* 87, pp. 67–77.

—— (1981), 'Genesis 22 in Syriac Tradition', in Cassetti, P., Keel, O., Schenker, A., *Mélanges D. Barthélemy, Fribourg/Gottingen*, pp. 2–30 (Orbis Biblicus et Orientalis 38).

—— (1984), 'Genesis 22: Where was Sarah?', *Expository Times* 96, pp. 14–17.

—— (1985), *The Luminous Eye: the Spiritual World Vision of St. Ephrem*, Rome.

—— (1986), 'Two Syriac verse homilies on the binding of Isaac', *Le Muséon* 99, pp. 61–129.

—— (1989), 'From Ephrem to Romanos', in Livingstone, E. A. (ed.), *Studia Patristica* 20, Leuven, pp. 139–51.

——, Harvey, S. Ashbrook (1987), *Holy Women of the Syrian Orient*, Berkeley and Los Angeles.

Brown, P. (1982), 'Dalla "Plebs romana" alla "Plebs dei": aspetti della cristianizzazione di Roma' in Brown, P., Cracco Ruggini, L., Mazza, M., *Governanti e intellettuali, populo di Roma e populo di Dio*, Torino, pp. 123–45.

—— (1986/1987), 'Late Antiquity', in Ariès, Duby (1986/1987), pp. 235–311.

—— (1988), *The Body and Society. Men, Women and Sexual Renunciation in Early Christianity*, New York.

Brown, R., Donfried, K. P., Fitzmyer, J. A., Reumann, J. (1978), *Mary in the New Testament*, London.

Brown, R. D. (1987), *Lucretius on Love and Sex*, Leiden.

Brunner, H. (1964), *Die Geburt des Gottkönigs*, Wiesbaden *(Studien zur Überlieferung eines altägyptischen Mythos, Ägyptologische Abhandlungen 10)*.

Bruyère, B. (1924–53), *Rapport sur les fouilles de Deir el Medineh*, Cairo (l'Institut français d'archéologie orientale du Caire).

Bryan, B. (1985), 'Evidence of female literacy from Theban tombs of the New Kingdom', *Bulletin of the Egyptological Seminar* 6, pp. 17–32.

Buchholz, H.-G., Karageorghis, V. (1973), *Prehistoric Greece and Cyprus*, London.

Bühler, G. (trans.) (1965), *Baudhāyanadharmasūtra*, Delhi.

—— (trans.) (1975), *Āpastambadharmasūtra*, Delhi.

—— (trans.) (1979), *Manusmrti*, Delhi.

Burlin, R. B. (ed.) (1968), *The Old English Advent Lyrics: a typological commentary*, New Haven.

Burnouf, E., Hauvette-Besnault, M. (trans.) (1840–98), *Bhāgavatapurānā*, Paris.

Busse, W. G., Holtei, R. (1981), 'Beowulf and the Tenth Century', *Bulletin of the John Rylands University Library of Manchester* 63/2, pp. 285–329.

Butler, B., Turner, D. M. (eds), (1987), *Children and Anthropological Research*, New York.

Bynum, C. (1987), *Holy Feast and Holy Fast*, Berkeley and Los Angeles.

Bynum C. Walker, Harrell, S., Richman, P. (1986) *Gender and Religion: on the Complexity of Symbols*, Boston.

Cadogan, G. (1976), *Palaces of Minoan Crete*, London.

Callahan, J. F. (1964), 'Plautus' "Mirror for a Mirror"', *Classical Philology* 59, pp. 1–10.

Cameron, Av. M. (1978), 'The *Theotokos* in Sixth-Century Constantinople', *Journal of Theological Studies* n.s. 29, pp. 79–108.

—— (1989), 'Virginity as Metaphor', in Cameron, Av. (ed.), *History as Text*, London, pp. 184–205.

—— (1990), 'Women in Early Christian Interpretation', in Coggins, R. J., Houlden, J. L. (eds), *Dictionary of Biblical Interpretation*, London, pp. 729–31.

—— (1991), *Christianity and the Rhetoric of Empire*, Berkeley and Los Angeles.

——, Kuhrt, A. (eds) (1983), *Images of Women in Antiquity*, London.

Caminos, R. A. (1954), *Late Egyptian Miscellanies*, London (Brown Egyptological Studies I).

Cannuyer, C. (1986), 'L'Obèse de Ptahhotep et de Samuel', *Zeitschrift für Ägyptische Sprache* 113, pp. 92–103.

—— (1989), 'Variations sur le thème de la ville dans les maximes sapientiales de l'ancienne Égypte', *Chronique d'Égypte* 64, pp. 44–54.

Carcopino, J. (1956), *Daily Life in Ancient Rome: the People and the City at the Height of the Empire*, London (trans. E. O. Lorimer).

Carp, T. (1981), 'Two Matrons of the Late Republic', in Foley (1981), pp. 343–54.

Carras, L. (ed.) (1984), 'Life of St. Athanasia' in Moffat, A. (ed.) (1984), *Maistor*, Canberra, pp. 199–211.

Carroll, M. P. (1986), *The Cult of the Virgin Mary. Psychological Origins*, Princeton.

Castner, C. J. (1981), 'Epicurean Hetairai as Dedicants to Healing Deities?', *Greek, Roman and Byzantine Studies* 23, pp. 51–7.

Černy, J. (1929), 'Papyrus Salt 124: (Brit. Mus. 10055)', *Journal of Egyptian Archaeology* 15, pp. 243–58.

—— (1945), 'The Will of Naunakht and related documents', *Journal of Egyptian Archaeology* 31, pp. 29–53.

—— (1957), 'A note on the Ancient Egyptian Family', *Studi in Onora di Aristide Calderini e Roberto Paribeni II*, Milan, pp. 51–5.

—— (1973), *A Community of Workmen at Thebes in the Ramesside Period*, Cairo (*Bibliotheque d'Étude* 50, l'Institut français d'archéologie orientale du Caire).

Chadwick, N. (1959), 'The Monsters and Beowulf', in Clemoes, P. (ed.) *The Anglo-Saxons: Studies in some aspects of their history and culture, presented to Bruce Dickins*, London, pp. 171–203.

Chambers, R. W., Forster, M., Flower, R. (1933), *The Exeter Book of Old English Poetry*, London.

Chance, J. (1986), *Woman as Hero in Old English Literature*, New York.

Chapkis, W. (1986), *Beauty Secrets: Women and the Politics of Appearance*, London.

Chase, C. (ed.) (1981), *The Dating of Beowulf*, Toronto.

Cherniss, M. D. (1969), 'Heroic Ideals and the Moral Climate of Genesis B', *Modern Language Quarterly* 30, pp. 479–97.

Childe, V. G. (1936, repr. 1981³), *Man Makes Himself*, Bradford-on-Avon.

Chippindale, C. (1989), 'Editorial', *Antiquity* 63/240, pp. 419–20.

Christie, A. G. I. (1938), *English Medieval Embroidery*, Oxford.

Cixous, H. (1981), 'Sorties', in Marks, de Courtivron (1981), pp. 90–8.

Clark, E. A. (1983), *Women in the Early Church*, Wilmington, Delaware.

—— (1984), *The Life of Melania the Younger*, New York and Toronto.

—— (1985), 'Authority and Humility: A Conflict of Values in Fourth-Century Female Monasticism', *Byzantinische Forschungen* 9.

—— (1986a), *Ascetic Piety and Women's Faith*, Wilmington, Delaware.

—— (1986b), 'Faltonia Betitia Proba and her Virgilian Poem: the Christian Matron as Artist', in Clark (1986a), pp. 124–52.

——, Hatch, D. F. (1986c), 'Jesus as Hero in the Vergilian *Cento* of Faltonia Betitia Proba', in Clark (1986a), pp. 153–71.

—— (1986d), 'Heresy, Asceticism, Adam and Eve: Interpretations of Genesis 1–3 in the Later Latin Fathers', in Clark (1986a), pp. 353–85.

—— (1986e), 'The Uses of the Song of Songs: Origen and the Later Latin Fathers', in Clark (1986a), pp. 386–427.

Clark, G. (1989), *Iamblichus: On the Pythagorean Life*, Liverpool.

Clark, S. R. L. (1975), *Aristotle's Man*, Oxford.

Clark Forbes, M. (1983), 'Variations on themes of male and female: reflections on gender bias in fieldwork in rural Greece', *Women's Studies* 10/2, pp. 117–33.

Clayton, M. (1984), 'Feasts of the Virgin in the Liturgy of the Anglo-Saxon Church', *Anglo-Saxon England* 13, pp. 209–33.

——, (1990), *The Cult of the Virgin Mary in Anglo-Saxon England*, Cambridge.

Clère, J. J. (1949), 'L'expression *dnśmhwt* des autobiographies égyptiennes', *Journal of Egyptian Archaeology* 35, pp. 38–42.

Colgrave, B., Mynors, R. A. B. (eds) (1969), *Bede's Ecclesiastical History of the English People*, Oxford.

Collingwood, R. G. (1945), *The Idea of Nature*, Oxford.

Conkey, M. W., Spector, J. D. (1984), 'Archaeology and the Study of Gender', in Schiffer, M. (ed.), *Advances in Archaeological Method and Theory* 7, Orlando, pp. 1–38.

Connelly, J. (1989), 'The CEO [Chief Executive Officer]'s Second Wife', *Fortune* 120/5, pp. 52–66.

Consolino, F. E. (1984), '*Veni huc a Libano: la sponsa del Cantico dei Cantici* come modello per le vergine negli scritti esortatori di Ambrogio', *Athenaeum* n.s. 62, pp. 399–415.

—— (1986), 'Modelli di comportamento e modi di santificazione per l'aristocrazia femminile d'Occidente', in Giardina, A. (ed.) *Società e impero tardoantico I. Instituzioni ceti economie*, Rome, pp. 273–306, 684–99.

—— (forthcoming), 'Sante o patrone? Le aristocratiche tardoantiche e il potere della curità, *Studi Storici*.

Corliss, R. (film review) (16 November 1987), *Time* 130, pp. 72–6 (US edition).

Cornford, F. M. (1939), *Plato and Parmenides*, London.

Coturri, E. (1968), 'Il ritrovamento di antichi testi di medicina nel primo secolo del Rinascimento', *Episteme*, pp. 91–110.

Coward, R. (1984), *Female Desire. Women's Sexuality Today*, London.

Cox, P. (1986), 'Pleasure of Text, Text of Pleasure: *Origen's Commentary on the Song of Songs*', *Journal of the American Academy of Religion* 54, pp. 241–51.

Crawford, S. J. (ed.) (rev. repr. 1969), *The Old English Version of the Heptateuch*, London (Early English Texts Society, OS, 160).

Cross, A. (1990), *The Players Come Again*, New York.

Crouzel, H. (trans.) (1989), *Origen*, Edinburgh.

Culham, P. (1982), 'The *lex Oppia*', *Latomus* 41, pp. 786–93.

—— (1986), 'Again, what meaning lies in colour!', *Zeitschrift für Papyrologie und Epigraphik* 64, pp. 235–45.

CUWAG: Cambridge University Women's Action Group (Survey Committee) (1988), *Forty Years On . . . The CUWAG Report on the Numbers and Status of Academic Women in the University of Cambridge*, Cambridge.

Damico, H., Hennessy Olsen, A. (eds) (1990), *New Readings on Women in Old English Literature*, Indiana.

Darby, W. J., Ghalioungui, P., Grivetti, L. (1977), *Food: The Gift of Osiris, I-II*, London.

Davidson, C. (1975), 'Erotic "Women's Songs" in Anglo-Saxon England', *Neophilologus* 59, pp. 451–62.

Davies, S. L. (1980), *The Revolt of the Widows. The Social World of the Apocryphal Acts*, London.

Dean-Jones, L. (1989), 'Menstrual bleeding according to the Hippocratics and Aristotle', *Transactions of the American Philological Association* 119, pp. 177–92.

—— (1992), *Women's Bodies in Classical Greek Science*, Oxford.

De Boor, C. (ed.) (1980 repr.), *Theophan, Chronographia* I and II, Leipzig.

De Buck, A. (1947), 'The Judicial Papyrus of Turin', *Journal of Egyptian Archaeology* 23, pp. 152–64.

De Cenival, F. (1988), *Le mythe de l'oeil du soleil*, Summerhausen (*Demotische Studien* 9).

Delcourt, M. (1961), *Hermaphrodite*, London.

De Marco, M., Glorie, F. (eds) (1968), *Aenigmata de Virtutibus et Vitiis I and II*, Turnhout (Corpus Christianorum, Ser. Lat. 133).

Demargne, P. (1964), *Aegean Art*, London.

Denby, D. (film review) (28 September, 1987), *New York* 20, pp. 116–18.

Denton, L. T. (1991), 'Varieties of Hindu Female Asceticism', in Leslie (1991a), pp. 211–31.

Derrett, J. D. M. (1973), *Dharmaśāstra and Juridical Literature*, Wiesbaden (A History of Indian Literature, 4/1).

De Ste Croix, G. E. M. (1981), *The Class Struggle in the Ancient Greek World*, London.

Dewing, H. B. (ed. and trans.) (1914–40), *Procopius* I–VII, London.

DeWitt, H., Nixon, L. (1988), 'Women and Men in Oxford', *Oxford Magazine* 36, pp. 11–13.

Diels, H., Kranz, W. (1951), *Die Fragmente der Vorsokratiker*[6] Berlin.

Dietrich, S. C. (1980), 'An Introduction to Women in Anglo-Saxon England, 600–1066', in Kanner (1980), pp. 32–56.

Dindorf, W. (ed.) (1832), *Themistius' Orationes*, Leipzig.

Dixon, S. (1983), 'A Family Business: Women's Role in Patronage and Politics at Rome, 80–44 B. C.', *Classica et Mediaevalia* 34, pp. 91–112.

—— (1986), 'Family Finances: Terentia and Tullia' in Rawson, B. (ed.), *The Family in Ancient Rome*, Kent, pp. 93–120.

—— (1988), *The Roman Mother*, London.

Doane, A. N. (ed.) (1978), *Genesis A*, Wisconsin.

Dodds, E. R. (1983), *Pagan and Christian in an Age of Anxiety*, Cambridge.

Dodwell, C. R. (1982), *Anglo-Saxon Art: A New Perspective*, Manchester.

Dover, K. J. (1971), *Theocritos*, London.

Drabble, M. (1975), *The Realms of Gold*, New York.

Dronke, P. (1984), *Women Writers of the Middle Ages*, Cambridge.

DuBois, P. (1988), *Sowing the Body: Psychoanalysis and Ancient Representations of Women*, Chicago.

Dudley, D. R. (1962), *The Civilization of Rome*, New York.

Dummler, E. (ed.) (1895), *Monumenta Germaniae Historica, Epistolae Selectae Caroli Aevi II: Alcuini Epistolae.*

Dupont, F. (1989), *La vie quotidienne du citoyen romain sous la republique*, Hachette.

Ebbell, B. (1937), *The Papyrus Ebers*, London.

Edwards, C. (forthcoming) *The Politics of Immorality in Ancient Rome*, Cambridge.

Edwards, I. E. S. (1965), 'Lord Dufferin's excavations at Deir el-Bahari and the Clandeboye Collection', *Journal of Egyptian Archaeology* 51, pp. 16–28.

Ehrenberg, M. (1989), *Women in Prehistory*, London.

Eisler, R. (1987), *The Chalice and the Blade*, San Francisco.

Engelhardt, H. T. (1974), 'The disease of masturbation: values and the concept of disease', *Bulletin of the History of Medicine* 48, pp. 234–48.

Evans, A. (1921–36), *The Palace of Minos at Knossos* I–IV, London.

Evans, J. (1943), *Time and Chance*, London.

Evans, J. M. (1963), 'Genesis B and its Background', *Review of English Studies* 14, pp. 1–16, 113–23.

Eyre, C. (1984), 'Crime and Adultery in Ancient Egypt', *Journal of Egyptian Archaeology* 70, pp. 92–105.

——, Baines, J. (1989), 'Interactions between Orality and Literacy in Ancient Egypt', in Schousboe, K., Trolle Larsen, M. (eds), *Literacy and Society*, Copenhagen, pp. 91–119.

Fell, C. E. (1981) 'Hild, Abbess of Streonaeshalch', in Bekker-Nielsen, H. *et al.* (eds.), *Hagiography and Medieval Literature: A Symposium*, Odense, pp. 76–99.

—— (1984), *Women in Anglo-Saxon England*, London.

—— (1990), 'Some implications of the Boniface Correspondence', in Damico, Hennessy Olsen (1990), pp. 29–43.

Festugière, A.-J. (ed.) (1970–1), *Vie de Théodore de Sykéôn* I and II, Brussels.

Finnegan, R. E. (1976), 'Eve and "Vincible Ignorance" in Genesis B', *Texas Studies in Literature and Language* 18, pp. 329–39.

Fiorenza, E. Schluesser (1979), 'Word, Spirit and Power: Women in early Christian communities', in Ruether, McLaughlin, pp. 29–70.

—— (1983), *In Memory of Her. A Feminist Reconstruction of Christian Origins*, New York.

Fischer, H. G. (1976), *Egyptian Studies I: Varia*, New York (The Metropolitan Museum of Art).

—— (1982), 'A Didactic Text of the Late Middle Kingdom', *Journal of Egyptian Archaeology* 68, pp. 45–50.

—— (1989), 'Women in the Old Kingdom and Heracleopolitan Period', in Lesko (1989a), pp. 5–24.

Fischler, S. (1989), *The Public Position of the Women of the Imperial Household in the Julio-Claudian Period*, Oxford (unpublished D. Phil. thesis).

Flax, J. (1983), 'Political Philosophy and the Patriarchal Unconscious: A Psychoanalytic Perspective on Epistemology and Metaphysics', in Harding S., Hintikka, M. (eds), *Discovering Reality: Feminist Perspectives on Epistemology, Metaphysics, Methodology and Philosophy of Science*, Dordrecht.

Foley, H. P. (ed.) (1981), *Reflections of Women in Antiquity*, New York.

Fortenbaugh, W. W. (1984), *Quellen zur Ethik Theophrasts*, Amsterdam.

Foucault, M. (1984/1985), *Histoire de la sexualité 2: L'usage des plaisirs*, Paris/*The History of Sexuality II: the Use of Pleasure*, London (trans. Hurley, R.).

Fowler, R. (ed.) (1972), *Wulfstan's Canons of Edgar*, Oxford (Early English Texts Society, OS, 266).

Frandsen, P. J. (1986), 'Tabu', *Lexikon der Ägyptologie* 6, col. 135–42.

Frankfort, H. (ed.) (1977), *The Intellectual Adventure of Ancient Man: An Essay on speculative thought in the Ancient Near East*, London.

Freeman, H., Simon, M. (1951), *Midrash Rabbah*, London.

Frend, W. H. C. (1965), *Martyrdom and Persecution in the Early Church*, Oxford.

Frese, D. W. (1983), 'Wulf and Eadwacer: the Adulterous Woman Reconsidered', repr. in Damico, Hennessy Olsen (1990), pp. 273–91.

Friedl, E. (1970), 'Fieldwork in a Greek Village', in Golde, P. (ed.), *Women in the Field*, Chicago, pp. 195–220.

Fry, D. K. (1970–1), 'Wulf and Eadwacer: a Wen Charm', *Chaucer Review* 5, pp. 247–63.

Frye, N. (1982), *The Great Code. The Bible as Literature*, London.

Gaballa, G. A. (1977), *The Memphite Tomb Chapel of Mose*, Warminster.

Gardiner, A. H. (1910), 'The Tomb of Amenemhet, High-Priest of Amun', *Zeitschrift für Ägyptische Sprache* 47, pp. 87–99.

—— (1940), 'Adoption Extraordinary', *Journal of Egyptian Archaeology* 26, pp. 23–9.

—— (1947), *Ancient Egyptian Onomastica. (The Ramesseum Onomasticon. The Onomasticon of Amenope)*, London.

—— (1957), 'A new moralising text', *Wiener Zeitschrift für die Kunde des Morgenlandes* 54, pp. 43–5.

—— (1961), *Egypt of the Pharaohs: An Introduction*, Oxford.

—— (1979), *Egyptian Grammar*, Oxford.

Gardner, J. (1986), *Women in Roman Law and Society*, London.

Garland, J. W. (1968), *The Concept of Isis during the Egyptian Old Kingdom based upon the Pyramid Texts*, Chicago.

Gedge, P. (1977), *Child of the Morning*, Toronto.

—— (1978), *The Eagle and the Raven*, Toronto.

Gero, J. (1985), 'Socio-politics and the Woman-at-Home Ideology', *American Antiquity* 50, pp. 342–50.

——, Conkey, M. W. (eds) (1991), *Engendering Archaeology. Women and Prehistory*, Oxford.

Ghalioungui, P. (1973), *The House of Life. Per Ankh. Magic and Medical Science in Ancient Egypt*, Amsterdam.

—— (1983), *The Physicians of Pharaonic Egypt*, Mainz am Rhein (Deutsches Archäologisches Institut Abteilung Kairo Sonderschrift 10).

Giannarelli, E. (1980), *La tipologia femminile nella biografia e nell'autobiografia cristiana del IV secolo*, Rome.

Giardina, A. (1988), 'Carità eversiva: le donazioni di Melania la giovane e gli equilibri della società tardoromano', *Studi Storici* 29, p. 127.

Gilligan, C. (1982), *In a Different Voice*, Cambridge.

Glotz, G. (1925), *The Aegean Civilization*, London.

Goedicke, H. (1963), 'Was magic used in the harem conspiracy against Ramesses III?', *Journal of Egyptian Archaeology* 49, pp. 71–92.

—— (1967), 'Unrecognised Sportings', *Journal of the American Research Center in Egypt*, pp. 97–102.

—— (1985), 'Rudjedet's Delivery', *Varia Aegyptiaca* 1/1–2, pp. 19–26.

Goody, J. (1983), *The Development of the Family and Marriage in Europe*, Cambridge.

Goolden, P. (ed.) (1956), *The Old English Apollonius of Tyre*, Oxford.

Gosling, J. C. B. (1973), *Plato*, London.

Gourevitch, D. (1984), *Le mal d'être femme: la femme et la médecine dans la Rome antique*, Paris.

Gow, A. S. F. (ed.) (1950), *Theocritus*, Cambridge.

Gradon, P. O. E. (ed.) (1977), *Cynewulf's Elene*, Exeter.

Graef, H. (1985), *Mary. A History of Doctrine and Devotion*, London.

Grant, R. J. (ed.) (1982), *Three Homilies from Cambridge Corpus Christi College* 41, Ottawa.

Green, M. (ed.) (1983), *Old English Elegies: New essays in criticism and research*, New Jersey.

Green, M. H. (1985), *The Transmission of Ancient Theories of Female Physiology and Disease through the Early Middle Ages*, Princeton (unpublished PhD dissertation).

Green, R. (1961), 'The Caputi Hydria', *Journal of Hellenic Studies* 81, pp. 73–5.

Greenfield, S. B. (1986), 'Wulf and Eadwacer: All Passion Pent', *Anglo-Saxon England* 15, pp. 5–14.

——, Calder, D. G. (1986), *A New Critical History of Old English Literature*, New York.

——, Robinson, F. C. (eds) (1980), *A Bibliography of Publications on Old English Literature to the End of 1972*, Toronto and Manchester.

Griffin, J. (1976), 'Augustan Poetry and the Life of Luxury', *Journal of Roman Studies* 66, pp. 87–105.

Griffiths, J. G. (1960), *The Conflict of Horus and Seth from Egyptian and Classical Sources*, Liverpool.

—— (1966), *The Origins of Osiris*, Berlin (Münchner Ägyptologische Studien 9).

Gross, M., Averill, M. B. (1983), 'Evolution and Patriarchal Myths of Scarcity and Competition', in Harding, S., Hintikka, M. (eds), *Discovering Reality. Feminist Perspectives on Epistemology, Metaphysics, Methodology, and Philosophy of Science*, Dordrecht, pp. 71–95.

Grumel, V. (ed.) (1947), *Les Regestes des Patriarches de Constantinople* I/3: *Les Actes (1043–1206)*, Kadiköy.

Guillou, A. (ed.) (1967–80), *Corpus des actes grecs d'Italie du sud et de Sicile* (Recherches d'histoire et de géographie), Vatican, Rome.

Gulick, C. B. (1927–41), *Athenaeus Deipnosophists*, Harvard.

Gupta, S. (1991), 'Women in the Śaiva/Śākta Ethos', in Leslie (1991a), pp. 194–209.

Guthrie, K. S. (1987), *The Pythagorean Sourcebook and Library*, Michigan.

Guthrie, W. K. C. (1962), *A History of Greek Philosophy I: The Earlier Presocratics and the Pythagoreans*, Cambridge.

Haddan, A. W., Stubbs, W. (eds) (1871), *Councils and Ecclesiastical Documents Relating to Great Britain and Ireland III*, Oxford.

Halkin, F. (ed.) (1973), 'Life of St Elizabeth', *Analecta Bollandiana* 91, pp. 249–64.

Hallett, J. P. (1984), *Fathers and Daughters in Roman Society: Women and the Elite Family*, Princeton.

Halperin, D. M. (1983), *Before Pastoral: Theocritus and the Ancient Tradition of Bucolic Poetry*, New Haven.

—— (1990), 'Why was Diotima a Woman? Platonic *Eros* and the Figuration of Gender', in Halperin, D. M., Winkler, J. J., Zeitlin, F. I. (eds), *Before Sexuality. The Construction of Erotic Experience in the Ancient Greek World*, Princeton, pp. 257–308.

Hanson, A. (1987), 'The eight months' child and the etiquette of birth: *Obsit omen!*', *Bulletin of the History of Medicine* 61, pp. 589–602.

—— (1990), 'The medical writers' woman', in Halperin, D. *et al.* (eds), *Before Sexuality*, Princeton, pp. 309–37.

Haraway, D. (1990), 'Investment Strategies for the Evolving Portfolio of Primate Females', in Jacobus, M., Keller, E. F., Shuttleworth, S. (eds), *Body/Politics. Women and the Discourses of Science*, New York, pp. 139–62.

Harpham, G. (1987), *The Ascetic Imperative in Culture and Criticism*, Chicago.

Harris, J. R. (ed.) (1971), *The Legacy of Egypt*, Oxford.

Harvey, S. Ashbrook (1983), 'Women in early Syrian Christianity', in Cameron, Kuhrt (1983), pp. 288–98.

Hayes, W. C. (1953) *The Scepter of Egypt: A Background for the Study of the Egyptian Antiquities in the Metropolitan Museum of Art 1*, New York.

Haynes, S. (1987), *The Augur's Daughter*, London.

Henderson, A. A. R. (ed.) (1979), *P. Ovidi Nasonis Remedia Amoris*, Edinburgh.

Henderson, J. (1989), 'Satire writes "woman": Gendersong', *Proceedings of the Cambridge Philological Society* 215, pp. 50–80.

Hercher, R. (ed.) (1873), *Epistolographi Graeci*, Leipzig.

Herrin, J. (1982), 'Women and the Faith in Icons in Early Christianity', in Samuel, R., Stedman Jones, G. (eds), *Culture, Ideology and Politics*, London, pp. 56–83.

—— (1983), 'In search of Byzantine women: three avenues of approach', in Cameron, Kuhrt (1983), pp. 167–89.

—— (1992), "Femina byzantina": Canons of the Council *in Trullo* on women', in Cutler, A., Franklin, S. (eds) *Homo byzantinus. Papers in honor of A. P. Kazhdan*, Dumbarton Oaks Papers 46, pp. 97–105, Washington, DC.

Hertzfeld, G. (ed.) (1900), *An Old English Martyrology*, London (*Early English Texts Society*, OS, 116).

Hertzfeld, M. (1990), 'Icons and Identity: Religious Orthodoxy and Social Practice in Rural Crete', *Anthropology Quarterly* 63, pp. 109–21.

Higgins, R. (1981), *Minoan and Mycenaean Art*, London.

Hill, J. (1990), '"paet waes geomuru ides!" A Female Stereotype Examined', in Damico, Hennessy Olsen (1990), pp. 235–47.

Hill, R. (1979), 'Marriage in Seventh Century England', in King, M. H., Stevens, W. M. (eds), *Saints, Scholars and Heroes: Studies in medieval culture in honour of C. W. Jones* I. Minnesota, pp. 67–75.

Hirschberg, L. (Interview with A. Lyne) (19 November 1987), *Rolling Stone Magazine*, p. 34.

Hoffman, M. A. (1979), *Egypt before the Pharaohs*, London.

Holum, K. (1982), *Theodosian Empresses*, Berkeley.

Hood, S. (1978), *The Arts in Prehistoric Greece*, Harmondsworth.

Hopkins, K. (1978), *Conquerors and Slaves*, Cambridge.

Hornung, E. (1982), *Conceptions of God in Ancient Egypt – The One and the Many*, London.

Hunter Blair, P. (1985), 'Whitby as a Centre of Learning in the seventh century', in Lapidge, M., Gneuss, H. (eds), *Learning and Literature in Anglo-Saxon England*, Cambridge, pp. 3–32.

Hurschon, R. (1981), 'Essential Objects and the Sacred', in Ardener (1981), pp. 72–88.

Irigaray, L. (1974), *Spéculum de l'autre femme*, Paris = (1985), *Speculum of the Other Woman*, Cornell (trans. G. C. Gill).

Irigoin, J. (1973), 'Tradition manuscrite et histoire du texte. Quelques problèmes relatifs à la Collection Hippocratique', *Revue d'histoire des textes* 3, pp. 1–13.

Jacobs, L. (1985), 'There is no problem of descent', *Judaism* 34, pp. 54–9.

Jacobson, D. (1978), 'The Chaste Wife', in Vatuk, S. (ed.), *American Studies in the Anthropology of India*, Delhi.

Jacoby, F. (ed.) (1923–), *Fragmente der griechischen Historiker*, Leiden.

Jagu, A. (1979), *Musonius Rufus: Entretiens et Fragments*, Hildesheim and New York.

James, T. G. H. (1962), *The Hekanakhte papers and other early Middle Kingdom documents*, New York (Publications of the Metropolitan Museum of Art Egyptian Expedition 19).

Janssen, J. J. (1975), *The Commodity Prices from the Ramessid Period: an economic study of the village of necropolis workmen at Thebes*, Leiden.

—— (1980), 'Absence from Work by the Necropolis Workmen of Thebes', *Studien zur altägyptischen Kultur* 8, pp. 127–50.

—— (1988), 'Marriage Problems and Public Relations', in Baines, J., James, T. G. H., Leahy, A., Shore, A. F. (eds), *Pyramid Studies and other essays presented to I. E. S. Edwards*, London, pp. 134–7. (Egypt Exploration Society).

——, Pestman, P. W. (1968), 'Burial and inheritance in the community of necropolis workmen at Thebes', *Journal of Economic and Social History of the Orient* 11, pp. 137–70.

Joannou, P. P. (1962), *Discipline générale antique* I and II, Rome.

Johanson, D. C., Edey, M. A. (1981), *Lucy. The Beginnings of Humankind*, London.

Joly, R. (1966), *Le niveau de la science hippocratique. Contribution à la psychologie de l'histoire des sciences*, Paris (Les Belles Lettres).

Kael, P. (film review) (19 October, 1987), *The New Yorker* 63, pp. 106–9.

Kampen, N. (1982), 'Social Status and Gender in Roman Art', in Broude, N., Garrard, M. (eds), *Feminism and Art History*, New York.

Kanner, B. (ed.) (1980), *The Women of England from Anglo-Saxon Times to the Present*, London.

Kaske, R. E. (1982), 'Sapientia et Fortitudo in Judith', in Benson, L., Wenzel, S., (eds), *The Wisdom of Poetry: essays in early English literature in honour of M. W. Bloomfield*, Kalamazoo, pp. 13–29.

Kassel, R., Austin, C. (1983–9), *Poetae Comici Graeci*, Berlin.

Kazhdan, A. P. (1973), 'Widows lost and regained', *Byzantion* 43, p. 509.

——, Constable, G. (1982), *People and Power in Byzantium*, Washington, DC.

Kelly, J. N. D. (1975), *Jerome*, London.

Kenna, M. E. (1985), 'Icons in Theory and Practice: an Orthodox Christian Example', *History of Religions* 24, pp. 345–68.

Kersenboom-Story, S. C. (1987), *Nityasumaṅgalī: Devadasi Tradition in South India*, Delhi.

—— (1991), 'The Traditional Repertoire of the Tiruttaṇi Temple Dancers', in Leslie (1991a), pp. 131–47.

Keynes, S. (1980), *The Diplomas of King Æthelred the Unready*, Cambridge.

——, Lapidge, M. (eds) (1983), *Alfred the Great*, Harmondsworth.

Kiernan, K. (1975), 'Cwene, The Old Profession of Riddle 95', *Modern Philology* 72, pp. 384–90.

King, H. (1983), 'Bound to Bleed: Artemis and Greek Women', in Cameron, Kuhrt (1983), pp. 109–27.

—— (1985), *From Parthenos to Gyne: The dynamics of category*, London (unpublished PhD dissertation).

—— (1987), 'Sacrificial blood: The role of the amnion in ancient gynecology', *Helios* 13/2, 117–26 = Skinner, M. B. (ed.), *Rescuing Creusa*, Texas.

—— (1989), 'The daughter of Leonides: reading the Hippocratic corpus', in Cameron, Av. M. (ed.), *History as Text*, London, pp. 11–32.

—— (1990), 'Making a man: becoming human in early Greek medicine', in Dunstan, G. R. (ed.), *The Human Embryo: Aristotle and the Arabic and European Traditions*, Exeter, pp. 10–19.

Kirschner, B. (1906), 'Alfabetische Akrosticha in der syrischen Kirchenpoesie', *Oriens Christianus* 6, pp. 44–69.

Kirshner, J., Wemple, S. F. (eds) (1985), *Women of the Medieval World*, Oxford.

Kishwar, M., Vanita, R. (eds) (1984), *In Search of Answers: Indian Women's Voices from Manushi*, London.

Kitchen, K. A. (1969), *Ramesside Inscriptions, historical and biographical*, Oxford.

—— (1979), 'The basic literary forms and formulations of Ancient Instructional Writings in Egypt', in Hornung, E., Keel, O. (eds), *Studien zu altägyptischen Lebenslehren*, pp. 260–82 (Orbis Biblicus et Orientalis 28).

—— (1980), 'Proverbs and Wisdom Books of the Ancient Near East: The factual history of a literary form', *Tyndale Bulletin* 29.

—— (1986), *The Third Intermediate Period in Egypt (1100–650 BC)*, Warminster.

Kliman, B. W. (1977), 'Women in Early English Literature. Beowulf to the Ancrene Wisse', *Nottingham Medieval Studies* 21, pp. 32–49.

Klinck, A. L. (1987), 'Animal Imagery in Wulf and Eadwacer: and the Possible Interpretation', *Papers in Language and Literature* 23, pp. 3–13.

Kock, T. (ed.), *Comicorum Atticorum Fragmenta* (1880–8), Leipzig.

Koerte, A. (1912), *Menandrea*, Leipzig.

Kors, A. C., Peters, E. (1972), *Witchcraft in Europe 1100–1700: A Documentary History*, Philadelphia.

Krapp, G. P., Dobbie, E. V. K. (eds) (1931–42), *Anglo-Saxon Poetic Records* I–VI, New York.

Kristeva, J. (1982), 'Motherhood according to Bellini', in *Desire and Language*, 237–70 (first published in *Peinture* (December 1975), repr. *Polylogue* (Paris, 1977, pp. 409–35).

—— (1986), 'Stabat Mater', in Moi, T. (ed.), *The Kristeva Reader*, Oxford, 161–86 (first published as 'Hérethique de l'amour', *Tel Quel* 74 (Winter, 1977).

Kudlien, F. (1968), 'Early Greek primitive medicine', *Clio Medica* 3, pp. 305–36.

Kurtz, E. (1889), 'Zwei griechische Texte über die Hl. Theophano . . . ', *Mémoires de l'Académie impériale de St. Petersbourg, hist.-philol classe, 8 e série* 3/2, St Petersburg.

Kyrtatas, D. J. (1987), *The Social Structure of the Early Christian Communities*, London.

La Belle, J. (1988), *Herself Beheld: The literature of the looking glass*, Ithaca.

Laiou, A. E. (1981), 'The Role of Women in Byzantine Society', *Jahrbuch der österreichischen Byzantinistik* 31/1, pp. 233–60.

—— (1985), 'Observations on the Life and Ideology of Byzantine Women', *Byzantinische Forschungen* 9, pp. 59–102.

—— (1986), 'The Festival of Agathe: Comments on the Life of Constantinopolitan Women', in *Byzantion. Aphieroma ston A. N. Strato* I, Athens, pp. 111–22.

—— (1977), *Peasant Society in the Late Byzantine Empire*, Princeton.

Lakoff, R. T., Scherr, R. L. (1984), *Face Value: the Politics of Beauty*, London.

Lane Fox, R. (1986), *Pagans and Christians*, Harmondsworth.

Lang, M. (1969), *The Palace of Nestor at Pylos in Western Messenia II: The Frescoes*, Princeton.

Lanowski, J. (ed.) (1953), *Szymon Szymonowic. Sielanka grecka z dodatkiem: Bukolika grecka w Polsce*, Wroclaw.

Lapidge, M., Herren, M. (eds) (1979), *Aldhelm: the Prose Works*, Cambridge.

——, Rosier, J. (eds) (1985), *Aldhelm: the Poetic Works*, Cambridge.

Lariviere, R. W. (forthcoming), 'Matrimonial Remedies for Women in Classical Indian Law: Alternatives to Divorce', in Leslie (1991c), pp. 37–45.

Larson, G. (1985), *The Far Side*, Kansas City.

Lausberg, M. (1970), *Untersuchungen zu Senecas Fragmenten*, Berlin.

Le Doeuff, M. (1987), 'Women and Philosophy', in Moi, T. (ed.), French *Feminist Thought: A Reader*, Oxford.

Lee, D. (trans.) (1965), *Plato. Timaeus*, Harmondsworth.

Lee, R. B., DeVore, I. (eds) (1968), *Man the Hunter*, Chicago.

Lefkowitz, M. R. (1981), *Heroines and Hysterics*, London.
—— (1986), *Women in Greek Myth*, London, pp. 15–29.
—— and Fant, M. B. (eds) (1982), *Women's Life in Greece and Rome*, London.
Lepsius, C. R. (1849–59), *Denkmaeler aus Aegypten und Aethiopien*, Berlin.
Lerch, D. (1950), *Isaaks Opferung christlich gedeutet*, Tübingen (Beiträge zur historischen Theologie 12).
Lesko, B. (ed.) (1989), *Women's Earliest Records from Ancient Egypt and Western Asia*, Atlanta (Brown Judaic Studies 166).
Lesko, L. H. (1989a), 'The Middle Kingdom', in Lesko (1989), pp. 31–2.
—— (1989b), 'The Egyptian New Kingdom', in Lesko (1989a), pp. 101–3.
—— (1990), 'Some Comments on Ancient Egyptian Literacy and *Literati*, in Israelit-Groll, S. (ed.), *Studies in Egyptology presented to Miriam Lichtheim II*, Jerusalem, pp. 656–67.
Leslie, I. J. (1983), 'Essence and Existence: Women and Religion in Ancient Indian Texts', in Holden, P. (ed.), *Women's Religious Experience*, London, pp. 89–112.
—— (1986), '*Strīsvabhāva*: The Inherent Nature of Women', in Allen, N. J., Gombrich, R. F., Raychaudhuri, T., Rizvi, G. (eds), *Oxford University Papers on India* 1/1, Delhi, pp. 28–58.
—— (1987/8), 'Suttee or Satī: Victim or Victor?', *Bulletin of the Center for the Study of World Religions* 14/2, pp. 5–23 (= repr. in Leslie (1991a), pp. 175–90.
—— (1989), *The Perfect Wife: The Orthodox Hindu Woman according to the Strīdharmapaddhati of Tryambakayajvan*, Delhi.
—— (ed.) (1991a), *Roles and Rituals for Hindu Women*, London.
—— (1991b), 'Śrī and Jyesthā: Ambivalent Role Models for Women', in Leslie (1991a), pp. 107–27.
—— (ed.) (1991c), *Rules and Remedies in Classical Indian Law*, Leiden.
—— (1991d), 'A Problem of Choice: The Heroic Satī or the Widow-Ascetic', in Leslie (1991c), pp. 46–61.
—— (1992), 'The Significance of the Dress of the Orthodox Hindu Woman', in Barnes, R., Eicher, J. (eds), *The Anthropology of Dress and Gender*, Oxford, pp. 198–213.
Levinson, R. (1975), 'From Olive Oyl to Sweet Polly Purebread: Sex Role Stereotypes and Televised Cartoons', *Journal of Popular Culture* 9/3, pp. 561–72.
Lichtheim, M. (1975–80), *Ancient Egyptian Literature I–III*, Berkeley.
Lightfoot, J. B. (ed.) (1889), *The Apostolic Fathers I–III*, London.
Ling Roth, H. (1978), *Ancient Egyptian and Greek Looms*, Carlton, Bedford (Repr.).

Lippi, D., Arieti, S. (1985), 'La ricezione del *Corpus hippocraticum* nell'Islam', in Mazzini, Fusco (1985), pp. 399–402.

Littré, E. (1839–61), *Oeuvres complètes d'Hippocrate*, Paris.

Lloyd, G. (1984), *The Man of Reason: 'Male' and 'Female' in Western Philosophy*, London.

Lloyd, G. E. R. (1975), 'The Hippocratic Question', *Classical Quarterly* 25, pp. 171–92.

—— (1983), *Science, Folklore and Ideology*, Cambridge.

Loewe, R. (1966), *The Position of Women in Judaism*, London.

Lonie, I. M. (1983), 'Literacy and the development of Hippocratic medicine', in Lasserre, F., Mudry, P. (eds), *Formes de pensée dans la collection hippocratique*, Geneva, pp. 145–61 (Actes du Colloque hippocratique de Lausanne).

Lorber, J., Farrell, S. A. (eds) (1991), *The Social Construction of Gender*, London.

Lord, L. E. (1947), *A History of the American School of Classical Studies at Athens 1882–1942. An Intercollegiate Project*, Cambridge.

Lossky, V. (1957), *The Mystical Theology of the Eastern Church*, Cambridge.

Lucas, A. (1983), *Women in the Middle Ages*, Brighton.

Lutz, C. E. (1947), '*Musonius Rufus: "The Roman Socrates"*', *Yale Classical Studies* 10, pp 3–147.

Maclean, A. J. (1919), *The Ministry of Women*, London, pp. 53–63. Report by a committee appointed by the Lord Archbishop of Canterbury.

Maclean, I. (1980), *The Renaissance Notion of Woman*, Cambridge.

MacMullen, R. (1984), *Christianizing the Roman Empire, AD 100–400*, New Haven.

Magdalino, P. (1991), 'Church, bath and *diakonia* in medieval Constantinople', in Morris (1991), pp. 165–88.

Malone, K. (1963), 'Two English Frauenlieder', in Greenfield, S. B. (ed.), *Studies in Old English Literature, in Honour of A. G. Brodeur*, Oregon, pp. 106–17.

Mango, C. (1972), *The Art of the Byzantine Empire 312–1453*, Englewood Cliffs, New Jersey.

—— (1982), 'St. Anthusa of Mantineon and the family of Constantine V', *Analecta Bollandiana* 100, pp. 401–9.

Mann, M. (1986), *The Sources of Social Power I. A History of Power from the beginnings to AD 1760*, Cambridge.

Manniche, L. (1978), *Sexual Life in Ancient Egypt*, London.

Manuli, P. (1980), 'Fisiologia e patologia del femminile negli scritti ippocratici dell'antica ginecologia greca', in Gronek, M. D. (ed.) *Hippocratica*, Actes du Colloque hippocratique de Paris, 1978, Paris.

—— (1983), 'Donne mascoline, femmine sterili, vergini perpetue. La ginecologia greca tra Ippocrate e Sorano', in Campese, S., Manuli, P., Sissa, G. (eds), *Madre Materia*, Turin, pp. 147–92.

Maraval, P. (ed.) (1983), *Vie de Ste. Macrine*, Paris.

Marglin, F. A. (1985), *Wives of the God–King: The Rituals of the Devadasis of Puri*, Delhi.

Marks, E., de Courtivron, I. (eds) (1981), *New French Feminisms: An Anthology*, Brighton.

Martimort, A. G. (1986) *Deaconesses. An Historical Study*, San Francisco.

Marzal, A. (1965), *La Enseñanza de Amenemope*, Madrid (Instituto Español de Estudios Eclesiasticos Monografias 4).

Mattingly, H. (1976), *Coins of the Roman Empire in the British Museum I: Augustus to Vitellius*, London.

Matz, F. (1962), *Crete and Early Greece*, London.

Maurin, J. (1983), 'Labor matronalis: aspects du travail féminin à Rome', in Levy, E. (ed.), *La femme dans les sociétés antique*, Strasbourg, pp. 139–55.

Mayr-Harting, H. M. R. E. (1972), *The Coming of Christianity to Anglo-Saxon England*, London.

Mazzini, I. (1985), 'Ippocrate latino dei secolo V–VI: tecnica di traduzione', in Mazzini, Fusco (1985), pp. 383–7.

——, Fusco, F. (1985), *I Testi di Medicina Latini Antichi: Problemi Filologici e Storici*, Macerata (Atti del I Convegno Internazionale).

McCullough, C. (1990), *The First Man in Rome*, New York.

McGee, M. (1991), 'Desired Fruits: Motive and Intention in the Votive Rites of Hindu Women', in Leslie (1991a), pp. 71–88.

McGuigan, C. (film review) (12 October 1987), *Newsweek* 110, pp. 76–7 (US edition).

McNamara, J. (1983), *A New Song: Celibate Women in the First Three Christian Centuries*, New York.

Menski, W. F. (1991), 'Marital Expectations as Dramatized in Hindu Marriage Rituals', in Leslie (1991a), pp. 47–67.

Mercati, S. I. (ed.) (1915), *S. Ephraem Syri Opera* I, Rome, pp. 43–83.

Merritt, L. S. (1984), *A History of the American School at Athens 1939–1980*, Princeton.

Meunier, M. (1932), *Femmes Pythagoriciennes: fragments et lettres de Théano, Périctioné, Phintys, Mélissa et Myia*, Paris.

Meyer, M. A. (1977), 'Women and the Tenth Century English Monastic Reform', *Révue Bénédictine* 87, pp. 34–61.

——, (1980), 'Land Charters and the Legal Position of Anglo-Saxon Women', in Kanner (1980), pp. 57–82.

Miller, F. G. B. (1977), *Emperor in the Roman World*, London.

Miller, H. (1941, repr. 1980), *The Colossus of Maroussi*, Harmondsworth.

Mills, B. (trans.) (1963), *The Idylls of Theocritus*, Indiana.

Möller, G. (1918), *Zwei Ägyptische Eheverträge aus Vorsaïtischer Zeit*, Berlin.

Momigliano, A. (1985), 'The Life of St. Macrina by Gregory of Nyssa', in Ober, J., Eadie, J. (eds), *The Craft of the Ancient Historian*, Lanham, Maryland, pp. 443–58.

Moore, L. (trans.) (1959), *St. John Climacus. The Ladder of Divine Ascent*, London.

Moore, T. (1956), *Poetical Works*, Oxford.

Morgenstern, J. (1966), *Rites of Birth, Marriage, Death and Kindred Occasions among the Semites*, Cincinnati.

Morris, R. (ed.) (1991), *Church and People in Byzantium*, Birmingham.

—— (ed.) (1967), *The Blickling Homilies*, Oxford (Early English Texts Society, OS, 58, 63, 73).

Mortley, R. (1981), *Womanhood. The Feminine in Ancient Hellenism, Gnosticism, Christianity and Islam*, Sydney.

—— (1988), *Désir et différence dans la tradition platonicienne*, Paris.

Müller-Rohlfsen, I. (1980), *Die Lateinische Ravennatische Übersetzung der hippokratischen Aphorismen aus dem 5./6. Jahrhundert n. chr.*, Hamburg (Geistes- und socialwissenschaftliche Dissertation 55).

Mustanoja, T. (1967), 'The Unnamed Woman's Song of Mourning over Beowulf and the Tradition of Ritual Lamentation', *Neuphilologische Mitteilungen* 68, pp. 1–35.

Musurillo, H. (ed.) (1963), *Méthode d'Olympe: Le banquet*, Paris (Sources chrétiennes 95).

Myerowitz, M. (1985), *Ovid's Games of Love*, Detroit.

Mynors, R. A. B. (ed.) (1969), *Vergil. Opera*, Oxford.

Naville, E. (1898), *The Temple of Deir el Bahari* 3, London.

Nelson, R. S. (1989), 'The Discourse of Icons: Then and Now', *Art History* 12, pp. 144–57.

Nesbitt, J., Wiita, J. (1975), 'A Confraternity of the Comnenian Era', *Byzantinische Zeitschrift* 68, pp. 360–84.

Newton, C. T. (1880), 'Dr. Schliemann's Discoveries at Mycenae', in *Essays in Art and Archaeology*, London, pp. 246–302.

Nichol, G. (1969), 'The clitoris martyr', *World Medicine* 4/16, pp. 59–65.

Nicholson, J. (1978), 'Women in the Age of Bede', in Baker (1978), pp. 15–29.

Nixon, L. (1983), 'Changing Views of Minoan Society', in Krzyszkowska, O., Nixon, L. (eds), *Minoan Society*, Bristol, pp. 237–43.

—— (1987), 'The Anthropology of Homecoming at Queen's', *Queen's Quarterly* 94, pp. 313–31.

Noailles, P., Dain, A. (eds) (1944), *Les Novelles de Léon le Sage*, Paris.

Norris, C. (1987), *Derrida*, London.

Nussbaum, M. C. (1986), *The Fragility of Goodness: Luck and Ethics in Greek Tragedy and Philosophy*, Cambridge.

Oakley, K. (1949), *Man the Tool-Maker*, London.

O'Donoghue, H. (ed.) (1986), *Art and Doctrine: Essays on medieval literature*, London.

Ogdon, J. R. (1986), 'An Exceptional Family of Priests of the Early Fifth Dynasty at Giza', *Gottingen Miszellen* 90, pp. 61–5.

Okin, S. M. (1980), *Women in Western Political Thought*, London.

Orton, P. (1985), 'An Approach to Wulf and Eadwacer', *Proceedings of the Royal Irish Academy* 85, pp. 223–58.

Osborn, M. (1983), 'The Text and Context of Wulf and Eadwacer', in Green (1983), pp. 174–89.

Owen, G. R. (1979), 'Wynflaed's Wardrobe', *Anglo-Saxon England* 8, pp. 195–222.

Page, R. I. (1970), *Life in Anglo-Saxon England*, London.

Pagels, E. (1990), *Adam, Eve and the Serpent*, London.

Papadopoulous-Kerameus, A. (1909), *Varia graeca sacra*, St Petersburg.

Parker, R. (1982), *Miasma*, Oxford.

Parkinson, R. B. (1991), *Voices of Ancient Egypt. An Anthology of Middle Kingdom Writings*, London.

Pater, W. (1893), *Plato and Platonism*, London.

Patlagean, E. (1976/1981), 'L'histoire de la femme déguisée en moine et l'évolution de la sainteté féminine à Byzance', *Studi medievali*³ 17/2, pp. 597–623/*Structure sociale, famille, chrétienté à Byzance*, London (Variorum).

Pflaum, H. G. (1960–1), *Les carrières procuratoriennes*, Paris.

Peet, T. E. (1930), *The Great Tomb Robberies of the Twentieth Egyptian Dynasty*, Oxford.

Pembroke, S. (1967), 'Women in Charge: The Function of Alternatives in Early Greek Tradition and the Ancient Idea of Matriarchy', *Journal of the Warburg and Courtauld Institutes* 30, pp. 1–35.

Percival, H. R. (ed.) (1900), *The Seven Ecumenical Councils. A Select Library of Nicene and Post Nicene Fathers* 14, Oxford.

Pestman, P. W. (1961), *Marriage and Matrimonial Property in Ancient Egypt*, Leiden (Papyrologica Lugduno-Batava 9).

Pillet, M. (1952), 'Les scènes de naissance et de circoncision dans le temple nord-est de Mout, à Karnak', *Annales du Service des Antiquités de l'Égypte* 52, pp. 77–104.

Pomeroy, S. B. (1977), 'Technikai kai Mousikai: The Education of Women in the Fourth Century and in the Hellenistic Period', *American Journal of Ancient History* 2, pp. 51–68.

—— (1984), *Women in Hellenistic Egypt*, New York.

Posener, G. (1951), 'Ostraca inédits du Musée de Turin (Recherches littérat 3)', *Revue d'Égyptologie* 8, pp. 171–89.

—— (1952), 'Le debut de l'enseignement de Hardjedef (Recherches Littéraires 4). Compléments aux "Richesses inconnues"', *Revue d'Égyptologie* 9, pp. 109–20.

Pringle, I. (1975), 'Judith: the Homily and the Poem', *Traditio* 31, pp. 83–97.

Pritchard, J. B. (ed.) (1950), *Ancient Near Eastern Texts Relating to the Old Testament*, Princeton.

Purcell, N. (1986), 'Livia and the Womanhood of Rome', *Proceedings of the Cambridge Philological Society*, 32, pp. 77–105.

Ralles, G. A., Potles, M. (eds) (1852–9), *Syntagmae ton theion kai ieron kanonon 1–6*, Athens.

Ramage, E. S. (1973), *Urbanitas: Ancient Sophistication and Refinement*, Oklahoma.

Ramanujan, A. K. (1982), 'On Women Saints', in Hawley, J. S., Wulff, D. M., *The Divine Consort: Rādhā and the Goddesses of India*, Delhi, pp. 316–24.

Raw, B. (1984), 'The Construction of Oxford, Bodleian Library, Junius 11', *Anglo-Saxon England* 13, pp. 187–205.

Rawson, E. (1969), *The Spartan Tradition in European Thought*, Oxford.

Redford, D. B. (1967), *History and Chronology of the Eighteenth Dynasty of Egypt. Seven Studies*, Toronto.

—— (1986), *Pharaonic King-lists, Annals and Day Books. A Contribution to the Study of the Egyptian Sense of History*, Mississauga (Society for the Study of Egyptian Antiquities, Publication 4).

Renault, M. (1958), *The King Must Die*, New York.

—— (1962), *The Bull from the Sea*, New York.

Renfrew, C. (1972), *The Emergence of Civilisation*, London.

Renoir, A. (1990), 'Eve's I. Q. Rating: Two Sexist Views of Genesis B', in Damico, Hennessy Olsen (1990), pp. 262–72.

Reynolds, J. (1982), *Aphrodisias and Rome*, London.

Richards, M. P., Stanfield, B. J. (1990), 'Concepts of Anglo-Saxon Women in the Laws', in Damico, Hennessy Olsen (1990), pp. 89–99.

Richlin, A. (1983), *The Garden of Priapus: Sexuality and Aggression in Roman Humor*, Yale.

—— (1984), 'Invective against Women in Roman Satire', *Arethusa* 17, pp. 67–80.

Ridgway, B. S. (1987), 'Ancient Women and Art', *American Journal of Archaeology* 91, pp. 399–409.

Riedinger, A. R. (1990), 'The Englishing of Arcestrate: Woman in Apollonius of Tyre', in Damico, Hennessy Olsen (1990), pp. 292–306.

Rist, A. (1978), *The Poems of Theocritus*, Chapel Hill.

Robertson, A. J. (ed.) (1925), *The Laws of the Kings of England from Edmund to Henry I*, Cambridge.

Robins, G. (1988), 'Ancient Egyptian Sexuality', *Discussions in Egyptology* 11, pp. 61–72.

—— (1990), 'While the Woman Looks On. Gender Inequality in New Kingdom Egypt', *KMT. A Modern Journal of Ancient Egypt* 1/3, pp. 18–65.

Robinson, F. C. (1964), 'Is Wealhtheow a Prince's Daughter', *English Studies* 45, pp. 36–9.

Rohrlich-Leavitt, R. (1977), 'Women in Transition: Crete and Sumer', in Bridenthal, R., Koonz, C. (eds), *Becoming Visible: Women in European Prehistory*, Boston, pp. 36–59.

Rome (1990), *Bellezza e Seduzione nella Roma Imperiale*, Rome (Exhibition Catalogue, De Luca Edizioni d'Arte with Laura Biagiotti).

Roper, L. (1987), '"The common man", "the common good", "the common women": gender and meaning in the German Reformation Commune'. *Social History* 12/1, pp. 1–21.

Rosaldo, M. (1974), 'Women, Culture and Society: A Theoretical Overview'. in Rosaldo and Lamphere (1974), pp. 17–42.

——, Lamphere, L. (eds) (1974), *Women, Culture and Society*, Stanford.

Rosati, G. (ed.) (1985), *I Cosmetici delle Donne*, Venezia Marsilio (Il convivo Coll. di class. greci. e lat.).

Rose, V. (ed.) (1886), *Aristotelis Fragmenta*, Leipzig.

Rosenqvist, J. O. (1986), *The Life of St. Irene Abbess of Chrysobalanton*. Uppsala.

Ross, W. D. (1924), *Aristotle's Metaphysics*, Oxford.

Rousselle, A. (1980), 'Images médicales du corps. Observation féminine et idéologie masculine: le corps de la femme d'après les médecins grecs' *Annales E. S. C.* 35, pp. 1089–1115.

—— (1983/1988), *Porneia, de la mâitrise du corps à la privation sensorielle*, Paris/*Porneia: On Desire and the Body in Antiquity*, Oxford.

Ruether, R. R. (ed.) (1974) *Religion and Sexism*, New York.

—— (1979), 'Mothers of the Church: Ascetic Women in the Late Patristic Age', in Ruether, McLaughlin (1979), pp. 71–98.

——, McLaughlin, E. (eds) (1979), *Women of Spirit: Female Leadership in the Jewish and Christian Traditions*, New York.

Ruffle, J. (1979), 'The Teachings of Amenemope and its connection with the Book of Proverbs', *The Tyndale Bulletin* 28, 1977, Cambridge, pp. 29–68.

Rundle-Clarke, R. T. (1978), *Myth and Symbol in Ancient Egypt*, London.

Russell, D. A. (1979), 'Rhetors at the Wedding', *Proceedings of the Classical Philological Society* 205 n.s. 25, pp. 104–17.

Ryberg, I. S. (1955), 'Rites of the State Religion in Roman Art'. *Memoirs of the American Academy at Rome* 22, Rome.

Safrai, S. et al. (eds) (1978), *Compendia Rerum Iudaicarum ad Novum Testamentun. The Jewish People in the First Century*, 1–2, Assen.

Said, E. (1978), *Orientalism*, London.

Sanday, P. R. (1974), 'Female Status in the Public Domain', in Rosaldo, Lamphere (1974), pp. 189–205.

Sayre, K. M. (1983), *Plato's Late Ontology: A Riddle Resolved*, Princeton.

Scaefer, U. (1986), 'Two Women in Need of a Friend: a Comparison of the Wife's Lament and Eangyth's Letter to Boniface', in Brogyanyi, B., Krommelbein, T. (eds), *Germanic Dialects: Linguistic and philological investigations*, Amsterdam and Philadelphia, pp. 491–524.

Schroeder, H. J. (1937), *Disciplinary Decrees of the General Councils*, London.

Schürer, E. (1973–87), *The History of the Jewish People in the Age of Jesus Christ*, 1–2, Edinburgh (ed. and rev. G. Vermes, F. Millar, M. Black); 3–4, Edinburgh (ed. and rev. G. Vermes, F. Millar, M. Goodman).

Scull, A., Favreau, D. (1986), 'The clitoridectomy craze', *Social Research* 53, pp. 243–60.

Seibt, W. (1973), 'Prosopographische Konsequenzen der Undatierung von Grumel, Regestes 933 (Patriarch Eustathios austelle von Eustratios)', *Jahrbuch der österreichischen Byzantinistik* 22, pp. 103–15.

Sethe, K., Helck, W. (eds) (1906–58), *Urkunden des ägyptischen Altertums, Abteilung 4: Urkunden der 18. Dynastie*, fasc. 1–22,/Leipzig.

Sewter, E. R. A. (1966), *Fourteen Byzantine Rulers*, Harmondsworth.

Shastri, H. P. (trans.) (1976), *Rāmāyana*, London.

Shirun-Grumach, I. (1985), 'Remarks on the Goddess Maat' in Israelit-Groll, S. (ed.), *Pharaonic Egypt. The Bible and Christianity*, Jerusalem, pp. 173–201.

Shupak, N. (1989), 'Instruction and Teaching Appellations in Egyptian Wisdom Literature', *Akten des 4. Internationalen Ägyptologen-Kongresses München 1985*, Hamburg (Studien zur Altägyptischen Kultur 3).

Simon, J. (film review) (4 December 1987), *National Review* 39, 56–7 (US edition).

Simpson, W. K. (ed.) (1973), *The Literature of Ancient Egypt*, London.

Sims-Williams, P. (1979), 'An Unpublished Seventh- or Eighth-Century Letter in Boulogne-sur-mer Ms 74 (82)', *Medium Ævum* 48, pp. 1–22.

Sisam, K. (1953), *Studies in the History of Old English Literature*, Oxford.

Sissa, G. (1983), 'Il corpo della donna. Lineamenti di una ginecologia filosofica', in Campese, S., Manuli, P., Sissa, G. (eds), *Madre Materia*, Turin, pp. 81–145.

—— (1987/1990), *Le corps virginal*, Paris/*Greek Virginity*, Cambridge, Massachusetts.

Skeat, W. W. (ed.) (1966), *Ælfric's Lives of the Saints*, London (Early English Texts Society OS 76, 82, pp. 94–114).

Sklute, L. M. (1970), 'Freððuwebbe in Old English Poetry', repr. in Damico, Hennessy Olsen (1990), 211–21.

Smith, F. M. (1991), 'Indra's Curse, Varuṇa's Noose, and the Suppression of Women in the Vedic Śrauta Ritual', in Leslie (1991a), pp. 17–35.

Smith, M. (1984), 'Sonnenauge, Demotische Mythos vom. A', *Lexikon der Ägyptologie* 5, col. 1082–7.

—— (1987), *The Mortuary Texts of Papyrus BM 10507*, London (Catalogue of Demotic Papyri in the British Museum 3).

Smith, W. D. (1979), *The Hippocratic Tradition*, Ithaca.

Sokolski, J. (ed.) (1985), *Szymon Szymonowic. Sielanki*, Wroclaw.

Sørensen, M.-L. (1988), 'Is there a feminist contribution to archaeology?', *Archaeological Review from Cambridge* 7/1, pp. 9–20.

Spelman, E. (1982), 'Woman as Body: Ancient and Contemporary Views', *Feminist Studies* 8/1, pp. 109–31.

Spender, D. (1980), *Man Made Language*, London.

—— (1989), 'Theorising about Theorising', in Bowles, G., Klein, R. D., *Theories of Women's Studies*, London. pp. 27–31.

Spengel, L. (1894), *Rhetores Graeci* 1/2, Leipzig (rev. L. Hammer).

Spiegel, S. (1969), *The Last Trial*, New York.

Stadele, A. (1980), *Die Briefe des Pythagoras und der Pythagoreer*, Meisenheim am Glan (Beitrage zur Klassichen Philologie 115).

Stafford, P. (1978), 'Sons and Mothers: Family Politics in the Early Middle Ages', in Baker (1978), pp. 79–100.

—— (1981), 'The King's Wife in Wessex, 800–1066', repr. in Damico, Hennessy Olsen (1990), pp. 56–78.

—— (1989), 'Women in Domesday', *Reading Medieval Studies* 15, pp. 75–94.

Stanley, E. G. (1966), 'Beowulf', in Stanley, E. G. (ed.), *Continuations and Beginnings: Studies in Old English Literature*, London, pp. 104–41.

Stenton, D. M. (1957), *The English Woman in History*, New York.

Stenton, F. M. (1970), 'The Historical Bearing of Place-Name Studies; the Place of Women in Anglo-Saxon Society', repr. in Damico, Hennessy Olsen (1990), pp. 79–88.

Stevens, M. (1968), 'The Narrator of the Wife's Lament', *Neuphilologische Mitteilungen* 79, pp. 72–90.

Stevenson, W. H. (ed.) (1904), *Asser's Life of King Alfred*, Oxford.

Stevick, R. D. (1960), 'Formal Aspects of the Wife's Lament', *Journal of English and Germanic Philology* 59, pp. 21–5.

Stewart, H. M. (1976), *Egyptian Stelae, Reliefs and Paintings from the Petrie Collection 1: The New Kingdom*, Warminster.

—— (1979), *Egyptian Stelae, Reliefs and Paintings from the Petrie Collection 2: Archaic Period to Second Intermediate Period*, Warminster.

Stocks, J. L. (1914), 'LOGOS and MESOTES in the *de Anima* of Aristotle', *Journal of Philology* 33, pp. 182–94.

Stone, L. (film review) (December 1987), *Ms* 16, 78–9 (US edition).

Stork, H. (1991), 'Mothering Rituals in Tamilnadu: Some Magico-Religious Beliefs', in Leslie (1991a), pp. 89–105.

Stubbs, W. (ed.) (1887), *Willelmi Malmesbiriensis Monachi de Gestis Regum Anglorum*, London, (Rolls Series 236).

Sutcliffe, R. (1978), *Song for a Dark Queen*, New York.

—— (1986), *The Flowers of Adonis*, London.

Swanton, M. (1987), *English Literature Before Chaucer*, London.

Syme, R. (1958), *Tacitus*, I and II, Oxford.

—— (1964), *Sallust*, London.

Talbert, R. J. A. (1984), *The Senate of Imperial Rome*, Princeton.

Talbot, A.-M. (1983), 'Bluestocking Nuns: Intellectual Life in the Convents of Late Byzantium', *Harvard Ukrainian Studies* 7, pp. 604–18.

—— (1985), 'Late Byzantine Nuns: by choice or necessity?', *Byzantinische Forschungen* 9, pp. 103–117.

Talbot, C. H. (ed.) (1954), *The Anglo-Saxon Missionaries in Germany*, London.

Tanner, T. H. (1867), 'On excision of the clitoris as a cure for hysteria', *Transactions of the Obstetrical Society of London* 8, pp. 360–84.

Tavard, G. H. (1973), *Woman in Christian Tradition*, Indiana.

Teeter, E. (1990), 'Wearer of the Royal Uraeus: Hatshepsut', KMT 1/1, pp. 4–12.

Teresa (Sr) (Joan White) (1989), 'The Development and Eclipse of the Deacon Abbess', *Studia Patristica* 19, pp. 111–16.

Te Velde, H. (1979/80), 'Towards a Minimal Definition of the Goddess Mut', *Jaarbericht: ex Oriente Lux* 26, pp. 3–9.

—— (1980), 'Horus and Seth', *Lexicon der Ägyptologie* 3, col. 25–7.

Théodoridès, A. (1971), 'The Concept of Law in Ancient Egypt', in Harris, J. (ed.), *The Legacy of Egypt*, Oxford, pp. 291–322.

Thesleff, H. (1961), *An Introduction to the Pythagorean Writings of the Hellenistic Period*, Abo.

—— (1965), *The Pythagorean Texts of the Hellenistic Period*, Abo.

Thorpe, B. (ed.) (1884), *Ælfric: Sermones Catholici I and II*, London.

Timmer, B. J. (ed.) (1978), *Judith*², Exeter.

Tonneau, R. (ed.) (1955), *Sancti Ephraem Syri in Genesim et in Exodum Commentarii*, Louvain (Corpus Scriptorum Christianorum Orientalium, Scr. Syri 71–2).

Topping, E. C. (1980), 'Thekla the Nun: In Praise of Women', *Greek Orthodox Theological Review* 25, pp. 353–70.

—— (1982–3), 'Byzantine Women Hymnographers', *Diptycha* 3, pp. 99–111.

Trapp, E. (ed.) (1971), *Digenes Akritas, Synoptische Ausgabe der ältesten Version*, Vienna.

Treggiari, S. (1979), 'Lower Class Women in the Roman Economy', *Florilegium* 1, pp. 65–86.

Trigger, B. (1989), *A History of Archaeological Thought*, Cambridge.

Troy, L. (1984), 'Good and Bad Women. Maxim 18/284–288 of the Instructions of Ptahhotep', *Gottingen Miszellen* 80, pp. 77–82.

—— (1986), *Patterns of Queenship in Ancient Egyptian Myth and History*, Stockholm (Uppsala Studies in Ancient Mediterranean and Near Eastern Civilisation 14).

Turner, B. S. (1984), *The Body and Society: Explorations in social theory*, Oxford.

Ucko, P. J., Tringham, R., Dimbleby, G. W. (eds) (1972), *Man, Settlement and Urbanism*, London.

Urbach, E. E. (1975), *The Sages. Their Concepts and Beliefs* 1–2, Jerusalem (trans. I. Abrahams).

Usener, H. (ed.) (1887), *Epicurea*, Leipzig.

Vallettas, N. (ed.) (1864), *Photiou Epistolai*, London.

Van den Bosch, L. P. (1991) 'The Marriage of the Dead in Ancient India: On the Interpretation of Vaikhānasasmārtasūtra V. 9.', in Leslie (1991c), pp. 62–79.

Van Geytenbeek, A. C. (1949), *Musonius Rufus en de Griekse Diatribe*, Amsterdam.

Van Rompay, L. (1978), 'Oratio de Abraham', *Amphilochii Iconiensis Opera*, Corpus Christianorum. Series Graeca III, Turnhout, pp. 274–303.

Vernant, J.-P. (1979), 'Manger aux pays du soleil', in Detienne, M., Vernant, J.-P. (eds), *La cuisine du sacrifice en pays grec*, Paris, pp. 239–49.

Veyne, P. (1978), 'L'amour et la famille dans le haut-empire', *Annales: Économies Societés Civilisations* 33, pp. 35–63.

—— (1985), 'Homosexuality in ancient Rome', in Ariès, P., Bejin, A. (eds), *Western Sexuality: Practice and Precept in Past and Present Times*, Oxford, pp. 26–35.

—— (1986), 'L'Empire romain', in Ariès, Duby (1986), pp. 19–224.

Vickrey, J. F. (1969), 'The Vision of Eve in Genesis B', *Speculum* 44, pp. 86–102.

—— (1971), 'The "micel wundor" of Genesis B', *Studies in Philology* 68, pp. 245–54.

Vilinsky, S. G. (ed.) (1911–13), 'Zhitie sv. Vasiliya Novogo v russkoi literature', *Zapiski Novorossiiskogo universiteta, Ist.-filol. fak.* 6–7.

Virgili, P. (1990), 'Culto della Bellezza e della Seduzione', in Rome (1990), pp. 17–62.

Vlastos, G. (1981), *Platonic Studies*², Princeton.

Volten, A. (1955), 'Die moralischen Lehren des demotischen Pap. Louvre 2414', *Studi in Memoria di Ippolito Rosellini nel primo centenario della morte* II, Pisa, pp. 269–80 (Universita degli studi di Pisa).

Von Arnim, H. (ed.) (1903), *Stoicorum Veterum Fragmenta*, Leipzig.

Von der Muehll, P. (1965), 'Was Diogenes Laertios der Dame, der er sein Buch widmen will, ankundigt', *Philologus* 109, pp. 313–15.

Waithe, M. E. (1987), (ed.), *A History of Women Philosophers I: 600 B.C.– A.D. 500*, Dordrecht, Boston and Lancaster.

Walcot, P. (1987), 'Plato's Mother and Other Terrible Women', *Greece and Rome* n.s. 34, pp. 12–31.

Walker, S. F. (1980), *Theocritus*, Boston.

Wainwright, F. T. (1959), 'Æthelflaed Lady of the Mercians', repr. in Damico, Hennessy Olsen (1990), pp. 44–55.

Ward, B. (ed.), Russell, N. (trans.) (1980), *The Lives of the Desert Fathers*, London.

—— (ed.) (1987), *Harlots of the Desert*, Oxford.

Ward, J. A. (1960), 'The Wife's Lament: an Interpretation', *Journal of English and Germanic Philology* 59, pp. 26–33.

Ward, W. A. (1989), 'Non-royal Women and their Occupations in the Middle Kingdom', in Lesko (1989a), pp. 33–43.

Warner, M. (1976), *Alone of All her Sex: The myth and cult of the Virgin Mary*, London.

Warner, R. D. N. (ed.) (1917), *Early English Homilies*, Oxford (Early English Texts Society, OS, 152).

Waterhouse, H. (1986), *The British School at Athens. The First One Hundred Years*, Oxford.

Watson, P. (1982), 'Ovid and *Cultus: Ars Amatoria* 3.113–28', *Transactions of the American Philological Association* 112, pp. 237–44.

Weaver, K., Brill, D. L., Matternes, J. H. (1985), 'The Search for our Ancestors', *National Geographic* 168/5, pp. 560–623.

Wehrli, F. (1944) *Die Schule des Aristotles*, Band 1: *Dicaearchus*, Basle.

Westerink, L. G. (1976), T*he Greek Commentaries on Plato's Phaedo 1: Olympiodorus*, Oxford.

Wheeler, E. P. (trans.) (1977), *Dorotheus of Gaza. Discourses and Sayings*, Kalamazoo.

Whitelock, D. (ed.) (1930), *Anglo-Saxon Wills*, Cambridge.

—— (ed.) (1979), *English Historical Documents I, c. 500–1042*, London.

Whitford, M. (1988), 'Luce Irigaray's Critique of Rationality' in Griffiths, M., Whitford, M. (eds), *Feminist Perspectives in Philosophy*, London, pp. 109–30.

Wicker, K. O'Brien (trans.) (1987), *Porphyry the Philosopher, To Marcella*, Atlanta, Georgia.

Williams, E. W. (1975), 'What's so New About the Sexual Revolution? Some Comments on Anglo-Saxon Attitudes Towards Sexuality in Women, Based on Four Exeter Book Riddles', repr. in Damico, Hennessy Olsen (1990), pp. 137–45.

Williamson, G. (1989), *Eusebius. Ecclesiastical History*, Harmondsworth (English trans. A. Louth).

Wilson, D. M. (1964), *Anglo-Saxon Ornamental Metalwork, 700–1100*, London.

—— (1985), *The Bayeux Tapestry*, London.

Wilson, E. (1985), *Adorned in Dreams: Fashion and Modernity*, London.

Wilson, J. A. (1977), 'Egypt', in Frankfort, H. (ed.), *The Intellectual Adventure of Ancient Man: An Essay on Speculative Thought in the Ancient Near East*, Chicago, pp. 31–122.

Wilson, R. M. (1970), *The Lost Literature of Medieval England²*, London.
Wilson-Kastner, P. (1981), *A Lost Tradition. Women Writers of the Early Church*, Washington, DC.
Wiseman, T. P. (1979), *Clio's Cosmetics: Three Studies in Greco-Roman Literature*, Leicester.
Witherington III, B. (1984), *Women in the Ministry of Jesus*, Cambridge.
—— (1988), *Women in the Earliest Churches*, Cambridge.
Wood, E. M., Wood, N. (1978), *Class Ideology in Ancient Political Theory*, Oxford.
Wood, M. (1985), *In Search of the Trojan War*, London.
Woolf, R. (1955), 'The Lost Opening to the Judith', repr. in O'Donoghue (1986), pp. 119–24.
—— (1963), 'The Fall of Man in Genesis B and the Mystère d'Adam', repr. in O'Donoghue (1986), pp. 15–28.
—— (1966), 'Saints' Lives', repr. in O'Donoghue (1986), pp. 219–44.
Wormald, C. P. (1977), 'The Uses of Literacy in Anglo-Saxon England and its Neighbours', *Transactions of the Royal Historical Society* 5th ser. 27, pp. 95–114.
—— (1978), 'Bede, Beowulf and the Conversion of the Anglo-Saxon Aristocracy', in Farrell, R. T. (ed.), *Bede and Anglo-Saxon England*, Oxford, pp. 32–89.
Wortley, J. (1987), *Les récits édifiants de Paul, évêque de Monemvasie et d'autres auteurs*, Paris.
Wyke, M. (1989), 'Mistress and Metaphor in Augustan Elegy', *Helios* 16, pp. 25–47.
Yorke, B. (1989), '"Sisters under the skin": Anglo-Saxon Nuns and Nunneries in Southern England', *Reading Medieval Studies* 15, pp. 95–117.
Young, F. (1983), *From Nicaea to Chalcedon*, London.
Zanker, P. (1988), *The Power of Images in the Age of Augustus*, Ann Arbor, Michigan (trans. A. Shapiro).
Zeller, A. C. (1987), 'A Role for Women in Hominid Evolution', *Man* n.s. 22, pp. 528–57.
Zepos, I., Zepos, P. (eds) (1931), *Jus Graecoromanum* 1–8, Athens.

Index

abbesses 184, 193, 206, 207; *see also* asceticism; nuns and nunneries

administration 124, 125, 211; *see also* labour, division of; power

adornment 134–48, 153, 162, 218, 219, 220; and the written word, 144–6

adultery 193, 194, 195, 210; 'strange woman', 43, 45ff; in Wisdom Literature, 36, 37, 45ff; Roman, 128, 136–7; modern, 262–4

aesthetics 95–6, 145

Agrippina II 115, 121–2, 124, 126

androgyny 137, 148, 152, 163; *see also* gender

anomalousness 106, 107, 116, 121–30, 137; *see also* social (dis)order

Antonia the Younger 123–4

Æthelflaed 208–19

Antony, St 154–5, 184

archaeology data analysis (gender bias), 2, 5, 6, 8, 9–11, 11–13, 17–20; orientalism, 11; Egyptian, 25; professional division of labour, 14, 15, 16–18; depiction in popular culture, 13, 14, 18; Minoan, Mycenaean *see under* place-names

architecture women's quarters, 9, 59; Minoan, 13; Knossos palace, 8–9; at Mycenae, 10

Arete 82, 84

Aristotle 74, 76, 83, 88–9, 106

art Mycenaean, 10–11, 13; Minoan, 13; murals 41; statues, 27, 34; Egyptian 32, 34; at Knossos, 9–10; use of female body, 144ff; toiletry articles, 143–4; relief sculpture, 129, 141–2; coin portraits, 129; *see also* adornment, icons

asceticism 154–7, 169–3, 165–6,

188–9, 193, 195–6, *see also* nuns and nunneries

Aspasia 72

Australopithecus afarensis *see* Lucy

authority, accorded men 116, 120, 121, 128, 129, 135, 136, 138, 139, 140, 147–8, 182, 184, 187, 191

Axiothea 73, 74

baptism, adult 191

Bible New Testament, 152, 183, 196, 208; Old Testament, 53–66, 157, 158, 169, 207

biology *see* medicine, social (dis)order

body, the human female control over own, 109, 110; and literary artistry, 144–6; and art, 144ff; as social category, 134–48; care of 134–48; texture, 106–7, 108, 110, 111, 112; *see also* social order, physical appearance, gender sexuality, medicine

Bronze Age *see* Minoans; Mycenaean society

caste *see* social order – Hindu

chaos, women representative of 26, 28, 38–9, 118–19, 127–30, 148, 188, 189, 249; *see also* social (dis)order

charity 162, 184, 186, 188, 189, 190, 192, 196

childbirth purification after, 59, 196–7; in Hippocratic corpus, 105, 107, 108, 112; miraculous, 195

children respect for parents, 40, 41; following divorce, 35; of adulterers, 45–6; care of, 45, 123, 124; inheritance by, 37–8, 49; Jewish, 65, 66; baptism, 183; Christian, 163, 187, 198; care of parents, 190; education,

187, 198; Isaac, 169ff; miraculous births of, 196; *see also* puberty

Christianity 152–66, 180, 181–199, 206–21, 260

Church Christian community, 152–66; women in community, 206–7, 180, 181ff; female officers, 183, 184, 191, 192, 193, 206, 207

Circe 254–5, 256, 265

circumcision female, 104; male, *see* men

citizenship Jewish, 62f; Greek, 92; Roman, 120, 135, 136, 137, 138, 139–40, 141, 142–3, 148

Claudia 117

Cleopatra 118

clothes 5, 73, 135, 137, 140, 142, 143, 153, 158, 162, 185, 188, 192, 218, 219, 220; *see also* cross-dressing

coinage, Roman 129

commandments, Jewish 58ff

community Christian, 152, 180, 181ff; Jewish, 53–6; exclusively female, 65–6; *see also* nuns and nunneries; social (dis)order

conception 103, 104, 106, 107, 108, 110, 111; *see also* sex

cosmetics 134–48; *see also* adornment; personal appearance

Crete, *see* Minoans

cross-dressing 73, 135, 160, 195

daily life prescriptive texts, 28ff, 156, 165, 181, 191, 194, 196, 240, 241, 245, 249; Christian, 186–90, 191–9; Hindu, 240ff, 245, 249

Damo 79

daughters Egyptian, 27, 29, 30, 48–9; Jewish, 56–7; Christian, 187, 188, 191, 195

deaconnesses 183–4, 191, 192, 194

death grave goods, 10; tombs at Thebes (Egypt) 25; rituals, 30, 31, 65, 185,

210; punishment for illicit sex, 36; tomb reliefs, 41; burial duties, 48–9; tomb inscriptions, 117, (124); suttee, 233, 247; keeners, 65; *see also* Eve; inheritance

deceitfulness 98–9, 146–8, 153, 154, 162

Devil, the 154–5, 159, 214–15, 216, 217, 260, 261

Diotima 72, 73, 156

divorce Christian, 188, 193; Egyptian, 34, 35, 36, 38, 42, 44, 46, 48

dress, *see* clothes

dualism 33, 36, 88–99, 135; *see also* gender

education 30, 156; Christian, 187, 196, 198; Egyptian, 40, 44, 45, 49; Greek, 72, 73, 82, 94; Jewish, 58; Hindu, 244; Anglo-Saxon, 206, 207–8; Educational Instructions, *see* Wisdom Literature; *see also* literacy

Elene, St 218–19, 225

empress, *see* imperial women

Epicureans 74, 79, 80, 81

epitaphs, *see* death

eroticism 136, 138, 144, 157–8, 163–6, 252, 254, 255, 256, 260, 261, 262, 263, 264

Evans, Arthur 9–10, 11

Eve 153–4, 157, 158, 161, 162, 165, 213–14, 215, 216, 264

evolution, reconstruction of human 6–8

Febronia 159

Galen 102, 103, 105, 146

gender definitions of, 88–99, 105–7, 116, 134ff, 148; binary oppositions, 12–13, 33, 36, 106–7, 110, 142–8, 156; and social status, 142, 194, 206, 207; within philosophy, 71, 73, 74,

76, 83, 88–99; bias in language, 5, 12, 18; crossing boundaries, 137, 147–8, 160, 214–15; stereotyping, 2ff, 8, 12, 14, 15, 16–18, 49, 71, 73, 74, 76, 83, 119, 246; concepts of 71, 73, 74, 76, 83, 153, 165–6, 243, 245, 246; constructs, 2ff, 6, 7, 123, 138–48, 161, 213, 214; *see also* power

Genesis Old Testament, 57, 158, 161, 169–80, 214; Old English, 213, 214
'gift-givers' 208, 211–12
goddesses 233, 247
Grendel's mother 212–13
gynaecology 102–12; *see also* medicine

Helena, St 186; *see also* Elene, St
Helvia 75, 137
Hild of Whitby 207–8, 219
Hinduism 233–49
Hippaechia 73, 74, 82, 83, 84
Hippocratic corpus 102–12
holy women, *see under* individual names
homily, *see* sermons
homosexuality, male *see* men
homophobia 260
honours, official 124, 129, 130, 139, 142, 211
household 2ff; Egyptian, 31, 33, 39, 43–4, 45, 47, 48; Roman, 117, 118, 122, 123, 126, 127, 128, 129; Hindu, 240ff, 248
hunter-gatherer, *see* Palaeolithic
hysteria 96–7, 105, 264; *see also* medicine

icons 159, 185, 193, 197–199
imperial women 115–30, 193, 198
inheritance 206, 209, 247; Egyptian, 35, 37, 38, 48, 49; Christian, 188, 189
intercession 122–3, 125, 126, 127, 192–3, 197–8, 211, 221; *see also* 'peace-weaver'
Irene of Chrysobalanton, St 193–4
irrationality 92, 96–7, 99
Isis 26–7
Islam 239
Israel the people, 57ff; the land, *see* Palestine

Jerome 154, 157, 158, 162
Jerusalem Temple of, 58ff, 65; Sanhedrin of, 63; pilgrimage to, 218–19
Jewish women 53–66
Judaism 53–66
Judith 209, 219–21
Julia the Elder 128
Juliana, St 216–18, 219, 225, 226
Julio-Claudians 115–30

Knossos, palace of 8

labour, division of 2, 6, 7, 8, 11, 12; domestic, 72, 76, 117, 123, 124, 140, 156, 185, 186ff, 196, 208, 209, 211, 239, 240, 241, 242ff, 245–6, 247, 252, 262, 265, 266; professions and non-domestic occupations, 19, 38, 39, 41, 65, 70–84, 107, 123, 124, 142, 187, 208–9, 210, 211, 239; producers, 19; in professional archaeology, 14, 15, 16–18
language, gender bias 6, 18, 20, 54ff
Lasthemia 73, 74, 81–2
law legal disabilities, 63–4; courts, 63, 125, 126; Jewish, 57ff; on illicit sex, 336; sumptuary legislation, 139, 141; legal entitlements, *see* property; inheritance; marriage contracts; *see also* text – prescriptive
Leontium 74, 80, 81
liturgy Jewish, 61; Anglo-Saxon, 207–8

literacy   in Egypt, 27–8; Christian, 196, 197; *see also* education
Livia   123–4, 126, 128
Lucy (*Australopithecus afarensis*)   7
luxury, Roman   139–41, 143

Macrina   156–7, 164, 187
man the hunter   14, 20
Marcia   75
magic, *see* witches
marriage   Christian, 163, 164, 165–6, 183, 185, 187, 188, 189, 190; Roman, 142, 143–4; maintenance, 32; contracts, 35, 42, 46; adultery, 36, 37, 45ff; Egyptian, 30, 31, 32ff, 42, 44, 46, 48; status bestowed by, 255, 261, 266, 267; aspirations for, 253–4, 261, 262–3; Hindu, 240, 244, 245, 247–8, 250; Greek, 94, 105, 108, 110, 111, 112; Anglo-Saxon, 206, 210, 211, 212, 223, 224; Pythagorean ideal, 72, 78
martyrdom   155, 183, 184, 186, 188, 196, 216–17, 221, 225
Mary Magdalene   159, 182, 186
Mary of Egypt   160, 185, 197
Mary, Virgin and Mother   152, 154, 158, 159, 160, 161, 162ff, 165, 185, 186, 196–7, 221; *see also* Eve
masculinisation   104, 105, 107, 160, 212–13, 218; *see also* androgyny
mathematics   gender and, 90–1, sexuality and, 91
matriarchy   265; Minoan, 9–10, 12, 13; imprecise term, 19; gender bias in archaeology, 13
matrilineality   56–7
matron (Roman)   115–30, 142; *see also* wife
Medea   102–12, 254, 256, 260
medical texts   representations of women, 102ff
medicine   concepts of gender, 102–12;

and cosmetics, 146; Hippocratic, 102–12; definition of normative, 104, 105; texts, 41, 102ff; icon veneration, 198; *see also* gynaecology
Medusa   265
men   as brothers, 156, 191, 193; as husbands, 30, 31, 32, 33ff, 39, 40, 43, 44, 48, 171ff, 187, 189, 206, 209, 233, 243, 244, 245, 262, *see also* wife; as sons, 28–9, 31, 40, 45, 48–9, 56, 57, 169–80, *see also* children; as fathers, 28, 30, 39, 40, 45, 91, 93, 128, 170ff, 210; as sexual beings, 95, 144, 147–8, 154, 155, 156, 158, 163, 164; fear of women, 125, 135, 137, 146, 152, 153, 155, 156, 159, 161, 165, 212–13, 219, 220, 246, 252, 264ff, *see also* power; unmanliness, 95, 98–9, 137, 147–8, 266–7; virility, 95, 137, 147–8; as rational, 70, 71, 72, 74, 92, 94, 97, 110, 138, 140, 214; beautifying selves, 135, 137, 138, 142–3; and homosexuality, 137, 261; male as ideal, 106; man the hunter model, 6; dominant in archaeology, 14–20; careers of, 29, 30, 40, 41, 43, 44, 47, 62, 64, 73; civil leaders, 62, 63, 64; dual nature, 33; adultery, 36, 37, 45ff; circumcision, 56–7, 58; Hindu religious duties, 241–2; as protectors and providers, 32, 266; male construct, 1ff, 6, 8, 12, 14; *see also* gender
Melania the Younger   183, 184, 188
menarche   111, 112
menopause   108, 111
menstrual taboo   59, 41–2, 104, 105, 106ff, 111, 112, 246, 247
Messalina   115, 124, 126
metaphysics, reproduction and   93–4
methodologies   feminist, 18–20, 64ff, 99, 152–3, 162, 254; Christian feminist, 152–3, 162; historiography (an-

cient and modern), 53ff, 103, 115–
16, 123, 127, 130, 169; presentism,
104, 153, 169, 261, 262; gender blind,
6, 7, 8, 17–20, 53ff; gender bias, 5, 6,
7, 9; archaeological, 2ff; problem of
sources, *see* text
midwives   65, 66
military   39, 124–5, 208, 213, 218–19,
220–1, 225; *see also* power
Minoans   8ff, 11
mothers   26–27; Christian, 169, 170,
185, 186–7, 189, 197, 198, *see also*
Mary, Virgin and Mother; Jewish, 58,
169, 170; Roman, 118, 123, 129, 137;
Egyptian, 29, 30, 31, 35, 38, 40, 42,
45, 47, 48; Hindu, 238, 246; Anglo-
Saxon, 210, 212, 221; Greek, 78–9,
91, 93; childbirth, 40, 41, 59, 65, 66;
inheritance from, 38; importance of
mother's father, 37
murderers   126, 254, 256, 260, 262–3
Mycenaean society   10–11
myth, *see* religion

nature–culture divide   92, 97, 99, 103,
104, 105, 107, 110, 111, 112, 135,
136, 138f, 140, 143, 145, 246, 264–5
nuns and nunneries   183–4, 188,
189–90, 191–5, 207, 226

Octavia   118, 122, 123
old age   108, 183, 187, 189, 190, 191,
195, 197
orientalism   11, 12, 118, 141, 147
Origen   154–5, 157, 164–5
orphans   39, 48

Palaeolithic   1–2
Palestine   53ff
patrilineality   56, 57
patronage   118, 122, 123, 124, 125, 127,
238
Paul, St   152, 158, 182, 195, 196
'peace-weaver' (Anglo-Saxon)   213

Pelagia   159–60
Perictione   73, 82
Perpetua   181
philosophy   representations of women
philosphers, 70–84; concepts of gender, 71, 73, 74, 75, 76, 83, 88–99,
163–4, 165–6, 135
physical appearance   34, 70–1, 73, 74,
82, 83, 104, 135–7, 138, 139, 142,
264–65, *see also* adornment
pilgrimage, pilgrims   58, 60, 186, 218
Poppaea Sabina   119–20, 121
Plato, (Neo-)Platonism   73, 88–99, 135,
156, 163–4, 165
popular culture   film, 13–14, 252–3,
261, 262–7; fiction, 14, 18, 115; cartoon, 2ff; television, 262
Postumia (Vestal Virgin)   143
power   danger of women, 33, 35–6, 39,
45, 46, 48, 49, 65, 71, 115, 116, 118ff,
121, 122, 126, 127–8, 130, 136, 146,
148, 152, 153, 155, 156, 160, 161,
212–13, 214, 246, 249, 254, 256,
262–3, 264, 265–6, 267; imperial
women, 115–16, 118, 121, 122, 123,
124, 125ff, 129, 130; intercession,
122–3, 125, 126, 127, 193–4, 198–9,
211, 221, *see also* peace-weaver;
military, 39, 124–5, 208, 213, 218–
19, 221, 225; patronage, 117, 121,
122, 123ff, 185–6, 127, 238; sought
through political rebellion, 39, 118,
119, 120, 121; control over own body,
109, 110; in religious communities,
152; formal authority accorded men,
29, 62ff, 64, 116, 118, 121, 162; judicial, 125–6; administration, 124,
125, 211; *see also* property and
wealth
pregnancy   66, 105, 107, 108, 110, 111,
112, 247
prescriptive text, *see* text
presentism   1ff, 5, 8, 19, 26, 243, 248
priestesses   72, (129), 143

property and wealth, business 122, 124, 185, 186, 187ff, 190, 192, 194, 195, 206, 208, 211, 239, 247; of widows, 47; Roman, 123, 124; Jewish 60, 63, 64; Egyptian, 31, 35, 37, 38, 49; women as consumers, 140, 141, 142, 143–4; *see also* power

proselytisers 186, 190, 191, 207, 219

prostitutes 159, 160, 193, 194; 'strange woman', 34, 45ff; Jewish, 66; Egyptian, 43, 45ff; Greek (courtesan), 74, 79–80, 81, 82, 135, 136

puberty Jewish, 56–7; Greek, 111–12

public roles for women, *see* labour, division of; power

purity in Jewish law, 39; Greek, 78

Pythagoras, Pythagoreans 71, 72, 73–4, 77, 78, 79, 88–99

queens, *see* royalty

rape 36, 111

rebellion 139, 254; *see also* power

relics 186, 219, 220

religion Christianity, 152–66, 181–199, 206–21; Judaism, 53–66; congregation, 56ff; Egyptian, 26–7, 28, 33; Mycenaean, 10–11, Minoan, 9; Roman, 36; liturgy, 170; Hinduism, 233–49; fundamentalism, revival 249; *see also* witches

rites of passage 56–7, 111, 142–3, 188, 240, 245

role models 196, 225–6

Rome 117ff

royalty Anglo-Saxon, 208, 210, 211–12, 218, 219; Egyptian, 38, 39, 118; *see also* imperial women

sacrifices, ritual of 59, 65, 243, 245; of Isaac, 169–80

saints, *see under* individual names

Sarah 169–80

saviour, of men 159, 160, 161

Schurer, Emil 54ff

segregation 59, 61; *see also* architecture

Sempronia 118, 119, 120, 128, 130

sermons 61, 165, 169–70, 171, 175

sex intercourse, 32, 36, 78, 111, 112; illicit intercourse, 36, 42, 43, 45ff, 193, 195, 261, 262; rape, 36; masturbation, 104; good exercise for women, 108; reproduction/procreation, 32, 48, 91, 93, 103, 104, 106, 108, 110, 111, 163, 186, 187–8; women as sexually active, 78; depiction in art, 144; *see also* childbirth, menstruation

sexuality women defined as sexual and/or physical, 70ff, 76, 79–80, 83, 84, 119–20, 134, 135, 136, 137, 140, 143, 144, 147–8, 152, 153–4, 155ff, 160, 161, 162ff, 209, 215, 216, 220, 246, 252, 253, 255, 260, 261ff, 265, 267; women sexually active, 43, 45ff, 49, 263–4, 267; *see also* asceticism

sexual differences, theories of 88–99, 106, 109, 134, 136, 137ff

sexual imagery 32, 47, 111, 154, 157, 163, 209, 260

Simaetha, Greek 253–7, 262

sisters 156, 191, 193

slaves 142

social (dis)order prescriptive texts, 44, 45, 48, 53–66, 72, 152, 154, 156, 161, 165, 181, 183, 191; elite, 9, 29, 30, 35, 38, 115–30, 142, 189–90, 193, 208, 210–11, 225, 239; non-elite, 40; Roman, 120, 121, 122, 124, 127, 129, 134–48; royalty, 9, 10, 27, 208, 210, 211–12; Platonic, 88–99; community, 53–66; Jewish, 61ff; xenophobia, 34, 45, 46; in Wisdom Literature, 28ff; power dynamics, 116, 121, 122, 124, 126, 127, 129, 130; political disruption of, 39, 118, 119, 120, 121, 214, 253; Hindu, 234, 239, 240, 244, 245;

adornment and dress, 135, 137, 141, 142–3, 148, 188, 192; symbolism, 103ff, 108ff, 129, 135ff, 139, 147, 140, 148, 156; reflected in nunneries, 194; Anglo-Saxon; woman anomalous, 71, 72, 76; imperial, 218–19, 225; Egyptian, 45; social mobility, 44, 48; *see also* power

Socrates 72, 73

Song of Songs 157, 158, 164–5

Soranus 102, 107

sorcery, *see* witches

spirituality 155ff, 160, 163–4, 164, 181–199

state, symbolism of 127–30, 138–41

stereotypes 252–3, 155–7, 261, 264, 265, 266; *see also* gender

sterility 110, 188, 197, 198, 248

Stoicism 75–6

Stone Age, *see* Palaeolithic

suttee 233, 247

symbolism for the state, 127–30, 138–41; of social order, *see* social (dis)order

synagogue 58, 60ff, 65

temptress 263–4; *see also* gender; sexuality

text prescriptive, 233, 234, 235, *see also* social order; problems as sources, 25–6, 71, 83, 99, 102–3, 104, 105, 121, 123, 127, 134f, 153, 156, 181–2, 204–5, 222, 223, 224, 226, 236; attributed to female authorship, 75, 77, 78, 80, 81, 82, 83, 105, 174–5, 181, 197, 222, 223, 224–5; ancient literary criticism, 144–6; textual transmission, 25–6, 27, 28, 83, 102–3, 169–70, 204–5, 233, 234–5, 236, 248, 252, 253–5, 257, 262, 265, 267

Thecla, St 157, 159, 182, 184, 195, 197

Theano 72, 76–9, 82, 84

Themista 74

Themistoclea 72

Theodora 187, 194

transvestism, *see* cross-dressing

Tryambaka 238, 239–40, 245, 247, 249

Urgulania 126

virginity 111, 143, 152, 154, 155ff, 159, 161, 162, 163–4, 166, 182, 183, 184, 188, 189, 192, 196, 216–17, 220, 221, 225; *see also* Mary, Virgin and Mother

wickedness 33, 118–19, 120, 121ff, 128, 130, 153–4, 162, 214, 215, 246, 249, 255, 256, 260, 264–5; *see also* dualism, power

widows Christian, 184, 187, 188, 189–90, 191, 192, 195; Hindu, 233, 247; Jewish, 65; Anglo-Saxon, 206, 219–20; Egyptian, 29, 35, 38ff, 47, 48; property, 47

wife Hindu, 233, 236, 239, 240–41, 242ff, 245–6, 247–8, 249; Greek, 76, 77–9, 94, 105, 108, 109, 111; Egyptian, 27, 29, 31, 32ff, 43ff; 48; Anglo-Saxon, 206, 209, 211, 222, 223, 224; Christian, 157, 171ff, 189, 195; Roman, 117, 118ff, 122, 123, 125ff, 129, 136–7, 137ff, 142; Jewish, 63, 171ff

Wisdom Literature 24–49

witches 65, 252–67; *see also* popular culture

womb in Hippocratic corpus, 105, 108, 109ff, 112; *see also* hysteria

woman the gatherer 7

Wulf 224–5

Xanthippe 73

xenophobia 34, 45, 46